WITH GOD ON THEIR SIDE

WITH GOD ON THEIR SIDE

How Christian Fundamentalists Trampled Science, Policy, and Democracy in George W. Bush's White House

ESTHER KAPLAN

THE NEW PRESS

NEW YORK
LONDON

Requests for permission to reproduce selections from this book should be mailed to:
Permissions Department, The New Press, 38 Greene Street, New York, NY 10013

Published in the United States by The New Press, New York, 2004
Distributed by W.W. Norton & Company, Inc., New York

LIBRARY OF CONGRESS CATALOGING-IN-PUBLICATION DATA

Kaplan, Esther.
  With God on their side : how Christian fundamentalists trampled science,
policy, and democracy in George W. Bush's White House / Esther Kaplan.
    p. cm.
  ISBN 1-56584-920-5
    1. Church and state—United States. 2. Bush, George W. (George Walker),
  1946—Religion. 3. Religion and state—United States. 4. Religion and
  politics—United States. 5. United States—Religion. I. Title.

  BR516.K34 2004
  322'.1'0973090511—dc22   2004050416

The New Press was established in 1990 as a not-for-profit alternative to the large,
commercial publishing houses currently dominating the book publishing industry.
The New Press operates in the public interest rather than for private gain, and is
committed to publishing, in innovative ways, works of educational, cultural, and
community value that are often deemed insufficiently profitable.

www.thenewpress.com

Composition by Westchester Book Composition
Copyediting by icopyedit
Printed in the United States of America

2   4   6   8   10   9   7   5   3   1

This book is dedicated to the memory of

Richie Perez
(1944–2004)
co-conspirator and visionary

and

Julien Mezey
(2001–2004)
who died of leukemia, one of the many illnesses for which stem
cell research holds such promise

CONTENTS

PREFACE AND ACKNOWLEDGMENTS

I GREW UP during the 1970s in King's Valley, Oregon, a small, down-and-out logging town reeling from recession. There wasn't much to do besides get lost in the woods—we had a grade school, a post office, a tavern, a 4-H club, and a church. Everyone in town was Christian—except us. What's more, many were fundamentalists, staunch believers that God's will played a direct role in their lives. One time, for someone who was chronically ill, there was a laying on of hands.

These were the people who seemed confused when my dad showed up at school to insist, unsuccessfully, that his daughters not be asked to sing Christian songs in the public-school choir, or to complain that the Good News Club met in our public-school building. Before encountering us, at least one of my schoolmates had only heard of Jews from anti-Semitic myths, and so believed Jews were horned creatures, not humans; others enjoyed the novelty of having some non-Christians around, ripe for conversion. I remember invitations to "play" at schoolmates' homes that somehow turned into Bible study sessions. Still, no one treated us with hostility. The town merely shared a worldview that couldn't imagine, much less accommodate, such an alien, non-Christian identity.

Indeed, this was my family's community, too: our friends and support network; the people from whom we borrowed farm equipment and adopted kittens; the kids with whom I raised animals, rode the school bus, learned to read and write and think. My relationship with these Christian fundamentalists was deeply familiar, even if it was always slightly fraught. I recall my mother phoning a neighbor early one morning and apologizing for the "ungodly hour," then catching herself, embarrassed for having misspoken. It was an early lesson in what was permissible speech.

I reached adulthood in very different circumstances, in the New York

City of the late 1980s, when AIDS deaths were climbing fast and seemed to be everywhere around me. It was in this context that I learned the harsher side of Christian fundamentalism. Not long after one of my closest friends died from AIDS, I happened to be in San Francisco on the day a public memorial was being held for Randy Shilts, the pioneering AIDS journalist and author of the searing AIDS history *And the Band Played On*. He had recently succumbed to the disease, and thousands turned out to mourn. Outside, Fred Phelps, a Baptist minister from Kansas and a marginal but flamboyant figure in the growing Christian right movement, showed up with a handful of followers who waved signs outside the church blaring Shilts in Hell and God Hates Fags. More than a decade later, the memory still devastates me.

This dichotomy was ever present as I researched this book. I met a man who worked for pennies at a humble drug treatment center and spent his nights on a narrow cot, living a life of service, and a woman who became a pro-life activist in part because she couldn't have children of her own. I also spoke with a Bush advisor and evangelical Christian who opposes condom education and told me that he frankly doesn't "believe in the homosexual lifestyle" and a family values activist who said that only "sloppy" people having "illicit" sex need access to contraception.

I share these experiences to address a question that dogs every journalist who writes critically about the Christian right: Isn't religion good? My answer is yes, it can be. Religion has fueled a long, rich tradition of service to the poor and prophetic activism against racism. It can help people struggling with loss and provide an ethical touchstone in people's lives. But religion can also be used to further a divisive, destructive political agenda. This book does not take up the role of Christianity in people's everyday lives, nor does it seek to promote or malign any particular faith. Instead it asks what impact the Christian right, as a dogma-driven *political* movement, has had in dictating American policy. What I found was that at the precise moment when we as a nation woke up to the threat of politicized religious fundamentalism abroad, George W. Bush invited our own fundamentalists to open up shop in the White House, offering this once marginal movement a degree of influence over the federal government that far outstrips their sway over any previous administration, even that of Ronald Reagan. This book is an effort to document the corrosive effects this fundamentalist influence has had on science, on sound social policy, on international relations, and on our basic national values of pluralism and democracy.

I'm grateful to Colin Robinson, my editor at The New Press, who saw right away that this book was an urgent political project, and I thank him for offering crucial insights that fundamentally shaped its direction and for pushing me to get it done on a tight schedule.

A climate of fear prevails in Washington today, so I'm especially grateful to all of the current and former government scientists and policy experts who risked jeopardizing their careers to speak with me, and to the AIDS, sex education, and reproductive rights researchers and advocates who risked jeopardizing their funding to do the same. This book leans on investigative reports by several not-for-profit advocacy groups including Americans United for the Separation of Church and State, the Alliance for Justice, the Center for Reproductive Rights, Human Rights Watch, NARAL, Office of Management and Budget Watch, People for the American Way, Political Research Associates, Population Action International, and the Union of Concerned Scientists. Thanks also to Abby Aguirre, who watchdogged several Freedom of Information Act requests, Gro Frank Rasmussen, and Lizzie Seidlin-Bernstein at The New Press, who offered invaluable research assistance; and to Roane Carey, Rebecca Casanova, Melanie Kaye/Kantrowitz, Richard Kim, Angela Pattatucci, Sean Strub, and Daniel Wolfe for commenting on chapter drafts, and offering thoughtful advice throughout.

Portions of this reporting, from the chapters on AIDS, abstinence, and gay rights, came from pieces I originally wrote for *POZ*, the national AIDS magazine, and for the *Nation*; I owe special thanks to my editors at those two magazines, Betsy Reed and Karen Rothmyer at the *Nation*, and David Thorpe, Tim Murphy, and especially Walter Armstrong at *POZ*, for their guidance on what turned out to be the seeds of this book. On the far end, this book would not have come together without the keen skill and hard work of my line editor, Bob Ickes, who midwifed the project in its final months, and excellent fact-checking by Kevin McCarthy and Kate Lansky.

The book would not have been possible without the support of my family and friends, in particular, extraordinarily generous material and moral support from my mother, Meredith McGovney Kaplan, my father, Hesh Kaplan, and my sisters, Sarah Kaplan, Sharon Kaplan, and Rachel Lanham; my friends Michelle Aronowitz, Bernhard Blythe, Eric Cadora, Cindra Feuver, Carl George, Jennifer Gonzalez, Darius James, Shana Krochmal, Julia Meltzer, Jenny Romaine, Ira Sachs, and Laurens Van Sluytman, who offered inspiration and assistance; and Naomi Braine, Nan Rubin, Alisa Solomon, and especially Marilyn Kleinberg Neimark, who shouldered extra duties so I could devote myself to the book. Above all, I offer thanks to my life partner, Andrew Hsiao, who intervened with advice, support, suggestions, and vision at every critical juncture along the way, and graciously allowed our lives to be turned upside down by deadline pressures.

INTRODUCTION

FOUR SHORT YEARS and a political lifetime ago, George W. Bush lost the 2000 popular election by more than half-a-million votes and assumed the leadership of a divided nation. He was expected then, by both the left and the right, to govern from the center. He promised to work closely with Republicans and Democrats "to heal whatever wounds may exist" from the bruising recounts and unprecedented electoral intervention by the Supreme Court.[1] The conciliatory tone that he struck in those early days was consistent with that of his general election campaign, where Bush had stumped for improving public schools and aiding charities, and that of his nominating convention, where he offered up to the nation a vision of a new Republican Party, one characterized by compassion and multiculturalism, where Christian right leaders were exiled from the stage in favor of his Latino nephew George P. Bush and African American general Colin Powell.

Four years ago, the Christian right was in an equally tenuous position. Its standard bearer, the Christian Coalition, was under investigation by the IRS and the Federal Election Commission, and many of its state chapters were in a state of collapse. Its lead organizers were fleeing so fast that one former field director called the organization "defunct."[2] Groups such as the Family Research Council and Concerned Women for America, undergoing their own leadership transitions, had not yet risen to take the coalition's place. The movement had staked its influence on the drive to impeach Bill Clinton, and after that effort collapsed, its leaders projected a palpable sense of gloom. Paul Weyrich, the man who had inspired Jerry Falwell to build a "moral majority" in America, wrote a Dear Friend letter that resounded with defeat. "I no longer believe that there is a moral majority," he wrote in February 1999. "I do not believe that a majority of Americans actually shares our values. . . . We got our people elected. But that did not result in the adoption of our agenda." He said the right had lost the culture war, and that instead of becoming more godly, America was becoming "an ever-wider sewer." He encouraged activists to give up, to quarantine them-selves from this infectious immorality, "to drop out of this culture, and find places . . . where we can live godly, righteous and sober lives."[3] Weyrich's letter sparked enormous controversy on the Christian right. But in light of a booming Christian home schooling movement and rising enrollment in fundamentalist Christian colleges, many saw his letter as the harbinger of a new evangelical separatism, marked by a retreat from political life.

At the close of Bush's first term in office, all this has changed. The Christian right has more political power than at any point in its his-tory, and Bush has governed from the far right. He has antagonized much of the world and a broad swath of the American people by launching a bold policy of preemptive war; by flouting international treaties on global warming, arms, and war crimes; and by invading Iraq despite global opposition. He has cemented a profoundly elite economic agenda, giving away hundreds of billions of tax dollars to corporations and to the wealthy while undermining labor unions and relaxing laws monitoring public lands, environmental pollutants, and media ownership. While a few of his tax policies arguably helped the middle class, most did not: slashing the tax on stock dividends mainly benefited the wealthiest 1 percent of Americans; revoking the tax on inheritance—already waived for small estates—aided only million-aires. When his tax cuts failed to produce millions of promised jobs, he vowed to implement more. Former Republican strategist Kevin Phillips has called these measures "stark class legislation."[4] Bush provided hun-dreds of millions in contracts to favored firms and bailouts to favored industries, while failing to aid states forced into draconian budget cuts to schools, public colleges, health care, and infrastructure by balloon-ing state deficits. He amassed a record federal deficit conservatively es-timated to exceed $500 billion and then threatened social-program austerity.

So how has George Bush managed to pamper the corporate elite, leave 2.5 million Americans jobless, trash the environment, reduce public services, and still maintain an electoral majority? This is not only a question about the political future of George W. Bush—it is a question about the future of American political life. For many analysts, this question was decisively answered by 9/11. "The terrorist attacks on September 11, 2001 created a new political era," veteran Washington reporter Fred Barnes wrote in the conservative *Weekly Standard* after Republicans swept the midterm elections. "We are no longer an equally divided, 50-50 nation. America is now at least 51-49 Republican and right of center."[5] The war on terror has indeed been the source of Bush's highest approval ratings and has offered the administration considerable leeway in its domestic and economic policies. But this national-security mandate is slim and tenuous, vulnerable to military setbacks, and dependent upon orange alerts and a perennial war footing to sustain itself. It can't be depended upon indefinitely.

We can see a second, far more permanent answer to this question in the president's intense devotion to his evangelical conservative supporters, whom he has decisively reenergized as a political force. Corporate donors may fill GOP coffers, but evangelicals are the party's institutional grass roots, its believers, its get-out-the-vote ground troops, as important to the Republicans as organized labor and African Americans are, combined, to the Democrats. Bush knows, and Christian right leaders know, that he couldn't have been elected without them. Though white evangelicals constitute only about 25 percent of the national population, this highly motivated voting bloc made up 40 percent of Bush's electorate in 2000, an amount he hopes to boost in 2004. When that number is combined with the most religiously observant Catholics, the total comes to 52 percent of all Bush votes in 2000.[6] The Christian right is not just another special interest group, like the NRA. This is Bush's *base*.

For the president, maintaining fealty from religious conservatives is a first principle. And to this end he has happily ceded huge swaths of his domestic and international policy to this lobby, from abortion and sex education to gay rights, social services, court appointments, and medical research. He has even used his global AIDS initiative, his foreign aid policy, and his war on terror to please religious radicals.

To be sure, the Christian right has periodically gained national influence in recent decades, successfully blocking the Equal Rights Amendment for women in the 1970s, shaping Reagan's social agenda in the 1980s, and pushing anti-abortion and antigay initiatives through state legislatures in the 1990s. But Bush's own, very public born-again Christianity, combined with the machinations of his brilliant political advisor Karl Rove, have conspired to provide Christian fundamentalists with an unprecedented level of influence on this White House and on government social policy.

Bush often cloaks his "faith-based" approach to governance in rhetoric about how religion has been wrongly banished from the public square, the idea, in the president's words, that "we're still fighting old attitudes, habits, and rules, that discriminate against religious groups for no good purpose."[7] But he isn't really interested in faith in general. The president didn't flick an eyelash when the National Council of Churches and the U.S. Conference of Catholic Bishops opposed his war on Iraq. He didn't listen when the Council on American-Islamic Relations filed a suit challenging the constitutionality of the Patriot Act. When the Union for Reform Judaism announced that an antigay marriage amendment would "defile the constitution," the president took no notice. Nor did Bush respond to a joint call, signed by fifty prominent Christian leaders, including Richard Cizik of the National Association of Evangelicals and Jim Wallis of Call to Renewal, for policies that promote "quality health care, decent housing, and a living income" for the poor.[8] His is not an embrace of spirituality or ethics broadly speaking, or of faith as an important voice among many in the national debate. It is, instead, an embrace of right-wing Christian fundamentalism.

"Poverty is a religious issue," says Wallis, who edits the liberal Christian journal *Sojourners*. "The environment is a religious issue. A war of choice fought on false pretenses is a theological issue. But Republicans have narrowed religious issues to a short list of four or five that happen to be very important to their constituency."

Conservative evangelicals were skeptical of Bush during the 2000 campaign because of his moderate presidential campaign and his relatively moderate father. But once Bush took office, he quickly won them over with his aggressive pro-life stance and his open declarations of faith. "Missed you at Bible study" were the first words speechwriter David Frum heard in the George Bush White House. The words weren't directed to Frum, an Orthodox Jew, but to his evangelical boss Michael Gerson. Still, Frum writes, "The news that this was a White House where attendance at Bible study was, if not compulsory, not quite uncompulsory, either, was disconcerting to a non-Christian like me."[9] This is an administration where weekly Bible study at the White House is attended by more than half the White House staff, and daily Bible study at the Department of Justice is presided over by the Attorney General. It is an administration where the staff at the General Services Administration hold revival meetings at lunch hour, making the building's front hall sound, in the words of the *Washington Post*, "more like the foyer of a Pentecostal storefront church."[10]

The Christian right is certainly not the Bush administration's only favored constituency, nor is it the only one to reap rewards for loyalty. The NRA, for example, which had wheeled out Charlton Heston for last-minute election-year rallies to help Bush in West Virginia, was promised the slackening of gun-control enforcement and got administration support for a bill offering legal immunity to gun sellers. The oil and energy industries got the abandonment of the Kyoto Protocol on global warming and an energy bill packed with tax breaks, subsidies, loan guarantees, and deregulation. For each sector of the conservative coalition, anti-tax advocate Grover Norquist told the *Weekly Standard*, Bush "got their hot button item and he got it right."[11] But after Bush's favored business interests, no constituency has snared more red meat than the Christian right.

"The libertarians and military hawks in the Republican tent don't care about gay marriage or abortion," says Jean Hardisty, a founder of Political Research Associates who has studied right-wing movements for more than two decades. "But there's an agreement that the Christian right got into the driver's seat in the 1990s, and the decision internally was that they're an important constituency and need to be responded to."

On his first day in office Bush reinstated the Reagan-era abortion "gag rule," instantaneously withdrawing federal funds from any family planning clinic in the developing world that voices support for abortion or even mentions it as an option to clients. Shortly thereafter, he launched his Office of Faith-Based and Community Initiatives, which would soon channel millions of federal dollars to such mainstays of the religious right as Pat Robertson and National Right to Life, as well as to church-run welfare and abstinence programs across the country. Bush proudly signed the partial-birth abortion ban and the Unborn Victims of Violence Act, which declares fetuses to be full persons for the purposes of criminal prosecution. He blocked federally funded embryonic stem cell research on all but a handful of existing cell lines in order to protect embryos' "potential for life."[12] He increased domestic funding for abstinence programs and allocated a third of his global HIV-prevention dollars to the same unproven approach. His nominees to the federal courts constitute a virtual religious right dream team, including adamant foes of church/state separation, gay rights, and abortion. When his Christian right base became so agitated about gay marriage that one leader, Operation Rescue founder Randall Terry, declared, "America's survival hangs in the balance," Bush proved he could be antigay as well.[13] First he issued a proclamation declaring "Marriage Protection Week," then he announced a multimillion dollar program to promote marriage, and, finally, at the start of the 2004 election season, he threw his weight behind a constitutional amendment banning same-sex marriage. "We have reason to be very, very thankful . . . that George Bush is in the White House," Christian radio host James Dobson told his followers a year into the Bush presidency. "I'm very thankful for those 350 votes in Florida."[14]

But that's just a catalog of Bush's headline-making initiatives. No condom fact sheet or obscure drug advisory panel is too small to escape the watchful eyes of the Family Research Council, Concerned Women for America, and the other power brokers in Washington's family values lobby—and when they set their sights on an issue, the

Bush administration responds. Bush has appointed Christian activists, not researchers, to scientific advisory councils, while administration officials distorted science on government Web pages to avoid offending fundamentalist sensibilities. While Bush doled out millions to churches for abstinence and marriage promotion, secular agencies that provide abortions or sex education faced punishing federal audits. The president invited in a team of extreme social conservatives, including a leading anti-abortion activist and a former representative of the Vatican, to join U.S. negotiating teams at every major UN conference touching on family values. And he gave them free reign to reverse U.S. stances on reproductive health, abortion, condoms, marriage, and parental rights—and used the force of the White House to bully other nations into offering their support. Bush Park Service officials have even approved the display of Christian symbols and Bible verses on public parkland, including a giant cross in the Mojave Desert.

Bush's religiosity is so widely embraced on the Christian right that when Pat Robertson resigned as president of the Christian Coalition at the end of 2001, American Values president Gary Bauer told the *Washington Post,* "I think Robertson stepped down because the position has already been filled. [Bush] is that leader right now." There is a shared sense among conservative evangelicals, Bauer said, "that a man of God is in the White House."[15] After 9/11, leaders on the Christian right began to speak of his presidency as divinely inspired and his reelection as divinely ordained—a view his staff has avidly cultivated. "I think President Bush is God's man at this hour," Bush's top evangelical liaison, Tim Goeglein, told a Christian magazine in October 2001.[16] This faith in his presidency has shielded Bush from accountability and from doubt. Since he believes, like his base, that "we are not the author" of our lives,[17] what does it matter if his claims that tax cuts would provide millions of jobs, that Iraqis would embrace American troops, and that Saddam Hussein harbored weapons of mass destruction have all unraveled? Bush and his conservative evangelical base are on the same team—God's team. This book charts the cost of their collaboration.

YES, VIRGINIA, IT IS A HOLY WAR

IT WAS ONE of George Bush's most statesmanlike moments. On June 4, 2003, flanked by dueling national leaders—the veteran Israeli hawk Ariel Sharon and the newly appointed Palestinian prime minister Mahmoud Abbas—the president assumed the role of Middle East peacemaker he had avoided for more than two years. "The Holy Land must be shared between the State of Palestine and the State of Israel, living in peace with each other and with every nation of the Middle East," he said, the sparkling blue waters of the Gulf of Aqaba at his back. The moment was carefully stage-managed, as so many Bush appearances are, with an attention to detail matched only by the president's "mission accomplished" photo op aboard the USS *Abraham Lincoln* the month before. In this case, American officials had ordered a wooden bridge built over the pool of their Jordanian host, King Abdullah, to allow the heads of state a grand entrance and engineered a hidden air-conditioning system beneath the podiums, to avoid any hint of nervous sweat.[1] But the event seemed to include some actual diplomacy along with the show: before the pageantry began, Bush sat down privately with Sharon and Abbas, first separately, and then together, in meetings closed to the press. The day's media reports widely assumed that Bush had used those private meetings to put some muscle behind his road map for Middle East peace, an assumption supported by the grudging concessions Sharon and Abbas made in their own speeches that day.

So what exactly did Bush say in those private meetings, his first serious intervention with two leaders engaged in a bloody conflict, each egged on by extremists—whether Muslim jihadists or ultra-Orthodox Jewish settlers—who arm themselves in the name of religion? A few weeks later, on June 26, the Israeli daily *Ha'aretz* published the minutes of a late June cease-fire negotiation during which the Palestinian prime minister relayed Bush's comments to militants from Hamas and Islamic Jihad. Abbas recalled that Bush said, "God told me to strike at al-Qaeda and I struck them, and then he instructed me to strike at Saddam, which I did, and now I am determined to solve the problem in the Middle East."[2]

This was the President of the United States telling a foreign head of state that he had waged wars in Afghanistan and Iraq on instructions from God.

In a July 1 press conference, Ari Fleischer insisted that Abbas's recollection was wrong, saying, "It's beyond a stretch. It's an invention. It was not said."[3] Perhaps. But the day before Bush met with Abbas and Sharon, his comments at another closed-door meeting were inadvertently recorded. At this June 3 meeting in Egypt, attended by Abbas along with the leaders of Egypt, Saudi Arabia, Bahrain, and Jordan, Bush again spoke of his religious convictions playing a role in his stance toward the Middle East. "I'm the kind of person who when I say something, I mean it," he said. "I mean that the world needs to have a Palestinian state that is free and at peace. And therefore, my government works with all parties concerned to achieve that vision. The Almighty God has endowed each individual on the face of the Earth . . . expecting each person to be treated with dignity. This is a universal call. It's the call of all religions—that each person must be free and treated with respect. And it is with that call that I feel passionate about the need to move forward so that the world can be more peaceful, more free, and more hopeful."[4] And these were not the only instances of Bush inserting his Christian beliefs into American diplomacy. The president has characterized his early connection with the president of Russia as rooted in their common Christian faith. "The first conversation I ever had with Vladimir Putin was about God," President Bush once recalled. "We'd never met each other, and the first discussion we had was about our personal beliefs."[5] Similarly, his strong bond with Tony Blair, who, like George Bush, found religion as an adult and has since made public display of his faith a habit. According to Stephen Mansfield, the author of *The Faith of George W. Bush,* a religious portrait of the president popular among Christian booksellers, presidential aides report that Bush and Blair have discussed scripture and prayed together.[6] In those cases, Bush used his Christian beliefs to build bonds, but he has also testified to his faith when it carried diplomatic risks: during the buildup to the war on Iraq, President Bush invited Turkish leader Recep Tayyip Erdogan to a meeting at the White House to woo Turkey's support. Erdogan is a devout Muslim, but as the leader of a secular nation that has often jailed Muslim leaders, he has thrown up a firm wall between his private religious beliefs and his public political life. According to an interview Erdogan's interpreter later gave to the *New York Times Magazine,* Bush startled Erdogan at the December 2002 meeting by saying, "You believe in the Almighty, and I believe in the Almighty. That's why we'll be great partners."[7] Conversely, as the *New York Times*' Bill Keller has pointed out, "it is probably not entirely irrelevant to our international relations that . . . Jacques Chirac of France and Gerhard Schröder of Germany are adamantly secular."[8]

Even if the president does not literally believe, as Abbas reported, that God told him to strike at al-Qaeda and Saddam Hussein, his unwavering certainty about every decision he has made regarding the war on terror is likely bolstered by the prevalence of such beliefs within his administration and among his most fervent supporters. From his chief speechwriter, his attorney general, and a high-ranking official in his Department of Defense to the many evangelical Christian leaders with whom he and his administration are in constant contact, the president regularly interacts with trusted supporters who believe the United States is engaged in a holy war and his presidency was ordained by God.

Bush has often spoken of his decision to run for president in divine terms. He's said that sitting in a church service in 1999, listening to a sermon straight out of Exodus about the reluctance of Moses, he heard "the call."[9] In *The Faith of George W. Bush,* televangelist James Robison recounts meeting with Bush and his political strategist Karl Rove shortly thereafter. "I feel like God wants me to run for president," Bush told Robison. "I can't explain it, but I sense my country is going to need me. Something is going to happen, and at that time, my country is going to need me. I know it won't be easy, on me or my family, but God wants me to do it." He'd rather not run, he told Robison, and would be happy being a retired governor someday "buying my fishing lures at

Wal-Mart. . . . But I feel God wants me to do this, and I must do it."[10] Other prominent evangelical leaders, such as Richard Land, a leader of the Southern Baptist Convention, recount similar conversations.[11] At one meeting in Dallas that Robison set up to introduce Bush to a group of major Pentecostal, charismatic, and Southern Baptist preachers, the pastors gathered around the governor to lay hands on him; at another, with Baptists and Methodists, one pastor led a prayer asking God to "put the mantle of a champion" on Bush.[12]

After September 11, the sense that Bush was chosen for the job caught fire inside and outside of Washington. "I've heard a lot of 'God knew something we didn't,'" former Christian Coalition director Ralph Reed told the *Washington Post* three months later, speaking of the shifting sentiment among evangelicals. "He had a knowledge nobody else had: He knew George Bush had the ability to lead in this compelling way." This idea soon permeated the White House. "I think President Bush is God's man at this hour, and I say this with a great sense of humility," Bush aide Tim Goeglein, one of Bush's main liaison's to religious conservatives, told the conservative Christian magazine *World*.[13] Former Bush speechwriter David Frum's account of the president's first year in office, *The Right Man*, is the story of how Frum, an Orthodox Jew, came around to this belief himself. Frum writes that at first he "strongly doubted" Bush was suited for the presidency, but Frum, seared by the experience of 9/11, closes his book by retelling a story from the book of Samuel, in which God speaks to the prophet and tells him he has chosen David, the unlikely youngest son, as the new leader of Israel. "Bush was hardly the obvious man for the job," Frum then writes. "But by a very strange fate, he turned out to be, of all unlikely things, the right man."[14] *Time* magazine reported on the anniversary of 9/11 that Bush had echoed these sentiments privately, speaking of being chosen by the grace of God to lead at this moment.[15] In *Plan of Attack*, Bob Woodward documents that Bush did not ask advice from his secretary of state or secretary of defense on whether to go to war; he didn't even seek guidance from his father, who had gone to war against Iraq twelve years before. "You know, he is the wrong father to appeal to in terms of strength," Bush told Woodward. "There is a higher father that I appeal to."[16]

Crusade

The danger of this view is especially apparent now, as the administration's original arguments for war on Iraq have dissolved. On the eve of the invasion, President Bush addressed a group of church leaders at the National Association of Religious Broadcasters conference in Nashville, where he spoke of Saddam Hussein as "evil" and said of the prospect of going to war, "If anyone can be at peace, I am at peace about this."[17] Yet less than a year after going to war, each of the administration's central claims about the Iraqi danger—that Saddam Hussein had aided al-Qaeda; that he possessed chemical, biological, and nuclear weapons of mass destruction; that he posed an "imminent threat"—had proved untrue. Each critical piece of intelligence used to bolster these claims—Iraq's importation of uranium from Niger; the meeting of an Iraqi official with an al-Qaeda contact in Prague; the reports from Iraqi dissidents about top-notch weapons programs—had been discredited. The administration's prediction that coalition forces would be met with open arms was undercut daily by the growing tally of American dead. Yet Bush's "peace" about his decision to invade remained unshakable. Political pundits characterized his refusal to admit any errors as either headstrong or politically calculated, but both views may have missed the point. If the president believed God wanted him to "strike at" Saddam Hussein, then what would inconclusive or contradictory intelligence have mattered? Each scrap of intelligence that supported invasion would have leaped from the page, an affirmation of God's will, while any intelligence that refuted such a necessity would have been received with suspicion, seeming to muddy God's plan. In *The Price of Loyalty*, the account of Paul O'Neill's tenure as Bush's treasury secretary, O'Neill recalls his discovery that ideology, not real world analysis, ruled the White House. "Ideology is a lot easier, because you don't have to know anything or search for anything," O'Neill says. "You already know the answer to everything. It's not penetrable by facts."[18] How much more so if that ideology is believed to be divine—and if it pertains to a war against evil itself.

It was David Frum who coined Bush's signature phrase in the new war on terrorism, "the axis of evil," words that powerfully associated Saddam

Hussein with both Nazism *(axis)*, the modern embodiment of horror for Jews, and Satan *(evil)*, the ancient embodiment of horror for Christians. And this idea of a war of good versus evil opened the door for the war on terror to be seen as a religious crusade by both Christian fundamentalists at home and Islamic fundamentalists abroad. While the World Trade Center was still in flames, evangelical leaders Jerry Falwell and Pat Robertson leapt to blame 9/11 on their favorite target, American liberalism, or, in the words of Falwell, "all of them who have tried to secularize America."[19] But the enemy within was soon eclipsed by the enemy without, as the Christian right redirected its anger at Islam, a message communicated most forcefully by those leaders who are closest to the administration. Within two months, Franklin Graham, the son of traveling evangelist Billy Graham, whom President Bush credits with his religious awakening—the same Franklin Graham who had led Bush's inaugural prayer—denounced Islam on television as "a very evil and wicked religion." Reverend Jerry Vines, a past president of the 16-million-member Southern Baptist Convention, a religious organization with strong ties to the administration, called the Muslim prophet Muhammad a "demon-obsessed pedophile." Both of these remarks were widely reported in the Arab press. Falwell and Robertson picked up the drumbeat: Robertson said Muslims were "worse than Nazis," while Falwell's characterization of Muhammad as "a terrorist" touched off a riot in Sholapur, India, that left nine people dead and one hundred injured.[20] And these comments were hardly anomalies. According to a poll published in early 2003 by the Ethics and Public Policy Center and Beliefnet, an online journal covering religion, 70 percent of evangelical leaders consider Islam to be "a religion of violence" and 66 percent believe Islam is dedicated to world domination. A Pew survey from 2002 found Islam had a far higher disapproval rating among white evangelicals than among any other American demographic.[21] "Evangelicals have substituted Islam for the Soviet Union," Reverend Richard Cizik, a vice president of the National Association of Evangelicals, told the *New York Times*. "The Muslims have become the modern-day equivalent of the Evil Empire."[22]

For evangelicals, who have long targeted Jews for conversion, the interest in Muslims is recent and intense. Five years ago, the Southern

Baptists reorganized their International Missions Board to focus on Islamic populations. Shortly thereafter, evangelicals formed the Window International Network, a campaign to target Muslims for conversion in a swath of the world they call the "10/40 window," comprising countries in North Africa, Asia, and the Middle East between 10 and 40 degrees north latitude. Participants include major missionary operations such as Nazarene Missions International, which claims to be active in thirty of the sixty-five "window" nations. Two years ago, Southwestern Baptist Theological Seminary in Texas created a master's degree program to train missionaries in how to convert Muslims. Since 1990, the *New York Times* reports, the number of missionaries in Islamic countries has quadrupled. As evangelical anger toward Muslims surged after 9/11, so did these activities. The Beliefnet survey found that by late 2002, 81 percent of evangelical leaders believed proselytizing Muslims abroad to be very important.[23] So with many countries in the 10/40 window off-limits to Christian missionaries due to laws against religious conversion efforts, the United States' invasion of Iraq was big news. "There is a tremendous amount of excitement about the opportunity," said Mark Kelly of the Southern Baptist Convention's International Mission Board when the war was just in its second month.[24]

Some missionaries stepped right into the war zone: "I can hear jets flying over the town, and I hear explosions from the distance," one missionary wrote home to the International Bible Society in early April 2003. "There are still a few of us in town. We go out to visit and distribute tracts and the Jesus video [an evangelizing film produced by Campus Crusade for Christ]. We are busy duplicating the video. We ran out of tracts and we need to print 10,000 more."[25] Others, many more, moved in after the fall of Iraq's Baathist regime, despite strong warnings by prominent theologians. (Chuck Campbell of the Columbia Theological Seminary said at the time, "I don't think Christians have any business trying to spread the Christian faith under the umbrella of U.S. military occupation. It really does lend the air of a crusade to this.")[26] The Southern Baptist Convention, which has more than a thousand missionaries in the 10/40 window, began sending boxes of food, with a label carrying the verse John 1:17 in Arabic: "The law indeed was given through Moses; grace and truth came through Jesus Christ."[27] Samaritan's Purse—whose president, Franklin Graham, called Islam "wicked"—made a decision to send missionaries as soon as heavy combat subsided, ready to tap its enormous $194 million budget for the effort. Samaritan's Purse has a spotty track record on such efforts. When providing aid to El Salvador after a 2001 earthquake through a grant from the US Agency for International Development, the group offered prayer services along with its construction project, incurring censure from the State Department. During the first Gulf War, Graham infuriated General Norman Schwarzkopf when he sent tens of thousands of Arabic-language Bibles to U.S. troops stationed in Saudi Arabia, asking that the soldiers pass them onto locals, in direct contravention of local laws against proselytizing and the language of a U.S.-Saudi agreement.[28] Other groups joined in: the Christian and Missionary Alliance decided to send food and supplies with the goal of evangelizing, In Touch Ministries made plans for Christian television broadcasts in Iraq, and the Center for Ministry to Muslims began to train some 20,000 missionaries to work with Muslims in Iraq and elsewhere in the Arab world. One evangelical training tour, run by Arab World Ministries, used Power-Point presentations claiming to prove that Islam is inherently violent; "You can tell me Islam is peaceful," a trainer said, according to one account in the *New York Times*, "but I've done my homework."[29]

Muslim leaders in the United States condemned this mix of aid and evangelism as coercive, while regional experts warned that such activities would only reinforce the image promoted by al-Qaeda that crusaders were out to undermine their religion. "It's going to be a public relations disaster for the Bush administration," said Ibrahim Hooper, spokesman for the Council on American-Islamic Relations, whose political action committee endorsed Bush in 2000. "It is very deceitful. They come with food in one hand and Bibles in the other."[30] A former senior CIA counterterrorism expert, Vincent Cannistraro, warned that "In the best of times, these people [evangelicals] excite passion among Islamists, and this is not the best of times; this is the worst of times. In the Arab media, this war is being portrayed as a clash of civilizations."[31]

Yet far from discouraging this explosion of missionary efforts in the

Arab world, Bush appeared in the Rose Garden with two evangelical missionaries who'd been imprisoned by the Taliban for breaking a ban on proselytizing and announced that one of the reasons he attacked Afghanistan was to secure their release.[32]

In early April 2003, just weeks after the launch of the war on Iraq, two reports emerged that this evangelizing spirit had infiltrated the American military itself. First, the Australian Broadcasting Corporation reported that a pamphlet called "A Christian's Duty," produced by the Atlanta-based In Touch Ministries, was being circulated by the thousands to American soldiers in Iraq. Though the pamphlet contains a tear-out form designed to be sent to the White House to confirm that "the soldier who sends it in has been praying for Bush," a spokesperson for In Touch claimed that it was not designed specifically for the military and that a member must have independently "shipped a bulk order over." Then the Miami Herald reported that a Southern Baptist Army chaplain based near Najaf had been offering soldiers a chance to bathe in a precious 500-gallon pool only if they sat through an hour-and-a-half sermon and agreed to get baptized. In each case, the reaction of U.S. officials was cavalier. Responding to questions about the prayer guide, Centcom spokesman Keith Oliver said he hadn't seen the pamphlet, but added that he's "not surprised at all that civilian ministries in the United States would be providing materials to our troops." The Army initiated a brief inquiry into the chaplain's baptism methods, but gave him the all-clear two weeks later, finding that he had not used coercion. More chillingly, prisoners tortured by U.S. guards at the notorious Abu Ghraib prison near Baghdad reported being forced to drink alcohol and eat pork, in violation of Muslim religious prohibitions, and said that anti-Islamic sentiment permeated the abuse. "They ordered me to curse Islam, and because they started to hit my broken leg, I cursed my religion," one former inmate said in sworn testimony to military investigators. "They ordered me to thank Jesus that I'm alive. And I did what they ordered me."[33]

While in the weeks after 9/11 he often emphasized that Islam was a religion of peace, Bush refused to condemn the growing demonization of Islam by the Christian right leadership. By the time Jerry Falwell called the prophet of Islam a terrorist in October 2002, the pressure began to mount for the president to offer a rebuke: "On their noxious mix of religious bigotry and anti-Muslim demagoguery," the *Washington Post* editorial page declared, "Mr. Bush's silence is deafening."[34] But the following excerpt from a subsequent press conference with Bush spokesperson Ari Fleischer typifies the careful dance the White House chose instead. The opening salvo was delivered by Les Kinsolving, a reporter with the right-wing online publication WorldNetDaily:

> Q: Ari, a *Washington Post* editorial on Sunday strongly criticized the president for what they termed "averting his gaze" from the defaming of Islam and the gross distortions which they attributed to the Reverend Franklin Graham, the Reverend Jerry Falwell, and to Pat Robertson. And my question is, does the president agree with the *Washington Post*'s claim that these three are defaming with great distortions, so that the *Washington Post* editors are better informed on comparative religion than these three Baptist Church leaders?
>
> MR. FLEISCHER: Les, I'm not familiar with the specific quotes you cited, so—
>
> Q: You didn't read the *Washington Post* on Sunday? [. . .] (Laughter.)
>
> Q: Falwell called Muhammad a terrorist, the Prophet Muhammad.
>
> MR. FLEISCHER: Assuming, of course, that that's an accurate quote—I haven't read it, myself—the president's views on Islam are well known. The president has said many times in his visits to mosques, and his visits with Muslim leaders, and his invitations for Muslim leaders to come here, as an important signal of America's openness and welcoming of Muslims, that Islam is a religion of peace.
>
> Q: And so he will disagree publicly with these three church leaders?
>
> MR. FLEISCHER: You know the president's position, it is exactly as I stated—

Q: Why can't you say whether he repudiates their remarks or not?

MR. FLEISCHER: Simply because I'm not aware of specifically what they've said, David. But there should be no—

Q: The remarks have been out there for some time and are pretty well documented.

MR. FLEISCHER: Again, I don't—I have a long pattern, as you know, if I haven't seen the remarks, I always want to make certain that everything I'm hearing is accurate.[35]

Bush couldn't quite endorse Falwell's, Robertson's, and Graham's inflammatory remarks about Islam, but he didn't want to risk condemning them either. Indeed, in ways both subtle and direct, the president and his staff were actively cultivating the idea that they were engaged in a holy war. Just a week after 9/11, the president himself called the war on terror a "crusade," a comment about which he later expressed regret, under fire from American Muslim leaders.[36] While the fighting in Iraq was still hot, Defense Department officials invited Franklin Graham to deliver a Good Friday homily at the Pentagon. After this, too, sparked protest by American Muslims—"It sends a completely horrible message to the Muslim world," Sarah Eltantawi of the Muslim Public Affairs Council told reporters—the Bush administration refused to retract the invitation, and Graham used the platform to tell his audience of soldiers, "There's no other way to God except through Christ."[37]

Bush has frequently made the association between God—even Jesus—and the American antiterror project, as Jim Wallis, the editor of the liberal Christian magazine Sojourners, has pointed out. "This ideal of America is the hope of all mankind," Bush said at Ellis Island on the first anniversary of 9/11. "That hope still lights our way. And the light shines in the darkness. And the darkness has not overcome it." Those final two sentences come straight from the New Testament's Gospel of John, except Bush changed its meaning, substituting America for God. In his 2003 State of the Union address, just before the launch of the invasion of Iraq, the president spoke of "power, wonder-working power, in the goodness and idealism and faith of the American people," a reference to a popular hymn, with Americans substituted for the sacrifice of Jesus ("the blood of the Lamb" in the original).[38] In his May 2003 speech on the USS *Lincoln*, where he declared an end to major combat in Iraq, Bush thanked American soldiers for serving not only America, but "our cause," "the highest calling of history," and said those who lost their lives died "fight[ing] a great evil." He closed by saying, "And wherever you go, you carry a message of hope—a message that is ancient and ever new. In the words of the prophet Isaiah, 'To the captives, come out, and to those in darkness, be free.'"[39] The Isaiah passage involves a commandment to spread God's word, which Bush here conflates with American democracy. (The verse also happens to be from a chapter in Isaiah used by Christian fundamentalists to show that the coming of Jesus was predicted in the Old Testament.)[40] "Bush seems to make this mistake over and over again," writes Wallis, "confusing nation, church, and God."

When Bush's Pentecostal attorney general, John Ashcroft, spoke to the National Religious Broadcasters, an evangelical association, at their annual conference in Nashville just five months after 9/11, he spoke of the war on terror in starkly religious terms. "Our fight against terrorism," Ashcroft said, according to a draft released by the Department of Justice, "is a defense of our freedom in the most profound sense: It is the defense of our right to make moral choices—to seek fellowship with God. . . . It is a conflict between those who believe that God grants us choice and those who seek to impose their choices on us. It is a conflict between inspiration and imposition, the way of peace and the way of destruction and chaos. It is a conflict between good and evil. And as President Bush has reminded us, we know that God is not neutral between the two."[41] That same month, comments surfaced from a radio interview Ashcroft had taken part in the previous November, in which he said, "Islam is a religion in which God requires you to send your son to die for him. Christianity is a faith in which God sends his son to die for you," comments Ashcroft later claimed referred only to terrorists.[42] During this same period, Ashcroft had begun to implement the Patriot Act in a way that aggressively targeted Muslims: shutting down Muslim charities, profiling Muslims at airports, and calling in some 5,000 legal Muslim foreign nationals for interrogation.[43]

The most incendiary remarks from inside the administration came a year and a half later, as insurgent attacks on the U.S. occupiers in Iraq began to mount. And they came from another significant player in the war on terror: a decorated lieutenant general and special ops expert who had just been assigned to head up efforts to track down Osama bin Laden and Saddam Hussein as the Pentagon's new deputy under-secretary of defense, Lieutenant General William "Jerry" Boykin.

BAPTISM BY FIRE

Jerry Boykin's anti-Muslim remarks caused an immediate stir when *NBC Nightly News* and the *Los Angeles Times* first reported them in October 2003.[44] But I first saw the complete videotape of his storied speech in late November, courtesy of former presidential candidate and Christian right leader Gary Bauer, whose organization, American Values, distributed copies for free in his defense. "We are engaged not only in a war against radical Jihadists whose sole aim is our complete destruction," Bauer wrote in his cover letter, "but a cultural war over our traditional values and common sense. The political correctness being so unfairly directed at General Boykin while he wages a concerted effort to capture or kill both Osama bin Laden and Saddam Hussein is a classic example of how the convergence of these two battles can hurt our country."[45]

The event documented on the tape was a "patriotic service" at the Good Shepard Community Church in Boring, Oregon, an annual event at which the congregation honors its members who are veterans or who are currently serving in the armed forces. The church choir kicked off the ceremony with a patriotic medley that folded in everything from "America the Beautiful" to "Auld Lang Syne"; men in uniform then filed onto the stage with their children and grandchildren, each planting a small flag in a giant bouquet of white carnations. Then came the star attraction, a man introduced as someone who "loves our nation, loves the Savior, and has been willing to risk his life to protect us." While the servicemen in the congregation attended in their dress uniforms, Boykin walked up to the stage in his battle fatigues, his pants tucked into polished combat boots. What surprised me most, viewing the grainy tape, was how scripted his speech seemed to be. His comments in print seemed so off-the-wall I assumed he had blurted them out spontaneously. But the general's talk was a multimedia affair, and his remarks on the tape seem well rehearsed, timed to coincide with the images in a lengthy slide show. He spends much of his talk telling war stories from his time in Mogadishu, Somalia (he figured in the *Black Hawk Down* events), and offering blow-by-blow battle details from the U.S. campaign in Afghanistan. Then he projects a series of graphic photographs from 9/11, followed by a shot of George W. Bush. "Then this man stepped forward and he looked America in the eye and he said, 'We will not forget, we will not falter and we will not fail,'" Boykin said. "Now ask yourself this: why is this man in the White House? The majority of Americans did not vote for him. Why is he there? And I tell you this morning he's in the White House because God put him there for such a time as this. God put him there to lead not only this nation but to lead the world, in such a time as this." "Such a time as this" is a phrase from the Bible, and it's a theme Boykin returns to again and again in his speech.

Then Boykin flashes slides of Osama bin Laden, Saddam Hussein, Kim Jong Il, and leaders of the Taliban, and asks each time, "Is this man the enemy? What about this man?" With a flourish, standing there in his combat fatigues, he offered his own answer: "The enemy is not a physical enemy. The enemy is none of these people that I showed you here. The enemy is a spiritual enemy. It's called the principality of darkness. We, ladies and gentlemen, are in a spiritual battle, not a physical battle. Oh, we've got soldiers fighting on the battlefields, we've got sailors, marines, airmen, coast guardsmen out there fighting against a physical enemy. But the battle this nation is in is a spiritual battle, it's a battle for our soul. And the enemy is a guy called Satan. . . . Satan wants to destroy this nation. He wants to destroy us as a nation and he wants to destroy us as a Christian army. I'm here on a recruiting trip. I'm here asking you to join this army."

Near the end of his talk, he clicks to a slide from Iraq, but this image isn't a battle scene. It's a soldier kneeling, with his head bowed, getting baptized, what Boykin calls "one of the greatest photographs to come out of the war." The deputy undersecretary of defense closes with a prayer. "We ask you Lord, in the name of Jesus, that if there is one among us here today that has never joined your army, that has never made the commitment to be part of your army, that in fact today will be the day of their salvation, Lord." He's in uniform, everyone around him is in uniform, and on the day he delivers the address he's just been put in charge of critical U.S. military operations—at this point, Jesus' army and the U.S. Army have become one and the same.

"Religious extremism is all over the world," Hussein Ibish, spokesperson for the American Arab Anti-Discrimination Committee, said on *Crossfire,* after Boykin's remarks had made headlines. "We don't need it in the Defense Department." Editorial pages across the country called for Boykin to be put on inactive duty, while Senator John Warner, the Republican chairman of the Armed Services Committee, demanded a formal probe. Yet Boykin's civilian boss, Defense Secretary Donald Rumsfeld, praised the general's "outstanding record," and his military superior, Joint Chiefs chairman Richard Myers, would say only, "It doesn't look like any rules were broken." Rumsfeld eventually announced that the Pentagon inspector general would launch an investigation into Boykin's remarks, but insisted he was doing so only at Boykin's request.[46] The same week the Boykin story broke, the president condemned anti-Jewish remarks by the prime minister of Malaysia as "reprehensible" and "divisive." But his response to Boykin recalled his earlier muted response to the anti-Muslim remarks of Falwell, Robertson, and Graham. The general he had just entrusted with the task of capturing Saddam and bin Laden had basically compared Islam to Satan, and Bush's response was this: "He doesn't reflect my point of view or the view of this administration."[47] After all, General Boykin was fast outpacing Alabama judge Roy Moore, the Ten Commandments hero, as the biggest cause célèbre on the Christian right, and caution was in order. After Bush's slight attempt to distance himself from the general's remarks, Bauer sent an action alert to his members, writing, "I must be missing something. The general has said that America is under attack because we are built on a Judeo-Christian values system; that ultimately the enemy is not flesh and blood, but rather the enemy is Satan; and that God's hand of protection prevented September 11 from being worse than it was . . . precisely which of those statements does the president take issue with?" The Christian Coalition began a petition drive urging Rumsfeld not to buckle under to the "intolerant liberal mob [that] has castigated General Boykin, a true American hero." And Focus on the Family Chairman James Dobson took to the airwaves, calling Boykin "a martyr" and imploring listeners to call the White House. Nihad Awad, director of the Council on American-Islamic Relations, articulated the concerns of many when he charged that "putting a man with such extremist views in a critical policy-making position sends entirely the wrong message to a Muslim world that is already skeptical about America's motives and intentions."[48] In this administration, the diplomatic risks of offending the Muslim world had proved a secondary concern when measured against the politicals risks of offending the administration's invaluable evangelical base.

MOTHER ISRAEL

Riding the enormous coattails of Ronald Reagan, George H. W. Bush won the presidency comfortably in 1988, and his more than respectable share of the Jewish vote that year—35 percent—didn't hurt. Partly because of the former CIA chief's tough stance toward Israel—he at one point threatened to withhold loan guarantees if Israel continued to expand Jewish settlements in the West Bank and Gaza—that support dropped to little more than 11 percent in 1992. And no lesson of Bush the elder's reelection defeat, however small, has been lost on the younger Bush's political mastermind, Karl Rove. Bush political advisors have pledged to boost President Bush's share of the Jewish vote from 20 percent in 2000 to as much as 40 percent in 2004, with special attention to such swing states as Florida and Pennsylvania. And he plans to do this mainly by easing U.S. pressure on Israel.[49] In the buildup to the midterm congressional elections, for example, Rove sent Bush to deliver a major Rose Garden address on the Israeli-Palestinian conflict, in which he firmly placed the Palestinian leadership on the wrong side of his "with us or against us" ledger, and then marginalized Yasir Arafat by "calling for the Palestinian people to elect new leaders."[50] Such gestures have achieved measurable results. According to the Jewish *Forward,* as of late summer 2003, some 2,000 Jewish "team leaders" had volunteered to support the campaign, along with several high-profile Jewish fundraisers, one of whom raised $4 million for the campaign at a single Manhattan event.[51] By early 2004, many leaders of major Jewish organizations, such as David Harris of the American Jewish Committee, agreed that "the Jewish vote is very much in play."[52] Regardless of international pressure to intervene more evenhandedly, strong support for Israel has generally been a win-win position from the perspective of Rove's electoral calculus. Not only might such a stance attract Jewish donors away from Democratic Party coffers, along with some Jewish votes, but the issue is also enormously popular among evangelical Christians, whom Rove has targeted for increased voter turnout in 2004.

While the pro-Israel lobby in Washington is usually identified with tightly organized Jewish lobbies such as the American Israel Public Affairs Committee, known as AIPAC, evangelical Christian support for Israel is much larger in sheer numbers and arguably far more influential, since conservative evangelicals have such close ties with Republican congressional leaders such as Tom DeLay. Rabbi Michael Lerner, a leader of the liberal Tikkun Community, recalls that when he visited Capitol Hill with some 400 Middle East peace activists in April 2004, most legislators he spoke with said they were feeling tremendous pressure from Christian Zionists to take a hard-line, pro-Israel stance. And one Christian Zionist leader, Robert Upton of the Apostolic Congress, has bragged that "we're in constant contact with the White House," including through weekly telephone briefings. Israel has held a fascination for Christian fundamentalists as far back as the formation of the modern state, which many viewed as a sign that millennial prophecies about Christ's return were beginning to unfold. During the Cold War this interest dovetailed nicely with right-wing views of Israel as a bulwark against Communism, as it does now with neoconservative views of Israel's role in the war against terror. A few projects took up the Christian Zionist cause as early as the 1970s, such as Americans for a Safe Israel, but many more have cropped up since: the Christians' Israel Public Action Campaign, a lobby group; the Friends of Israel Gospel Ministry, whose emphasis is prayer; Christian Friends of Israel; Christians United for Israel; and on and on. The first Christian Congress on Biblical Zionism was held in 1985, where delegates from around the world honed their case for supporting Israel based on a literal reading of the Bible. The proclamation of their most recent congress, held "at the onset of a new millennium" in February 2001, lays out fairly clearly the role Israel plays in a Christian millennialist view of history. The document asserts "the firm belief that God chose the Jewish people and bequeathed to them as an everlasting possession the Land of Canaan," and that "the modern restoration of Israel is . . . evidence of God's ongoing faithfulness to His people." It urges Jews around the world to "return" to Israel, a prerequisite for "the coming of the Lord," and concludes by saying, "Ultimately, we affirm that the restoration of Israel will usher in the coming of the Messiah."[53]

Rabbi Yechiel Eckstein, who has been cultivating evangelical support for Israel for more than twenty-five years, first at the Anti-Defamation League (ADL) and starting in 1983 as founder of the International Fellowship of Christians and Jews, says interest from Christian fundamentalists really took off about eight years ago. His Fellowship now boasts 330,000 Christian donors who in 2002 contributed $20 million to projects in Israel and millions more to support Jewish resettlement to Israel, rocketing the group onto the *Chronicle of Philanthropy*'s top 400 list. "Since 9/11, the Christian community has become more intense," Eckstein says. "Now everywhere you go it's Jews and conservative Christians linked together as a base of support for Israel, and Christians as natural allies. You have Ralph Reed addressing the ADL, Gary Bauer addressing AIPAC—these are major changes." Eckstein dismisses concerns that evangelical Christian support for Israel is rooted in theological beliefs about the End Times, what he calls "this image that they support Israel just so Jews will go back there and accept Christ and those who don't will be killed," and his organization commissioned a poll to put the issue to rest. What the Tarrance Group survey found instead is that a substantial minority of conservative Christians, 28 percent, cite "reasons related to the end times" as the source of their support for Israel, and a majority, 59 percent, cite "the Biblical promise to bless Israel." An independent survey conducted by the Pew Forum on Religion and Public Life found

even higher numbers: 63 percent of white evangelicals believe Israel ful-
fills the biblical prophecy about Jesus' second coming.[54]

When I ask Eckstein if he thinks the alliance unwise, in light of persistent evangelical efforts to convert Jews and to break down a church/ state
divide that has protected religious minorities, Eckstein says he has his
"finger on the pulse of the evangelical community better than any Jew in
the world," and that they simply don't offer a threat to the Jewish community. "It's a question of trust," he says. "Ralph Reed, even if he had the
opportunity, he's not going to try to make it into a Christian nation and
erode Jewish liberties." In fact, in the months after 9/11 Eckstein teamed
up with Reed, who served as director of the Christian Coalition during
its heyday in the mid-1990s, to form Stand for Israel, a campaign to
deepen support for Israel throughout the Christian evangelical church.

Stand for Israel's biggest operation is its annual Day of Prayer and
Solidarity with Israel. Some 25,000 churches and 7 million worshippers
across America and around the world had pledged to participate in the
second such event, in October 2003.[55] I stopped by the flagship event at
Mount Paran Church of God in Atlanta, Ralph Reed's home church.
Mount Paran is a massive operation, with a hundred-person choir and
two morning services to accommodate the thousand-plus attendees who
arrive each Sunday. It sits in a fabulously wealthy outlying area of Atlanta, with seven-bedroom stone mansions on wooded six-acre lots, a
setting that seems to suit the style of Pastor David Cooper, who preaches
a kind of muscular Christianity, emphasizing God's commandment to
"produce something" and using the stock market, industrial production,
and the information economy as metaphors. He's also a strict fundamentalist, who insists, according to his church's Web site, that the Bible is
"God's only inspired, inerrant and authoritative revelation of Himself to
man in written form."[56] While Reed, the master tactician, gave a politically savvy speech, never going farther than to quote a psalm about God
blessing Zion, Cooper showed his cards. "We pray, Lord God, that you be
a wall of fire around the city, a hedge of divine protection," Cooper said,
right on script. "We pray, Lord God, for peace in Israel, and peace in the
Middle East." Then he prayed for something else, conversion: "We pray
for the Good News of Jesus to bring the peace of God, the greatest of all

peace, to the hearts and the lives of those in Israel, in the Middle East, and in the world." He is, after all, the author of *Apocalypse!*, which interprets current events in light of the book of Revelation, and predicts such events as the rise of the Antichrist, the Great Tribulation, and the Second Coming of Jesus.[57] For Cooper, as for many evangelical supporters of Israel, Jewish migration to Israel will just be stage one, followed by their acceptance of Christ as their Savior.

Jean Hardisty is the founder of the Massachusetts-based Political Research Associates, a watchdog of the American far right, and she has long tracked Christian fundamentalist thought. "Throughout U.S. history, conservative Christians who were evangelical or fundamentalist and have taken the word of the Bible literally, have believed that the creation of Israel was a necessity for the fulfillment of Christian prophecy," she says. "So it's in the interest of Christians focused on the ultimate accomplishment of the Second Coming of Christ that the Jews go back to Israel, and this creates a natural affinity with Jews around the issue of Israel. But the real story is that the Jewish conquest of the land of Israel advances Christian prophecy to the moment when redemption comes. And at that moment, Jews will have converted, or they will be left out. They will not be redeemed." The double-sided nature of this support is clear in countless comments by major evangelical leaders: Jerry Falwell, for example, in a single passage of his 1980 book *Listen America!* writes of the importance of Jews "returning to their land" and of Jews being "spiritually blind and desperately in need of their Messiah and Savior."[58]

When I spoke with Reed after the prayer service, he, like Eckstein, denied that such visions have anything to do with evangelical support for Israel. But since Reed is now head of the Georgia GOP and southern regional chairman of Bush/Cheney 2004, it's impossible to separate his take on things from his aspirations to play a decisive role in delivering the White House to George Bush. He offered up a kind of enemy-of-my-enemy analysis, saying Christian conservatives support Israel "because Israel is our most reliable ally and a critical ally in the war on terror," and, sounding very much like the president in that 2002 Rose Garden speech, "because we've learned that the same infrastructure of terror responsible for the attacks on the United States is the enemy of

Israel." When I push him on whether Stand for Israel is ultimately designed to serve the president's reelection campaign, he slides into his pitch: "I think whether we existed or not, a lot of Jews are taking a second look at the president and the Republican Party. Because the president has been an outstanding leader in the war on terror, and such a strong defender of Israel, it's undeniable that if things continue as they have, this president will overperform in the Jewish community in historic terms." If Reed helps produce such an outcome, Rove won't soon forget him. But even if Christian Zionism doesn't attract Jewish votes, it has already exerted substantial pressure on Bush administration policy.

The Christians' Israel Public Action Campaign claims to lobby Capitol Hill daily on behalf of "policies that support Israel on biblical grounds," putting pressure on the House, the Senate, and the White House.[59] When Bush called for Israel to withdraw its tanks from West Bank cities after the army's reoccupation in April 2002, Falwell helped get 100,000 e-mails to the White House in protest. Bush silenced his criticism, and the Israeli army stayed put. That September, responding to international pressure to intervene in the escalating Israel/Palestine crisis, the United States joined Russia, Europe, and the United Nations, a group known as "the Quartet," in endorsing a road map for a peace agreement and a Palestinian state. Falwell, Robertson, and Christian right groups such as the Christian Coalition responded by turning out thousands to Washington for a Christian Support for Israel Rally to demand "no negotiations with terrorists," "no dismantling of Jewish communities in biblical Israel," and "no to a Palestinian state." As President Bush held meetings with the Quartet in December to discuss the road map, a dozen Christian Zionist groups took ads out in conservative papers, condemning the plan as "a path that would deny the Jewish people its rightful claims, those derived explicitly from God's covenant with the Jews." When Bush officially rolled out the road map in May 2003, Gary Bauer organized more than twenty major religious right leaders—Paul Weyrich of the Free Congress Foundation; Lou Sheldon of the Traditional Values Coalition; televangelist D. James Kennedy; and Richard Land, a leader in the Southern Baptist Convention, among others—to sign onto a letter insisting it would be "morally reprehensible for the United States to be 'evenhanded' between democratic Israel . . . and the terrorist infested Palestinian infrastructure." Meanwhile, members of Upton's Apostolic Congress sent in some 50,000 postcards to protest the plan.[60] With each small step Bush took to support the road map, Christian Zionists sent up a warning flare.

While most American Jews and most Israelis support an independent Palestinian state and support some dismantling of Jewish settlements to achieve that end, Christian Zionists believe that all of biblical Palestine—including the West Bank—must be under Jewish control. They donate millions of dollars to projects in Jewish settlements, long recognized by American officials as obstacles to peace. Their demands are more hard-line than those of either AIPAC or Israel's hawkish Likud Party, and far more aligned with the religious extremists of the Jewish settler movement. Rabbi David Saperstein, director of the Religious Action Center, the lobbying arm of Reform Judaism, has called this biblically based support for Israel "dangerous to Israel, to the Arabs, and to America."[61] In late 2003 and early 2004, as Israel's construction of a security wall incurred UN censure, and as Sharon's assassination of top Hamas leaders triggered Muslim anger as far away as Baghdad, it's hard not to imagine that the relentless pressure of the Christian right encouraged Bush to hold his tongue. Certainly they seemed to have access: according to far-right media sources, in August 2001 Bush's evangelical liaison, Tim Goeglein, held an intimate sit-down with leaders of the Christian Zionist movement, including the heads of Americans for a Safe Israel and Christian Friends of Israel, to discuss Mideast policy. And according to a memo obtained by the *Village Voice*, before President Bush endorsed Israeli Prime Minister Ariel Sharon's pullout plan from Gaza in spring 2004, Bush's senior Middle East advisor, Elliott Abrams, sat down with dozens of ministers affiliated with the Apostolic Congress to reassure them that "the Gaza strip had no significant Biblical influence . . . and therefore is a piece of land that can be sacrificed." [62] As Yechiel Eckstein points out, "Christian conservatives are a very important constituency for the administration. Jews have very few eggs in the Republican basket, but these people constitute that basket, and have a strong influence on Karl Rove and President Bush and in elections."

Bully Pulpit

Evangelical leader Tim LaHaye, the husband of Concerned Women for America founder Beverly LaHaye, has built a media empire out of his blockbuster "Left Behind" apocalyptic novels. The books lay out a detailed fictional account of LaHaye's literal reading of the book of Revelation, telling the story of the Rapture, when Christian believers will be whisked up to heaven; the period of Tribulation that follows on earth for nonbelievers "left behind"; the rise of the Antichrist, who will try to establish a world government; and the Second Coming of Jesus, who will establish a thousand-year reign on earth. The twelve novels in the series have together sold 55 million copies, and when the series' final installment, *Glorious Appearing*, was released in April 2004, it jetted to the number one spot on the *New York Times* fiction bestseller list. This empire includes videotapes, audiobooks, graphic novels, children's books, and study guides, as well as a series of branded calendars, gift cards, and apparel.[63] It also includes a weekly subscription e-mail, the Left Behind Prophecy Club, which helps readers "understand how current events may actually relate to End Times prophecy." In one posting from early 2004, LaHaye listed his top two "signs of the End Times" in 2003 as:

1) Israel claims her land. The return of the Jewish people to Israel is the "super-sign" of prophecy. . . .

2) Saddam's removal clears the way for rebuilding Babylon.

In other words, from his unflinching support of Israel's far right government to his invasion of Iraq, Bush's Middle East policy perfectly aligns with the religious worldview of LaHaye and his millions of readers. And beyond the Middle East, the novels point to an additional synchronicity between Bush foreign policy and the beliefs of LaHaye and other "premillenialist" End Times believers. In the series, LaHaye imagines the Antichrist as the charismatic Nicolae Carpathia, an advocate for global disarmament, a single world currency, and a more powerful United Nations. Carpathia eventually becomes the United Nation's secretary general. Here LaHaye sounds the deep suspicion of internationalism and multilateral institutions on the far right, bodies the right associated with Communism throughout the Cold War, but which, to many Christian fundamentalists, carry the taint of Satan, too. "There are some passages in the book of Revelation that suggest a player in the End Times is a one-world-government type with Satanic influence," says Randall Balmer, a professor of religious history at Columbia University, "which has created a long-standing suspicion of the United Nations or any confederation of countries."

Christian right outfits such as Phyllis Schlafly's Eagle Forum have long taken a strong stand against the United Nations. In one 1995 essay, titled "The United Nations: An Enemy in Our Midst," she claims the United Nations served as "a headquarters for Soviet espionage," "a conduit to bleed the U.S. taxpayers," and a "Trojan Horse" that "lures Americans to ride under alien insignia to fight and die in faraway lands." The Eagle Forum has called for the United States to pull out of the United Nations, or short of that, to refuse to pay its UN dues (a campaign joined by Beverly LaHaye and Concerned Women for America). During the Clinton years, the group circulated a videotape broadside against the institution called *Global Governance: The Quiet War Against American Independence,* which included interviews with, among others, Pentecostalist John Ashcroft, then a U.S. senator.[64] Religious right groups have particularly raised the alarm that the United Nations threatens to reach down into the privacy of American homes to legislate sexual mores and dictate how parents should raise their children. Concerned Women for America has insisted that the UN Convention on the Elimination of All Forms of Discrimination Against Women would "hand over our right" to decide our own laws on such issues as "family law, parental rights, religious exercise, education, abortion regulation, employment pay scales, quotas in educational institutions, workplaces and elected offices, and homosexual privileges" and "forbid us" from recognizing "that men and women are fundamentally different." In the essay "The New World Order Wants Your Children," the Eagle Forum warned that the UN Convention on the Rights of the Child would prohibit parents from forcing their children to do their homework and open the door for parents who home-school their children to be arrested for neglect. Austin Ruse's

Catholic Family and Research Institute, a Christian right advocacy group that focuses specifically on the United Nations, has charged the UN Population Fund with coercing abortions and UNICEF, the UN children's fund, with falling under the sway of "radical feminism."[65]

In the early 1980s, Tim LaHaye was predicting the fall of Communism and warning of a rising tide of interest in world government; in his 1984 book *The Coming Peace in the Middle East,* he wrote that this Satanic development would emerge "under the guise of 'the new world order.' "[66] So after the Soviet Union did collapse, the senior George Bush's use of that very phrase stoked fears on the Christian right, most publicly articulated in Pat Robertson's 1992 book *The New World Order,* which warned of conspiracies (many of them tinged with anti-Semitic paranoia) involving the United Nations and other international bodies. In this context, many on the Christian right viewed with alarm the senior Bush's decision to go to war against Iraq under the multilateral auspices of the United Nations.

How welcome then, when the younger George Bush shaped a tough unilateral foreign policy instead. His new policy, operating from ideas articulated in the early 1990s by deputy defense secretary Paul Wolfowitz and others while they were Washington outsiders (but fully embraced by the administration after 9/11), would be to celebrate and defend America's role as a sole superpower, and to ensure that no rivals emerged. Despite warnings from credentialed Republicans like Brent Scowcroft that this "go-it-alone strategy," at least with regard to Iraq, could produce both "a serious degradation in international cooperation with us against terrorism" and "an explosion of outrage against us" in the Middle East, Bush refused to make concessions at the United Nations and went to war on Iraq backed only by a small coalition of nations willing to accept U.S. leadership.[67] In his 2004 State of the Union address, delivered as the human and financial costs of unilateralism were becoming evident in Iraq, Bush reasserted his opposition to international give and take. "There is a difference, however, between leading a coalition of many nations, and submitting to the objections of a few," he said. "America will never seek a permission slip to defend the security of our country."[68]

The administration has made shows of unilateralism its hallmark.

Over objections from his own EPA chief, Christine Todd Whitman, Bush pulled out of the Kyoto Protocol on global warming. He opposed ratification of the Comprehensive Test Ban Treaty on nuclear arms and withdrew from the Anti-Ballistic Missile Treaty with Russia. In May of 2002, he "unsigned" the treaty negotiated by the Clinton administration to establish an international criminal court. And his administration charged into UN negotiations on such issues as AIDS, children's health, population policy, and women's rights with a new delegation staffed by Christian conservatives from such organizations as the Heritage Foundation, the Independent Women's Forum, Concerned Women for America, the Family Research Council, and the Vatican. "I saw it through Iraq, and I've seen it in all the special sessions, all the general assemblies," says Loreto Leyton, a diplomat at Chile's mission to the United Nations, a country the Bush administration sought to strong-arm on Iraq and on various negotiations around women's and children's rights. "It's 'Take it or leave it.' It's a very tough approach, a very careless approach in terms of the rest of the world." What angered foreign diplomats, however, was enormously pleasing to premillenialists on the Christian right. In their view, by shedding international entanglements and undermining the authority of the United Nations, Bush just may have been shedding the influence of Satan himself. As Austin Ruse, the Christian right lobbyist at the United Nations, gleefully declared in February 2001, "There's a new sheriff in town."[69]

2

CHRISTIAN NATION

ATTORNEY GENERAL John Ashcroft, the son and grandson of barn-storming Pentecostal preachers, is, without a doubt, one of the most visible symbols of the Bush administration's thoroughgoing religiosity. He famously refuses to drink, smoke, or even dance and, for religious reasons, remained a virgin until his marriage at age twenty-five. One of his first acts in office was to drape the exposed breast of the giant Spirit of Justice statue in the Justice Department's Great Hall. He has long viewed his political career in theological terms: in his memoir, he describes each of his many electoral defeats as a crucifixion and every important political victory as a resurrection, and recounts scenes in which he had friends and family anoint him with oil in the manner of "the ancient kings of Israel" with each new public office.[1] He says that he seeks God's presence when he makes political decisions and staunchly defends the legislation of morality: he did this so successfully during his one term in the Senate that he earned a 100 percent rating from the Christian Coalition every year.[2] "I don't particularly care if I do what's right in the sight of men," he has said. "The important thing is for me to do right in God's sight."[3] Until the war on terrorism intervened, necessitating that the attorney general attend early morning briefings at the White House, Ashcroft proceeded over daily morning prayer meetings in his own private office for Justice Department staff. The man who once told an audience at the fundamentalist Bob Jones University, "Unique among the nations, America recognized the source of our character as being godly and eternal, not being civic and temporal. . . . We have no King but Jesus" has long seen the wall between church and state as "a wall of religious oppression," and he's made every effort to knock it down as U.S. attorney general.[4]

Indeed, Ashcroft has shown himself to be a faithful channel not only for his own personal religiosity, but for the priorities of the Christian right. He has devoted significant Justice Department resources to investigating and prosecuting the pornography industry, but defended abortion clinics from threats and violence only after intense pressure from pro-choice advocates. And he has done battle against secularism whenever the opportunity arises. Early in his tenure, he expunged a pro forma phrase, "there is no higher calling than public service," from Justice Department letters to constituents and Congress, arguing, "There is a higher calling than public service, which is service to God."[5] In June 2002, when the Ninth Circuit Court ruled that asking public school children to use the phrase "under God" in the pledge of allegiance violated the First Amendment, evangelical conservatives flew into a rage, with Jerry Falwell, for example, calling the decision "probably the worst ruling of any federal appellate court in history." Ashcroft formally requested a rehearing of the case.[6] In spring of 2003, the Justice Department filed amicus briefs in two landmark cases regarding the intrusion of religion into the public schools—both briefs in support of an international missionary group, Child Evangelism Fellowship, that sought to have public schools in Maryland and New Jersey distribute its invitations to after school Bible study sessions.[7] That September, Justice filed an amicus brief in another carefully watched church/state case, this one in Washington State; again, Ashcroft argued on behalf of the plaintiff, a university student who sought to receive government funds to pay for religious training.[8] "Whenever cases deal with government funding or promotion of religion," says Rob Boston, spokesperson for Americans United for the Separation of Church and State, "the Justice Department under Ashcroft is always on the side of bringing church and state together."

But with Ashcroft waving a red flag for civil libertarians, other Bush administration officials and departments have escaped the same degree of scrutiny. Consider the Department of Education, whose secretary, Rod Paige, briefly became the subject of controversy when he told an interviewer with the *Baptist Press* that "all things being equal," he'd prefer to have a child in a school where there's a strong appreciation for Christian values. The matter blew over after Paige reiterated his support for church/state separation and the reporter was fired over some minor inaccuracies in his article. But according to a full transcript of the April 2003 interview, Paige's expressions of support for eroding the church/state divide were more substantial than the original article indicated. When asked if the nation should embrace religious values in our schools, he answered "absolutely." He called the Ninth Circuit Court decision about God language in the pledge "one of the worst decisions we could imagine" and expressed support for a Supreme Court decision allowing a Cleveland school voucher program to go forward, saying it would "foster a growth of our students' ability to get into schools, and in religious schools as well as secular schools." He praised the president for letting faith guide his political decisions, and when asked what he would say to critics of such religiosity, he responded, "I would offer them my prayers." And he said he begins each day with twenty-five minutes of scripture reading and—here he sounds remarkably like Ashcroft—that his own decisions at work were "a product of God's grace."[9] And Paige's religious views have shaped Department of Education policy.

Paige, for example, received strong praise from Christian conservatives for issuing a new set of federal guidelines on prayer in the schools, which stipulate that schools must allow students to organize prayer groups and religious clubs in school facilities and that teachers and administrators must be allowed to meet for prayer or Bible study on-site as well, as long as they aren't doing so in their "official capacities." Paige also threatened to withhold federal funding from public schools that he found to be out of compliance.[10] "Secretary Paige's guidelines make it abundantly clear that our nation's public school systems do not leave their First Amendment rights of religious expression at the boundary of public school property," Richard Land of the conservative Southern Baptist Convention told the *Baptist Press*. "This helps in that there are consequences for ignoring the First Amendment in a public school— immediate and real consequences."[11]

Or consider the National Park Service, governed by Secretary of the Interior Gale Norton, the woman who, as Colorado attorney general, paid a Christian advocate of gay reparative therapy as an "expert witness" in her effort to fight a gay civil rights measure.[12] A videotape that had been screening at the Lincoln Memorial since 1995, which documents the use of the monument as a soapbox for dissent, was suddenly recalled after Christian right organizations raised a fuss about a few seconds of footage of gay rights, pro-choice, and anti–Vietnam War demonstrations. According to Jeff Ruch, executive director of the watchdog group Public Employees for Environmental Responsibility, whose members went public with the story, Park Service officials responded by ordering the video to be re-edited to include footage of a Promise Keepers march and a prowar event from the Gulf War. Then there were the brass plaques, engraved with Christian Bible verses, that a group called the Evangelical Sisters of Mercy had installed on public lands at Grand Canyon National Park. After Judge Roy Moore was ordered to remove his Ten Commandments monument from the Alabama Supreme Court, the Grand Canyon superintendent consulted with Department of the Interior lawyers about the plaques and was advised to remove them, which he did. Well, as Ruch jokes, the sisters must have had a line not just to Mary but to top Park Service officials, because suddenly the Park Service deputy director ordered the plaques restored, reprimanded the superintendent, and wrote a humble letter of apology to the sisters. By far the most bizarre intervention on behalf of public religion took place in the Mojave National Preserve in California. There, under pressure from the ACLU, assistant superintendent Frank Buono arranged to remove a giant, eight-foot-tall cross that had been erected on a thirty-foot-high rock outcropping on public park land. After his retirement in 1995—he's since joined the board of Ruch's organization—Buono discovered that his decision had been reversed, and so he sued, in a case that he won in a California district court. The Bush administration appealed to the Ninth Circuit, and when it lost there, asked for a hearing by a full panel—the last recourse before a Supreme Court review. Then secretly, according to Ruch, as *Buono v. Norton* awaited its final hearing, the White House worked with Republican members of Congress to slip a provision into the 2004 defense appropriations bill after it had been approved by the

House and Senate—while it was in conference committee—to authorize a trade of the single acre of land on which the cross sits for five private acres at the park entrance. "So you'd have this one acre of private religious memorial right in the middle of this 1.5-million-acre national park," Ruch says. "Of course, given that this one-acre exchange is conditional upon the private group maintaining the cross, it remains a government establishment of religion."

Or recall one of the more spectacular explosions of Christian morality, at the Federal Communications Commission (FCC), after Janet Jackson briefly bared her breast before millions of Super Bowl viewers in February 2004. The family values lobby had recently flexed its muscles by forcing CBS to cancel an airing of its docudrama *The Reagans*—reputed to offer a critical view of their great hero—and its leaders quickly beat their own breasts about Janet's. Gary Bauer, Focus on the Family, and the Family Research Council immediately sent out action alerts to their members, and the phone calls and e-mails poured into Washington and CBS. Focus on the Family's Pete Winn declared that Jackson's display was a "symptom of how diseased pop culture has become"; if we don't draw the line, he said, "our society and our very freedom are at stake." FCC Commissioner Michael Powell, who had bucked popular discontent by taking a hard-line antiregulatory stance up till that point, responded quite differently to pressure from this important constituency, announcing that he would personally helm an investigation. The FCC hardball had immediate repercussions: Clear Channel radio network fired one shock jock, Todd Clem, and dumped Howard Stern's syndicated show from its stations. Viacom announced a similar zero tolerance policy; several awards broadcasts, and even the children's network Nickelodeon, imposed time delays to allow the censoring of improprieties; PBS deleted a cleavage shot from a biopic about free-love advocate Emma Goldman; a Los Angeles radio commentator was fired after an engineer neglected to bleep an expletive in her prerecorded editorial; and the House passed legislation that bumped up maximum FCC fines from $27,500 to $500,000.[13] Altogether, it was an unusual Republican assault on unfettered corporate power, but the rewards were great. "We are glad the FCC has thrown a flag on the halftime show," Family

Research Council president Tony Perkins wrote to his members, while Bauer wrote to his American Values list that Powell's actions are "a chance for the FCC to regain some credibility." Focus on the Family declared Powell "deserving of applause."[14]

But nowhere has the Bush administration experimented more directly with theocracy than in the centerpiece of Bush's compassionate conservatism: his faith-based initiative. The initiative's political origins lie, not unsurprisingly, with none other than John Ashcroft, who, as a senator, successfully attached what he called "charitable choice" amendments to Clinton's welfare reform legislation and other bills. In Ashcroft's arguments for the measures, which made it easier for states to turn welfare and other social services over to religious organizations, his desire to legislate Christian morality was barely under the surface. "Until now, Washington's failed welfare system has rewarded behavior that keeps the needy dependent," he said in a celebratory press release upon passage of the welfare bill in 1996. "Successful reform must minister to the deeper needs of people."[15] As the governor of Texas, Bush had often sought advice from Marvin Olasky, a Christian magazine editor who coined the term "compassionate conservatism" and wrote books arguing that churches were better suited to help the poor than government. Once the Ashcroft amendments passed, Governor Bush took advantage of the new provisions with more speed and enthusiasm than any other state executive, and he went on to promote the idea of faith-based social services throughout his presidential campaign. When Bush took office as president, he immediately tried to muscle an ambitious faith-based bill through Congress, one that would have eased restrictions on religious grantees and increased tax deductions for charitable giving. But legislators balked at some of its more extreme provisions—especially those exempting religious groups from federal antidiscrimination laws—and the bill stalled. The president's faith-based initiative, as currently constituted, was created instead by a series of executive orders in 2001, 2002, and 2003 that created an Office of Faith-Based and Community Initiatives (so named because the office can't legally discriminate between secular and religious charities) and lifted any number of long-standing regulations that once safeguarded the church/state divide. The initiative is now administered by a White House faith czar along with faith-based offices in seven federal departments, from Labor to Justice to Health and Human Services. Since President Bush typically speaks of the initiative as no more than a broad embrace of volunteerism and good works, an effort "to welcome people of faith in helping meet social objectives,"[16] the idea may appear as innocuous as his father's "thousand points of light." But the younger Bush's initiative actually marks a significant new effort to bring Christian faith into the government arena.

THE FAITH-BASED IDEA

For George W. Bush, giving a speech before the audience assembled at Nashville's Opryland Hotel on February 10, 2003, was a bit like having home-court advantage. This was a crowd who spoke his language, adored him, and was in a position to offer him a tremendous amount of political support. He'd come to address the annual conference of the National Religious Broadcasters, a media lobby led by politically connected evangelical leaders such as Jerry Falwell and Pat Robertson that represents some 1,700 Christian media operations, which reach a combined audience of hundreds of millions. "Religious" is perhaps too loose a term for what the association represents, since members are required to believe that those who aren't saved through Jesus Christ are condemned to eternal damnation and to "believe the Bible to be inspired, the only infallible, authoritative Word of God."[17] Surveying the crowd of 5,000, Bush said, "I see Evans," meaning Dallas-based evangelical broadcaster Tony Evans, who preaches on hundreds of radio stations across the country. "I see Gramm," meaning Texas' conservative former senator Phil Gramm. "It's good to see friendly faces."

The president used the opportunity to plug his faith-based initiative, offering up yet another version of a speech he's given, on tape or in person, before religious audiences from Los Angeles to Dallas to Pittsburgh. "The role of government is limited, because government cannot put hope in people's hearts or a sense of purpose in people's lives," he said, clarifying for the small-government conservatives in the audience that this effort was a critique, not an embrace, of the welfare state. "That happens when someone puts an arm around a neighbor and says, 'God loves you.'" He warned of the harms of "discriminating against religious groups just because they're religious," playing to the perception among Christian conservatives that liberals have sought to exile believers from the public square. He also dangled the promise of largesse. First he proposed an addiction recovery voucher program that would privilege organizations with "the capacity to change heart"—an evangelical catch phrase—"and, therefore, change habit"; then he mentioned a series of teach-ins his administration had organized across the country "to help faith-based groups to understand how they can qualify for government grants without compromising their mission." As he always does when discussing the faith-based initiative, President Bush trotted out his mantra of religious pluralism, which this crowd of Christian evangelizers must have greeted with a wink: If "the charity's helping the needy, it should not matter if there's a rabbi on the board or a cross on the wall or a crescent on the wall or religious commitment in the charter." Yes, Muslim, Jew, and Buddhist alike were all invited to join Bush's "armies of compassion."[18]

The broadcasters drank it all in and capped off the festivities by passing a resolution honoring Bush for his "godly" leadership, from recognizing "the sanctity of life in all its forms" to "advocating tax relief." The document concluded: "We recognize in all of the above that God has appointed President George W. Bush to leadership at this critical period."[19] Though the broadcasters association, as a tax-exempt organization, is barred from endorsing the president, they had done one better, simply declaring that God had taken sides already.

IT'S A CHRISTIAN THING

That October, I found myself in an unusually long line at the Memphis Convention Center, waiting to pass through a metal detector and a security check as invasive as an international airport's. The crowd of 1,600 white and African American clergy, church elders, social service providers, and professional grant writers were elbowing their way into a White House Conference on Faith-Based and Community Initiatives—one of the teach-ins Bush had promoted in his speech—lured by the promise that they'd learn how to reel in hundreds of thousands of dollars in federal grants. Some attendees came from established Christian charities such as Heifer International, which promotes sustainable agriculture in the developing world; others came from small congregations in Alabama or Georgia with vague plans to start what they called a "ministry" to feed the homeless. All of them, I slowly realized as the day progressed, were Christian.

When I slipped into a workshop on international programs run by the U.S. Agency for International Development (USAID), one of the seven federal departments and agencies that now house a special faith-based office, I noticed that everyone else who'd signed in had a Christian organizational affiliation. Every single religious presenter, handpicked by the faith-based office as a model for "successful partnerships," represented a Christian outfit—whether a small grass-roots operation, such as the program at Nashville's Metropolitan Interdenominational Church that supports an AIDS orphanage in South Africa, or a major not-for-profit corporation, such as MAP International, the $176 million Christian relief organization.

The day began with a videotaped greeting from President Bush, in which he again spoke of the pluralistic vision he has for his faith-based program. (This time he said, "It shouldn't matter to the government if the group has a cross on the wall, a mezuzah on the door, or a mullah on the board of directors.") But wandering through other workshops, focused on substance abuse, homelessness, and community development, I found the same Christian-only pattern as at the workshop run by USAID. In the session on home ownership, presenter Phil Reed, of Jackson, Mississippi's Voice of Cavalry Ministries, said, "Our mission was to spread the Gospel of Jesus Christ throughout the world. We put that in our proposals and said, 'If we don't get funded, so be it.' And we got the money. You no longer need to compromise your faith to get federal funding. If you want a Bible verse to wrap around that, if Cyrus wants to give us the money to build God's kingdom, we'll take it." In a session on homeless services, one woman in the audience, a lay church leader who'd faced community opposition when she tried to start up a shelter at her church, said, "We need to, as Christians, pray—" She then hesitated, asking, "I guess most of us are Christians here?" Hearing a quiet murmur of assent, she continued "—we need to pray that the municipalities will support us in this thing." As these incidents accumulated through the course of the day, I began to wonder whether the morning's presidential videotape, with its interfaith veneer, was actually a sectarian Christian message offered in a kind of code for the faithful. "Together we will find ways to break down bureaucratic barriers," he had said, "and expand the reach of programs that save and transform lives." What, precisely, did he mean by "save"?

The pervasive Christian vibe of the faith-based initiative is reinforced by a quick look at its key staff. The office's original director, John DiIulio, calls himself a "born-again Catholic" and credits his 1996 Palm Sunday "reawakening" for his faith in religiously run social services.[20] He was replaced after less than a year on the job by Jim Towey, another avowedly pro-life Catholic. At the conference, Towey made jokes about the sex workers he had aided at a homeless shelter ("I've spent a good bit of my life with prostitutes—ha ha—I should explain that—ha ha—'Hi mom!'"), then described them as "animals in the street" until they found their "God-given dignity." He also claimed dramatically that past administrations had engaged in a "ruthless" effort to clear the public square of religious influence, to the point that even "Mother Teresa's smile" was made illegal, and that congregations had been forced to "sell their soul" to provide a social service. His executive assistant, Catharine Ryun, who served as the Memphis event's upbeat MC, is the daughter of Republican Representative Jim Ryun of Kansas, a member of a group of "family values" lawmakers known as the Values Action Team.[21] She spent her early career running Christian sports camps, and, not long after the Memphis conference, I saw her participating in a major pro-life march on the Capitol demanding that *Roe v. Wade* be overturned. Brent Orrell, who runs the faith-based office at the Department of Labor, was legislative director for Senator Sam Brownback, the dean of pro-life forces in the Senate and head of its Values Action Team. Brownback, whose recent conversion to Catholicism was officiated by a priest affiliated with the far-right Opus Dei, a sect that rejects the reforms of Vatican II, is known for initiating prayer sessions in the Senate chambers. Robert Polito, who runs the faith-based office at Health and Human Services, was the founder of Faith Works, a Christian evangelical welfare-to-work program that has since faced lawsuits in Wisconsin over church/state separation.[22] Bush's staffing choices replicate a pattern he began as governor in Texas, where all but one person on his sixteen-member Task Force on Faith-Based Programs was Christian.[23]

Christianity dominates in the official publications of the White House faith-based office as well, as evidenced in the array of glossy brochures being pedaled from the government booths in Memphis. A Department of Justice handout trumpets nine faith-based victim assistance programs, whose institutional sponsors constitute a religious mosaic that ranges from Catholic Charities to the Abundant Grace Fellowship Church in Memphis to, well, the U.S. Catholic Conference. Not a mezuzah or mullah in sight. The brochure from the Department of Labor's faith-based office features on its cover a luscious four-color print of a bush in flames and bears the title, "Not everyone has a burning bush to tell them their life's calling," a text-and-image combination that seems to equate religiosity with the Bible.

At day's end, I cornered Jeremy White, a former Brookings Institution analyst who is now outreach director for the White House faith-based office, and asked him why he thought there were so few Asians and Latinos at the conference, and so very few non-Christians—if, indeed, there were any at all. He ducked the question, insisting that attendance was self-selective, and that Hispanic and Muslim faith-based groups just don't have the well-established communications networks the black church enjoys. I also asked him about who was getting the money.

It's difficult to get a complete list of all the recipients of faith-based grants since Bush first launched his initiative in January 2001. But in examining announcements of hundreds of grants from the faith-based offices at Labor and at Health and Human Services, in such areas as job training, work placement, child support, and abstinence education, I found that—with the exception of a few interfaith groups—every single religious organization that had won a grant was Christian. A sizable number of grants went to secular community organizations, but not one to a religious group that was identifiable by name as Jewish or Muslim or, for that matter, Hindu, Buddhist, Sikh, or any other non-Christian member of the American religious community. When I asked White about what appeared to be a pro-Christian bias in the grant-making, he said he wasn't familiar with the full list of grantees and couldn't comment. But a month after the Memphis event, in a White House–sponsored online chat timed for Thanksgiving, faith-based director Jim Towey indicated that some bias was indeed coming from the top. Asked whether he'd give equal consideration to pagan applicants for faith-based funds, Towey disparaged them as "fringe groups" who lacked the necessary "loving hearts."[24]

Some months later, Jim Towey told me that his office sends notices of these faith-based conferences to all registered charities in the area, so attendance is primarily a question of self-selection, as is who does and doesn't apply for grants. "The quality we're looking for is organizations interested in working with the poor, so we've reached across racial and ethnic lines," he says. "But I think we've been careful to communicate that there shouldn't be some kind of quota system." He says that grants are going to Christian groups, secular organizations, and, indirectly, through Compassion Capital Fund (CCF) subgrants, to Jewish groups. (His office could document only five grants to Jewish organizations, and only one to a Muslim group—all CCF subgrants over which the federal government has no control.) Other religious charities, he says, simply haven't competed for the money. "With Muslim organizations, what I understand is they tend to want to serve only Muslims in their social programs because they're an insular community," he said. "And some groups in the Orthodox Jewish community may not be interested in serving the general public." Religious sensitivity, Bush administration style.

THE POLITICAL USES OF FAITH

At the heart of Bush's faith-based project beats the gospel of privatization, the old-school right-wing ideal of pushing any responsibility for social welfare from the government onto the private sector. Reagan budget director David Stockman's strategy for this was, in his poetic phrase, to "starve the beast"—first push through tax cuts so drastic they empty the federal till, then force Congress to slash domestic spending in response.[25] President Bush has wholeheartedly embraced the Stockman strategy: for him, its two pillars are, on the one hand, huge tax cuts for the capitalist class and, on the other, transferring social services over to religious and private community organizations. As DiIulio, the former faith-based director, put it in early 2001, "The president's compassionate conservatism enlists government effort but resists government growth."[26] Even if the ideas are close cousins, "compassionate conservatism," in the form of faith-based grants and increased charitable deductions, sounds far kinder and gentler than "starving the beast."

The intellectual underpinnings of the faith-based initiative can be found in *The Dream and the Nightmare,* a furious indictment of liberalism by Myron Magnet, a fellow at the conservative Manhattan Institute. Karl Rove has often cited the book as his political bible, and it was one of the first books he gave to George W. Bush in the very early days of Bush's presidential bid. (The cover of the paperback edition boasts, "the book that helped make George W. Bush president.") The 1993 book argues that all of our social ills, from violent crime to drug addiction to poverty itself, are "the fruit not of economic deprivation but of inner defect."[27] What the poor need to succeed, Magnet concludes, is not higher wages or protections on the job, not child care programs or health care or affordable college tuition, but "an authoritative link to traditional values."[28] He lays out a worldview, which Rove ingested and regurgitated to Bush, that provides a perfect excuse for slashing government social programs and asking churches to solve our problems instead. This view, that what the poor really need is spiritual uplift, *even if they don't desire it themselves,* is also highly attractive to the evangelical right's soul-hungry ground troops. When Bush says, as he did in his speech to religious broadcasters, "Welfare policy will not solve the deepest problems of the spirit," one can imagine Magnet's applause.

Magnet's influence also seems to hover over the introduction George W. Bush wrote, during his presidential bid, to Marvin Olasky's

Compassionate Conservatism, one of two books in which Olasky lays out the theory and practice of the idea that would become Bush's trademark. "We started to see ourselves as a compassionate country because government was spending large sums of money and building an immense bureaucracy to help the poor," the then-governor writes. "In practice, we hurt the very people we meant to help."[29] How much more compassionate, then, to cut back on government social spending, to be a government that "knows its limits" and "rallies these armies of compassion" instead.[30] Olasky is himself a religious conservative, editor of the right-wing Christian magazine *World* and the former chairman of a crisis pregnancy center, one of those storefront agencies that pressure young women not to abort. But he fancies himself a moderate, steering between liberals "enamored with big government" and conservatives content to let the poor eat cake. Olasky spends much of the book profiling churches and community groups that run social service programs, mostly without government help, but his central argument is clear: we need government policy that "exercis[es] effective compassion rather than merely pushing for . . . income redistribution."[31] It is easy to see the usefulness of this idea for both economic and social conservatives: it implies that you can change the circumstances of the poor without changing the circumstances of the very rich; that you can send hundreds of billions of public dollars to the very wealthy through tax cuts, slash government social programs, and still be . . . compassionate. It was the perfect political packaging for George W. Bush.

"Essentially the faith-based initiative is a huge privatization scheme, a bait and switch," says Rob Boston of Americans United for the Separation of Church and State. "Because everyone thinks religious groups are great and deserve funding. The switch comes when the funding is cut off. A lot of people will suffer when that happens." So far, Bush has been careful to insist that the federal government will continue to play a role in providing social services.[32] But his words have sent a clear signal to those conservatives for whom downsizing government is a top priority. "If the President's rhetoric is taken seriously, no social problem would be immunized from the civilizing influence of religion," writes Heritage Foundation religion fellow Joseph Loconte. "If he confronts the deepest flaws of the welfare state, he could help shift resources from failed secu-lar programs toward those with a moral backbone. While liberals are willing to speak approvingly of the benefits of faith, they are unwilling to allow religious organizations to assume any of the social service functions controlled by government. If Bush pushes the logic of his own initiative, this is exactly the direction his reforms are headed."[33]

Of course, for an initiative to become so central to Bush's campaign and his administration, it had to do more than delight small-government conservatives. From the start, the faith-based idea was also designed to appeal to two seemingly contradictory constituencies: the president's white, conservative evangelical base and the traditionally Democratic black church. As for the latter, it is no secret that part of Karl Rove's formula for creating a Republican electoral majority in the United States is to skim off bits of the African American churchgoing vote (President Bush won a remarkably low portion of the black vote, 8 per-cent, in 2000, the worst showing by a presidential candidate since Barry Goldwater in 1964), or, perhaps more nefariously, to silence op-position to Bush by African American clergy who would normally help turn their (Democratic) flock out to the polls. African American GOP strategist Kenneth Blackwell has expressed this goal most ambi-tiously, telling the *Boston Globe* in 2001 that the White House was en-gaged in a "tightly choreographed effort" to attract as much as 30 percent of the African American vote in future presidential elections.[34] At any rate, visible attempts to reach out to African Americans and Latinos would help burnish George Bush's centrist veneer with subur-ban swing voters.

Several early signs indicated the faith-based initiative would serve as the cornerstone of administration efforts to woo African American support: The appointment of DiIulio to head up the project, someone with close ties to religious leaders in Philadelphia's African American community and a close ally of Reverend Eugene Rivers, a high-profile African American leader in Boston. The special invitation to the White House for prominent African American ministers, including Rivers, to discuss the initiative.[35] The targeted outreach to African American congregations through the Office of Faith-Based and Community Initiatives road shows, such as the one I attended in Memphis. The appointment of two successive African Americans, Rivers protégé Reverend Mark Scott and later Jeremy White, with whom I spoke in Memphis, to the role of outreach director at the White House's faith-based office, when almost every other person holding a senior position in the initiative is white.

Two months into Bush's presidency, Reverend Jesse Jackson, along with other African American civil rights leaders and members of the Congressional Black Caucus, accused the Bush White House of using faith-based dollars to bribe African American clergy into silence. "The same forces that sought to deny us the right to vote in Florida now are trying to neutralize the strength and the voice of black churches," Jackson said. "It is all about voter suppression." While officials in the faith-based office denied the charge—"This initiative is not George Bush's political ploy to win black votes," Scott responded at the time—subsequent events would support Jackson's contention.[36] As the *Washington Post* reported in the fall of 2002, top officials from the White House faith-based office appeared at Republican Party events in six states with close races, and most of these events targeted the African American community. At one event in South Carolina, where Republicans were fighting hard to keep the seat vacated by segregationist Senator Strom Thurmond, Jeremy White gave the keynote address to a crowd of 300, composed mostly of local African American ministers. White spoke of the millions of federal dollars that would be disbursed through the initiative, and everyone who attended received a follow-up note, on GOP stationery, explaining how to apply for the faith-based grants. In another tight race, in Kentucky, Republican Anne Northup brought Jim Towey along to discuss the faith-based initiative when she toured a black neighborhood in Louisville.[37]

When I was at the faith-based meeting in Memphis, I asked White whether the significant number of African Americans in attendance was indicative of any targeted outreach on his part, and whether such outreach was related to the president's electoral intentions. "Definitely not," he said sharply. "We haven't targeted any specific area. We work in urban areas, rural areas—we're targeting the whole country." Republican pollster Frank Luntz has quite a different assessment; he's characterized Bush's faith-based initiative as the "first successful effort I have seen to penetrate the black mind-set."[38]

Bush's efforts to use his faith-based initiative to deepen the loyalty of his white evangelical base got off to a rockier start. Marquee names on the Christian right quickly signaled their concern that "aberrant" groups (Pat Robertson's word) might receive public funds—and therefore legitimacy. While Robertson sounded the alarm about Hare Krishnas, Scientologists, and followers of the Reverend Sun Myung Moon, his counterpart, Jerry Falwell, singled out Muslims, insisting that "Islam should be out the door before they knock"—disqualified for even applying for grants.[39] Anxiety about the initiative on the Christian right was only exacerbated when John DiIulio made a speech before the National Association of Evangelicals in March 2001. He not only declared that "I strongly respect the separation of church and state" (a stance that was likely anathema to many in the room) and emphasized the need for "empirical data" showing that programs work (an irrelevancy for those whose ultimate goal is saving souls), but he made a less-than-subtle dig at the Robertsons and Falwells in the room. "With all due respect, and in all good fellowship, predominately white, ex-urban evangelical, and national para-church leaders should be careful not to presume to speak for any persons other than themselves and their own churches," he said, in one of the most strongly worded moments of a generally wonkish presentation. "Literally hundreds of millions of dollars raised and spent each year by national para-church organizations seems hardly to reach, and only weakly and episodically to benefit, the community-serving urban churches that witness 'truth and action' to the poor every blessed day."[40]

For a staffer in the Bush White House, that kind of attitude just would not do. While White House spokesman Scott McClellan defended DiIulio publicly, a senior Bush advisor told the *Boston Globe*, "I would not expect there to be a repetition of such remarks." Sure enough, within a week, senior White House officials met with leading evangelical social conservatives, where Lou Sheldon, chairman of the Traditional Values Coalition, a conservative lobby group that, it so happens, does not provide any social services, called for DiIulio's head. Reverend Richard Land, a leader with the conservative Southern Baptist Convention, told the *Boston Globe,* "My friends at the White House didn't disagree when I said DiIulio's statements were inaccurate and imprudent."[41] Whatever participants were told in that hastily convened meeting must have profoundly reassured them. Or perhaps the launch of an intensive lobbying campaign against the faith-based initiative by the Christian right's most despised foes—NOW, the ACLU, People for the American Way, Americans United for the Separation of Church and State, and liberal religious denominations including Unitarians and Reform Jews—helped clarify which side they were on.[42] Either way, Jerry Falwell, once a chief critic of the initiative, declared a week after the White House meeting that he "fully supports" the program and was "excited" to see it implemented.[43] In mid-April, a new Coalition for Compassion (likely a nod to the ACLU-led effort, the Coalition Against Religious Discrimination) held a press conference in Washington to announce its enthusiasm for the faith-based initiative. Its members included not only Olasky, the father of compassionate conservatism, but Lou Sheldon, Gary Bauer, Paul Weyrich's Free Congress Foundation, the Family Research Council, Concerned Women for America, the Eagle Forum, and more than a dozen other prominent family values lobbies. DiIulio, with egg on his face, joined the press conference, where he listened as coalition chairwoman Connie Marshner spoke of the great potential for proselytizing through social services (warning that "it would truly be a tragedy if a single church were to change its mission one nanometer because of government money") and for accessing government money to construct church buildings. She closed by shaking DiIulio's hand "to show that he is in accord with us on these principles."[44]

As the grant money began to flow from the federal government's various faith-based offices, and several politically connected evangelical organizations won major grants, any remaining doubts on the Christian right evaporated. Pat Robertson's Operation Blessing—despite having recently been investigated by the state of Virginia for misusing relief funds to haul equipment for Robertson's for-profit diamond mining firm—was one of the first organizations to receive a faith-based grant. Robertson received $500,000, renewable for three years, for a total of $1.5 million.[45] The money pays for Operation Blessing to offer technical assistance to smaller faith-based outfits, so they can compete for federal dollars of their own—and given that Robertson had already disparaged several religious groups as "aberrant" and insisted they not be considered for federal funding, he'll likely use the $1.5 million to leverage grants to like-minded evangelical organizations. Chuck Colson—a regular at White House meetings of religious leaders, and someone who had legal troubles of his own after Watergate—was another significant beneficiary, through his evangelical organization, Prison Fellowship Ministries, which was chosen by the faith-based office as one of only four "national nonprofit partners" for a $22.5 million workplace reentry program for ex-offenders.[46] And beyond these high-profile names, dozens of grants have gone to support the less familiar grass roots infrastructure of the religious right. The Tri-County Right-to-Life Education Foundation in Ohio received more than $600,000 in 2001 and 2002, for example, and Metro Atlanta Youth for Christ, whose goal is "reaching the young people of metro Atlanta with the Gospel of Jesus Christ," received a 2003 grant for $364,000.[47] The Institute for Youth Development, which distributes scientifically unsound literature debunking condom effectiveness to abstinence programs around the country, received $71,000 in 2002—not entirely surprising, since Health and Human Services officials appointed the group's president, Shepherd Smith, to join the panel that decides who gets the grants, along with dozens of others figures on the Christian right. And more than a dozen crisis pregnancy centers received grants of up to $800,000. "The inclusion of a right-to-life organization and several crisis pregnancy centers among the federal programs," says Bill Smith, director of public policy at SIECUS, the Sexuality Information and Education Council (of the United States), "suggests there is a great deal more going on here than merely the promotion of abstinence."

As if to offer final confirmation that the conservative evangelical movement had won out over DiIulio's urban serve-the-poor ethic in the battle over the president's faith-based initiative, DiIulio announced his resignation in August, after only six months on the job. The academic had not only openly criticized conservative evangelicals at their convention, he had taken far too seriously the idea that the faith-based initiative was designed to solve questions of poverty, not politics. And anyway, he'd always sounded a bit soft on big government with his comments that religious groups can only "complement, but not replace, state services."[48] Eugene Rivers, the religious antiviolence organizer from Boston, was floored. "With John DiIulio's departure, the Bush administration has formally told the black and brown of the inner cities to go to hell," Rivers said. "It sends a signal that the faith-based office will just be a financial watering hole for the right-wing white evangelists." DiIulio's critics passed up the opportunity to be gracious. "Anyone will be an improvement," Jerry Falwell said.[49]

Jim Towey, who took over the initiative when DiIulio left, finds the allegations of political opportunism offensive. "That was a very sexy charge," he told me, "but I don't see the proof. You could just as easily say that funding secular social services was payback to the secular, Democratic base. You can make a stronger case for that rather than that Bush is funding the religious right."

True Believers

Looking back on his brief tenure at the White House, DiIulio told *Esquire*, "The lack of even basic policy knowledge, and the only casual interest in knowing more, was somewhat breathtaking."[50] This was especially true of the faith-based initiative, and with good reason. For evangelical Christians, for whom winning souls to Jesus Christ is a central tenet of practicing their faith, starting a soup kitchen or running a homeless shelter or counseling a drug addict may be a welcome opportunity to do good, but it is really only a means to an end. The real prize these activities offer is the chance to "witness" to someone in crisis and bring that person to Jesus Christ. What happens in this life—whether it be preventing an infection or getting someone a decent job—is second-ary to what happens in the life to come. Policy, in DiIulio's sense—mean-ing the process of using research to define a social problem, analyze the potential efficacy of various approaches to solving it, and generate data-driven means of measuring success—thus matters little to these true be-lievers, and even less to the elected officials wooing their votes. A central part of the mission of Operation Blessing, the Pat Robertson relief or-ganization that is set to receive up to $1.5 million in federal faith-based funds, is "worldwide evangelization."[51] Barry Farrah, a board member of Faith Partners, a welfare-to-work program in Colorado Springs that has received $100,000 in public money through a federal welfare block grant, described his organization's mission in this way to NPR: "The first step is to love them and to care for them, and not to attempt to share with them necessarily any of the concepts surrounding the Christian faith, but just to be the faith to them, love them and accept them. And that takes a few months of the program, and that's phase one. And then the next phase is inviting them to explore the concepts of the faith in God through Jesus Christ, which is the Christian faith. And I think it's some-where in the 85 percent range that come to some relationship with God through Christ as a consequence of our participation with them."[52] Nod-ding to constitutional prohibitions against state-sponsored religion, faith-based initiative guidelines state that organizations can't directly use federal money for worship or prosyletizing. But the document also em-phasizes that these religious activities can occur right after the federally funded service, or right next door, as long they're covered by an indepen-dent funding stream or by volunteers.[53]

I saw this evangelical imperative reflected in all of the faith-based programs I visited, even the most well designed. The most impressive of the four federally funded abstinence programs I encountered, for exam-ple, was a program called the Journey, run out of the Christ Community Medical Clinic in Memphis. Unlike many abstinence programs, which target white suburbanites, the Journey serves African American kids at high risk for drug addiction, teen parenthood, and HIV. Its leaders wrap the abstinence idea in a message of empowerment, encouraging their charges over the course of eight months to make ambitious plans for their lives despite the fact that their public school teachers or friends may expect very little. Yet even this program, which felt truly grounded in the kids' experiences, and which offers them such tangible support as help filling out an ACT application, is undergirded by evangelism. "We have an opportunity to witness," Journey health educator Janon Wilson told me, "and that is our ultimate goal, to find a way to fund this that could allow us to talk about faith." She says they can't do that inside program hours, because of their federal funding, "but we do find opportunities to talk to the children outside of the program." During a session at another federally funded Memphis abstinence program, run by Creative Life International, junior high–age kids sang gospel songs in a room decorated with verses from the New Testament.

In his State of the Union Address in January 2003, President Bush proposed a way around these inconvenient restrictions: a three-year, $600 million, drug treatment voucher program.[54] By channeling the funds to individuals, through vouchers, rather than to institutions, through grants, Bush's proposal could achieve what has been the holy grail for faith-based advocates such as Marvin Olasky: the chance to spend federal money on pervasively religious programs—even on evangelizing itself. Just six months earlier, the Supreme Court upheld the legality of school voucher programs that direct public money to Catholic schools, so the president's scheme to fund religious drug treatment may well stand up in court, too. "Our nation is blessed with recovery programs that do amazing work," the president said. "One of them is found at the Healing Place Church in Baton Rouge, Louisiana. A man in that program said, 'God does miracles in people's lives, and you never think it could be you.' Tonight, let us bring to all Americans who struggle with drug addiction this message of hope: The miracle of recovery is possible, and it could be you." Just four months earlier, to a more selective audience, Bush had spoken of his own recovery from drinking in miraculous terms. In a private White House meeting with members of the clergy, Bush told them, "You know, I had a drinking problem. Right now I should be in a bar in Texas, not the Oval Office. There is only one reason that I am in the Oval Office and not in a bar. I found faith. I found God. I am here because of the power of prayer."[55] That night, at the State of the Union, religious healers were offered pride of place. Seated next to the First Lady was the charismatic founder of the Healing Place program, Tonja Myles, as well as the leader of another evangelical drug treatment operation that has earned Bush's praise, a forty-year-old national residential program called Teen Challenge, which has roots in Pentecostalism.[56] I headed to Louisiana to visit them both—and to find out what our federal tax dollars may soon fund.

The Teen Challenge program in New Orleans is just a ten-minute drive from the French Quarter, but the neighborhood feels a world away from that quarter's preciously restored inns and tourist-crammed boîtes. It sits in the crime-plagued Ninth Ward, on Franklin Avenue, where the rutted roads look like they haven't seen a repair crew in years, and peeling paint and sagging awnings decorate the small wooden houses. You can only tell which ramshackle building houses Teen Challenge because two of its clients are selling snow cones and pork rinds from a small cart out front. It's equally humble inside: a few spartan barracks upstairs, a printing press in the back—like the snack cart, an income generator—and a common room filled with threadbare couches. With a bar next door and drug transactions on the corner, addicts could easily be tempted off the wagon. But inside, says Michael Miller, a Teen Challenge counselor and alumnus known here as "Brother Mike," the men "eat, drink, and breathe Jesus twenty-four hours a day," including prayer every morning and night and two-and-a-half hours of Bible study each day. "We believe in Christ as the only way someone's going to be set free from their addiction," he says. Being "set free" is a popular metaphor among Christian treatment programs. The words refer to a New Testament verse that reads, in a popular translation, "If the Son sets you free, you will be free indeed." Using the term in the context of drug addiction conflates freedom from addiction with Christian conversion, which captures the worldview of Teen Challenge trench workers like Brother Mike.

Teen Challenge participants often travel to area churches, and Brother Mike says that's how most participants come their way; self-referred, or referred by pastors, they likely already feel comfortable with the Christian message. But he says they also get referrals from detox programs and the courts, and this is where the Teen Challenge approach gets a bit troubling. When I ask him what they do when someone who's not Christian gets sent their way by the government, he says he tries to convince people to stay, by offering success statistics as well as statistics about what will happen to them if they go back to the street. He says he does not offer referrals to secular programs. "Jesus can come into that person's heart," he says, "whether they're court-ordered or whatever, and He can change them." He tells me the story of one court-ordered client of his who didn't want to stick with the program, but after Mike encouraged him to stay on, the client found Jesus; "God was speaking through me," Brother Mike says. A couple of years ago, John Castellani, the Teen Challenge president—he was a special guest at Bush's January 2001 launch of the faith-based initiative—bragged to a congressional committee that several Jewish participants in his program had become "completed Jews," an evangelical term for Jews who convert to Christianity.[57]

The statistics Brother Mike has been taught, and which he proudly recites to me, turn out to be a bit suspect. Teen Challenge cites a National Institute on Drug Abuse study from 1975 and a study conducted by Aaron Bicknese, PhD, of Northwestern University, to bolster claims that "86.6 percent of graduates after seven years remain drug and crime free." The 1975 study did find that 67 percent of Teen Challenge participants who completed the nearly year-long program were still drug-free seven years later, which compares favorably to a literature review by the federal General Accounting Office in 1998, which found a 40 to 50 percent success rate for those heroin and cocaine users who completed a three-month residential program, and found that "clients who stay in treatment for longer periods report better outcomes." But the sample size in the 1975 study was too small—just 186 participants—to be statistically significant. More troubling, only 18 percent of those who began the program finished it, and a third of those who dropped out cited an "excess of religion" as the reason.[58] The 86.6 percent rate came from Bicknese, whose "study" turns out to be a political science graduate thesis based on interviews with only 59 Teen Challenge graduates.[59]

Nevertheless, the program has received strong backing from George

W. Bush, dating from his days as governor of Texas. When state regula-
tors threatened to shut down a San Antonio Teen Challenge in 1995 for
failing to employ licensed drug counselors, Marvin Olasky organized a
major protest—at the Alamo, no less—and Governor Bush swooped in
to save the day. He first granted Teen Challenge a legal exemption and
then pushed through a law exempting all faith-based social programs
in Texas from state oversight.[60] The effects of Bush's deregulation
haven't been pretty. Since the law went into effect, a counselor in another Christian program, a church-run shelter in Corpus Christi
known as the Roloff Homes, was arrested after teen residents claimed
they were beaten and bound. The facility had been shuttered previously (after a girl there was found tied up with duct tape), but regula-
tors had to reopen it once Bush placed such groups outside of state
oversight.[61] An October 2002 report from the nonpartisan Texas Freedom Network assessing the impact of five years of Governor Bush's
faith-based initiatives in Texas, found that deregulation of religious
service providers had "provided a refuge for facilities with a history of
regulatory violations . . . and lowered standards of client health, safety,
and quality of care." The report also concluded that religious groups
had received "preferential treatment" in government contracting and
had spent money on "overtly religious activities."[62]

Data doesn't drive the Christian recovery movement, anyway. Stories
do. And at Set Free Indeed, the recovery program in Baton Rouge that
was lauded by Bush, Tonja Myles tells hers to a crowd of one hundred
every Friday night. "I might not have killed anyone, but I did some stuff
that would come close," Myles said the night I was there, ticking off her
addiction to cocaine and crack and the strangers she slept with to feed
these habits. Myles calls Set Free Indeed a ministry, but it pretty much
feels like church. The evening sessions close with small group discussions along the 12-Step model, but the rest of the program is devoted to
praise songs and Myles' powerful preaching. "I don't care where you've
been, His arm is not so short that He can't reach out to you," she began
that night. "That's good news. That's good news to a person with a past."
It was hard, sitting there, to imagine how her message would work for a
non-Christian, and yet I could see it was tremendously seductive. She

spoke over and over of forgiveness, love, and transformation, all tremendous prospects for people whose addiction has driven them to some pretty dark places. "People will say I remember what you did last week, what you did two months ago, what you did last year, and you will never change," she said. "Yes, you can change. Yes, you can be made whole. Yes, you can be set free. Who so the Son has set free is free indeed." God loves you, she said over and over, God loves you, God loves you, God loves you. I'm sure for many of the people in the room, this was exactly what they needed to hear. But civil libertarians and religious minorities have expressed mounting concern that this is how the federal government may choose to spend its drug treatment dollars.

WHAT WALL?

The Anti-Defamation League, a national Jewish watchdog organization, has called faith-based grants "patently unconstitutional" and a "serious breach of the church/state wall."[63] ACLU legislative council Christopher Anders called the initiative a "sweeping affirmation of tax-funded religion and religious discrimination."[64] Indeed, as federal block grants have made their way to faith-based programs around the country, court challenges have followed in their path. One prominent case involved a Milwaukee-based program called Faith Works, which has received $600,000 in federal grants through the state of Wisconsin even though it uses, according to its literature, an "inherently Christian" approach to treating drug addiction, including Bible study, prayer meetings, and "spiritual direction." A local organization filed suit, charging that the program unconstitutionally blurred the church/state line. Faith Works was founded by Robert Polito, the man who now runs the president's faith-based office in the Department of Health and Human Services, and received its first taxpayer dollars from then Wisconsin governor Tommy Thompson, now the secretary of HHS. In January 2002, a federal judge found that "the Faith Works program indoctrinates its participants in religion," making any public subsidies unconstitutional; she ordered the state to stop the direct grants.[65] In July 2002, a federal judge in Louisiana ordered that state to stop using federal abstinence dollars to fund organizations that "advance religion." Court records revealed that publicly funded Louisiana groups were teaching abstinence through stories about the virgin birth and telling students sex outside of marriage is "offensive to the Lord"; one program, Passion 4 Purity, which I later visited, was cited for teaching abstinence through "a Scriptural view of human sexuality" and "Biblical instruction on purity."[66] In April 2003, the state of Florida was forced to withdraw a publicly funded brochure, "A Christian Response to AIDS," under threats of legal action from the ACLU. The brochure, created and distributed by the Florida Health Department, contained no HIV-prevention information, but instead proffered Bible verses and images of Jesus healing the sick.[67] And there's a promise of more to come.

Reverend Barry Lynn, an ordained United Church of Christ minister who now runs Americans United for the Separation of Church and State, has testified before Congress against the slippery slope the faith-based initiative is on when it comes to the Constitution. "We continue to career dangerously down the path of government-supported religion," Lynn told Congress in March 2004. "Congress has a duty to apply the brakes."[68] In that case he warned about an improper role for government. But he is also deeply concerned about the initiative's corrosive effects on religious belief. "Throughout America's history, and indeed world history, it is always dangerous for religious groups to become dependent on the largesse of the government, and it's also dangerous for them to feel that if they help the ruler, the president, the king, that somehow that will help them in the long run," he said to me. "The strength and vitality of religion around the world is clearest and strongest when governments simply leave religion alone, and let it be nurtured by volunteer support, not by the resources of the government." The Unitarian Universalist Association, the Union of American Herbrew Congregations, and several Baptist and Catholic organizations each wrote the president out of concern that the faith-based initiative would result in hiring discrimination and an "excessive entanglement between religion and government."[69]

But the advocates of faith-based funding take a very different view. Marvin Olasky argues in *Compassionate Conservatism* that the constitution does not put a wall up between church and state at all, that the First Amendment has been taken out of context.[70] Another administration favorite, televangelist D. James Kennedy, whose *Coral Ridge Hour* airs on some 500 stations, has called separation a "false doctrine" and "a lie" and wrote in his 1996 book *The Gates of Hell Shall Not Prevail* that "Our job is to reclaim America for Christ, *whatever the cost.*"[71] Many other leaders within the president's Conservative Christian base concur. Pat Robertson, founder of the Christian Coalition, as well as Focus on the Family chairman James Dobson and Concerned Women for America founder Beverly LaHaye, have often argued that America was founded as a Christian nation, as has Jerry Falwell, who once said, from the pulpit, "We must never allow our children to forget that this is a Christian nation. We must take back what is rightfully ours."[72] These views, writes Sara Diamond, an expert on the religious right, in her book *Roads to Dominion,* have their roots in a set of tenets called "dominion theology," the view that Christians are biblically mandated to take control of all secular and government institutions until Christ returns. In some versions, this involves civil disobedience as a tool for restoring biblical norms (thus Randall Terry's abortion clinic blockades); in others, writes Diamond, it involves "the application of God's law to all spheres of everyday life"—in a word, theocracy.[73]

Elliot Mincberg, vice president of People for the American Way, says this desire to break down the church/state divide permeates the president's faith-based initiative. "They say, 'You can't fund prayer on Uncle Sam's dime,' but can you, on Uncle Sam's dime, encourage people to go to a prayer service that starts right after?" he asks. "Can you have a prayer going on at the same time, as long as someone else is paying for it? These areas are very vague, and we're very concerned about the possibilities. The administration wants to limit the prohibitions on funding inherently religious activities, and some would argue the regulations are deliberately fuzzy on this subject." And concerns that the president's initiative would promote religious bigotry were a significant reason his "charitable choice" proposal failed in Congress. Republican Bobby Scott, a member of the Congressional Black Caucus and a leader of the opposition, pointed out that religious charities, from Lutheran Services to Catholic

Charities to the Jewish Federation, had long competed for and won government contracts. "There are only two reasons 'charitable choice' is necessary," he said at one press conference, where he was flanked by liberal religious leaders, "to advance your religion in a publicly funded program and to discriminate in your employment based on religion when using taxpayer dollars."[74] The White House holds that these regulatory changes were necessary to protect religious organizations from discrimination. That Bush also intended to allow grant recipients to discriminate against people who are out of step with their conservative Christian mores became incontrovertible in July 2001, when the *Washington Post* revealed Karl Rove had been negotiating with the Salvation Army to assure that government-funded religious groups would be exempt from gay antidiscrimination laws.[75] When I asked White House faith-based director Jim Towey whether antigay discrimination had proved to be a practice among grantees, he said, "I don't think that's an issue. Because a gay or lesbian is not going to work in Jerry Falwell's soup kitchen. Typically they'll go where they feel welcome, where there are simpatico views." As with his take on why no Muslim charities have received direct grants, Towey sees any patterns of bias as self-imposed.

When Bush lost this battle in Congress, he proposed the same regulatory changes through a series of executive orders, the first of which he announced in late 2002. In detailed public comments issued at the time, People for the American Way argued that changes to the welfare program would allow a Baptist organization receiving federal funds to place a help-wanted ad saying "No Jews Need Apply." The organization found that changes to the Housing and Urban Development program, which would allow government funds to help build churches if even a portion of the space was used for a social service program, "contrary to Supreme Court decisions that prohibit spending government funds on structures that are not 'exclusively secular.'" It found that changes to the community service block grant program would "threaten to entangle a religious message with the provision of social services." The president has often complained of "activist judges" who don't respect the balance of powers, but with his rash of faith-based orders, he'd taken the law into his own hands, softening the line between church and state to the point of illegibility. The effects have already begun to be felt on the ground. In September 2003, the Salvation Army instituted a rule requiring its 850 New York City–area employees to sign a form identifying their church affiliation, cataloging their church attendance for the past decade, and pledging to adhere to the Salvation Army's religious principles, which include Christian evangelism, a policy that the New York Civil Liberties Union has challenged in court.[76]

DAMNED IF YOU DON'T

The special treatment Christian organizations receive from the Bush administration is perhaps most visible in contrast to the administration's treatment of its secular critics. Christian fundamentalists have such close ties to the White House that Jeff Ruch, the Park Service watchdog, has concluded, "What bothers them today becomes policy tomorrow." And the centerpiece of Bush's compassionate conservatism agenda, the faith-based initiative, has proved to be, at least in part, what Boston's Reverend Eugene Rivers calls "a financial watering hole for the right-wing white evangelicals." But critics of Bush administration policy—especially policy designed to please the Republicans' Christian right base, and especially organizations that are deemed important Democratic constituencies—receive none of this largesse. Instead, these groups get a steady diet of financial audits, criminal investigations, onerous reporting requirements, and outright defunding. The pattern had become so prominent by mid-2003 that the nonpartisan good-government group OMB (Office of Management and Budget) Watch issued a report, *An Attack on Nonprofit Speech,* in which the authors conclude that "this administration—and its conservative allies—is stifling free expression and using the heavy hand of government to quash dissent."[77] In fact, the idea of using government powers to harass and defund the liberal opposition dates back to the early Reagan years—but it has never been so fully implemented as under George W. Bush.

It was Richard Viguerie, the direct-mail guru who helped forge the religious right as a political force, and Howard Phillips, a former Nixon official who went on to become head of the Conservative Caucus, who pulled together some eighty right-wing organizations in 1981 in a joint campaign to "defund the left."[78] Viguerie and Phillips targeted organizations representing important Democratic issues—from women's rights to civil rights and the environment—that were also important elements of the Democratic base, such as the Audubon Society, the Urban League, Planned Parenthood, and other organizations the two believed were using federal funds to "subsidize liberal antifamily values."[79] "Our opposition receives almost 70 percent of its funds from the government," said Viguerie in 1982. "We want to stop that."[80] In concert with their Reagan administration ally, David Stockman, Viguerie and Phillips battled for a series of rule changes to accomplish their aims throughout the Reagan years, many of which were rebuffed, but some of which, such as the Mexico City Policy (known as the global abortion "gag rule"), became government policy. This drive to "defund the left" was revived in the mid-1990s by the conservative true believers of the Gingrich revolution, in conjunction with think tanks such as the Heritage Foundation; Representative Ernest Istook took the lead in introducing a series of proposals to quash nonprofit advocacy, all of which were defeated.[81] Most recently, the American Enterprise Institute, a think tank so close to Bush that dozens of its former associates have joined the administration, launched NGO Watch, an effort to target nongovernmental organizations the group views as promoting an anticorporate agenda.

Following in this tradition, the Bush White House has targeted its opponents in multiple ways. Mainstream scientific, professional, and policy organizations, whose constituencies often lean Democratic, have been removed from influential federal advisory positions and replaced by ideologues. The American Medical Association no longer advises American delegations to UN summits on children's issues; Concerned Women for America does instead. Leaders of the National Association of People with AIDS no longer sit on the presidential AIDS advisory council, though religious abstinence advocates do; and members of the right-wing Federalist Society now vet judicial nominees rather than the mainstream American Bar Association.

Organizations bucking administration policy or protesting too publicly have become the target of audits and investigations. Greenpeace, for example, a strong critic of Bush administration environmental policy, became the target of federal prosecutors, who used an obscure nineteenth-century law to hold the organization criminally responsible for an act of civil disobedience by two of its members. Labor unions, who have protested Bush's economic policies, were targeted with rules requiring elaborate new financial reporting, rules so Byzantine that a federal judge stayed their implementation; AFL-CIO president John Sweeney said they were "craftily designed to weaken unions . . . and go far beyond what is required of corporations or other not-for-profit organizations." This pattern is particularly evident when it comes to Bush policies that were designed to please the Christian right. After Planned Parenthood, along with the sex education groups SIECUS and Advocates for Youth, launched a privately funded campaign to oppose federal spending on abstinence education, all three groups received multiple federal audits. Fifteen of the country's most prominent AIDS organizations were financially investigated by the federal government after they joined in a protest of Health Secretary Tommy Thompson at an international AIDS conference, while Stop AIDS and another gay HIV-prevention group were hit with audits that were months long. Head Start program directors received a harsh warning letter—and a federal financial inquiry—after they raised their voices against administration plans to restructure the program, changes that would open the door for church groups to administer local Head Starts.[82] "Generally, I don't think there's much history of the audit powers being used in such a targeted way, or being triggered by policy disagreements," says Kay Guinane, an author of the OMB Watch report, which documents several of these incidents. "Nonprofits can lobby with their private funds, and many of them do, and that's never triggered audits before. It's been settled since the early 1980s that that's legitimate. In other administrations there just hasn't been this level of reports of audits of organizations with political or policy differences from the administration. It's fairly unusual." Guinane notes that organizations that are in sync with administration policy do not face financial audits, even when they seem to be in open breach of the law. She points to the Black Alliance for Educational Options (BAEO), which received a $600,000 federal grant to educate parents about school choices available to them—including private religious schools. One BAEO board member, Pennsylvania state representative Dwight Evans, said Philadelphia's portion of the grant would be used to lobby for legislation he sponsored that would give a public subsidy to homeschooling parents.[83] Using federal dollars to lobby is in fact illegal, Guinane says, but "that hasn't triggered an audit."

While these groups have been audited, others have been defunded outright. The International Planned Parenthood Federation and other international family planning groups, long targets of the Christian right, lost millions when Bush reinstituted the Reagan-era Mexico City Policy, which denies funding to any organization that even takes a pro-choice position in public policy debates. The UN Population Fund and several nongovernmental organizations were defunded to the tune of tens of millions of dollars after Christian right groups inaccurately claimed that they supported China's restrictive one-child policy. Under the auspices of the Patriot Act, the federal government shut down several legitimate Muslim charities, and, as noted above, no Muslim groups have received grants through the administration's faith-based initiative. "The burden of proof has shifted to the organizations, which must prove their innocence," says an OMB Watch report on the impact of the Patriot Act, "even though, in many cases, the government has not specified wrongdoing."[84] Evidence has begun to accumulate that the faith-based initiative itself, which cannot legally favor religious over secular grant applicants, has starved the latter in favor of the former. One organization, United Veterans of America, which had received federal grants in the past to run a homeless shelter for veterans, was denied a $415,000 grant renewal in 2003; a year later, after the group registered as a faith-based organization, the group received almost $2 million in federal funds.[85]

If the president has his way, even more money will flow to faith-based organizations, with even fewer restrictions on its overtly religious use. After years of pushing Congress to support a school voucher program, Bush won his first victory in early 2004 with the passage of an appropriations bill that included $14 million in private school vouchers for Washington, D.C., schoolchildren—the first ever federally funded school choice program. While school voucher programs, in theory, offer parents the chance to send their child to a secular or religious private school, the small voucher scholarships typically only cover Catholic school tuition, and local voucher programs have become a means to channel millions of taxpayer dollars into the Catholic Church. In Cleveland, which has one of the nation's most well-established programs, 96 percent of voucher dollars in 2000 went to Catholic schools.[86] The president, true to form, announced the victory at a Catholic school in Washington, D.C., where he called Catholic schools a model for education in America.[87] And he hopes to build on this win: his 2005 proposed budget contains $50 million for a national school voucher program.[88] If he succeeds on this front, he may build momentum to push through his $600 million drug treatment voucher program as well. If all goes according to plan, Tonya Myles and Brother Mike will soon be able to help struggling addicts accept Jesus using our tax dollars.

MOST FAVORED CONSTITUENCY

GEORGE W. BUSH's courtship of the Christian right began almost immediately after he became born again. In his memoir, Bush attributes his acceptance of Jesus, after years of wild living and heavy drinking, to a walk on the beach Bush took with the Reverend Billy Graham, arguably the nation's most prominent evangelist, in the summer of 1985 at the Bush clan's Kennebunkport home. There, as Bush wrote, "Reverend Graham planted a mustard seed in my soul."[1] The seed took its time to germinate—Bush didn't give up drink until the following year—but by the time it sprouted, Bush was already chest-deep in evangelical politics as an operative on his father's presidential campaign. As *Dallas Morning News* reporter Bill Minutaglio documents in his biography of the younger Bush, *First Son*, by late 1986, George W. was working closely with a former Assemblies of God evangelist (and associate of Jim and Tammy Faye Bakker) to woo Paul Weyrich's support and oversee the production of a religiously inflected authorized biography of his father. According to Minutaglio, Bush "plowed through receiving lines, acting as his father's surrogate at swings through the southern states; glad-handing evangelicals at the Washington campaign headquarters and being the family spokesman in the intense and often uncomfortable mating ritual between Team Bush and the Christian Right."[2] George W. Bush was fluent in the language of religious conservatives from his time spent in 1985 and 1986 attending a Community Bible Study Program, a weekly devotional group of bankers and corporate leaders in Midland, Texas.[3] And it showed. His "I was lost and then I was found" narrative—he used these very words in a private meeting with religious leaders during his first week in office—and his frequent public confessionals of faith appealed enormously to evangelicals compared with his father's traditional, and far more private, Episcopalianism.[4]

From his first encounter with the young George W. Bush, political consultant Karl Rove was starstruck. A political operator from his days in the early 1970s rigging elections as a College Republican, Rove learned the tricks of the trade working side-by-side with Lee Atwater, the architect of Reagan's victory, at the Republican National Committee and then set up shop as a campaign consultant in Texas, where he soon emerged as the state's unofficial Republican Party boss. Like Richard Viguerie before him (the man credited with coalescing the Christian right as a political force), Rove was master of the direct-mail list. He built up jealously guarded lists during each campaign he ran and cannibalized others, matching names up with issues, and dubbing them, say, "Texas Oilmen and Fat Cats," or "Texans Opposed to Labor Unions."[5] He was also attuned to expanding the Republican Party's religious conservative base, pouncing on an analysis by Catholic magazine editor Deal Hudson that devout Catholics tended to be more politically conservative than their less churchgoing counterparts, and importing Hudson out to Texas to host meet-and-greets with Catholic activists.[6] As political reporter Nicholas Lemann wrote in his 2003 profile of Rove in the *New Yorker*, "If you have an idea involving a hitherto undiscovered but distinct group of voters that the Republican Party might be able to attract, chances are that you have heard from Rove."[7] In little more than twelve years, Rove turned a blue state red, running every important campaign along the way, from judgeships to agricultural commissioners, including those of George W. Bush. It was Rove who first urged Bush to run for governor of Texas back in 1990, seeing in him an explosive blend of corporate-friendly, religiously conservative, and, in Rove's words, "more charisma than any one individual should be allowed to have,"[8] but Bush demurred. Within a few months of the father's 1992 electoral defeat, however, Rove began grooming his dream candidate for the 1994 gubernatorial run, which Rove viewed from the start as a platform for the presidency.[9] The careers, political priorities, and strategic thinking of the two became so close over the years, so merged, that Rove came to be called "Bush's brain."

Before Bush announced his presidential run in June 1999, Rove made sure he'd won the blessing of top officials in such key Republican issue-based lobby groups as the National Rifle Association, the National Right to Life Committee, and Americans for Tax Reform.[10] Rove lined up so many major business-sector donors that within three weeks of Bush's announcement, he'd secured $36 million in contributions, and Rove also reeled in a string of endorsements from such respected party players as former secretary of state George Shultz.[11] Most importantly, Rove orchestrated a campaign to woo powerhouse evangelical pastors and Christian right leaders to Bush's side. After Bush "heard the call" to run, an event that he says happened during a service at a Methodist church, he just happened to dial one of the most popular televangelists in the nation, James Robison, to discuss the idea. Robison, who has a television audience of 100 million through his Texas-based program, *Life Today,* and a reputation for connecting the Christian right with friendly politicians, sat down with Rove and Bush and gave his imprimatur—just as he had, twenty years earlier, to Ronald Reagan. He then organized a series of gatherings with other major church leaders, who, at meeting after meeting, laid hands on the future president to bless his run. Robison also called up heavyweights of the Christian right's political arm, securing the endorsement of Pat Robertson and neutralizing potential opposition from James Dobson.[12]

Their support was an essential element in Rove's campaign strategy for Bush, which involved bringing in record donations from the business sector through a strong stance against taxes, regulation, and unions; arousing the evangelical base through the candidate's religiosity, firm pro-life views, and support for public funding of religious schools and social services; and using Bush's vaguely defined "compassionate conservatism" and rhetoric about improving education to carve into traditionally Democratic constituencies such as Catholics, Latinos, suburban women, blue-collar union workers, and workers in industries, like coal or farming, that are threatened by regulation. "Rove is the conceptualizer of Bush as a 'different kind of Republican,'" wrote the *Weekly Standard*'s Fred Barnes in an early profile of Rove, "whose presidency transforms the GOP into a majority party by adding new constituencies (Latinos, Catholics, wired workers) to a conservative base."[13] Rove has said he doesn't believe America has a political middle; he prefers to call those voters "unattached." So Rove never searches for consensus or middle ground; he considers it his job to nab those unattached voters by attaching them to issues, preferably, as he told one Texas client, those that "*compel* people to vote for you."[14]

But for all Bush's and Rove's efforts to broaden the party base in 2000, their instinct was to veer right whenever danger loomed. When John McCain's Republican primary victory in New Hampshire rattled Bush's campaign, Rove immediately dispatched his candidate to speak at Bob Jones University, a fundamentalist Christian college based in South Carolina, and launched a direct-mail campaign claiming (falsely) that McCain wanted to remove the party's pro-life plank—both efforts to marshal evangelical conservatives to stop McCain cold in the South Carolina primary.[15] Bob Jones University's interracial-dating ban— and its leaders' public anti-Catholic comments—would later pose problems for the campaign and hinder Bush's crossover appeal, but in extremis, those concerns were tellingly trumped.

Evangelicals and the Rise of the Right

The Christian right's coming-out party as a formidable political bloc was Ronald Reagan's 1980 election, their enthusiastic turnout for the former actor made all the more remarkable because Reagan was up against the nation's first evangelical president, the liberal Jimmy Carter. But religious conservatives had been a pillar of the new right coalition from its formation out of the ashes Barry Goldwater's disastrous 1964 presidential bid. The conservative economic agenda of lower taxes, deregulation, and downsizing government seemed perfectly tailored to fundamentalist Christians, who'd had their fill of liberalism, secularism, and modernity. Unlike Catholicism, which emphasized service to the poor, the exploding evangelical movement emphasized personal responsibility, through the life-changing experience of being born again. The movement's suspicion of government and equation of wealth with God's blessings made its millions of followers far more amenable than Catholics, Jews, or mainline Protestants to the agenda of lowering taxes and slashing social services. As the right sought to modernize and broaden its appeal, the new generation of conservative leaders downplayed the old right's overt support for segregation and opposition to civil rights measures and cultivated a new Southern strategy based on conservative Christian values.

The Christian right as we currently know it began to coalesce in the 1970s, through the direct-mail solicitations of Richard Viguerie and the coalition-building efforts of Paul Weyrich, who sought both to politicize evangelical Christians and to lure them into the broader right-wing tent. In its early years, the Christian right movement depended heavily on the influence of a small group of charismatic leaders, most notably Reverend Jerry Falwell, whose television broadcasts from his Thomas Road Baptist Church, at their height, reached four out of every ten households in the United States.[16] But it was beginning to build institutional power. Think tanks, such as the Heritage Foundation; issue-based lobbies, such as the National Right to Life Committee; and family values media empires such as Focus on the Family cropped up throughout the 1970s; by the 1980s, the Christian Coalition had arrived on the scene with its national network and powerful ability to mobilize the grass roots.[17]

A remarkable maturity now distinguishes the Christian right. It has an ornate and stable infrastructure made up of hundreds of national and local membership organizations, many with $100 million budgets, as well as thousands of radio and television outfits reaching tens of millions of listeners, several well-funded think tanks and political action committees, professional associations and journals, deep-pocketed funders dedicated to long-term institution building, and a massive network of tens of thousands of churches and ministries. It has a fertile farm system, too, which attracts young people through campus publications and youth ministries and cultivates new political leaders by running Christian right activists as candidates for school boards and city councils. The movement has remained obstinately independent of the Republican Party, willing to bolt for third-party candidacies rather than back Republican moderates (as Focus on the Family chairman James Dobson did when he supported Taxpayers Party candidate Howard Phillips against Bob Dole in 1996).[18] Yet it has also worked to remake the party from within, sending delegates to Republican conventions to influence the platform and commandeering state party machinery. A 2002 analysis in the trade journal *Campaigns and Elections* found that in forty-four states, Christian conservatives controlled at least a quarter of the GOP's state committees, up from thirty-one states just six years earlier; in eighteen of them, Christian conservatives dominate the state committee altogether—not just in the South, but in the Midwest and West.[19] Christian right leaders have also ascended to top party positions, such as former Christian Coalition executive director Ralph Reed, who now chairs the Georgia GOP and runs Bush's southern regional reelection campaign, and David Barton, a leading promoter of the idea that America was founded as a "Christian nation," who's now vice chair of the Texas GOP. The Christian right took over religious denominations as well, purging moderates from leadership positions in the 16-million-strong Southern Baptist Convention during the 1980s.[20] "What began as an outreach effort by the New Right leadership," writes Jean Hardisty in her book on conservative populism, *Mobilizing Resentment,* "has become the force that now controls the entire movement."[21]

The Christian right has also matured strategically and ideologically. Long regarded as harsh and judgmental, the movement took steps to soften its image over the past decade. The movement's anti-abortion stance seemed to blame women and disregard infants once they were born, so the movement launched a network of "crisis pregnancy centers," whose numbers exploded in the 1990s, which provide pregnancy counseling, parenting classes, and donated baby clothes. Leaders softened their hate-based antigay stance by nurturing an "ex-gay" movement, which allows them to "love the sinner" by praying for him or her to become heterosexual through accepting Jesus. Their view of AIDS as

God's punishment for sin seemed cruel, so they fashioned abstinence as a faith-based solution. They papered over their hostility toward Jews with language about a common Judeo-Christian heritage and with avid support for Israel. At the same time, leaders bridged denominational divides, not only forging a common identity among born-again Christians of the Pentecostal or Southern Baptist stripe, but healing tensions between evangelicals in general and other socially conservative Christian denominations such as Catholics and Mormons that they had previously reviled as "the church of the Antichrist" (Bob Jones Jr., 1982) and "a cult" (the Southern Baptist Convention, 1998), respectively.[22] Occasionally, the movement even reached out to Orthodox Jews. "As the issues have become increasingly more common, and the concerns more common, there's been increasing cooperation," says Janice Crouse, a former speechwriter for the first President Bush and now a senior staffer at the Washington, D.C.–based lobby group Concerned Women for America. Turf wars subsided further as networking structures took root, such as the Council for National Policy, which links the Christian right with corporate conservatives, and a variety of single issue coalitions focused on issues such as gay marriage, abortion, and judicial appointments that coordinate the work of Christian broadcasters, grass-roots organizations, and Washington lobby groups. The gulf that separates fundamentalists and religious social moderates is now so extreme that it often eclipses differences between religions: while Catholics in the Christian right insist their pro-choice coreligionists are bound for hell, they have made common cause with Muslims in opposing abortion rights at the United Nations. Throughout this period, the movement's base has grown. While mainline Protestant denominations such as Presbyterians and the United Church of Christ, which lean toward a social justice gospel, shrank during the decade of the 1990s, Catholic Churches, Pentecostal Assemblies, the Mormon Church, and the Churches of Christ, all part of the emerging Christian right coalition, each grew by 16 to 19 percent.[23]

The movement's political maturity is best illustrated by the stark contrast between the 1992 Republican National Convention and Bush's convention in 2000. In Houston in 1992, ultraconservatives hogged the spotlight and then alienated the electorate by openly declaring a culture war. By 2000, the movement had learned to accept the big tent show for what it was and willingly traded visibility for more discreet victories, such as strong party-platform language on marriage and the sanctity of life. "Social conservatives have become increasingly mature and sophisticated about the political process, and understand that a political party is not a church, and that becoming a governing majority requires that you work with others with whom you occasionally disagree," Ralph Reed said during the convention. "If there wasn't a full understanding of that eight or ten years ago, there certainly is now."[24]

That November, Bush's polling numbers exposed how deep the family-values fault line had become—and how important the Christian right has become to the contemporary Republican Party. In an extremely close race, Bush beat Al Gore by 14 percentage points among married people with children and by 30 points among frequent churchgoers; whereas Gore beat Bush among working mothers by 20 points, and among nonchurchgoers by 38 points. Bush also won almost two-thirds of voters who described the nation's moral climate as off on the wrong track.[25] While Reagan and Bush Sr. did well among white evangelicals, Bush Jr. scored a wipe out: 75 percent of all white evangelicals and 84 percent among the most observant. Evangelical conservatives made up only 12 to 15 percent of Reagan's electorate, but they added up to 40 percent of Bush's.[26]

In a testament to the power of Christian right organizations to mobilize this base, one poll showed that 79 percent of the evangelicals who voted for Bush did so after being contacted at least once by a religious right organization.[27] "I think that the White House understands that the largest constituency in the Republican Party on Election Day are people who are regularly in church on Sunday, and then are in the voting booth on Tuesday," Gary Bauer, the Christian right leader who was an early contender for the Republican nomination in 2000, told the Christian Broadcasting Network. "We've gone way beyond the point where we need a seat at the table, for example. We're in a position to offer others a seat at the table, because we really are the heart of the party."[28]

The Art of the Narrowcast

In George W. Bush's presidential campaign, as well as in his presidency, the secret of his appeal has been his artful combination of the broadcast and the narrowcast—an approach that is particularly important when religious extremists are an indispensable part of your base. The broadcast component, under the guidance of longtime Bush advisor Karen Hughes, a former Dallas television reporter, is what the nation sees on television: the warmth, compassion, and multiculturalism of the Republicans' 2000 convention; Bush's initiatives on education standards, global AIDS, and faith-based social services; his post-9/11 calls for national unity in the war on terror. The narrowcast, on the other hand, with its targeted, even inflammatory appeals to the base, is Rove's provenance. As a Bush advisor told the *New York Times,* "Karen's job is to articulate the message, and Karl's job is to cater and pander to the base. Karl is trying to work in the Grover Norquist and Ralph Reed message, and Karen is listening to the soccer moms."[29] The broadcast messages often work through indirection. Texas journalists James Moore and Wayne Slater, in their Rove biography, *Bush's Brain,* print excerpts of a remarkable early campaign memo Rove wrote to Bill Clements, whose successful Texas gubernatorial race Rove ran in 1986, which exposes some of the thinking behind the strategy: "The purpose of saying you gave teachers a record pay increase is to reassure suburban voters with kids, not to win the votes of teachers. Similarly, emphasizing your appointments of women and minorities will not win you the support of feminists and the leaders of the minority community, but it will bolster your support among Republican primary voters and urban independents."[30] While the broadcast messages are meant for primetime TV, the narrowcast travels through less visible channels.

For controversial issues and negative campaigning, Rove once told a group of students at the University of Texas, "it's better to narrowcast." "Radio is really good for a negative attack," he continued, because it's "tough to figure out what the opposition is doing. The only thing worse to face is mail," since direct mail is "immune from press coverage."[31]

The broadcast and the narrowcast work in tandem: Thus in the hotly contested South Carolina Republican primary, Hughes reinvented Bush as "a reformer with results," while Rove conducted the below-board dirty tricks: sending Bush to Bob Jones to speak, putting out the direct-mail warnings that McCain was not pro-life, and using surrogates, such as a Bob Jones professor, to circulate rumors that McCain had fathered an illegitimate child. Likewise, while Bush fashioned himself a conservationist to national audiences, he appeared with out-of-work miners in West Virginia and blamed their hardship on Clinton/Gore environmental regulation.[32] It was this same broadcast/narrowcast strategy that led Bush to assiduously court the Christian right during his campaign—but keep them from the microphone at the 2000 convention.

Rove is known as a close reader of Machiavelli and he's said to live by the Italian philosopher's insight that "the great majority of mankind is satisfied with appearances, as though they were realities."[33] This idea implies a formula: as long as the broadcast message has wide appeal (war on terror, educational standards, compassionate conservatism), almost anything can be doled out under the table. The danger comes when this campaign strategy is transferred into government, as Rove has done, through his transformation from campaign manager to "senior counselor," where, as Fred Barnes details in his Rove profile, he now rules as "first among equals" and his various schemes propel the presidency. This politically driven White House employs a carefully managed set of themes and messages to shape the president's national image, while delivering to favored constituencies cherished agenda items, unvarnished, and, when possible, below the public radar, avoiding the rough and tumble of public debate and legislative compromise through the use of private meetings, executive orders, and discretionary funds. Delivering the goods, of course, falls to Rove. "Rove assigned himself one of the most important tasks at the White House," Barnes writes, "keeping the Republican Party's conservative base solidly behind Bush. This is virtually a full-time job."[34] Every speech, appointment, and policy initiative crosses his desk.[35] And given that the Christian right, with its hard-line social conservative agenda, stands first among cherished conservative constituencies (Rove has often complained that only 15 million of the nation's 19 million evangelical conservative voters actually came to the polls in 2000, a number he's vowed to change),[36] Rove's strategy is a recipe for the triumph of marginal, radical ideas.

Once you start looking, you see the Rove philosophy at work everywhere in Washington. Every year, for instance, a few thousand anti-abortion activists hold a March for Life in Washington on the anniversary of *Roe v. Wade,* at which, every year, they call for *Roe*'s repeal. Though openly pro-life, President Bush has never appeared at the march, which might make headlines and energize the pro-choice opposition. Instead, finding himself conveniently out of town, Bush always dispatches an emissary with pro-life bona fides to deliver his speech (one year it was Chris Smith, a leading abortion foe in Congress) or calls it in by phone, offering up strong pro-life language that gets plastered all over the evangelical press, but rarely gets picked up in the mainstream media. Still, if Bush avoids a personal appearance, he goes the extra mile to ensure that pro-life forces get the care and attention they deserve. On the eve of one of the marches, in January 2002, Bush held a private meeting in the White House with twenty-five leaders of the National Right to Life Committee, the leading anti-abortion lobby, an event reported only in such outlets as the *National Catholic Register* and *National Right to Life News.*[37] Sometimes Bush combines the broadcast and the narrowcast in a single speech, as theologian Bruce Lincoln has outlined in his book *Holy Terrors,* an examination of the religious rhetoric surrounding the events of 9/11. Lincoln points out that in the president's October 2001 speech announcing U.S. military strikes on Afghanistan, he insisted that this was not a religious war, that "we are the friends of almost a billion people worldwide who practice the Islamic faith."[38] However, Bush ended the speech by noticeably twisting a familiar formula, saying, "May God continue to bless America," what Lincoln considers "the tip of a vast subtextual iceberg."[39] Those familiar with Christian scripture, Lincoln says, would find in Bush's talk of terrorists who "burrow deeper into caves," of the "lonely path" of those who side with terror, of "killers of innocents," clear references to the Gospels of John and Matthew and to the books of Isaiah, Job, Exodus, Jeremiah, and Ezekiel in a seemingly secular speech. And even that final, seemingly innocent phrase, about God "continuing" to bless America, could be read as an allusion to the fear expressed in far harsher terms after 9/11 by Jerry Falwell and Pat Robertson that "God Almighty is lifting his protection from us" because of those "who have tried to secularize America." Bush's language so closely reflects evangelical ways of speaking and habits of mind that one missionary leader, invited to the White House for a talk by the president on his faith-based initiative, wrote to his members, "I thought for a minute I had written his speech."[40]

One of the administration's great political challenges is how to send its evangelical base these private or sub-rosa signals without seeming to openly express bigotry or religious intolerance, or to openly declare a full-scale culture war. Even many advocates who have opposed Bush policies say the effort has been quite successful. "They can gut so many policies and laws and go under the radar," says Donna Crane, deputy director of the pro-choice group NARAL. "There's a level of sophistication on how to attack these issues. They're incredibly attuned to the threshold of the public's awareness." When, on occasion, a message narrowcast to the Christian right does make headlines, the administration often beats a hasty retreat—a pattern that exposes just how much the president hopes to hide his close ties to hard-liners. Consider the president's 2002 nomination of Jerry Thacker to his AIDS advisory council. Thacker, a marketing consultant and Bob Jones University alumnus, had called AIDS "the gay plague" and homosexuality a "sinful deathstyle." He supports efforts to "rescue the homosexual" through Christian conversion. And he had ignorantly claimed that "pores in a latex condom are up to 450 times larger than a single cell of the HIV virus."[41] The administration was fully aware of Thacker's record, since gay Republican activists had raised these issues behind the scenes in an effort to block his nomination. Yet the nomination proceeded—with the enthusiastic support of family values groups including Concerned Women for America and Donald Wildmon's Tupelo, Mississippi–based American Family Association.[42] It wasn't until the story broke onto page A1 of the *Washington Post*, above the fold, and presidential hopeful John Kerry took the issue to the airwaves, that the administration cooled on Thacker, who withdrew his name less than a week before he was set to be sworn in.

But in the relentless backstage courtship of the Christian right, the brief flap over Thacker has proved the exception rather than the rule. As one evangelical churchgoer put it to the *New York Times*, "I know what Bush is like behind the scenes, things that don't get in the press, because I read Christian publications."[43]

THE ENDLESS ROMANCE

After spending his final months on the campaign trail seeking to portray himself as a moderate, George W. Bush reassured his Christian right supporters the moment he arrived in Washington. Even before his inauguration, Karl Rove privately met with a group of influential members of the family values lobby, convened by Paul Weyrich, to guarantee that Bush would govern as "a philosophically driven president who is a conservative," and that he would pursue this agenda despite the closeness of the election. He offered right-wingers a special role at his inauguration, tapping Franklin Graham, Billy Graham's son, to offer the invocation, and giving what Richard Land, who represents the conservative, 16-million-member Southern Baptist Convention in Washington, warmly characterized as the "most overtly religious speech in its tone of any inaugural address in living memory."[44] Once in office, Bush staffers set up a system of frequent conference calls with evangelical conservatives and, separately, with Catholic conservatives, calls Rove himself often joins.[45] Special closed-door meetings with the president are common, such as one during Bush's first week in office preceding the launch of his faith-based initiative, which included partisan evangelical leaders such as Chuck Colson, the born-again former Watergate felon who now runs a proselytizing operation called Prison Fellowship Ministries. Marvin Olasky, a former Bush advisor who coined the concept of "compassionate conservatism," said the gathering felt like "a revival."[46] Karl Rove has served as the star attraction at the

Conservative Political Action Conference, an A-list event for the far right, where everyone from the NRA to antitax activists to elements of the religious right attend; "Rove was as eager to be there," the *Weekly Standard* reported, "as the group was to have him."[47] Rove has head-lined the Family Research Council's annual Washington Briefing, where conservative evangelicals from across the country huddle to plan their political strategy, an event where a parade of the Bush administration's evangelical darlings have also appeared, such as John Ashcroft, faith-based director Jim Towey, and White House evangelical liaison Tim Goeglein.[48] When the Council for National Policy, another meeting ground for economic and social right-wingers, held its twentieth an-niversary conference in Washington, its elite "gold circle club" got a private audience with Rove and Bush at the White House.[49] Bush aides, often from Rove's office, regularly attend Washington's two weekly meetings for conservative activists, one run by Grover Norquist, head of Americans for Tax Reform, and the other by Weyrich.[50] Officials as diverse as domestic policy advisor Margaret Spellings, economic advi-sor Larry Lindsey, and Secretary of the Interior Gale Norton have of-fered Christian television and print outlets privileged access.[51] And the president himself has often addressed important evangelical audi-ences, such as the National Association of Religious Broadcasters.[52]

James Dobson, chairman of the Colorado Springs Christian media giant Focus on the Family and an enormously popular Christian radio host, had been a holdout in endorsing Bush before the election; he was wooed back into the fold by the president's full-throated endorsement, early in his tenure, of the National Day of Prayer, an annual event or-chestrated by Dobson's wife Shirley.[53] Christian right leaders such as Dobson and Tony Perkins, president of Focus on the Family's Wash-ington, DC–based offshoot, the Family Research Council, brag to their members of the constant special perks they receive, such as being in-vited to a private gathering with the president before he signed the Par-tial Birth Abortion bill, and getting to ride along in his motorcade to the signing. Even after 9/11, as Bush sought to project a message of tol-erance, Bush put Goeglein, praised by one conservative Christian pub-lication as a "strong evangelical," in charge of planning the national prayer service and arranging an intimate gathering of religious leaders with the president the following week. That meeting featured evangelical right-wingers such as Franklin Graham, who would, just weeks later, call Islam "a very evil and wicked religion."[54]

When staffers dare to hamper this evangelical courtship, they are swiftly reprimanded. After Colin Powell spoke on MTV about the importance of condoms for sexually active youth, Dobson and Focus on the Family pounced, prompting Bush to reiterate his "abstinence only" philosophy a few days later.[55] After John DiIulio, the former director of the Office of Faith-Based Initiatives, insulted evangelical "parachurches" for ignoring the poor at a gathering of Christian broadcasters, Rove took him aside and urged him to bury the hatchet. DiIulio responded feistily, saying, "I'm not taking any shit off Jerry Falwell"— but then he resigned before the year was out.[56]

Bush has also lavished special attention on Catholic conservatives. During his first week in office, he and national security advisor Condoleezza Rice joined Washington, D.C.'s Cardinal Theodore McCarrick and several bishops for dinner at McCarrick's home; Bush invited Cardinal Bernard Law of Boston for a one-on-one meeting in the White House a couple of weeks later. He pointedly delivered his first commencement address as president at Notre Dame, and when traveling, he often takes time to meet with a local bishop or cardinal. He has lavished praise on the Pope to Catholic audiences, receiving a standing ovation at one gathering when he spoke in glowing terms of the Pope's commitment to a "culture of life" and his call that "we must defend in love the innocent child waiting to be born."[57]

"I've been through five Republican administrations, and the effort to communicate with conservatives and to understand our concerns and address our concerns and involve us in the process is the best of any of the Republican administrations, including Ronald Reagan," Weyrich told the *New York Times* a few months into the new administration. "In fact, far superior to Ronald Reagan."[58] Richard Land of the Southern Baptist Convention echoed these words to the *Christian Science Monitor*: "In the Reagan administration, they took our calls," he said; now, "they call us."[59] It's no coincidence that the only defections on Rove's watch have been moderates: Jim Jeffords, who bolted the GOP in the Senate, giving the Democrats a brief majority there; Treasury Secretary Paul O'Neill and Environmental Protection Agency chief Christine Todd Whitman, both moderate Republicans; and DiIulio, a Democrat, all of whom resigned their posts in frustration.

FRIENDS IN HIGH PLACES

All this access has paid off handsomely—by producing more access. Aside from Rove and Cheney, Bush's inner circle are all deeply religious: Rice is a minister's daughter, chief of staff Andrew Card is a minister's husband, Karen Hughes is a church elder, and head speechwriter Michael Gerson is a born-again evangelical, a movement insider who's earned the president's admiration for his "deep and animating religious faith."[60] And far-right conservatives, including leaders of the Christian right, populate the administration at all levels. Lawyers from the right-wing Federalist Society staff the office of the White House counsel, while fellows from the socially and economically conservative think tanks the Heritage Foundation and the American Enterprise Institute are scattered around the administration, including Frum, who coined the term "axis of evil," foreign policy advisor Richard Perle, and economic advisor Lawrence Lindsey.[61] Family Research Council (FRC) lobbyist Connie Mackey has bragged that her people are sprinkled throughout the government. "Lobbying works now from both ends of Pennsylvania Avenue and everything in between—that means all the federal agencies," she told the crowd at the group's annual gathering in 2002. "The good news is that with President Bush in office a lot of FRC people are in place. And that's the good part that makes our life a lot easier."[62]

High-profile favorites of the Christian right include Geoglein, Bush's evangelical wrangler; Wade Horn, past president of the National Fatherhood Initiative, a group dedicated to "solving the problem of father absence";[63] and of course attorney general John Ashcroft, the strict Pentecostal who promoted the "family values" agenda while in the Senate. The story of his nomination—and confirmation—illustrates the close cooperation and joint strategy that characterize the Christian right's relationship with the current White House. According to the authors of *Boy Genius,* another Rove biography, Bush originally wanted to offer the post to Montana Governor Marc Racicot for his tenacity during the Florida recount, but on one of those regular White House conference calls with conservative evangelicals, the ground troops insisted on Ashcroft.[64] Ashcroft's nomination went forward, but then an even more interesting development occurred, as recounted by Grover Norquist in the *American Spectator*: "Far from assuming that Bush's White House was responsible for winning on the Ashcroft nomination, conservative groups organized to phone, fax and e-mail in his support. The ACU [American Conservative Union] formed Americans for the Bush Cabinet and 154 state and local groups joined through the Internet to generate 900,000 e-mail messages to the Senate. The Family Research Council organized conservative women in a series of press conferences, demonstrations and Hill visits that out-hustled the feminists and won more press coverage than Ashcroft's opponents. The Capital Research Center, led by Terry Scanlon, documented that many of the liberal groups attacking Ashcroft had received federal funds during the Clinton years totaling hundreds of millions of dollars."[65] Religious conservatives who had been known for making demands and sulking when they weren't met in full were now rallying their troops in close cooperation with the White House and winning results.

Bush put religious conservative Kay Cole James, a former dean at Pat Robertson's Regent University and a former vice president of the Family Research Council, in charge of his Office of Personnel.[66] For a window into her worldview, one can look to her 1995 book, *Transforming America from the Inside Out,* in which James likened gay people to alcoholics, adulterers, and drug addicts.[67] With Rove directing from above, and James watchdogging the details, an avalanche of religious right appointments followed. Bush named Alma Golden, an abstinence proponent from Texas, to oversee the nation's family planning program. He named Claude Allen, a pro-lifer, Christian homeschooler, and abstinence advocate as deputy secretary of Health and Human Services. He named David Hager, a physician and Christian book author who led the Christian right's effort to block FDA approval of RU-486, the early abortion pill, to the FDA's Reproductive Drugs Advisory Committee. His nominee to head the National Labor Relations Board, Robert Brame, had been a board member of the Atlanta-based American Vision, which supports putting the United States under biblical law.[68] Bush named Tom Coburn, an antigay former congressman who had served on the Family Research Council board of directors, to cochair his Presidential Advisory Council on HIV/AIDS. He named Reverend Lou Sheldon, founder of the Traditional Values Coalition, a virulently antigay group based in Washington, D.C., that advocates discrimination, as an advisor for a spring 2001 Faith-Based Summit, the launching pad for the president's cherished initiative.[69] And the list goes on, deep into the bowels of Health and Human Services, the State Department, the Justice Department, and the White House. As Ralph Reed told the *Washington Post,* "You're no longer throwing rocks at the building; you're in the building."[70]

This assignment of Christian right players to so many key administration positions has allowed administration hard-liners, congressional conservatives, and leaders of the Christian right to closely coordinate. Conservative publications report that social conservatives are "thrilled" by their level of access to friendlies in the administration, and that close alliance has proved extraordinarily useful for the administration as well. "If you want to say, 'Hey, guys, we'd like your help on x, y, and z,' there are 110 guys there," Norquist said of the administration's relationship to his Wednesday gathering of prominent business and social conservatives. "They come out of that meeting, go back to their groups, and they're talking to thousands of people."[71] Michael Schwartz, the top lobbyist for Concerned Women for America, describes the workings of the Values Action Team, a far-right congressional caucus that meets weekly with its grass-roots family values allies, in a similar way. "Serious strategy meetings take place separate from the Values Action Team meetings, but the communication that takes place at those meetings is critically important," he says. "You know that twenty-five groups will be coming together at the Values Action Team meeting, and you can bring an issue to them, and maybe fifteen of them will do something about it." This collaboration is apparent even on initiatives that are not at the heart of the Christian right agenda. For instance, as the president was building support for his first round of tax cuts in 2001, the *Wall Street Journal* reported, Tim Goeglein and Karl Rove enlisted help from the Christian right in promoting the proposal through a series of private meetings with social conservatives in Washington. When at one stage officials floated the idea of dropping the tax break for married couples, these religious leaders protested and the idea was dropped. Evangelicals returned the favor, as leaders such as Pat Robertson promoted the tax-cut package on popular programs such as his *700 Club*. The day Bush was set to sign the bill, Christian radio stations across the country gave Goeglein access to their airwaves to praise it. "With this president and this White House, the religious right is trying to be part of the team," says Tim Graham, White House correspondent for the conservative Christian magazine *World*.[72]

All Politics, All the Time

The White House under George W. Bush is a famously closed shop. But a few notable defectors have given us disturbing glimpses of what life is like in an administration that orbits around Karl Rove. When the *New Yorker*'s Nicholas Lemann asked Rove to define the Democratic base, he wisecracked, "Somebody with a doctorate."[73] And whether Rove sees them as members of the enemy camp, or just inconvenient obstacles to his political agenda, policy wonks are certainly unwelcome at this White House. As are the things that somebody with a doctorate might value, like accurate data, honest research, and thorough policy analysis.

Some of the administration's defectors, such as Christine Todd Whitman, have chosen only to issue gentle warnings, as she did on the editorial page of the *New York Times*, characterizing Bush as "one of the more conservative presidents in recent history" and noting that "many moderate Republicans feel even less certain of their place in the party."[74] John DiIulio, a major influence on Bush's faith-based initiative who was brought on to head up the office, was the first to speak in detail about his concerns. DiIulio, a working-class Italian Catholic who's had a career as an Ivy League professor, is a controversial figure—he fashioned the concept of urban youth as "superpredators," then later disavowed it, emphasizing instead the role urban churches have to play in helping at-risk youth—but he is roundly considered an intellectual heavyweight. He has close ties with black church leaders in Philadelphia and Boston, and the assumption was that he would provide serious heft to Bush's compassionate conservatism agenda and its centerpiece, the faith-based initiative. But what he found instead at the White House, according to a series of interviews and e-mail exchanges with journalist Ron Suskind, was "a complete lack of a policy apparatus," something he saw as unprecedented. "What you've got is everything—and I mean everything—being run by the political arm." He mentions, in particular, the enormous weight given to right-wing think tanks and the Christian right: While "Clinton was the policy-wonk-in-chief," devoted to "information-rich decision-making," DiIulio wrote in a memo to Suskind, this White House was nearly devoid of "meaningful, substantive policy discussions" and produced decisions that were often "slap-dash" and "politically-timed." DiIulio says he argued the president should sell the faith-based initiative in bipartisan venues like the U.S. Mayors Conference, "But they could not see it, and instead went back to courting religious conservative leaders and groups." DiIulio, whose charges were dismissed by the White House as "groundless and baseless," later issued an apology.[75] But another, higher level defector, soon affirmed DiIulio's portrait of the Bush White House—Treasury Secretary Paul O'Neill.

O'Neill, a former corporate CEO, had worked side-by-side with Dick Cheney in the Nixon and Ford administrations, and Cheney personally wooed O'Neill to join the Bush team. As one of the top-ranking members of Bush's cabinet, O'Neill had regular one-on-ones with the president, took part in meetings of the National Security Council, and shaped policies on everything from tax cuts to global warming. His account of his time in the White House, told by Suskind in *The Price of Loyalty*, includes some stunning revelations such as the administration's single-minded focus on regime change in Iraq from the very first National Security Council meeting in January 2001. It also documents a disturbing pattern of disregard for the facts. O'Neill discovers, to his horror, that the president's first State of the Union used cooked numbers to bolster his tax-cut plans.[76] When O'Neill made the case for canceling pieces of the tax cut if the deficit began to balloon, the president responded, "I won't negotiate with myself. . . . If someone comes to me with a plan for this, *and they have a significant amount of political backing,* I'll sit down with them—talk it out. But until then, it's a closed issue" (emphasis added).[77] He watches as the president decides—betraying his campaign promises—to oppose the Kyoto protocol before he and Whitman even have their first sit-down.[78] O'Neill suspects that Bush never looked at the research on global warming that he and Whitman had painstakingly compiled, but rather, it was a decision "based on simply, 'The base likes this and who the hell knows anyway.'"[79] "What became clear to me at that point is that the presence of me and Colin and Christie helped convince people that this would, actually, be an administration that would look hard for best solutions, without regard for which party had claimed an idea first or some passing political calculation. . . . Thinking back about how all of us started to be banged up so early on, from the inside, it now seems like we inadvertently may have been there, in large part, as cover."[80] It's notable that, of the three, only Powell is left standing.

All of my conversations with lower level staff at other federal departments and agencies (those who have left and those who are still there and so chose not to speak on the record) echo the portrait DiIulio and O'Neill paint of an administration where inconvenient facts are ignored in the interest of politics—especially the politics of pleasing the Christian right. One former State Department staffer, for example, who worked in the Bureau of Population, Refugees, and Migration under Clinton and then Bush, said that part of her job was to prepare U.S. delegations who were heading into U.N. negotiations on population and health issues. "We would normally provide these delegations with memoranda recommending specific language [on reproductive health]. . . . We literally got those memos bounced back to us with e-mails and phone calls saying, 'These positions are not in line with the administration's positions.' In effect saying, 'We don't care what you say, or what the facts are. . . .' We as health policy professionals were not only being ignored but told to shut up."

Judy Auerbach, a former director of AIDS social science research at the National Institutes of Health, describes administration efforts to intimidate scientific peer reviewers—the ones who decide which research proposals get funding—in areas of particular concern to the Christian right such as HIV and sexuality. "The department [HHS officials] starting visiting AIDS and infectious-disease-related study sections, to listen in on the peer review process. And the peer reviewers I spoke to said, 'Shoot, are these people going to take notes, go after the folks sitting in on the study section? If they vote for a [politically sensitive] proposal, will HHS start targeting them?'" Margaret Scarlett, a former scientist at the Centers for Disease Control and Prevention, reports that the agency pulled information about condoms from its Web site, information that contradicted the christian right's preferred abstinence-only message, without even consulting the relevant agency staff. "People who are the condom experts in the HIV/AIDS division, who've written textbook chapters, they said, 'Oh, I hadn't seen that, no one came to me about that,'" Scarlett says. "It's not uncommon for changes to be generated at high levels, but then you would always go to the content experts. All those protocols have been circumvented. And that's what's disturbing."

If facts and expertise can bolster a policy that is prized by a key Bush constituency, the administration is all for it. When they don't, there seems to be little interest in grappling with them at all. This attitude echoes that of the faith-based social service providers I spoke with around the country, many of whom cared far less about the results of their programs (pregnancies prevented, addiction defeated) than in the fact that the message they were sending (live a pure lifestyle, accept Christ as your Savior) was morally right. And what is morally right in these circles is politically right in Washington. O'Neill once described the president, functioning in this vacuum of inconvenient information and ideas, as "a blind man in a roomful of deaf people."[81] Perhaps that's too harsh. But as Rove himself has said, "History is really littered with people who agonized over decisions. . . . Even in this White House, I've seen people agonizing over decisions, but I've never seen [Bush]."[82]

Bush's rule is simple, and he follows it always. If an idea has "a significant amount of political backing" from a valued constituency, he'll do what he can regardless of the facts. And when it comes to the Christian right, he will do a lot.

4

WEIRD SCIENCE

WITH ITS PAIRS of birds and beasts and creeping things, its ferocious forty-day flood, and its final beautiful image of the dove of peace, Noah's ark is one of the most dramatic tales in the Bible. But the story that has inspired endless Sunday school yarns has also posed enormous challenges for biblical literalists, who engage in elaborate calculations to prove that a sampler of all the earth's animals could have fit on the ark, lead expeditions to find the ark's remains, and hunt for geological evidence of the flood. It's also pretty close to what passes for science in the Bush White House. From public parks to public health, in this administration, when scientific consensus clashes with conservative Christian worldviews, the latter often wins.

Noah's ark and the Bush administration first intersected in Grand Canyon National Park in July 2003, when the park's chief of interpretation approved a glossy coffee table book, *Grand Canyon: A Different View*, for sale in the park's official bookstore. The book, edited by Tom Vail, who leads "Christ-centered" tours through the canyon, includes beautiful shots of the canyon along with essays by more than a dozen creationists. According to decades of accumulated geological study, rocks deep in the canyon date back 2 billion years, while the canyon itself was created some 6 million years ago, as the Colorado River slowly eroded layer upon layer of rock.[1] The contributors to *A Different View* attack that science, accepted by geologists around the world, and claim the canyon was forged by a single "catastrophic" event a few thousand years ago—the great flood that launched Noah's ark. The decision to approve the book appears minor, but it was notable. Like everything under Park Service control, the canyon's bookstore operates under a Congressional mandate to promote scientific understanding. According to documents obtained by the advocacy group Public Employees for Environmental Responsibility, of twenty-six products suggested for the bookstore by a private advisory body over the past two years, only one, Vail's creationist book, was approved for sale. (On her product evaluation form, dated July 22, 2003, the park's chief of interpretation avoiding checking a box declaring the book to be accurate or inaccurate, but rather drew a circle between the two and scrawled, "Interpretation of the canyon from a different perspective—interesting timing in light of recent events!" She was likely referring to the decision, a week earlier, by Donald Murphy, deputy director of the National Park Service, to restore a set of brass plaques bearing Christian Bible verses that the Grand Canyon superintendent had removed from the canyon's rim on First Amendment grounds.)[2]

The Grand Canyon has long been a subject of special interest for creationists, especially for advocates of that new brand of pseudoscience known as "intelligent design," which uses fragments of real geological evidence to argue the view that the earth is only a few thousand years old, a timeline based in their literal reading of the book of Genesis. Answers in Genesis, an international Christian ministry dedicated to "uphold the authority of the Bible from the very first verse" that opened a U.S. office in 1994, argues that the Grand Canyon's rock formation "dramatically demonstrates the reality of the catastrophic global Flood of Noah's day." To bolster their claims, they cite a growing pool of creationist literature, books like *The Young Earth* and *Grand Canyon: Monument to Catastrophe*. In the latter, creationist Steven Austin claims to identify in the canyon "tectonics associated with the formation of an ocean basin midway through Creation Week" and "ocean deposits from the post-Creation, but pre-Flood world."[3] The president of Answers in Genesis contributed an essay to *A Different View*, and the group mobilized its 17,000 members to email the Park Service in support of the book.[4] Answers in Genesis has a friend in the Institute for Creation Research, which runs its own creationist graduate school and published *A Different View*. ICR has been leading creationist "field study tours" into the canyon for 24 years. The Alliance Defense Fund, founded by such Christian right leaders as Focus on the Family leader James Dobson and televangelist D. James Kennedy to "keep the door open for the spread of the Gospel" through litigation, serves as the legal arm of the creationist movement; the group has chosen to represent Vail, *A Different View*'s editor, in his efforts to keep the book stocked in Park Service stores.[5]

In December 2003, the heads of seven leading national geological associations got wind that the Grand Canyon had begun to sell *A Different View* and sent a letter to Joseph Alston, the Grand Canyon superintendent. Its tone was one of barely contained alarm. "The National Park Service should be extremely careful about giving the impression that it approves of the anti-science movement known as young Earth creationism or endorses the advancement of religious tenets as science," the letter reads. "The book aggressively attacks modern science and broadly accepted interpretations of the geologic history of the Grand Canyon. As such, any implied approval or endorsement by the NPS [National Park Service] for the book and others like it undermines efforts to educate the public about the scientific understanding of Grand Canyon geology."[6] The Alliance Defense Fund responded with a seven-page letter, in early January 2004, to Interior Secretary Gale Norton threatening legal action if the book was pulled from the Canyon's store shelves.[7] Later that month, after conducting an official review of the book, the government's top geologist, David Shaver, head of the Department of Interior's Geologic Resources Division, issued a strong recommendation that the national park pull the book. He said *A Different View* "purports to be science when it is not" and in fact "repudiates science" by promoting a " 'creation science' worldview which is not supported by scientific observations of the natural world and cannot be meaningfully tested" and by making "claims that are counter to widely accepted geological evidence." Shaver concluded, "Its sale in the park bookstores directly conflicts with the Service's statutory mandate to promote the use of sound science in all its programs."[8]

But the book controversy was picking up steam on the religious right. As alerts circulated on Christian news services and among Christian lobby groups—including the influential Family Research Council and Focus on the Family—the chances of the book's removal slimmed. By late February 2004, religion had won out: the Grand

Canyon bookstore had reordered A Different View, which was being stocked on the bookstore shelves and marketed on the Grand Canyon's official Web site as "natural history."[9] Ruch, the director of Public Employees for Environmental Responsibility, was the first to bring media attention to the book controversy after park workers called in about the incident to PEER's anonymous tip line. During this same period, Park Service employees reported to PEER about another federal intervention on behalf of creationists. In 2000, in response to requests from park interpreters, the Geologic Resources Division drafted a document offering guidance to park geologists and rangers on how to address visitors' questions about creationism. The draft, according to Ruch, who obtained a copy, states clearly that there is no valid scientific data showing that the earth is only a few thousand years old and says that since creationists' assertions cannot be meaningfully tested, their claims cannot be considered to be a legitimate scientific perspective. The guidance, originally expected to gain approval and be issued to park workers in 2001, has yet to be released; sources tell Ruch that it has been permanently quashed. Whether these decisions were made due to pressure from Christian right lobby groups or trickled down from a president who once told a New York Times reporter that he believes the jury is still out on creationism—that's left for the rest of us to theorize.[10] "Creationists have become more aggressive about pushing their view as a form of science that should be given equal time," says Ruch. "And with the entrée that Christian fundamentalists have with top administrators in both the Department of the Interior and the White House, the National Park Service has been forced to adopt a position of geologic agnosticism. This incident may not seem very large, but it reverberates not only through the park, but throughout the entire Park Service."

A large-scale survey of Park Service employees published in late 2003 by the environmental group Campaign to Protect America's Lands found nearly nine out of ten employees had a great deal of concern that "decisions are being influenced by politics rather than professional experience/science," with nearly eight in ten saying political decision making is more prevalent than it was just a few years ago.[11] But such political interference in scientific decisions has hardly been confined to the public parks under President Bush; in fact, it has become rife throughout the administration. In fact, the pattern of interference became so visible by February 2004 that more than sixty leading scientists—including twenty Nobel Prize winners—wrote a public letter expressing their outrage. "When scientific knowledge has been found to be in conflict with its political goals, the administration has often manipulated the process through which science enters into its decisions," the letter reads. "This has been done by placing people who are professionally unqualified or who have clear conflicts of interest in official posts and on scientific advisory committees; by disbanding existing advisory committees; by censoring and suppressing reports by the government's own scientists; and by simply not seeking independent scientific advice. Other administrations have, on occasion, engaged in such practices, but not so systematically nor on so wide a front. Furthermore, in advocating policies that are not scientifically sound, the administration has sometimes misrepresented scientific knowledge and misled the public about the implications of its policies. . . . The distortion of scientific knowledge for partisan political ends must cease."[12] Almost two months later, White House science advisor John Marburger quietly issued a twenty-page rebuttal. "I can attest from my personal experience and direct knowledge that this Administration is implementing the President's policy of strongly supporting science and applying the highest scientific standards in decision-making," Marburger wrote. "This administration also believes in tapping the best scientific minds—both inside and outside the government—for policy input and advice."[13] In an interview with the *New York Times*, he charged the Nobel laureates with peddling a "conspiracy theory."[14] But after a review of the evidence, their charges hardly seem paranoid. From global warming to lead poisoning, from AIDS research to pregnancy prevention, the Bush administration has chosen to sacrifice science whenever it conflicts with the needs of Bush's corporate patrons or his evangelical base. Administration officials have attacked and investigated scientists and public health experts working in fields that offend Christian right sensibilities; stacked scientific committees with believers who filter data through a religious prism; censored government science when its conclusions are inconvenient to the family values agenda; and based policy decisions on unsound science, contorted to please the Republicans' most favored constituency.

ENDLESS INQUISITIONS

Early in 2003, scientists at the National Institutes of Health (NIH), the most prestigious and moneyed scientific institution in the world, discovered that avid Republican congressional staffers were spending their idle hours online, scouring CRISP, a database of federally funded biomedical research, the way seventh graders might scan *The Color Purple* for the dirty parts. They seemed to be searching for terms like "sex worker," "gay men," and "anal sex"—terms that might signal endorsement of homosexuality or prostitution to the Christian right—and NIH personnel began to fear real consequences for researchers in these areas. So that spring, NIH project officers started calling scientists and telling them to purge such terms from their grant proposals if they hoped to get funded—and stay funded. "I have been asked to camouflage abstracts so as not to mention 'men who have sex with men' or 'gay' or 'anal sex'—there are lots of words that can trigger an investigation," says one HIV-prevention researcher who asked not be named in order to protect his research. "It's absurd because these words describe the main population or topic you're after and it's very difficult to camouflage." The scientist would not risk discussing the particulars of his research but did speak hypothetically. "Let's say that you're going to explore HIV risk behavior in bareback parties," places where gay men meet to have sex without condoms, a new area of study for HIV-prevention researchers. "you cannot say 'bareback,' you cannot say 'men who have sex with men,' you cannot even say 'sexual risk.' You can just say something vague like men in your city who are intentionally engaging in risk behavior. They are especially concerned about anything that might be construed as using taxpayers' money to support same-sex behavior. So if you wanted to study risk behavior at a bathhouse, and for an ethnographer to enter the bathhouse he has to pay a $5 entrance fee, that can be construed as using taxpayer money to support same-sex practices." That researcher rewrote a grant application to avoid offending words, as did others with whom I spoke. Two other researchers, who likewise asked not to be named, told me that they had been warned to censor all of their written communications, including e-mails. "My experience with project officers at NIH," said one of them, "is I have been encouraged to mask my populations in all communications except verbal where the project officer indicates safety."

The changes were made mostly in titles and abstracts—the short summary that shows up on CRISP—not the substance of the grant proposals. But even these small acts of censorship have compromised the scientific review process. Research proposals are assigned to the appropriate experts for review based on the proposals' titles and abstracts. According to a researcher who serves as an NIH peer reviewer in the field of HIV prevention (one of those who was told to censor his e-mails), this process has broken down due to efforts by researchers to avoid unwanted attentions from the Christian right. "At a recent review," he says, "there was a study in my area that I couldn't recognize because its description was full of generalities. I later found out it was a prevention study involving gay men, which is my area of expertise, but I couldn't recognize it as such from the vaguely worded abstract." So the grant application went to another behavioral scientist for review, someone who wasn't an expert in gay HIV prevention and who likely had a difficult time judging the proposal on its merits. In the end, while these efforts at euphemism and self-censorship disrupted the grant review process, they did not succeed at protecting grantees from the watchful eyes of the Christian right.

In October 2003, top scientists across the country began to receive a new, far more aggressive round of warning calls from the NIH. These public health researchers, working in the fields of AIDS, sexually transmitted diseases, drug and alcohol addiction, and pregnancy prevention, had all been awarded grants by the federal agency after a rigorous, sometimes years-long scientific review process, led by the top minds in their fields. Now these researchers were being told that their funding—much of it already spent—was in jeopardy.[15]

Tooru Nemoto, a researcher at the Center for AIDS Prevention

Studies at the University of California at San Francisco who has done pioneering research into HIV risk among immigrant communities and the transgendered, got one of those calls. His came from a project officer at the NIH's National Institute on Drug Abuse. "It was a friendly call," says Nemoto, "but it scared many of my colleagues. He was warning me that someone else might contact me, that my name was on a list. He didn't say where it came from." A look at where that list originated, and how it generated such a massive organizational response at NIH, provides a window into how the federal government treats scientists these days—or at least scientists in controversial fields.

Earlier that October, the House Energy and Commerce Committee held a big public hearing on NIH spending. A bipartisan effort in Congress had nearly doubled the NIH's budget in recent years, and the hearing was meant to determine what new accountability measures should be introduced. NIH head Elias Zerhouni and his predecessor Harold Varmus each made lengthy presentations about the challenges facing the sprawling agency (Varmus, a Nobel laureate, would later sign onto the critical February 2004 letter), but then the topic swerved. Several Republican congressmen on the committee, led by Pennsylvania's Joe Pitts, demanded that Zerhouni defend ten research projects the legislators deemed frivolous. All but two were related to sexuality or HIV.[16] The grants in question received a total of $2.3 million in 2002, or less than $\frac{1}{100}$ of 1 percent of the NIH's annual budget.[17] Their list included five grants that Pitts' Republican colleague Pat Toomey had singled out for defunding two months earlier through an amendment to a labor spending bill. (Unlike AIDS, he said at the time, "there are real diseases that are affecting real people and that's what this kind of money should be used for.")[18] In that case, even after powerful Republicans like Ralph Regula, who chairs the appropriations subcommittee that oversees the NIH, warned that Congress would "put a chill on medical research if we start to micromanage individual NIH grants," the Toomey amendment was barely defeated, 212 to 210.[19]

After the hearing, when NIH staff called for a list of the projects in question, an unnamed Republican committee staffer faxed them a list of 289 NIH grants, almost all of which funded research into AIDS, sexually transmitted diseases, addiction, and pregnancy prevention—the very list, it turns out, on which Nemoto's name had appeared. Immediately afterward, Nemoto and other scientists started to receive the warning calls. The list itself is a curious document. Many of the grant titles are accompanied by brief remarks that alternate between the squeamish and the sarcastic. They note that one study of HIV risk among homeless heroin users "looks at 'risky' injection practices" and that a study of HIV risk among Latino men includes "discussion on reducing 'unprotected' anal sex." The quotes around *risky* and *unprotected* signal a rejection of the distinction between safe and unsafe practices; to those who created this list, gay sex and drug injection are apparently just plain wrong, and shouldn't be made safe from HIV. The comments often veer into prurience, quoting with relish any street terminology that appears in the grant language: "rock," "crystal," "public sex," "lot lizards," "truck chasers." One study on HIV prevention in South Africa notes "Awarded to Abortionist."[20] Though drug addiction is a massive epidemic, affecting 22 million Americans, though 1 million Americans are HIV infected, and though some 300,000 American teenagers become pregnant each year, the commentary on this list indicates a deep skepticism about—if not outright hostility toward—the government devoting any resources to public health research in these areas. "They seem to find AIDS research that's not focused only on the basic biology bizarre, weird, and unimportant," says Judy Auerbach, a vice president of the American Foundation for AIDS Research who until recently served as director of the behavioral and social science program in the Office of AIDS Research at NIH. "They clearly are motivated by a particular religious ideology that condemns prostitutes, homosexuals, transsexuals, and drug users—not just their behaviors, but the actual people themselves. But they are also political conservatives who want to decrease federal programs, and they figured out that NIH was a huge, well-funded agency. They couldn't take on cancer or Parkinson's, but they could easily take on AIDS, because it's about 'queers and junkies and whores.' So the content of these grants allows them also to pursue this larger Republican project of defunding government programs."

The warnings might have remained the subject of anxious murmurs within the scientific community if it weren't for Democratic Representative Henry Waxman, who had set up an anonymous tip line some months earlier, when he first became concerned about political interference with science in the Bush administration. E-mails to the tip line poured in from researchers who'd received NIH warnings, and Waxman wrote to Health Secretary Tommy Thompson asking him to identify the source of the list. "Collectively, this research aims to promote scientific understanding that could save millions of lives around the world," he wrote. "I urge you in the strongest possible terms to denounce this scientific McCarthyism."[21] Only then did the Traditional Values Coalition (TVC), one of the most aggressively antigay organizations on the Christian right, claim authorship of the list and launch its director, Andrea Lafferty, onto the talk show circuit. "We know for a fact that millions and millions of dollars have been flushed down the toilet over years on this HIV/AIDS scam and sham," she told the Associated Press. To the *Washington Post* she said, "There needs to be some adult supervision at NIH."[22]

"It's no surprise that the Traditional Values Coalition would generate a list like this," says Ken Haller, MD, president of the Gay and Lesbian Medical Association, a number of whose members were on the TVC list. "But the fact that it received credence in government speaks volumes about the lack of respect this administration has for science when good science conflicts with ideology."

It's hard to fathom how a hit list created by a fringe organization like the TVC, whose founder once called for AIDS leper colonies, created an agency-wide response at NIH. Waxman noticed details on the list that weren't easily available to the public, and asked about the involvement of Health and Human Services (HHS) staff—which would go far to explain the NIH's strong reaction. But Health Secretary Thompson issued a testy response to Waxman denying any departmental collusion. "I must emphatically set the record straight regarding your assertions that HHS created a 'hit list,' " his letter read. "HHS and its leadership team create and support an environment of solid scientific research. The integrity of the leaders of our institutions is beyond reproach."[23] Congressman Pitts' spokesman Derek Karchner insists his boss played no role in forwarding the TVC list and had yet to even see it when the story broke. And in fact Pitts had famously feuded with the group the previous summer when TVC attacked pro-life members of Congress for supporting cheap drug imports from Canada, a stance that Pitts considered a breach of loyalty. TVC claimed the import law would ease access to RU-486, the early abortion pill, but it turned out the group was on the payroll of the pharmaceutical lobby.[24] So perhaps the forwarding of the TVC's list to the NIH was merely a simple mistake, a misunderstanding created by—Karchner's words—a "confused" congressional staffer.

"Confused" is an apt word for the entire incident. Even experienced beltway AIDS advocates and longtime NIH scientists had difficulty connecting the dots between the TVC's list, Republican congressional staffers, and the strong response by NIH. "They do a pretty good job of a no fingerprints thing," says Terje Anderson, executive director of the National Association of People with AIDS and a member of the presidential AIDS council during the Clinton years. What is clear is strong ties exist between Joe Pitts, HHS staffers, and the Christian right lobby. Whether or not she played a hand in circulating the sprawling TVC list, Sheila Moloney, policy director of the Republican Study Committee, a far-right congressional caucus, is listed as the author of Joe Pitts' shorter ten-grant list. And Moloney is a well-known quantity within religious right circles. She's a former editor with the conservative *Policy Review*, the former executive director of the Eagle Forum, and a former senior staffer at the Family Research Council. Pitts himself is the winner of a True Blue Award from the Family Research Council for his unwavering commitment to the family values agenda, and he includes a link to the Family Research Council on his official congressional Web site.[25] He also serves as chairman of the powerful Values Action Team (VAT), a far right congressional caucus that brings together Christian right lobby groups with their allies in Congress.

The VAT, a project of the Republican Study Committee, was launched in 1998 when James Dobson, head of Focus on the Family and host of its influential Christian radio program, threatened to bolt the Republican Party and back a Gary Bauer insurgency against Bush.[26] But if it was created merely to mollify malcontents, the weekly VAT meetings have become a central address for coordinating the strategy of Christian right lobby groups and congressional true believers. At the invite-only meetings, Christian right power brokers—including the Christian Coalition, Focus on the Family, the Family Research Council, Concerned Women for American, the Eagle Forum, and the right-wing Southern Baptist Convention—meet with such congressional attack dogs as Pitts, leading abortion-opponent Representative Chris Smith, and AIDS-foe Representative Mark Souder.[27] The TVC, too, is a card-carrying member—despite being briefly exiled over the pharmaceutical imbroglio. So it's easy to see how a TVC document reflecting the shared concerns of the family values set about addiction and sexuality would reach the hands of a staffer like Moloney.

Pitts and company have become experts at using their majority congressional power to demand information from federal agencies and to instigate investigations of government grantees who set off morality alarms on the Christian right. Congressional staffer Roland Foster, a top Souder aide on a House Government Reform subcommittee, has mastered this skill, several AIDS lobbyists, Democratic congressional aides, and former government staffers report. "This is how it usually works," says Judy Auerbach, the former NIH AIDS researcher. "Foster sends an e-mail to somebody in the department, to the secretary of HHS or the director of NIH, and he names people and he names grants, and lists everything that's wrong with the studies. HHS forwards the e-mail to NIH with no comment, just a forward. And then everybody scurries around having to formulate a response." She adds, "I asked the question many times how was it that a Congressional staffer had this kind of authority and was told that if a communication came from a committee staffer, NIH had to treat it as if it came from a member of Congress. I asked, 'How do we know that this reflects the committee?' and was told, 'We know that Souder doesn't object, and he's the subcommittee chair.' "

Moralizing about scientific research and government waste is hardly unheard of in the annals of Capitol Hill. Back in the 1970s, Senator William Proxmire used to give out his annual Golden Fleece Awards after combing government databases for studies he thought preposterous, and Senator Jesse Helms made a habit of rooting out grants he thought advanced the homosexual agenda. What's new is the level of administration involvement. "The kinds of ideological influence, coercion, and fear that both NIH program staff and their grantees are feeling is something that has been experienced before," says Auerbach, "but everyone will say it's much worse now than it has ever been."

The warnings directed at HIV researchers only began in the wake of the Republicans' sweep of the 2002 midterm elections, when the party's right wing—and its evangelical base—were feeling newly energized. But the harassment of public health providers in the fields of HIV, STDs, and pregnancy prevention began early on in Bush's tenure, in the summer of 2001, when, through a seemingly unending series of audits, they were charged with everything from obscenity to financial impropriety to practicing unsound science. A telling episode involved the Stop AIDS Project in San Francisco, which conducts explicit HIV-prevention workshops for sexually active gay men. Once Stop AIDS became the target of the Traditional Values Coalition and the Values Action Team, the group experienced three audits over a period of two years, during which the group was accused of everything from obscenity to financial impropriety to public health malpractice. In the end, Centers for Disease Control (CDC) head Julie Gerberding affirmed the group's approach to prevention was "based on current and accepted behavioral science"[28]—though she was later forced to retract her conclusion under political pressure. Aggressive audits of half a dozen other HIV-prevention and sex-education groups followed.

As the events of 2003 moved along, from whispers of grant censorship to snowballing audits to the unexpectedly close vote on the Toomey amendment to that extensive Traditional Values Coalition hit list, the scientific community ignited. The leading medical journals published furious editorials, and at least two dozen major professional associations issued statements condemning political interference with scientific research. "The hallmark of an advanced free society is ethical but politically unfettered empirical investigation that (1) yields trustworthy, valid, important, and responsible scientific results; (2) does not recoil from what might be considered politically sensitive or distasteful topics by some; and (3) courageously allows intellectual independence and objectivity on scientifically legitimate topics that a minority may find 'objectionable,'" reads the declaration of the American Sociological Association, one of many professional bodies that weighed in during this period. "America's respect for rational science is based on the common understanding that serious health, economic and social consequences are at stake."[29]

The Fake Science Industry

Multinational corporations have a long and fairly well-known tradition of seeking to undermine—or outflank—independent scientific research. They sometimes put scientists on their payroll, who are charged with conducting research to support predetermined outcomes—say, that hormones in meat don't pose health risks, or that lead does not harm children. These scientists may also trawl for shreds of data in the independent research that supports the industry position and selectively present it in official-sounding reports. The industry likewise creates institutions that have the air of scientific expertise, with names like the American Meat Institute Foundation, the American Petroleum Institute, and the Chemical Industry Institute of Toxicology. These organizations sometimes invent fake "citizen activists" who circulate scientific misinformation through e-mails to newspapers and elected officials.[30] An American Chemical Council strategy memo leaked to the environmental group Greenpeace speaks openly about recruiting "highly credible third party allies" and creating front groups "to provide testimony, demonstrations, press conferences and other defensive and proactive situations."[31] Fred Smith Jr., president of the antiregulatory Competitive Enterprise Institute, expressed the thinking behind these initiatives perfectly when he told the *Washington Post*, "I'm afraid that in politics, science just becomes a tool to be manipulated by both sides."[32] The Union of Concerned

Scientists has denounced such spin as "junk science," which in their view includes the "presentation of selective results, politically motivated distortions of scientifically sound papers, or the publishing of quasi-scientific non-reviewed journals," and any other efforts to lend "undeserved respectability" to "opinion and speculation."[33]

The two most visible recent examples of this corporate manipulation of government science involved the Environmental Protection Agency; both were humiliating experiences for the agency's politically moderate head, Christine Todd Whitman, and were widely regarded as having contributed to her decision to resign. The first uproar ensued in early 2001 when Whitman suspended a Clinton-era regulation tightening acceptable limits for arsenic in drinking water, claiming that there was "no consensus on a particular safe level" and that the issue required further scientific study. After Bush's poll numbers dropped and a National Academy of Sciences study came back saying the Clinton limit was, if anything, not cautious enough, Whitman reinstated the arsenic limits.[34] The second controversy concerned global warming, which, though a top priority of environmentalists, was mysteriously absent from the EPA's June 2003 Draft Report on the Environment, which claimed to be a "comprehensive road map." The National Wildlife Federation soon uncovered an earlier draft that had contained a section on global warming. The group found that a reference in that draft to a National Academy of Sciences report on industrial contributions to global warming had been replaced by the White House with a reference to a study funded by the American Petroleum Institute that questioned the evidence on the causes of climate change. An internal EPA memo revealed that agency staffers found the revisions embarrassing and complained that the revised draft "no longer accurately represents scientific consensus on climate change."[35] Greenpeace, which would soon be targeted for prosecution by the Justice Department, later uncovered a memo detailing cooperation between the White House and the Exxon-funded Competitive Enterprise Institute in Bush's decision to repudiate an earlier, far more critical report on climate change that the EPA had sent to the United Nations.[36]

In recent years, Christian social conservatives have developed an alternative science apparatus of their own, using many of the methods of the industrial giants. In her book *The Battle for God*, theologian Karen Armstrong explains the roots of this strategy. Religious fundamentalism around the world rose in reaction against modernity and scientific rationalism, yet fundamentalists absorbed many of science's tenets. "Because by the end of the nineteenth century science and rationalism were the watchwords of the day, religion had to be rational too if it was to be taken seriously," she writes. "It must be . . . clear, demonstrable, and objective."[37] It was during this period that American Protestant fundamentalists began to insist that the Bible was literally true, without error, and that the first religious attacks against the theory of evolution emerged. By April 2004, according to a Pew survey, 40 percent of Americans believed the Bible to be literally true.[38] With the political rise of the Christian right in the 1980s and 1990s, the movement began to build institutions that could (pseudo-)scientifically demonstrate the truth of their worldview. The earliest examples were groups defending creationism, such as the organizations that rallied behind *A Different View*, the creationist book about the Grand Canyon. A particularly influential group is the Seattle-based Discovery Institute, founded in 1990, which exploits scientific disagreements about various evolutionary mechanisms to argue that science has disproven evolutionary theory in its entirety. The group, which receives substantial funding from donors who support the imposition of biblical law in the United States, often provides pseudoscientific arguments to community members fighting to get creationism or "intelligent design" taught in public schools.[39] Professional associations formed as well, based not on field of expertise, but on ideology. Members of the Tennessee-based Christian Medical Association may be cardiologists or endocrinologists, but they must commit to "living out the character of Christ in their homes, practices, communities and around the world." They must also believe in "the divine inspiration, integrity, and final authority of the Bible as the Word of God"—not easy to square with the scientific spirit of inquiry—and commit to be "controlled by the Holy Spirit" in everything they do.[40]

Other influential institutions within the Christian right include the National Association for the Research and Therapy of Homosexuality (NARTH) and the Medical Institute for Sexual Health, each founded in

1992. NARTH claims to have found scientific evidence for the long-debunked idea that homosexuality is a mental illness that can be cured through therapy. The group also uses shoddy survey data to associate gay sexuality with pedophilia, extreme promiscuity, and suicide, and during the 1990s offered a veneer of scientific legitimacy for antigay measures in Colorado and Oregon.[41] (In Colorado, NARTH founder Joseph Nicolosi presented his questionable data as a paid expert witness on behalf of the state's attorney general, Gale Norton, now President Bush's secretary of the interior.)[42] The Medical Institute, founded by former Austin gynecologist Joe McIlhaney, who has become one of the most prominent peddlers of fake science in the Bush administration, marshals data, discounted by experts in the field, that abstinence-only education works to prevent sexually transmitted diseases but that condoms don't. While he has a slim track record of publishing peer-reviewed studies, he has authored a brochure, *Why Condoms Aren't Safe*, which uses discredited science to argue that condoms are ineffective, and is the star of a video with a similar message, *The Myth of Safe Sex*, with Focus on the Family's James Dobson.[43] A sister organization, the Institute for Youth Development (IYD), has launched a peer-reviewed journal, *Adolescent & Family Health*.[44] Of course, all of the scientific peers associated with IYD's journal have passed an ideological litmus test and tend to clear articles for publication that undermine the case for safer sex, but just to be able to claim the studies are "peer reviewed" offers this morality-based research a new degree of credibility. "For years, our basic line in arguing against abstinence-only education was, 'There's no peer evaluated research,'" says Debra Hauser, vice president of Advocates for Youth, a sex education advocacy organization based in Washington, D.C. "Now that they've created their own peer-reviewed journal, we've got a real problem. We can no longer say there are no articles in peer-reviewed journals. It's pretty insidious." Focus on the Family launched the Physicians' Consortium in 1999 to give its attacks on sex education and condoms a professional veneer; doctors representing the group appeared with right-wing members of Congress in 2001 to call for the resignation of then CDC head Jeffrey Koplan, charging him with misleading the public by encouraging condom use.[45] The Heritage Foundation has recently joined in the effort to produce biased reports on sexuality for use by family values outfits, such as their June 2003 report, *Sexually Active Teenagers Are More Likely to Be Depressed and to Attempt Suicide*, which selectively interprets other researchers' data and ends with the unsupported conclusions that comprehensive sex education has failed and that "abstinence education programs are uniquely suited to meeting both the emotional and the physical needs of America's youth."[46]

Jean Hardisty, the founder of Political Research Associates and the author of several books on the far right, says attracting scores of MDs and PhDs to head up these scientific front groups has taken years of cultivation by the Christian right. "Focus on the Family has worked for years with doctors; they even have a magazine for doctors," she says. "So this is the fruition of an old tactic. What happens when you start working with a professional sector and organizing and politicizing them is you get payback—you get them on the board of your bogus organization. What a group like Focus on the Family is doing is drawing these doctors into a community of like-minded people and motivating them to get involved. There's a lot of honey in the recruitment process. The experience for a doctor coming across these groups is a love bomb: they tell you, 'You're a physician, you're important in this society, you can affect all of society if you speak out.'" What's new is the extent to which these shady science promoters—whether corporate or Christian—have been invited inside the administration, offering a significant opportunity for both of the Republican Party's most significant constituencies to exert enormous influence on policy without attracting undue public attention. Indeed, much of the Republican assault on science is taking place deep within the bowels of the administration, away from public view. And it has involved an audacious restructuring of the way the federal government receives scientific advice.

COUNCILS OF QUACKS

Federal law requires that federal scientific advisory bodies be "fairly balanced in terms of the point of view represented" and "not be inappropriately influenced by the appointing authority or any special interest."[47] But this administration openly flouts such rules. Nominees to scientific panels have been vetted for their views on litmus-test issues such as the death penalty, stem cell research, and needle exchange, even when those issues are irrelevant to their committee work. According to the medical journal *Science*, a White House liaison to the Department of Health gave one nominee to a National Institute on Drug Abuse panel, psychologist William Miller of the University of New Mexico, a running tally on the political acceptability of his responses on these topics ("You're two for three," said the White House staffer at one point) and then asked Miller whether he voted for Bush in 2000. When the candidate answered in the negative he was chastised: "Why didn't you support the president?"[48]

The White House engineered the wholesale replacement of advisors to the CDC's National Center for Environmental Health, without even consulting the center's director. New members include one scientist, Roger McClellan, the former director of an industry front, the Chemical Industry Institute of Toxicology, and another scientist, Dennis Paustenbach, who testified on the side of Pacific Gas and Electric in a trial over poisoned drinking water that served as the basis for the film *Erin Brockovich*. They're joined by Becky Norton Dunlap, a vice president of the Heritage Foundation, a strong foe of government regulation who fought environmental protections while serving as an official in Virginia, and two Christian doctrinaires who appear to have little expertise in environmental toxins.[49] One, Sharon Falkenheimer, is a member of the Christian Medical Association; the other, Harold Koenig, has written about the power of prayer in healing.[50] They replace such respected researchers as Thomas Burke, a public health professor at Johns Hopkins School of Public Health who served as chair of the advisory committee for five years.[51] Burke, whose term President Bush did not renew, told *Science* that before its makeover the committee was "very activist," known for irritating pesticide and chemical manufacturers with its cutting reports and aggressive human exposure tracking programs. It would be a surprise to see such activism emerge from the new gang.[52] Other committees that gained a reputation for aggressive oversight during the Clinton years, such as a committee on lead poisoning and one on gene testing, met similar fates, as experts were replaced by industry consultants.[53]

A standing HHS advisory committee on human research protections was scrapped, renamed, and entirely restaffed. The old body had angered the pharmaceutical industry by strengthening conflict-of-interest rules. The new body, the Secretary's Advisory Committee on Human Research Protections, was formed in the fall of 2002 with a mix of appointees that would change its role from corporate regulator to watchdog of fundamentalist Christian morality. The new body includes doctors who base their practices in Christian beliefs, such as Nancy Jones, a member of the Christian Medical Association and a fellow with the Center for Bioethics and Human Dignity, which promotes "explicit Christian engagement" in scientific decision making.[54] Jones argued against scientific consensus in formal testimony before another federal committee, saying "justifying our decisions based on subjective aspects of science is more analogous to faith in the enterprise of science, rather than justification based on 'proven' fact." She also referred to science as merely another "ideology" that "has been preferred over other dogmatic methods historically ascribed to philosophy and theology." Even more apropos to her new role, Jones argued that science has nothing to contribute to the debate over when to consider a fetus a person.[55] HHS wrote into the committee's new charter a "particular emphasis" on "pregnant women, embryos, and fetuses," a development that thrilled the National Right to Life Committee, whose legislative director Douglas Johnson said, "We applaud the administration for explicitly recognizing in the charter that the term 'human subjects' includes all living members of the species Homo sapiens at every stage of their development."[56] If most Americans are barely aware of the government's complex network of some 250 scientific advisory committees, these pro-life activists are keenly attuned to the role they can play in changing legal precedent—and public policy.

The president's FDA commissioner (until spring 2004), Mark McClellan, is an old Bush family friend who was charged in that post with ensuring that Americans' food and prescription drugs are safe. At his confirmation hearings in the fall of 2002, long after much of this corporate and religious bias had come to light, he defended George Bush's choice of scientific advisors along these lines: "Expertise and objectivity are important criteria for selection," he told the Senate, but so is "diversity of viewpoints."[57] Legitimate debates over the implications of scientific data were once the hallmark of diversity on these committees. But the Bush administration's new take on diversity sidelines expertise and has already produced its intended effect: derailing scientific debate by setting up an irreconcilable conflict between those who are willing to be guided by the data and those who choose to be guided by industry interests—or by a literal reading of the Bible. Few would question that questions of corporate profit or religious dogma are legitimate parts of the broad chorus of public policy debate, but scientific advisory committees have a different and narrower role: to produce guidance for the administration on how to navigate those debates in relation to what the science tells us. The new diversity serves to obfuscate the science itself. And far from reflecting the nation's extremely diverse perspectives on public health, one sees that these new appointments actually display a rather disturbing sameness, coming as they do from such a small, intense, interconnected network of far-right social conservatives. At a handful of company picnics in Texas or Virginia, one could probably run into a great number of the president's newly "diverse" advisors.

Some of these morality-based medical outfits, such as the Christian Medical Association and Joe McIlhaney's Medical Institute for Sexual Health, have become veritable placement agencies, elbowing out prestigious academic research institutions as advisory committee farm teams. McIlhaney serves on both the president's AIDS advisory council and the board that advises CDC director Julie Gerberding.[58] The Institute, beginning with its clinical sounding name, projects an image of scientific respectability. But it is in the habit of quoting unpublished graduate student papers as if they were legitimate peer-reviewed research (as McIlhaney did before Congress in April of 2002, in an effort to claim success for unproven abstinence-education programs) and of drawing fanciful conclusions from legitimate studies, as the Institute did in response to a highly technical 2001 NIH review of condom efficacy studies, falsely implying in a press statement that federal scientists concluded there is "only one way" of avoiding sexually transmitted diseases: "sex within the context of marriage."[59] And McIlhaney is the patriarch of an extended family of Bush science advisors who share his questionable scientific methods.

Two of McIlhaney's board members, Shepherd Smith, publisher of that peer-reviewed journal *Adolescent & Family Health*, and Marilyn Billingsly, who provides Christian medical advice through Focus on the Family, are companions on Gerberding's nine-person advisory committee. Smith's wife, Anita, with whom he runs the Children's AIDS Fund, a pro-abstinence outfit whose major contribution to AIDS seems to be providing gifts to children with AIDS at Christmastime, is on the president's AIDS advisory council. Follow these leads one step further, and you'll notice that Pat Ware, who first served as director of the AIDS council under Bush and now has a senior post at HHS, was a top staffer at the Smiths' group in the 1990s. Congressional aide Roland Foster is also affiliated with the Children's AIDS Fund and sends out their press releases and news updates, which have often featured sensational articles on the oft-audited Stop AIDS.[60]

Another Medical Institute board member, the Christian book author David Hager, was named to the FDA's newly reconstituted Reproductive Drugs Advisory Committee, and yet another, Freda McKissic Bush, was appointed to the CDC's advisory committee on STD prevention. According to her Medical Institute biography, she is an opponent of abortion and a partner in an ob-gyn practice in Jackson, Mississippi, "whose mission statement begins acknowledging the Lordship of Jesus Christ in their personal and professional lives." She is the co-president of the Mississippi Family Council, a state affiliate of Focus on the Family and the Family Research Council.[61] Everywhere you look, this family values circle tightens: Tom Coburn, the former congressman who now co-chairs the president's AIDS advisory council, recently served on the Family Research Council board of directors and Marilyn Billingsly, the CDC advisor, sits on the editorial board of Shepherd Smith's journal.[62]

In addition to the stacking of public science advisory panels, evidence began to accumulate in early 2003 that closed-door grant review panels were subject to political interference as well—at times to please industry, and at other times to please the Christian right. Pamela Kidd, an expert on ergonomics, was nominated by NIH scientists to serve as a grant reviewer for the National Institute of Occupational Safety and Health, which looks into workplace injuries; her nomination was rejected by Tommy Thompson, a move the panel's chairman said was clearly because Kidd "has publicly supported a workplace ergonomics standard."[63] An abstinence grantmaking panel at HHS was filled with family values advocates from such groups as the Family Research Council, the Christian Coalition, and Concerned Women for America.[64] And Judy Auerbach, the former NIH AIDS researcher, says that for a short time in 2003, federal staffers with no direct relationship to the awarding or managing of grants began to show up at scientific peer-review meetings. This was legal, but unprecedented. "The perception among the people who are the reviewers and the NIH staff is that these folks were sent by HHS to monitor the discussion," Auerbach told the radio program *Democracy Now.* "The reviewers themselves are getting nervous they're going to be on a list of people who are sympathetic to certain kinds of research" and that their studies will be targeted, too.[65]

As this unscientific stacking of scientific advisory committees came to light, the medical community again rallied, and starting in late 2002 prestigious medical journals published a wave of critical editorials. "Every administration advances its agenda by making political appointments of scientists and managers to direct its agencies," wrote *Science* in an editorial entitled "Advice Without Dissent." "But disbanding and stacking these public committees out of fear that they may offer advice that conflicts with administration policies devalues the entire federal advisory committee structure."[66] "Science policy that affects public health should be above party politics, and seen to be so, wrote the British medical journal *Lancet.* "Members of expert panels need to be impartial and credible, and free of partisan conflicts of interest, especially in industry links or in right-wing or religious ideology. . . . The current U.S. administration is certainly pro-industry, pro-family, and on the religious right. Any threat to impartial science-policy advice, especially advice that affects health and health care choices, will harm most those whose voices are unheeded by the right-wing—the poor, minorities, those without health insurance, those living in the shadow of polluting industries, those at risk of sexually transmitted infection (especially young people), young people who need realistic contraceptive advice, single mothers, and intravenous drug users."[67]

David Hager, the Kentucky ob-gyn and Christian book author, boasts all the right credentials for the Bush era: member of the Christian Medical Association, board member of the Medical Institute for Sexual Health, and such a staunch opponent of abortion that he refuses to perform the procedure. His pro-life values are so pure he won't even prescribe RU-486, the early abortion pill, or insert an IUD. (Though scientific consensus marks the implantation of a fertilized egg in the uterus as the start of pregnancy, and thus classifies the IUD, which blocks implantation, as a contraceptive, Hager believes human life begins days earlier, when sperm first meets egg. By this logic, and contradicting accepted scientific definitions, Hager insists the IUD is an abortion agent.) At any rate, two sources close to his practice told *Time,* he refuses to prescribe any contraceptives to unmarried women. As he said in a Focus on the Family roundtable discussion, "My first option for them is abstinence," and, failing that, "secondary virginity," the term used by abstinence proponents for people who have had sex and then choose chastity.[68]

Hager is a favorite of Christian right organizations like Focus on the Family for his authorship of two volumes on how to approach gynecologic care from a Christian perspective. In *As Jesus Cared for Women,* easily available from Christian book clubs, Hager argues that "a person's age, position, or experience is not the deciding factor" in the struggle of infertile couples to conceive. "God is looking for people of faith who will trust Him in every part of life. . . . Remarkable miracles of conception still occur." And he writes glowingly of a patient experiencing heavy vaginal bleeding who chose to ask her pastor to pray for her, rather than undergo medical treatment, a story with obvious parallels to a New Testament parable about a bleeding woman healed by touching Jesus' cloak. "What a lesson I learned from this woman of faith," he writes, adding that he would go on to share this lesson with many other women "needing the touch of the Master Physician."[69] In his other popular book, *Stress and the Woman's Body* (co-written, in the habit of so many evangelical Christian guidebooks, with his wife), Hager offers Christian prayers as treatments for headaches, PMS, and cancer.[70] In August 2002, Hager served as the spokesman for the Christian Medical Association in presenting a ninety-page "citizen's petition" to the Bush administration, calling on the FDA to suspend its decision to approve RU-486. (In this effort he worked closely with Beverly LaHaye's lobby group Concerned Women for America.)[71] The FDA had okayed the drug in 2000 based on data from controlled studies and on the advice of its Advisory Committee for Reproductive Health Drugs.

Now, thanks to a quiet Christmas Eve appointment just four months after his protest, Hager sits on that committee himself. The newly politicized panel, which hadn't met once since its high-profile RU-486 decision, met twice in the first year after Bush replaced its members. At the first meeting, in September 2003, Hager insinuated his religious perspective into a debate over fertility drugs, successfully pushing to change the clinical end point in fertility drug trials from live birth to "fetal heart motion."[72] One small step for the man, perhaps, but a large step for all of those abortion foes who seek to move back the definition of when human life begins.

At the next meeting, in December 2003, the debate was far more contentious, and FDA officials expected such a large crowd that they moved the meeting to a large suburban hotel in Gaithersburg, Maryland. The entire agenda was devoted to debating whether Plan B, an emergency contraception pill, should be available over-the-counter, and the ballroom was indeed jammed, not only with scientists, clinic workers, and gynecologists, but with advocates from Planned Parenthood, the Feminist Majority Foundation, and NOW sandwiched in next to their counterparts from Concerned Women for America, the abstinence organization TeenStar, and the American Life League. The makers of Plan B, which blocks a pregnancy if taken within seventy-two hours of unprotected intercourse, argued speed was so essential for this drug that women should be able to skip visiting their physician and go straight to the drugstore; the question put to the advisory committee was whether the pill was safe enough for use without a prescription.

The public comments strayed far from this mark. Though the FDA and the drug's makers had offered detailed evidence that Plan B (unlike RU-486) works by preventing pregnancy and showed that the pill hadn't been associated with a single serious complication or death, Judie Brown of the American Life League, the Catholic antiabortion group, insisted that the pill causes abortions and that it was "not only dangerous, but potentially deadly." Jennifer Taylor of Human Life International, a group whose pro-life position is so hard-line they organized a boycott of pharmaceutical giant Merck for engaging in stem cell research, complained that such a pill wouldn't be necessary if it weren't for "the inability of women to control themselves in sexual situations," and then proselytized for the rhythm method—the only contraceptive method sanctioned by the Catholic Church. Jill Stanek, a nurse with Concerned Women for America, objected to drug store access because "sexual predators could keep a stash [of Plan B] in their pockets to give to their victims." Thanks to Bush's appointments to the panel, these comments were hardly confined to the peanut gallery.

Point by point, Hager echoed their sentiments from within the committee, as did two other Bush appointees who shared his tendency toward what *Scientific American* has termed "faith-based reasoning."[73] Like Hager, these other two appointees are staunchly anti-abortion and deeply skeptical of contraception of all kinds. Joseph Stanford is an advocate of the rhythm method who refuses to prescribe contraceptives to his patients and even avoids vasectomies and tubal ligations, because he believes they are "detrimental to marriages" and against the guidance of the Mormon Church. He wrote in 1999, in the religious journal *First Things,* that the Catholic Church encyclical against contraception "could only have come from divine inspiration."[74] Here he

was now on a government panel, weighing in on a pill made of proges-
terone, a hormone often used to *protect* pregnancies, listening to evidence that it works by preventing ovulation or by inhibiting sperm
movement; that if a woman is already pregnant when she takes Plan B,
the drug will not harm the pregnancy; and that widespread use of the
pill could reduce the number of abortions in this country by half. Yet
again and again he offered the opinion that Plan B might theoretically
work, in some rare cases, by blocking a fertilized egg from implantation, the same concern that made him pledge as a young med student
never to prescribe contraceptives.

Susan Crockett, a leader of the American Association of Pro-Life
Obstetricians and Gynecologists, is the third member of Bush's Christian right trio. (While Crockett's organization claims 2,500 members, a
representative of the mainstream, 45,000-member American College
of Obstetricians and Gynecologists was restricted to a brief prepared
comment.)[75] Crockett used her time to ask repeatedly about the dangers of some women misusing the pill as everyday contraception—
even after a federal researcher pointed out that the pill has been used
exactly that way, and safely, in Europe for years. For his part, Hager
kept asking why safety data had not been collected separately for teens
(a government researcher tactfully informed him the FDA doesn't require this). As a stopgap measure, all three insisted Plan B include on
its label a detailed discussion of its "mechanism of action," including
any "potential" mechanisms, such as blocking implantation of a fertilized egg.

In the end, with the exception of Hager, Crockett, Stanford, and one
other, the vote followed the science. To the shock—even the tears—of
those who'd fought for this contraceptive technology for decades, the
panel approved Plan B for drugstore access. But the result owed much
to the extremely narrow questions posed to the advisors by the FDA,
each of which had to do exclusively with evaluating the data; and with
the unusual circumstance that for this particular decision, the advisors
on the politicized reproductive drug committee were joined by advisors on a drug access committee that had escaped Bush's political
notice—and political stacking. Afterward, I spoke to a defeated and

frustrated Hager. "Although the sponsors indicated that it's not a method of abortion," he said, "there is some data that it has an endometrial effect. The key is when do you define a pregnancy. If you define it at fertilization, when all the DNA is present to form a human being, to me, that's when life begins. If you define it as implantation, the so-called medical definition, you don't have the same problem." His comments had all the hallmarks of Bush's new experts: a rejection of the scientific consensus (about when pregnancy begins) and an insistence that there is data to support his position when there is none.

Though he felt defeated that day, Hager's efforts to cloud the data ultimately bore fruit. Formal FDA approval was expected in February 2004, a rubber stamp of the advisory committee's vote; but when February came around, the FDA announced it would delay its decision for another ninety days. "I am afraid that this could be a stalling tactic, resulting from political pressure exerted by conservative opponents of this measure," said Congresswoman Louise Slaughter, cochair of the House's prochoice caucus, who joined seventy members of Congress in writing a letter of protest.[76] Indeed, three months later, the FDA's acting commissioner, Lester Crawford, rejected the Plan B application, over the objections of his own staff. Slaughter and a dozen other members of Congress called for Crawford to step down and demanded an investigation.

THE DISAPPEARANCE OF DISAGREEABLE FACTS

President Clinton was, for all his charisma, a bit of a technocrat. Certainly his celebration of high tech as the driver of the 1990s economic boom extended to a warm embrace of the scientific enterprise as a whole. His remarks in 1999 as he bestowed the National Medal of Science were typical. "The United States is the strongest it has ever been, thanks in large measure to the remarkable pace and scope of American science and technology in the last fifty years," he said. "Our scientific progress has been fueled by a unique partnership between government, academia, and the private sector. . . . Vannevar Bush"—here Clinton spoke of the scientist who mobilized scientific research during World War II and whose theories many credit with prefiguring the structure of the Web—"helped to convince the American people that government must support science, that the best way to do it would be to fund the work of independent university researchers. This ensured that, in our nation, scientists would be in charge of science." He closed with a vision of the foundational link between science and the American project. "From its birth, we have been built by bold, restless, searching people. We have always sought new frontiers. The spirit of America is, in that sense, truly the spirit of scientific inquiry."[77]

President Bush, however, has never quoted Vannevar Bush (no relation), or anyone like him. He has allied himself with old technologies, like oil and coal, not innovative research. His temperament and his political strategy link him with religious ideologues, not PhDs. Scientific inquiry has no romance for him, and its spirit—to seek out answers through the relentless examination of information—escapes him in every area. Not just in public health or scientific research, but in environmental policy, foreign policy, war planning, and diplomacy. For Bush, at critical moments, the spirit of inquiry seems to be trumped by spirit itself, where his task is not to question, but to follow God's path.

Data that stands in the way of that path often gets sidelined or suppressed. This tendency exploded into the public view around the question of the administration's justification for going to war against Iraq and the president's use of shaky, even false evidence to bolster his claim that Saddam Hussein possessed weapons of mass destruction and was ready to use them. His desire to project a muscular homeland defense led to a plan to inoculate some 10 million first responders with a high-risk smallpox vaccine against the recommendations of many public health experts—plans that were only scaled back after three vaccine recipients died.[78] At other times, Bush's allegiance to an oil-based energy policy, and to his corporate supporters in the oil sector, led him to suppress inconvenient information about caribou habitats in an Alaska preserve and the fast-melting polar ice caps.[79] And the Bush administration's commitment to pleasing the Christian right has led officials to censor public health information that offends their view that gay sex, extramarital sex, and promiscuity are sins.

If you happened to search out the federal government's fact sheet on condoms any time during 2002, you came upon this abrupt message: "Being Revised." If you were a teacher looking for curricula with proven success at reducing young people's HIV risk, you were told the following: "Thank you for your interest in Programs that Work (PTW). The CDC has discontinued PTW."[80] The CDC is the federal government's public health arm, in charge of tracking disease outbreaks and educating the public about how to prevent everything from the flu to obesity to HIV. Its Web site is generally responsive and user friendly, with easily clickable sections on flu shots or mad cow disease popping up as soon as these threats hit the headlines. So it was extremely unusual for such useful information to unceremoniously disappear. "Usually the CDC leaves hopelessly out-of-date stuff on the Web site for years until they're ready to make a change," says Margaret Scarlett, who worked in federal HIV policy for several years, first at the White House Office of AIDS Policy and then at the CDC. "Even with SARS, where information was changing so quickly, they just leave what's there up until it's updated. Yet the condom fact sheet was singled out to be taken off the Web, unlike CDC policy for anything else. I checked around to find out whether there was any new science to justify doing that, and no one says there is." Not until year's end was information on condoms restored—or, rather, redacted. The new fact sheet, to quote a December 2002 letter from Representative Henry Waxman and a dozen colleagues, was "carefully edited to deny the public important information about the role condoms can play in reducing sexually transmitted diseases and pregnancies." The alterations, the politicians dryly added, "are certainly not in the interest of the public health."[81]

A document that once advised, unequivocally, "The correct and consistent use of latex condoms during sexual intercourse—vaginal, anal, or oral—can greatly reduce a person's risk of acquiring or transmitting most STDs, including HIV infection, gonorrhea, Chlamydia, trichomonas, human papilloma virus infection (HPV), and hepatitis B," was now far more guarded, echoing the language of Joe McIlhaney and his ilk. The new document reads: "The surest way to avoid transmission of sexually transmitted diseases is to abstain from sexual intercourse, or to be in a long-term mutually monogamous relationship"—remember, this is the government's fact sheet on *condoms*. "For persons whose sexual behaviors place them at risk for STDs, correct and consistent use of the male latex condom can reduce the rate of STD transmission. However, no protective method is 100 percent effective, and condom use cannot guarantee absolute protection." It emphasizes right up top the dangers of slippage, of breakage, of inconsistent use—while to read about the protections condoms offer a viewer must scroll far down the page.[82] Scarlett says the agency's main condom experts weren't even consulted on the new language. "This is really cutting away at the CDC's mission," she said. "It's endangering people's lives."

A source at the CDC told the Union of Concerned Scientists that "higher-ups in the Bush administration" had ordered the suppression of the information on the CDC Web site, and CDC officials have declined to offer any information about what motivated the decision, saying only that it was the result of a routine scientific review.[83] But it seems more than coincidence that the Web pages had recently attracted negative attention on the Christian right. On April 10, 2002, the Physicians Consortium, a 2,000-member organization affiliated with Focus on the Family, released a report complaining that materials on the CDC's Web site include "graphic depictions of sexual behavior and promiscuity" and charging that the CDC's "Programs that Work" initiative lauded programs that "are preoccupied with promoting condom use and sexual experimentation among young people." Two weeks later, Joe McIlhaney repeated the charges in testimony before the House Energy and Commerce Committee during a hearing on abstinence education.[84] Not long after, the information on "Programs that Work" was removed from the CDC site. In response to a query, CDC spokeswoman Kathryn Bina wrote that "Programs that Work" was removed because of "concerns and suggestions from the field" and will be replaced by a new initiative in late 2004.

Similar shenanigans occurred on other government Web sites. On the National Cancer Institute Web site, a fact sheet on the fabled link between abortion and breast cancer was suddenly replaced. Up until early 2002, the page stated clearly that despite some mixed data a decade ago, newer, large-scale studies found "no association" between breast cancer risk and previous abortion. The new language, posted in November 2002, asserted that the earlier, smaller studies had found "significant evidence of an increased risk of breast cancer in women who have had abortions" and announced a special conference to re-open the scientific debate.[85] Again, this was not prompted by new science. But it was consistent with the work of pro-life activists, who have managed to push through bills in several states requiring doctors to warn women of the alleged link.

Two condom fact sheets on the USAID Web site, each calling condoms "highly effective" in preventing HIV, met similar fates: one was permanently removed, the other altered to emphasize that "no barrier method is 100 percent effective." The Department of Education issued a memo instructing staff to remove all studies dated before February 2001 unless they are "consistent with the Administration's philosophy."[86] A CDC notice announcing the availability of federal funds to support public health conferences appeared in mid-2003 with the following caveat: scientists would have to assure "active participation by CDC . . . in the development and approval of the conference agenda to make sure there are no subjects that would embarrass the Government."[87] "In many ways what they're doing around reproductive health and HIV is not about public health, but propaganda," says one longtime Democratic congressional staffer. He says the Christian right pushed its traditional values agenda hard during the Clinton years as well, but this kind of censorship simply didn't happen. What's changed is the administration, what he calls the "invisible" staff people in the health secretary's office, a "truth squad within the department from radically conservative backgrounds who serve as enforcers. . . . These are people who genuinely don't care what the mainstream medical associations think," he adds, "and if your message doesn't fit their mold, they just pull it."

This truth squad is helmed by HHS Deputy Secretary Claude Allen, a former Jesse Helms aide who gained a reputation as a fierce pro-lifer and abstinence-only advocate during his years as the top health official in the state of Virginia, and his senior advisor, Pat Ware, who during her brief tenure as the director of Bush's presidential AIDS advisory council interrupted one meeting for half an hour to give an unscheduled speech on the benefits of marriage. It includes Wade Horn, the assistant secretary for family support and the brains behind Bush's initiative to promote marriage among the poor and Alma Golden, the deputy assistant secretary for population affairs, a Texas transplant who once headed up an abstinence-only organization. And it includes lesser known figures, such as legislative analyst Maggie Wynne, a pro-life activist and former staffer to Congressional Values Action Team member Chris Smith.

The truth squad has not only vetoed NIH nominees to advisory committees and stopped by NIH grant review meetings to observe and intimidate, it has even interfered with civil service hires, positions that are supposed to be free of political influence. According to several sources close to the process, one HIV expert, Frank Beadle de Palomo, a frequent consultant to the CDC on HIV prevention matters, was up for the job of director of the division of HIV prevention. He was the top choice of Harold Jaffe, director of the CDC's Center for HIV, STD, and TB Prevention, and the only name Jaffe forwarded to CDC head Julie Gerberding. After a positive interview with Gerberding herself, all systems were go when Beadle de Palomo's name was forwarded, completely outside of protocol, to the top guns at HHS. Soon his colleagues were getting phone calls from congressional aide Roland Foster and from Pat Ware, then director of the president's AIDS advisory council, asking about Beadle de Palomo's stance on condom effectiveness, his ties to the AIDS community, and his support for gay rights. The hire never happened, and the position—in an administration that has staked much of its compassion agenda around AIDS—remained unfilled three and a half years into the Bush administration. (CDC officials declined to comment.)[88]

Stem Cell Games

It's not easy to remember our pre–9/11 president, or what exactly he did during those months before al-Qaeda attacked. That summer began with James Jeffords' defection from the Republican Party, giving the Democrats control of the Senate, and ended with the resignation of John DiIulio, the chief of the office of faith-based initiatives, Bush's pet program. Bush's education bill, the centerpiece of his domestic agenda, had stalled, and his top political advisor, Karl Rove, was embroiled in a scandal over a deal he'd cut with the Salvation Army to exempt the group from laws banning antigay discrimination. During these doldrums, the president made one prime-time televised address to the nation, and it was on stem cell research. This is a complex, quickly evolving scientific field (stem cells were first isolated in 1998) that is little understood by most Americans—but a near obsession among the pro-life movement. And the president's stance on this issue was the earliest high-profile indication that he would use illegitimate science to justify morality-driven policies.

Embryonic stem cells, undifferentiated cells that can be culled from a few-day-old embryo, have the ability to specialize into virtually any kind of cell in the human body. Researchers are far from being able to develop applications, but the potential is vast: the ability to produce specialized dopamine cells to treat Parkinson's, bone marrow cells to treat cancers, insulin-producing cells for diabetes, cells to repair heart tissue and spinal cords—lifesaving interventions for intractable and often fatal diseases. The advocacy movements that have sprung up around these diseases have placed intense hope on this line of research, and it has generated excitement throughout the scientific community: in early 2001, eighty Nobel Prize–winners wrote a letter to the president calling the discovery of stem cells "a significant milestone" with the potential to save millions of lives and urging him not to restrict research.[89] Just days before the president's speech, a Gallup poll found that 54 percent of Americans support stem cell research, while 38 percent said such study is morally wrong.[90]

The president spent enormous amounts of time sequestered in the Oval Office during the summer of 2001, holding lengthy meetings on the issue with self-styled "embryo destruction" opponents such as the National Right to Life Committee and research advocates such as the Juvenile Diabetes Foundation. His closest advisors—Karl Rove, Karen Hughes, and Andrew Card—all sat in on the debates. During his campaign, Bush had pledged to oppose any research that involves destroying human embryos, as part of his across-the-board pro-life stance; once in office he had put a hold on all related federal grants.[91] Now he was face-to-face with a pharmaceutical lobby favoring the research and a bipartisan rainbow of disease advocates that included people like Fox News commentator Morton Kondracke, who became a proponent of stem cell research after his wife was diagnosed with Parkinson's, and Nancy Reagan.

Former Bush speechwriter David Frum, in his hagiographic memoir of the first year of the Bush White House, devotes significant space to Bush's stem cell speech. Frum argues that the stakes were extremely high, calling stem cell research "an issue with the power to shatter Bush's image as a social moderate."[92] The president's final compromise, Frum writes, was "inspired." He would permit federal funding on adult stem cells and on existing embryonic stem cell lines, ones already being cultivated in labs, but he would ban all other embryonic stem cell research. Here is Frum's characterization of this "masterstroke":

> Bush had defended on national television the most unflinchingly pro-life position ever expressed by a president before a mass audience: "I . . . believe human life is a sacred gift from our Creator. I worry about a culture that devalues life, and believe as your president I have an important obligation to foster and encourage respect for life in America and throughout the world." And he had not only protected but actually expanded his image as a moderate.

"We are delighted," announced Laura Echevarria, spokeswoman for the National Right to Life Committee.[93] "A few minutes before Mr. Bush made his speech, Karl Rove, the president's senior advisor, called and gave me a 'heads up' on what was about to take place," Focus on the Family president James Dobson wrote to his members in September 2001. "Needless to say, I was elated to learn that, contrary to our fears, Mr. Bush was planning to act on behalf of unborn life!"[94] Researchers did not share his elation. Bush's complicated compromise was based on invented science. Banning embryonic stem cell research does not save embryos: the vast majority of frozen embryos are destroyed and discarded anyway. Adult stem cells have nowhere near the versatility or therapeutic potential of embryonic stem cells. And the sixty existing stem cell lines Bush touted in his speech turned out to be a total fiction. According to a subsequent investigation by *Time* magazine, "in the weeks before the President's speech, an order came down to the NIH from Thompson: Work the scientific grapevine to find out how many cell lines might conceivably exist." Jay Lefkowitz, then a White House liaison to the evangelical community and the official most closely involved in Bush's stem cell decision, said it was "at the president's direct instigation" that he asked the NIH "to press further" in its search for more potential stem cell lines.[95] A year after the president's speech, the medical journal *Science* completed an intensive search for all stem cell lines available at the time of Bush's decision—the only lines scientists with federal funding can now use—and found only sixteen. Of those sixteen, the journal discovered, no more than four were actually available to U.S. researchers not directly collaborating with the labs that had developed the lines.[96]

Michael Manganiello is a leader of the Coalition to Advance Medical Research, which was founded in early 2001 to save American embryonic stem cell research. The Coalition represents professional medical associations as well as organizations advocating research into diabetes, Parkinson's, cancer, paralysis, and infertility; Manganiello doubles as vice president of the Christopher Reeve Paralysis Foundation, where his boss is a passionate supporter of stem cell research as well. While Manganiello is deeply concerned that the president's decision will delay scientific breakthroughs that could aid people struggling to survive life-threatening illnesses, he also sees signs that Bush's decision will harm the American scientific community. It was researchers at American universities who discovered embryonic stem cells, Manganiello says, but now "the research is moving offshore." According to Manganiello, China is spending an enormous amount on stem cell research, Sweden is lining up to be the world leader in the field, Israel has become a player, and Singapore, seeing in stem cell research the next high-tech boom, is actively wooing away American researchers.[97] Manganiello recalls a trip Reeve made to Yale Medical School, where he learned that the prestigious institution had decided not to enter the field; researchers there told him they couldn't establish a lab and expect to fund it in a politicized research climate that might never improve. "We don't want to overpromise the potential of stem cell research, but there are going to be clinical applications and the average American won't be able to access them," Manganiello says. "Why would we want to lose the edge? Biotech is one of the only growing sectors in the economy, and we've cut it off at the knees."

He says the tide was beginning to turn before Bush's speech—polling data, major newspaper editorials, and many visible conservatives were on the side of saving stem cell research. When Manganiello testified before the President's Council on Bioethics, convened to advise Bush on the stem cell decision, "the prestige gap between our scientists and their scientists was overwhelming," he says, referring to the scientists marshaled by the Christian right. "Most of them weren't even stem cell researchers, or researchers at all." But, in the end, Manganiello says, "on our side were all these hard-working, fact-finding advocates, and on their side, well, there was the Family Research Council. And they have the ear of the president."

During the Clinton years, policy did not always follow the recommendations of scientists, but science itself mostly remained above the fray. In one famous incident in 1998, Clinton announced that he would not lift a ban on federal funding of needle exchange programs—even as his health secretary Donna Shalala and his NIH director Harold Varmus affirmed the conclusions of scientists that needle exchange programs decrease HIV infection without increasing drug use. Clinton instead came down on the side of his drug czar, Barry McCaffrey, who insisted that lifting the ban would send the wrong message to the nation's children. Clinton was open that science pointed one way, and he had chosen another, exposing himself to protest from his own AIDS advisors.

In the Bush administration, the dynamic is quite different. Rather than affirming the scientific importance of embryonic stem cell research but explaining that he would halt it for religious and political ends, Bush chose to misrepresent the science, setting in motion an administration-wide pattern. "There is significant evidence that the scope and scale of the manipulation, suppression, and misrepresentation of science by the Bush administration is unprecedented," the Union of Concerned Scientists concluded in its February 2004 investigation, *Scientific Integrity in Policymaking.* "World-renowned scientific institutions such as the CDC and the National Institutes of Health take decades to build a team of world-class scientific expertise and talent. But they can be severely damaged in short order by the scientifically unethical behavior such as that displayed by the current administration."[98]

GOOD-BYE *ROE*

FOR MANY IN the trenches of the Christian right it must have felt like a dream—or a miraculous vision. Everyone was there—Reverend Lou Sheldon, head of the Traditional Values Coalition; televangelist Jerry Falwell; Christian radio host James Dobson; Adrian Rogers, who used to run the Southern Baptist Convention; former Jews for Jesus attorney and right-wing radio personality Jay Sekulow; and the entire legislative staffs of the Christian Coalition and the Family Research Council. On that day in early November 2003, in a building named for Ronald Reagan, the man the National Right to Life Committee calls "our first unabashedly pro-life president," a crowd of dedicated pro-life activists packed the cavernous hall. And then the President of the United States himself strode onto the stage and, surrounded by American flags and flanked by some of the leading social conservatives in Congress, signed a "partial-birth abortion" ban into law, the first national ban on an abortion procedure since abortion became legal in 1973. The applause was explosive.[1]

It was a victory eight years in the making, and the superlatives flowed like wine. The Family Research Council declared it "a turning point in the debate over abortion"; Concerned Women for America, "one of the most important milestones in the history of the thirty-year struggle to regain legal protection for the right to life." The reaction of pro-lifers was downright "giddy" in the words of David Andrusko of the National Right to Life Committee, as activists expressed "joy," "camaraderie," and "obvious affection and love" for the president. These groups had watched in exasperation as President Clinton vetoed similar abortion bans, not once, but twice. But now the pro-life movement was at last in from the cold, and they were enjoying the moment. Family Research Council president Tony Perkins boasted to his e-mail list that he was "honored to be invited to the White House for a private meeting with President Bush as he prepared" for the big event and to be able "to travel with the president's motorcade to the signing," while Dobson shared similar warm memories with his radio audience.[2] And the president's speech, from its first lines, was perfectly crafted to delight the faithful.

"The most basic duty of government is to defend the life of the innocent," the president said between standing ovations. "Every person however frail or vulnerable has a place and a purpose in this world. Every person has a special dignity. This right to life cannot be granted or denied by government because it does not come from government, it comes from the Creator of life."[3] A Right to Life report later marveled that Bush "described partial-birth abortion, not as the killing of a 'fetus' or even a baby, but as the 'partial delivery of a live boy or girl, and a sudden, violent end of that life.'"[4] The Family Research Council sent out the text of president's speech to its e-mail list; National Right to Life posted it on their Web site; and through their syndicated programs, Concerned Women for America and Focus on the Family replayed his words to Christian radio audiences across America.[5] Even their hero Ronald Reagan, limited by a Democratic House, had never been able to deliver anything like this.

On his Focus on the Family radio broadcast, a few days later, Dobson recalled breaking down in tears with fellow evangelical Chuck Colson when President Clinton vetoed a similar bill and contrasted that with the "excitement" he felt when he joined President Bush, Tony Perkins, and other evangelical conservatives in the Oval Office that day. "I tell you, I've been in the Oval Office many times, going back nearly twenty years, with three presidents. I've never had a more satisfying time with a President of the United States than Wednesday of this week. . . . This president is more committed to the unborn and to life in general than any president in our history, including Ronald Reagan and President Bush's own father. It is incredible the stand that he has taken. And he means it and he believes it and you could see it on his face."[6]

For pro-choice advocates, the scene at the Ronald Reagan Building looked more like a nightmare. NOW posted an image on its Web site of President Bush, seated at the signing table, surrounded by half a dozen smiling, laughing, and applauding middle-aged men—Trent Lott, Denny Hastert, Rick Santorum, Orrin Hatch, the all-male Republican team who had pushed this bill through Congress, and thereby orchestrated, in the words of NOW president Kim Gandy, "the theft of our reproductive freedom." For her, the day was a milestone, too. "By signing the deceptively named Partial-Birth Abortion Ban into law," she said, "Bush confirms that his administration and Congress have both the power and the will to overturn *Roe v. Wade,* one step at a time."[7]

THE LONG HAUL

Much of the contemporary Christian right has its roots in the *Roe v. Wade* decision of 1973. To evangelical conservatives and pro-life Catholics, the ruling was nothing less than cataclysmic. It not only launched a national movement—the National Right to Life Committee, now a $12 million organization with close to 3,000 chapters in all fifty states, was formed within four months of the decision, while Judie Brown founded the American Life League, Beverly LaHaye founded Concerned Women for America, James Dobson founded Focus on the Family, and Phyllis Schlafly founded the Eagle Forum within the next few years—but forever discredited the federal courts in their eyes.[8] To this day, the Web sites of groups such as Focus on the Family, the American Life League, and National Right to Life prominently clock the abortions conducted in the United States since 1973, which they calculate at more than 40 million—and abortion remains the most important political test for the family values lobby.[9]

Movement heavyweights such as LaHaye, Dobson, Schlafly, and Gary Bauer campaigned heavily before the 2000 Republican Convention for a word-for-word readoption of the party's hard-line pro-life plank, which includes an anti-abortion litmus test for judicial nominees.[10] Scorecards of congressional votes on abortion measures, compiled by such groups as National Right to Life to influence close races, hold enormous sway over Republican politicians. (Thirty-three Republican Senators earned a 100 percent score from National Right to Life for 2003–2004, including Majority Leader Bill Frist, while only two Democrats did.) Pro-life lobbyists threaten to jeopardize legislators' sterling pro-life ratings if they vote the wrong way on any obscure abortion-related amendment, as the pro-life Eagle Forum did with regard to a bankruptcy provision that would have made clinic blockaders more vulnerable to lawsuits. Conversely, members of Congress try to intervene in those scorecards when they worry their perfect score is at risk, as Values Action Team chairman Joe Pitts (100 percent pro-life rating) did in an urgent November 2003 letter about the drug reimportation bill, which National Right to Life claimed would ease access to RU-486. "Dear Wanda," he and his colleagues wrote to the group's president, Wanda Franz, "The decision of the National Right to Life Committee (NRLC) to include the Medicare Prescription Drug and Modernization Act as a key pro-life vote on your Congressional scorecards is of grave concern to us."[11] While pro-life lobbyists give elected officials a pass for supporting the death penalty, the American Life League took out ads warning pro-choice Catholics in Congress such as Ted Kennedy and John Kerry that by supporting legal abortion they "risk their eternal salvation."[12] At the same time, they attack pro-choice Republicans such as Senator Olympia Snowe as "RINOs"—Republicans in name only.

In the immediate wake of Roe, pro-life activists sought to overturn the right to abortion wholesale, through a constitutional amendment introduced by Jesse Helms in 1975. Embarrassingly unable to muster enough votes, abortion foes soon turned to the more piecemeal strategy we know today, what Gandy referred to as the effort to overturn Roe "one step at a time." The first major victory in this strategy was the Hyde Amendment, legislation that excluded abortion coverage from Medicaid, which Congress passed in 1976 and the Supreme Court upheld in 1980.

This strategy of death-by-a-thousand-cuts has four major elements: The first, in the spirit of the Hyde Amendment, is to chip away at actual access, through restricting public funds, threatening clinics, and throwing up roadblocks such as parental consent requirements. The second would remake the nonprofit sector by taking away funds from organizations that support and provide abortions, while increasing the cash flow to pro-life organizations such as crisis pregnancy centers. The third, a purely ideological battle, aims to establish the precedent that life—and thus human rights protections—begins at conception, a project that plays itself out in countless congressional amendments and scientific regulations. The final strategy trumps all the others: to remake the courts through pro-life judicial nominees who will eventually have the power to overturn *Roe*.

The pro-life movement has accomplished much by circumventing Congress and going directly to the states, a project made significantly easier by the 1992 *Planned Parenthood v. Casey* case, argued before the Supreme Court by then Solicitor General Ken Starr, which allows any abortion restriction to stand unless plaintiffs can prove it causes an "undue burden" on a woman's right to abortion.[13] By the end of 2002, these efforts had triumphed: thirty states now mandate counseling prior to an abortion, following a strict script that, in many cases, includes frightening and scientifically inaccurate claims. Three-quarters of all states require minors to receive parental consent—or a judicial bypass—before getting an abortion; more than half of all states prohibit state funds from being used to cover the cost of abortions. What's more, thirty-five states have passed laws that single out abortion providers for often absurd regulatory oversight (like a law in South Carolina mandating that abortion clinic lawns be kept free of grass that could harbor insects).[14] Other victories have come through public protest—and violence. The seven murders of abortion providers, 209 abortion clinic bombings and arsons, and hundreds of death threats to clinic staffers since the late 1970s have surely contributed to the one-third reduction in willing providers during that same period—to the point that six out of every seven U.S. counties have none.[15] But the triple threat of a Republican House, a Republican Senate, and an avidly pro-life president in George W. Bush have thrown open the door for some significant gains in Washington for the pro-life cause.

Even the most war-weary pro-life advocates acknowledge there's a new kind of motion against abortion in Washington now. "I've been involved in the pro-life movement since the 1960s," Michael Schwartz told me. He's vice president of Concerned Women for America, in charge of their lobbying on abortion and other issues on the Hill, and he's also a former congressional aide and an old Washington hand. "With Reagan, there were open doors in every agency, but the social conservatives didn't have any other friends in town besides the president. During the old Bush administration in 1989, '90, '91, the pro-life movement was as down as down could get. The president was officially on our side but anyone could tell he didn't want to be and our image was bad because of the clinic blockades. But with the shift in Congress in 1994, we had friendly committee chairmen, and around this time, we got a lock on the Republican presidential candidate. And of course with a pro-life president you're going to be able to do a whole lot more."

THE BUSH RECORD

Bush sent his first bouquet to the far right before he'd even taken office, by nominating John Ashcroft, the handpicked choice of the Christian right, for attorney general. Evangelicals adore Ashcroft as a devout believer and an uncompromising pro-life ideologue, which he is: Ashcroft opposes abortion even in the case of rape or incest and has declared the anniversary of *Roe v. Wade* a "day in memoriam" for aborted fetuses.[16] While in the Senate, Ashcroft earned a 100 percent voting score from National Right to Life and even sponsored a proposed constitutional amendment that gave the "unborn" legal protections "at every stage of their biological development, including fertilization," a measure that could have turned even certain forms of birth control into an act of murder. When he explored a presidential run in 1997 and 1998, almost all his financial backing came from conservative evangelical donors such as Pat Robertson.[17] His confirmation as attorney general was a delicious twist of fate for pro-life advocates: who better to charge with "protecting" women's access to abortion clinics than the man who'd voted against those protections as senator?

Even after 9/11, when terrorism became his major focus, Ashcroft found time to deliver on many items topping the pro-life and family values agenda. In late 2001, Ashcroft announced that federally controlled drugs could not be used for assisted suicides, even in states like Oregon where it is legal (a policy later overturned in federal court).[18] In early 2002, Ashcroft filed a brief in support of an Ohio partial-birth abortion ban that had been declared unconstitutional for failing to provide an exception to protect a woman's health. Responding to lobbyists from the American Family Association, the Family Research Council, and Concerned Women for America, he dramatically increased the number of federal pornography prosecutions, and he served as the front man in the administration's turnabout on an international women's rights treaty known as CEDAW, shelving it for "careful review."[19] And the moment Bush put pen to paper to sign the federal ban into law, Ashcroft pulled off a pro-life pièce de résistance, assigning enforcement of the law to the civil rights division, an "Orwellian" move, in the words of a protest letter signed by several Democrats on the House judiciary committee, designed to institutionalize the idea that fetuses have civil rights.[20] Three months later, Ashcroft subpoenaed hundreds of hospital records of women who had undergone abortions, claiming he needed access to the private files in order to defend the partial-birth ban, a maneuver that Republican Eliot Engel said was an invasion of privacy worthy of "Big Brother."[21]

Ashcroft has exerted his influence less publicly, too. After he was nominated as attorney general, Ashcroft pledged to destroy a special Department of Justice task force to thwart violence against abortion providers, created by Janet Reno in the wake of the murder of New York State ob-gyn Barnett Slepian by an anti-abortion fanatic. Ashcroft retracted the inflammatory position once it threatened to jeopardize his confirmation hearings, but his actions in office indicate that he never completely abandoned his earlier stance. Vicki Saporta, who directs the National Abortion Federation, recalls meeting with ATF and FBI agents and U.S. marshals regularly during Janet Reno's tenure as attorney general and characterizes Reno's Justice Department as extremely responsive to threats on abortion providers. Reno, for example, put two members of the radical anti-abortion group Army of God on the FBI's Ten Most Wanted List—Eric Rudolph, who had bombed a clinic, and

James Kopp, Slepian's killer—and sent federal marshals to Buffalo after Slepian was shot. In contrast, as violent clinic protests accelerated throughout 2001 and a doctor in Wichita was targeted with death threats, Ashcroft kept refusing requests for marshals from Saporta's group and local abortion providers. He relented only after Saporta and other pro-choice advocates called a press conference in protest. When another anti-abortion murderer, Clayton Waagner, escaped from federal custody during this same period—the man who would later be tied to abortion clinic anthrax threats—Ashcroft refused multiple requests for a meeting and shunted Saporta off to the FBI.

One would think overlooking domestic terrorism would have been difficult after 9/11. Yet just a few weeks after the attacks, when some 250 family planning clinics across the country received mailed anthrax threats, it was the National Abortion Federation, not the Department of Justice, that warned clinics, provided them with a suspicious mail protocol, and established a national database of incidents. It wasn't until Waagner began to use the National Abortion Federation's Fed Ex account to send the group's clinic affiliates anthrax threats that Saporta finally secured a meeting with Department of Justice staff, where she insisted on the need for Ashcroft himself to publicly confront the matter. But the number of anthrax threats to abortion clinics had reached 550 before Ashcroft made a televised statement denouncing them—which led, just a few days later, to Waagner's arrest. "They moaned and groaned and said they weren't sure it was wise for him to make such a statement," says Saporta. "But what we asked them to do was effective."

Bush's second grand pro-life gesture, after nominating Ashcroft, was also his very first presidential act: his January 2001 institution of a global gag rule, pioneered by Ronald Reagan, that withdraws U.S. family planning assistance from any organization, worldwide, that offers abortion or promotes abortion access—even if it does so with private funds. The executive order, delivered on the anniversary of the *Roe v. Wade* decision, accomplished two sacred goals of the Christian pro-life movement: to make abortions harder, and riskier, around the globe; and to defund groups such as International Planned Parenthood that the movement sees as potent political foes. When Congress debated an amendment to overturn the aid ban, the White House sent a written message to House members threatening a veto.[22] Influential conservative Grover Norquist called the victory "huge" for the pro-life movement.[23]

The gag rule, the Ashcroft appointment, and the president's signing of the ban on partial-birth abortion were his most spectacular contributions to the pro-life agenda. But God was in the details, too. In often invisible ways, President Bush has made contributions to each element of the pro-life movement's incremental strategy to undermine *Roe*. Bush has used the Health and Human Services (HHS) population office, which oversees family planning, to chip away at access to abortion and reproductive health. He appointed an acquaintance from Texas, abstinence advocate Alma Golden, as deputy assistant of population affairs, meaning that a woman affiliated with both the Medical Institute of Sexual Health and the Institute of Youth Development—two organizations that disparage condoms and birth control in their efforts to insist that young people avoid sex altogether—would oversee the country's federally funded Title X family planning clinics, which are mandated to offer contraception and pregnancy counseling to both adults and youth.[24]

As part of its attack on the provision of these services to minors, the Texas-based anti-abortion group Life Dynamics has accused family planning clinics of failing to report statutory rape and child abuse. They argue that any sexually active minor should be reported to the state as a potential abuse victim and claim to have found, in a 2002 survey, that most minors who have had sex with adults are not reported to authorities.[25] When, in early 2003, pro-life Congressman Chris Smith asked HHS to look into the Life Dynamics charges, Golden initiated two full-scale investigations, one by the HHS inspector general and another by a private firm advised by the Medical Institute for Sexual Health.[26] "It's quite subtle," says Marilyn Keefe, vice president of the National Family Planning and Reproductive Health Association, which represents Title X clinics. "Golden cites the Life Dynamics data approvingly and uses it as an argument for limiting confidential access to family planning services for teens."

Golden has also sought to inject a pro-life bias into Title X pregnancy counseling. By federal mandate, the counseling is supposed to be neutral and nondirective, impartially laying out choices including abortion and adoption. But pro-life advocates have often insisted that adoption should get more emphasis, and under Golden's watch, counselor training has gone in this direction. According to a letter of complaint from one Title X counseling supervisor who attended an HHS training session in Los Angeles in late 2003, "the training environment was distinctly antichoice." Several of the trainers represented overtly Christian agencies, the supervisor wrote, and the majority of participants were staffers of crisis pregnancy centers—whose mission is specifically to discourage young women from choosing abortion. (According to Keefe, Golden "always talks about the fact that she'd like to see 'new kinds of providers' on the scene, which is code for exiling Planned Parenthood," a major recipient of Title X funds, and inviting in pro-life crisis pregnancy centers.) Participants, the supervisor wrote, were encouraged to tell their young clients that adoption is "a courageous decision," while trainers characterized other choices as "inhumane"; throughout, some choices were framed as "right" and others as "wrong." One training video used Christian Bible quotes, and the tenor of the discussions was overtly Christian, an experience the supervisor found to be "disconcerting and unnecessary, especially as I was attending a federally funded workshop and expecting a neutral training environment."[27] In addition to these new, adoption-centered trainings, Golden also sent out program guidance to Title X clinics placing a new emphasis on encouraging abstinence.[28]

Golden is hardly isolated at HHS, as Bush's key health appointments all claim impeccable pro-life credentials. HHS Secretary Tommy Thompson is generally considered a probusiness conservative, but as governor of Wisconsin he enacted several measures restricting abortion access, from mandatory waiting periods to a partial-birth ban.[29] His deputy, Claude Allen, is also strongly anti-abortion. He has characterized it as genocidal for the African American community, and he won acclaim in the pro-life movement for having intervened in a high-profile right-to-die case, blocking a woman from having her vegetative husband's feeding tube removed, while Allen was the top health official in Virginia. Indeed, HHS teems with avid pro-lifers, such as legislative analyst Maggie Wynne. Wynne was the pro-life movement's main congressional liaison for years in her post as staff director of the House Pro-Life Caucus.[30] Her Thomas Aquinas alumnus bio, written during that time, proclaims: "keeping a well-trod path to her door are representatives of the Christian Coalition, National Right to Life, Family Research Council, American Life League, and the U.S. Catholic Conference." She represented International Right to Life at the landmark UN population conference in Cairo in 1994 and has picketed clinics for more than a decade. Now she's on the inside.[31] All in all, Connie Mackey, chief lobbyist for the Family Research Council, told a Christian paper, "there are many good people at HHS who are doing good work in redefining the regulations."[32]

Bush has made effective use of international policy to make progress on a second important goal of the pro-life movement: starving pro-choice organizations and abortion providers of federal funds. Bush withheld $34 million in aid that Congress had set aside for the UN Population Fund, which supports family planning services around the world, asserting that the organization supported forced abortions in China—despite a contrary finding by his own investigative team. He cut off $1 million in grants to the Reproductive Health for Refugees Consortium, again based on the unsupported contention that one of its member organizations supports China's coercive family planning policy. And his global gag rule, known as the Mexico City Policy, had the effect of withdrawing tens of millions of dollars from International Planned Parenthood.

In the battle for fetal personhood, Bush scored three important victories. In 2002, Bush issued an order extending coverage through the State Children's Health Insurance Program (SCHIP, which offers health services to children in low-income families) to fetuses and embryos—but not to pregnant mothers themselves. Experts in maternal/child health, pointing out that a healthy infant depends entirely on the health of the mother during pregnancy, had long sought to extend SCHIP benefits to pregnant women, but Bush's regulation had the pro-life twist of defining a set of benefits exclusively for embryos.[33] The president likewise modified the charter of a human research advisory committee to declare that embryos are to be considered "human subjects," a bit of bureaucratic finesse that attracted little media attention but glowing words from National Right to Life and the U.S. Conference of Catholic Bishops.[34] And he turned over more than a million dollars to the Christian pro-life group Snowflakes to promote "embryo adoption"—a term the group prefers because it implies an equivalence between embryo and child, even though most frozen embryos are not healthy enough to ever grow to full term, even if implanted.[35]

Finally, Bush's nominations to the powerful federal appeals courts reflect a commitment to the pro-life movement's long-term vision of undermining *Roe* in the courts. Bush nominee Michael McConnell has called *Roe v. Wade* a "gross misinterpretation of the Constitution" and nominee Bill Pryor went further, calling *Roe* "the worst abomination of constitutional law in our history," a decision in which "seven members of our highest court ripped the Constitution and ripped out the life of millions of unborn children." Other Bush picks are more than pro-life sympathizers; their actions have marked them as pro-life activists. Nominee Carolyn Kuhl once submitted a brief to the Supreme Court arguing for the overturn of *Roe,* and nominee Timothy Tymkovich, as Colorado Solicitor General, defended an amendment to his state's constitution that blocked the state from paying for abortions even in the case of rape or incest. While a district court judge, nominee Dennis Shedd excused South Carolina Citizens for Life from complying with campaign finance laws and struck down a law that would have prevented anti-abortion fanatics from using DMV records to track down the names and addresses of abortion clinic doctors and their patients. After two of Bush's pro-life nominees were rejected by Senate Democrats as too extreme, he waited until the Senate changed hands and nominated them again. One of these, Priscilla Owen, had, while serving as a judge in Texas, gutted a judicial bypass mechanism for minors seeking a waiver from parental consent requirements, an act that Owen's colleague on the court (now White House counsel), Alberto Gonzales, called "an unconscionable act of judicial activism." The other, Charles Pickering, helped push through a Republican Party plank calling for an anti-abortion constitutional amendment just three years after *Roe* was decided.[36] All but two of these nominees, Owen and Kuhl, were approved by the Senate and made it onto the federal bench.

There are many items still on the Washington agenda of the pro-life movement, all of which its close allies in the House are doggedly pushing through. One bill bolsters the case for fetal rights: a complete ban on embryonic cloning. Two others are just the latest efforts in the traditional strategy to restrict abortion access: the Child Custody Protection Act, which would make transporting a minor across state lines to seek an abortion a federal crime, and the Abortion Non-Discrimination Act, which would allow publicly funded hospitals, clinics, and individual health care workers to refuse to provide abortions. The Family Research Council has vowed to push all four bills through, while Douglas Johnson, legislative director of the National Right to Life Committee, told the *Washington Post* in late 2002, "We're very happy with the support the White House has given on all of these bills. We expect that to continue."[37]

"People always believe that something will stop these policies or modify them," says Donna Crane, deputy director of NARAL, the pro-choice organization. "They believe that you have to overturn *Roe* to gut women's access to abortion. But once these Bush administration policies are in place and the effects are felt, it's like an epidemic—you can never go back." Shortly before President Bush signed the partial-birth abortion ban, *USA Today* asked then president of Concerned Women for America, Sandy Rios, whether all abortion could be banned if Bush were reelected. "It's possible," she said. "I don't think we're there yet, but we're moving in the right direction."[38]

TENDING THE GRASS ROOTS

Even more than his accomplishments inside the beltway, what has endeared President Bush to the pro-life movement is his warm embrace of their core values, their language, and their grass-roots activism. At the 2002 March for Life, when President Bush called in his greetings, he made a special point to offer personal thanks to organizer Nellie Gray and to each one of the participants for "working and marching on behalf of a noble cause." In his speech, he took care to list every cherished item on the pro-life agenda: "That is why my administration opposes partial-birth abortion and public funding for abortion," he said, to applause, "why we support teen abstinence and crisis pregnancy programs [applause], adoption and parental notification laws [applause], and why we are against all forms of human cloning."[39] The day before the march, Bush invited twenty-five leaders of the National Right to Life Committee for a private meeting in the Roosevelt Room and a personal tour of the Oval Office. There, according to one report, Bush linked the pro-life cause to the war on terror, saying that the response to 9/11 must be to create "a culture of respect for life." The participants reported feeling "deeply impressed."[40]

In a gesture that's invisible to most Americans, Bush often signals his close pro-life affinity by lifting language directly from the movement's leadership. One of Bush's favorite turns of phrase projects a day "when every child is welcomed in life and protected in law"; he used these words, for example, when he signed a pro-life bill called the Born Alive Infant Protection Act. It turns out Bush lifted it verbatim from a Clinton-era pro-life manifesto, "A Statement of Pro-life Principle and Concern," signed by movement heavies such as the Family Research Council, Concerned Women for America, the Southern Baptist Convention, Focus on the Family, the Christian Coalition, and National Right to Life.[41] On the rare occasion when he does not narrowly hew to the hard-line pro-life position, the president takes pains to assure pro-lifers they are listened to and in the loop. Leading up to the announcement of his stem cell compromise in the summer of 2001, pro-life advocates, including National Right to Life, were invited to high-powered White House meetings with Karl Rove, Karen Hughes, and Andrew Card to share their views.[42] Thirty minutes before the president took to the airwaves to present his tightly guarded decision, Rove placed a conference call to Senator Brownback, Representative Smith, and Values Action Team chair Joe Pitts, to alert them and win them over to the compromise; he also phoned James Dobson of Focus on the Family.[43]

Bush has shored up the grass-roots anti-abortion movement in a number of concrete ways, by supporting crisis pregnancy centers, legitimizing spurious claims about the health risks of abortion, and giving pro-life doctors a say over access to contraception. Crisis pregnancy centers have a special place in the pro-life movement, serving as local outposts for community involvement in the cause, and they've experienced a boom in recent years, growing from 2,000 centers to more than 3,200 during the 1990s. A center I visited in Louisiana was typical—a small strip mall storefront decorated with rose-print wainscoting, religious literature, and posters of developing fetuses, with a small video screening room in back to show abortions in a gory light. The soft-spoken director, Cindy Collins, has no medical or public health background, but she proudly showed me a display of photos of babies she had "saved" and a closet stocked with donated baby clothes for those who "choose life." The goal of crisis pregnancy centers, in the words of one how-to manual from the right-wing Pearson Foundation, is to "compete with the abortion chambers"; the manual's author refers to pregnant girls as potential "killers" and describes the centers as engaged in a fight against Satan. For deceptively presenting this theological and ideological project as medical service, centers have faced injunctions and other legal action in New York, Ohio, and California.[44] Yet in his addresses to pro-life groups, Bush has consistently expressed his support for these questionable centers, and he has extended praise to the pro-life leaders who run them, singling out Marvin Olasky's role as the chairman of one such center in his glowing introduction to Olasky's book, *Compassionate Conservatism*.[45]

Pro-lifers in Congress, perhaps taking a cue from the president, introduced a bill that would channel $3 million in federal dollars to crisis pregnancy centers, to fund the purchase of sonogram machines, the pro-life deus ex machina. Focus on the Family claims to have conducted a survey showing that 79 percent of "abortion-minded women" changed their minds after viewing ultrasound images of their fetus; the group has devoted $1.2 million to purchasing these machines, citing one center director in Iowa who says, "Having an ultrasound is like

walking in the door as a missionary with the complete Scriptures translated into their own tongue. It is light-years ahead of just sitting there
and talking to a girl." [46]

As that bill crawls forward, Bush has found another, far less visible
way to channel federal dollars to the crisis pregnancy center network—
his abstinence-only-until-marriage program. Much of the federal abstinence money goes through the states, but one funding stream is
doled out directly by the Department of Health and Human Services.
And though crisis pregnancy centers have no background in sexuality
education or STD prevention, they've received a larger and larger share
of these HHS grants during each year of the Bush administration. In
2001, HHS gave $1.1 million to at least four crisis pregnancy centers.
In 2002, that number rose to $2.2 million dollars and at least seven cri-
sis pregnancy centers. In 2003, the grants totaled $2.8 million to at least
six crisis pregnancy centers—or one in every five grantees.[47] And
though the federal government doesn't track which groups receive abstinence money through state block grants, the Tennessee record
echoes the pattern at HHS: five of that state's twenty-two funded abstinence programs are at crisis pregnancy centers, or nearly one of every
four grantees.[48] These abstinence grants have taken small, volunteer-
run organizations and turn them into substantial institutions; one
crisis pregnancy center in Boston, A Woman's Concern, received a
$488,000 grant that allowed the group to bump its staff up from two to
twelve. "Basically, they have created an industry," says Adrienne Verrilli,
a spokesperson for the sex education group SIECUS.[49]

For years, the pro-life movement embodied a combative concern
for fetuses at the expense of pregnant women, and this prompted a
movement makeover in the 1990s. Crisis pregnancy centers helped to
soften that image—and so did a new argument that abortions hurt not
just fetuses, but women, too. Women pay "a huge price for abortion,"
according to a 1996 movement manifesto.[50] This message is spread
through videos, books, and pamphlets such as "You're Considering an
Abortion—What Can Happen to You?" published by Heavenly Bounties, which claims that abortion poses "spiritual . . . emotional . . . and
physical risks," language echoed by Concerned Women for America

and Focus on the Family. Though the life-threatening risks of child birth go unmentioned, these pamphlets warn ominously that abortions can cause hemorrhage, infection, laceration, perforation, future miscarriages, sterility, and, a special favorite, an increased risk of breast cancer. Scientists, who once saw potential evidence of an abortion–breast cancer link, now point to definitive, large-scale studies showing that no such connection exists. Yet the Heavenly Bounties pamphlet, which I picked up at the Louisiana crisis pregnancy center, still claims that "women who have aborted have significantly higher rates of breast cancer later in life. Breast cancer has risen by 50% in America since abortion became legal."

In 1996, Christ's Bride Ministries, an antichoice organization, put up billboards in Maryland, Pennsylvania, and Washington, D.C., warning: "Women Who Choose Abortion Suffer More and Deadlier Breast Cancer!" Other anti-abortion groups put up similar billboards in Florida and North Dakota.[51] Pro-life groups have filed suit against abortion clinics in several states charging that health providers had failed to warn women of the nonexistent breast cancer risk. And in 2001 alone, activists worked with local legislators to introduce thirty-four measures in eighteen states that would force doctors to warn women of the apocryphal link. As of late 2002, two states had such laws on the books.[52] Clearly, playing on women's fear of breast cancer has become an important ideological tool. Concerned Women for America even lists building "public awareness of the harm of abortion to women and their families, including the link between abortion and breast cancer" as one of its top fourteen organizational goals.[53] So it hardly seemed coincidental when, in mid-2002, a page on the National Cancer Institute (NCI) Web site, "Abortion and Breast Cancer," which sharply debunked the alleged abortion–breast cancer link, quietly disappeared.

Only after Democratic Representative Henry Waxman and several other members of Congress complained to Tommy Thompson was the missing page replaced—by a brief statement referring to "inconsistent" data and a promise to hold a federal workshop to reevaluate the research. In a letter of protest, Waxman and his bipartisan co-signers wrote that "the new NCI fact sheet appears to have been changed to reflect the political agenda of the White House, not scientific facts."[54] In February 2003, the NCI finally held its workshop, where researchers came to the same conclusion as before—that abortion does not increase breast cancer risk.[55] But the revised Web page wasn't completed until the end of May—too late for the women of Minnesota and Texas. In those states, during April and May, pro-life legislators each passed bills called the Women's Right to Know Act, heavily backed by Texas Right to Life and Minnesota Citizens Concerned for Life, respectively, which force doctors to inform women of the breast cancer–abortion link, even though the link has no scientific merit. "I am happy to see state lawmakers putting women's health and safety over politics," a delighted Wendy Wright, of Concerned Women for America, told the conservative *Washington Times*. The *Christian Science Monitor* attributed the passage of the Texas bill to the growing influence of the Christian right there—but the movement's allies in Washington may have tipped the balance by deliberately confusing the science.[56] Waxman has twice formally requested that Thompson reveal who requested the abortion–breast cancer information be removed in the first place, but he has yet to receive a response.

THE NEW "CULTURE OF LIFE"

On April 1, President Bush held his second major pro-life bill signing in less than five months, to the cheers of another packed family values audience. This time around, he was careful to surround himself by women onstage—the family members of pregnant crime victims. "As these and the other families understand," Bush said as he signed the Unborn Victims of Violence Act (UVVA), which would recognize a fetus as a second legal victim when a pregnant woman is killed. Calling the bill by its pro-life vernacular, "Laci and Conner's Law," a reference to California murder victim Laci Peterson, Bush said, "Any time an expectant mother is a victim of violence, two lives are in the balance, each deserving protection, and each deserving justice."[57] But the law, which the National Right to Life Committee helped to draft back in 1999, may do far more than offer stiffer penalties when a pregnant woman is murdered. "What the UVVA does is give legal recognition to life in the womb," said Focus on the Family spokesperson Carrie Gordon Earll. Family Research Council president Tony Perkins, who brought one of the largest contingents to the signing, was ebullient, calling the bill a "tremendous victory" in the effort to end abortion. "We are now one giant step closer to rebuilding a culture of life, where every child—born and unborn—is given the protections they so clearly deserve."[58]

As Bush signed the law, its potential uses could be seen in Salt Lake City, Utah, where "unborn children" are already protected by a similar criminal statute. There, prosecutors charged twenty-eight-year-old Melissa Ann Rowland with murder after one of her twins was stillborn in January, claiming that Rowland's decision to delay a C-section caused the death.[59] "This is an example of 'fetal rights' replacing the bodily integrity and autonomy of women under the law," said NOW President Kim Gandy.[60] (After Rowland spent months in jail, the murder charge was finally dropped.)

At the same time, cases unfolded in three states challenging the partial-birth abortion ban that Bush had signed the previous fall. While David Stevens, head of the Christian Medical Association, said he hoped the cases would serve to make the "gruesomeness of this procedure . . . a matter of court record," the plaintiffs, including Planned Parenthood and the National Abortion Federation, argued in court that the law Bush signed is so "hopelessly unclear" that it could outlaw common abortion procedures performed as early as thirteen weeks into a pregnancy. To the plaintiffs, the partial-birth ban, like so many other Bush initiatives, is, in the words of Planned Parenthood President Gloria Feldt, "part of a larger agenda, and that agenda is to outlaw all abortions, at any time during pregnancy, for any reason."[61] One more marker along the road to overturning *Roe*.

WHOSE GAY AGENDA?

ON ABORTION AND the constellation of issues such as stem cell research, fetal personhood, and judicial appointments that constitute the pro-life agenda, there can be little doubt that President Bush identifies closely with social conservatives. On gay rights, the other bedrock concern of the Christian right, that's far less clear. Yes, his record as Texas governor was antigay down the line: he spoke out against gay adoptions, expressed support for the state's sodomy law (the same law that would be overturned by the Supreme Court in *Lawrence v. Texas*) as a "symbolic gesture of traditional values," and opposed a hate-crimes bill that would have included gay and lesbian victims.[1] And early on in his presidential campaign he made a public show of refusing to meet with the Log Cabin Republicans, a national gay organization, prompting them to endorse his rival in the primary, John McCain. But once Bush had locked in his party's endorsement, his stance toward gays quickly softened—at least for the time being.

Working closely with gay Republican activists Carl Schmid, a former leader within the Log Cabin group, and Charles Francis, who had launched his own conservative gay rights organization to endorse Bush against McCain, Bush's campaign met with a dozen gay Republicans in April of the election year. The Austin meeting was seen on all sides as a landmark event for the Republican Party, one Schmid believes has pried open doors for gays and lesbians. "Bush is conservative on gay issues," he says, "but he's not as conservative as the religious right. When we met with him, he didn't embrace their agenda completely, and told us that, if not in so many words." A sticking point at the meeting, Schmid says, was gay hiring, but Bush came around on that and soon announced that sexual orientation would not be a factor in his staffing decisions if he became president.[2] He gave openly gay Arizona

Congressman Jim Kolbe a speaking slot at his nominating convention, and directed Tommy Thompson, who was riding herd over the GOP platform process, to eliminate planks opposing gay marriage, gays in the military, and gay civil rights protections (though, in the end, social conservatives successfully fought to get the planks restored).[3] Log Cabin Republicans in turn endorsed Bush in the general election and, after coordinating an ambitious get-out-the-vote operation in key Florida counties, boasted that the gay vote had provided Bush's margin of victory there. "We were the difference," said Kevin Ivers, then Log Cabin's public affairs director. "The Bush campaign knew what we did for them in Florida because high-level officials told us after the election how much they appreciated our work. They told us what we did there would not be forgotten."[4]

Once in office, Bush kept his word and fast became the first Republican president to appoint openly gay people throughout his administration. Most visible was Bush's choice for AIDS czar, Wisconsin Log Cabin head Scott Evertz. According to Schmid, the appointment was Karl Rove's reward for Evertz's decision to break ranks with Log Cabin leadership over the group's McCain endorsement—Evertz backed Bush in the Republican primary instead. Bush also appointed openly gay men to two other visible posts, making Michael Guest ambassador to Romania and giving Stephen Herbits, a vocal opponent of the military's gay ban, a top personnel post at the Defense Department. Over time, the president named several openly gay men to his AIDS council: Republican politicos David Greer, who'd organized a gay welcome for Bush in Philadelphia in 2000; James Driscoll, a former AIDS advisor to the Log Cabin Republicans; and Abner Mason, a former top staff advisor to Republican Massachusetts Governor Jane Swift, as well as HIV-positive liberals Brent Minor and Don Sneed. Gay Republican activists were invited to the White House early on, and were invited, even more unexpectedly, to meet with Attorney General John Ashcroft, who during his years as a senator often referred to homosexuality as a sin. "There's a dawning realization with this administration that they need to build a political infrastructure in the gay community, just as they do in the black and Latino communities," Driscoll told me, not long after he was appointed to the AIDS council. "I was brought on mainly because through the process and struggle of deciding who should be on the council, they decided they needed some gay Republicans." Bush also made other pro-gay gestures, such as extending 9/11 benefits to gay partners.[5]

The strategy was classic Rove: by making a handful of gay appointments Bush could both neutralize opposition from gay lobby groups and present an image of tolerance to moderate suburbanites. Being the first Republican president to break the lavender barrier likely sat well with the private George Bush, too. Vice President Dick Cheney, one of the most influential voices in the administration, has a warm relationship with his lesbian daughter, Mary. She's Cheney's close political advisor in the Bush/Cheney reelection bid, and she has been known to bring her partner Heather Poe to official GOP functions.[6] During the 2000 vice-presidential debate, Cheney took a laissez-faire attitude toward gay marriage, saying, "People should be free to enter into any kind of relationship they want to enter into" and that any regulation was best left to the states.[7] Bush considers Charles Francis, a participant in that landmark gay meeting in Austin, a loyal family friend. Francis's endorsement of Bush in the 2000 presidential primary had come at a critical time in the race—and long before that, Francis's brother, Jim, chaired Bush's first successful political campaign, his 1994 gubernatorial bid against Ann Richards. In light of his almost familial ties to Mary Cheney and Charles Francis and his quick decision to hire gay staff as president, it's a very real possibility that Bush's antigay orthodoxy in Texas may have sprung more from political necessity—social conservatives own the Texas GOP—than from personal conviction.[8]

But as Bush embraced gay conservatives the family values backlash was swift and strong. The Evertz appointment "was major," says Schmid, who meets regularly with administration officials, "and the right-wing went berserk. They went crazy over it. I don't think the gay community realizes the heat the administration has had to face." Donald Wildmon's American Family Association sent out an urgent action alert in April 2001, citing the Evertz and Herbits appointments as a sign the Bush team was "opening its arms to homosexual activists."

Wildmon asked his half-a-million American Family Association members to contact the president and remind him that "he campaigned as a conservative Christian who supported pro-family positions. Ask him to please stop granting powerful appointments to openly homosexual activists who have been working diligently to overthrow the traditional values of Western civilization regarding human sexuality, marriage and family." The Traditional Values Coalition found the Evertz appointment outrageous as well, saying that if the AIDS czar "fails to recognize that homosexual sex is a destructive and dysfunctional behavior disorder," AIDS will spread. Concerned Women for America released a harsh report, *The Bush Administration's Republican Homosexual Agenda,* outlining the many "pro-homosexual actions" taken by the new president.[9]

Over the course of the next year the administration took several steps to reassure its base. Bush ended the Clinton-era practice of issuing gay pride declarations in June and eliminated the position of White House liaison to the gay and lesbian community. His personnel director, Kay Cole James, a former vice president of the Family Research Council, blocked domestic partners of federal workers from buying into the government health plan. Stephen Herbits stepped down from his post at DOD. Even in the midst of the war on terror, the army, with administration support, discharged seven gay Arab-language experts. And Tommy Thompson unleashed that series of audits of gay AIDS organizations whose prevention messages had been singled out as "shocking" by groups such as the Family Research Council.[10]

None of these gestures went unnoticed—or uncelebrated—in family values circles, but a few of the president's actions had special symbolic importance to his antigay constituency. Bush appointed Michael McConnell to a federal appeals court, the same attorney who had become a hero to the Christian right when he argued before the Supreme Court for the Boy Scouts' right to discriminate against gay youth. He appointed another antigay legal star, Timothy Tymkovich, to an appeals court seat: in *Romer v. Evans,* Tymkovich argued before the Supreme Court in defense of Colorado's antigay Amendment 2, which prohibited local governments from enacting gay and lesbian civil rights protections. Another Bush appeals court choice, Alabama attorney general William Pryor, wrote a brief supporting the State of Colorado in the *Romer* case and supporting Texas in the sodomy case *Lawrence v. Texas*. In the Lawrence brief he compared gay sexuality to prostitution, adultery, necrophilia, incest, pedophilia, and bestiality. And Bush nominated his pro-life deputy secretary of health, Claude Allen, to another appeals court seat. Allen was the first African American staffer for Jesse Helms, the most aggressively antigay legislator in the U.S. Senate; as a staffer in Helms' 1984 reelection campaign, Allen derided Helms' opponent as having links "with the queers."[11] All four of these nominees are not only antigay, but well-known figures within the Christian right lobby; all but Allen have made it onto the federal bench.

The president asked former Congressman Tom Coburn, a practicing medical doctor who openly disapproves of what he calls "the homosexual lifestyle," to co-chair his presidential AIDS council. Coburn, who described himself to me as a "man of faith" is a Christian evangelical insider. He was a board member of the Family Research Council; one of his top aides from his days in Congress, Michael Schwartz, is now vice president of Concerned Women for America; and he has collaborated with Focus on the Family's James Dobson on such efforts as the attempt to force the resignation of CDC director Jeffrey Koplan over his promotion of condom use, rather than abstinence until marriage, to prevent sexually transmitted diseases. While editorial pages across the country condemned Coburn's selection, the family values lobby applauded, calling him the ideal man for the job. With his near obsessive focus on "AIDS babies"—despite the fact that mother-to-child transmission has nearly disappeared in the United States—Coburn could be trusted to sideline the squeamish topic of gay sex on the AIDS council. Meanwhile, Bush's AIDS czar Scott Evertz, who had become something of a lightening rod for defending explicit HIV prevention for gay men, stepped down in June 2002 under increasing pressure from family values groups. Though he was replaced by another openly gay man, HIV doctor and career civil servant Joe O'Neill, the switch seemed to satisfy religious conservatives. "AIDS policy is unfortunately wrapped up in gay politics," Michael Schwartz told me,

·

"but it's a health issue and O'Neill has always treated it as a health issue. His record shows that his private life doesn't enter into his public life."

In December of that year, the president issued new regulations, in conjunction with his faith-based initiative, that would allow religious organizations receiving federal funds to discriminate on religious grounds. Bush repeatedly emphasized that the rules were designed simply to protect religious service providers from being "forced to change their character or compromise their prophetic role," but gay advocates insisted they were actually meant to pave the way for Christian fundamentalists to refuse to hire gays.[12] They point to the July 2001 revelation that Karl Rove had been secretly negotiating with the Salvation Army—who sought assurance that the religious charity would be exempt from gay antidiscrimination laws—as evidence that antigay sentiment was indeed a driving force behind the new Bush regulations.[13] Also in December 2002, health officials convened an invitation-only closed-door meeting in Atlanta with the goal of rethinking HIV prevention. There, longtime AIDS service providers were confronted by antigay staff from Concerned Women for America, the Traditional Values Coalition, and other Christian right organizations. Paul Kawata, executive director of the National Minority AIDS Council, says Concerned Women for America's Peter LaBarbera approached him just to say, "I think you're sick and demented." Several attendees advocated for "reparative therapy" as a solution to AIDS, reflecting the common belief of Christian right groups such as the American Family Association and Exodus International that "freedom from homosexuality is possible through repentance and faith in Jesus Christ as Savior and Lord."[14]

This avalanche of Bush administration concessions to the Christian right only subsided when one of the president's antigay gestures—each designed to appeal, sub rosa, to his family values constituency—broke into the news. In this case, it was one of Bush's second-round appointments to his AIDS advisory council, marketing consultant and Bob Jones University graduate Jerry Thacker, in January 2003. Bush stood by his choice despite private warnings from gay Republican activist

Carl Schmid and reports in a Washington gay paper that Thacker had called AIDS the "gay plague" and homosexuality a "sinful deathstyle," and supported efforts to "rescue the homosexual" through Christian conversion. But once the story won an A1 headline in the *Washington Post* and surfaced on the evening political talk shows, Bush spokesperson Ari Fleischer hurried to insist that "the views [Thacker] holds are far, far removed from what the president believes"—and Thacker petulantly withdrew his name.[15] Sandy Rios, then president of Concerned Women for America, was dumbfounded: "With which of Mr. Thacker's views does the president disagree? Does he not believe that homosexual behavior is sinful and dangerous?"[16]

The same month Bush backed away from Thacker, he made an even grander gesture to reassure gay Republicans and swing voters alike: he used his State of the Union address to announce an ambitious five-year, $15 billion plan to combat global AIDS. Carl Schmid was impressed: not only had Bush "stepped up to the plate on AIDS" with an ambitious plan, but he had devoted precious real estate during his State of the Union address to the issue. Even outspoken critics of the Bush administration recall being cautiously supportive. "The cynical read on this was that if he handled domestic AIDS wrong he would appear to be too aligned with Falwell and that crowd, and the global epidemic was the right opportunity to focus on compassion and treatment," says Terje Anderson, executive director of the National Association of People with AIDS. "My noncynical version is that George W. Bush is a deeply religious man and, confronted with this apocalypse around HIV in the developing world, he wanted to do the right thing. At any rate, he is doing more than Clinton ever did, and he deserves credit for that."

When Rick Santorum, the third-ranking Senate Republican, went so far as to compare homosexuality to bestiality in April 2003, family values advocates rallied to his side, saying he was "exactly right."[17] The White House, taking its cue, stayed silent—but also sought to cover its lavender flank. As the Santorum controversy persisted, Bush sent emissaries including AIDS czar Joe O'Neill to meet with some 200 members of the Log Cabin Republicans at their national convention and patch things up.[18]

On balance, though, Bush was sending enough of the right signals to convince his Christian evangelical base that he wasn't soft on gays. A case in point: his handling of a dustup surrounding Republican National Committee chairman Marc Racicot. Social conservatives had never forgiven Racicot for signing an executive order while governor of Montana that established sexual orientation as a protected class. Imagine conservative reaction, then, when Racicot met with a national gay lobby group, the Human Rights Campaign, in March 2003. Ken Connor, then president of the Family Research Council, wrote an editorial in the *National Review* calling him "utterly tone deaf—or openly hostile—to traditional values voters who comprise the vast bulk of the Republican political base." Connor then threatened consequences, saying that he had "warn[ed] the White House that the GOP drift on marriage and such aspects of the gay agenda as domestic partner benefits, hate crimes, and such, could cause some social-conservative voters to stay home" in 2004. In early May, a dozen major family values players, including Gary Bauer, Lou Sheldon, and Paul Weyrich, angrily confronted Racicot; according to one participant, Racicot kept insisting that gay people had "a right to be involved in the public discussion," while Weyrich demanded "a clear, strong, unequivocal statement" from the GOP leader that homosexuality is immoral.[19] Racicot is a favorite of George W. Bush; in fact, the governor was his first choice for attorney general until the Christian right insisted on Ashcroft. But within a month of that contentious meeting with Weyrich and company, Racicot was out as GOP head, moved horizontally to head Bush's reelection campaign. The top Republican Party slot was turned over to the more enthusiastically antigay Ed Gillespie.

AN EARTHQUAKE AT THE SUPREME COURT

Soon, none of Bush's low-profile antigay maneuvers would prove sufficient. In the summer of 2003, the Supreme Court's surprisingly broad decision legalizing sodomy—coming just two weeks after a Canadian court decision that opened the door for gay marriage—sent shock waves through the religious right. Justice Antonin Scalia's ferocious dissent was circulated widely, and its assertion that "state laws against bigamy, same-sex marriage, adult incest, prostitution, masturbation, adultery, fornication, bestiality, and obscenity" were all "called into question by today's decision," resonated with a movement experiencing a profound sense of siege. In one decision, declared Concerned Women for America, the Supreme Court had knocked down "3,000 years of Judeo-Christian-based law." Suddenly, the antigay backlash kicked ferociously into high gear. Commentator Joel Belz, writing in the conservative Christian magazine *World,* reported that the decision had "terrorized and energized this group of pro-family Bush supporters . . . a group of people for whom this may be the biggest public issue of their lifetimes." He added, "The position the president stakes out . . . will prove a key test of his largely happy alliance so far with the so-called religious right." After the *Lawrence* decision, and with a Massachusetts Supreme Court decision on gay marriage in the offing, Focus on the Family head James Dobson wrote to his supporters that the fight against gay marriage would be "our D-Day, or Gettysburg or Stalingrad."[20]

Belz characterized this new outcry as not another "noisy ultimatum" from a family values movement known for noisy ultimatums, but rather a question of "quiet resolve." Evidence of that resolve surfaced everywhere. The Republican Policy Committee, the home of Senate ultraconservatives, released a report in July, "The Threat to Marriage from the Courts," making the case for a constitutional amendment restricting marriage to one man and one woman as the final bastion against same-sex marriage.[21] The Traditional Values Coalition began sending out 1.5 million mailings a month asking voters to push for such an amendment, while Focus on the Family launched a media campaign and its president, James Dobson, announced that he would take a leave from his post to free himself from the constraints of nonprofit advocacy so he could fight gay marriage "on the political level."[22] Randall Terry, known for his leadership of the radical arm of the pro-life movement, sent out a national letter to Christian activists rallying them to fight "homosexual perversion." The man who once egged on his Operation Rescue troops to throw themselves in the path of women seeking abortions was now saying the *Lawrence v. Texas* decision "put our Republic in great danger. . . . Our children's and grandchildren's future is surely at stake. . . . America's survival hangs in the balance."[23] Family Values leaders who didn't rally to the cause were purged: Ken Connor, who'd served as head of the Family Research Council since founder Gary Bauer stepped down to run for president in 1999, disagreed about redirecting the organization's resources to fight for a federal marriage amendment. "There have been 1,700 proposed constitutional amendments," he told *Christianity Today*. "We have only added twenty-six to the Constitution. That tells you something."[24] That was the wrong attitude. By mid-July, Connor had been forced out, replaced by former Louisiana state representative Tony Perkins, who had authored a "covenant marriage" law there, the country's first, which created a legally binding biblical marriage in which couples give up their right to no-fault divorce.

Evangelical conservatives often work on the same issues, but they don't often work well together. So when, in July, some two dozen Christian right groups dropped their territorial tendencies to coordinate their defense of traditional marriage, it was notable. "This is larger than anything we've ever done before," said Tony Perkins. "Groups that are normally very independent are in lockstep on this."[25] So when this coalition, called the Arlington Group after the location of its first meeting, launched Marriage Protection Week, the president immediately signed on, issuing a national proclamation. The coalition includes movement founder Paul Weyrich; beltway influentials the Christian Coalition, the Family Research Council, Concerned Women for America, and the Traditional Values Coalition; and major Christian broadcasters including Coral Ridge Ministries, Focus on the Family, and the entire National Religious Broadcasters Association; together, these organizations announced plans to support a constitutional amendment by distributing literature to 70,000 churches and taking to the airwaves to get the message out to their audience of millions.[26] For his part, Bush announced that "Marriage is a sacred institution, and its protection is essential to the continued strength of society. . . . Marriage is a union between a man and a woman, and my administration is working to support the institution of marriage." The proclamation was so closely coordinated with Christian right advocates that Concerned Women for America announced it to the press before the White House did.[27]

Afraid to alienate Republican moderates by endorsing a constitutional ban on gay marriage, the president nevertheless began inching toward his far right base. *World* magazine reported in October that the White House had developed its own, mildly worded, draft amendment, just in case. In December, Bush offered tentative support for an amendment on a primetime interview with Diane Sawyer, saying he would do so "if necessary," while seeming to keep the door open for civil unions, adding "the position of this administration is that whatever legal arrangements people want to make, they're allowed to make, so long as it's embraced by the state." Increasingly uneasy in this charged climate of making any misstep with his evangelical base, Bush declined to endorse Arnold Schwarzenegger's California gubernatorial bid. Though political commentators predicted that a Schwarzenegger victory would boost Bush's chances for winning the state in 2004, the Traditional Values Coalition was sending out hundreds of thousands of voter guides and some 10,000 letters to pastors complaining about the star's pro-gay record. Bush likely stayed mum to keep the peace. For someone who began his term extending a historical Republican embrace to gay men and lesbians, President Bush had been decisively forced into retreat by his family values base.[28]

During these same volatile months, I spoke with Patrick Guerriero, the new national director of the Log Cabin Republicans. Guerriero is a political prodigy, a small government, strong-defense Republican true believer who, though openly gay and working class, became a state representative in Massachusetts at twenty-five. He's convinced the Republican Party can accommodate social conservatives, libertarians, and social progressives—and that any advances in gay civil rights will require movement on that side of the aisle. Republicans dominate every branch of government, he pointed out, "so with that in mind, we have a job to do, which is figure out how do you navigate the new political landscape in America." Guerriero speaks regularly with party leaders in Congress and senior White House staffers, and he likes to use words like "personal responsibility" and "family" when talking about the gay community because he believes in finding a common language with the party's right wing. He picks his battles, and criticizes liberal gay advocates for "overreacting" to symbolic acts such as Bush's proclamation in defense of marriage.

But he was deeply concerned by the growing storm in opposition to gay marriage, and the movement for a constitutional amendment that he believes would institutionalize discrimination. "Social conservatives are attempting to use the marriage issue as a wedge to divide not only the Republican Party but the entire American family," he says. "As much as I've argued for avoiding it, I think we're entering into a couple of years of a full-fledged culture war in America." Though Guerriero personally supports Bush and has donated to his reelection campaign, he told me Log Cabin would withhold an endorsement if the president firmly backed an amendment. "The White House has given a lot of things to the far right in this administration," he said. "Partial-birth abortion, the faith-based initiative, global AIDS—there are a lot of projects that mean a lot to the evangelical community, and I'm not sure they need to add another. Gay marriage is a brand-new issue for this country, it brings up a lot of complex emotions. And I've always thought one thing you don't do when your country is just starting to deal with something is start rewriting the Constitution."

Bush tried one last time to avoid supporting a constitutional ban on same-sex marriage and preserve his moderate credentials. In mid-January, he announced a $1.5 billion five-year initiative to promote "healthy marriage" among welfare recipients through advertising campaigns, mentoring programs, and skills workshops. The day before the announcement, unnamed administration officials told the *New York Times* they were confident his marriage promotion plan would please conservatives. " 'Healthy marriages' sounds like a traditional value, which is red meat to married voters," pollster John Zogby concurred.[29] But for a Christian right movement newly energized by its resounding opposition to gay marriage, marriage promotion just wasn't enough.

"The Bush administration must recognize that co-habitation and divorce are not the only threats to the institution of marriage," said Tony Perkins, the Family Research Council's new anti-gay attack dog. "Efforts to redefine marriage out of existence must be stopped, and the president's support of a federal marriage amendment would go a long way in making sure that marriage is not only promoted, but also protected." "We have a hard time understanding why the reserve," said Glenn Stanton, a policy analyst at Focus on the Family. "You see him inching in the right direction. But the question for us is, why this inching? Why not just get there?" The Family Research Council, Focus on the Family, the Traditional Values Coalition, and the conservative Southern Baptist Convention all continued to push for firm presidential backing for an amendment. They showered their members with e-mails, they hit the political talk show circuit, they took it to the Christian airwaves, and, of course, they quietly approached Karl Rove.[30]

In February 2004, the president threw in the towel, declaring to the nation in a televised speech from the Roosevelt Room that "activist judges and local officials have made an aggressive attempt to redefine marriage" and had forced his hand. "If we are to prevent the meaning of marriage from being changed forever, our nation must enact a constitutional amendment to protect marriage in America," he said. Then, to make his intent crystal clear, he added, "Today I call upon the Congress to promptly pass, and to send to the states for ratification, an amendment to our Constitution defining and protecting marriage as a union of man and woman as husband and wife."[31] His base had laid down the gauntlet, and he had responded. He hadn't called any of his closest gay supporters to give them a heads up, not even family friend Charles Francis.[32]

"We applaud President Bush's unequivocal support of a Federal Marriage Amendment," said James Dobson. "President Bush has shown outstanding leadership," said Matthew Spalding of the Heritage Foundation. "The president's statement was eloquent and powerful," said Gary Bauer to his American Values membership, "precisely the kind of moral clarity that is needed." Bauer then described the "nonstop media blitz" he'd been on, praising the president's statement on all the major networks and leading newspapers, and declared, "Make no mistake, my friends, the sanctity of marriage will be the defining issue of 2004." Payoff. For the Bush team, losing the endorsements of gay conservative organizations and weathering the $1 million campaign Log Cabin immediately launched to defeat the amendment was just the price of the ticket. Bush won only a quarter of the openly gay vote in 2000, anyway—not more than a million votes. A White House aide coolly said to *Newsweek* that Bush has friends "who are homosexual . . . but they might understand that he has his principles."[33]

THE DESTRUCTION OF MARRIAGE, AND OTHER CONCERNS

While members of the Arlington Group were up in arms when the threat of same-sex marriage was merely hypothetical in the fall of 2003, once renegade mayors from San Francisco, California, to New Paltz, New York, began to actually perform gay weddings in early 2004, the situation, in Gary Bauer's words, had spun "out of control." Christian right leaders spoke in panicked tones that everything from child rearing to sex education would be undone by the mainstreaming of gay relationships, but no threat loomed larger than the threat to traditional, heterosexual marriage. "Marriage is under assault as never before," Concerned Women for America said in a typical alert to its members. Focus on the Family's Glenn Stanton called gay weddings "the death of marriage."[34]

University of Minnesota sociologist William Doherty is one of the leading academic experts on marriage and family. He is a respected researcher, the past president of the National Council on Family Relations, and the author of eight books on family issues, including *Take Back Your Marriage* and *Putting Family First*. He agrees with the Christian right that heterosexual marriages are in crisis—he just disagrees about the cause. He says infidelity and addiction often lead to divorce, and that stressful life events—whether illness, job loss, falling into poverty, or having a new child—put tremendous strain on couples. And he says an emerging culprit is overwork: "Work schedules come first, and the family gets the dregs." Doherty reels off a list of public policies that contribute to marital stress: lack of access to affordable health care and child care, which often chain one spouse to an unhappy job; stingy vacation policies that leave little time for restoring relationships; a minimum wage that requires families to work extra jobs; and mandatory overtime. On many of these fronts, Bush has made matters worse.

He has opposed any hike to the minimum wage and fought for changes to the Fair Labor Standard Act that would expand mandatory overtime to some 8 million police officers, nurses, store supervisors, and other workers. His economy has leached some 2.5 million jobs since he took office, pushing up unemployment rates and pushing down wages. While official unemployment rates have increased by less than 1 percent since the recovery began, long-term unemployment has skyrocketed, especially among white-collar workers: the rate tripled among those with college degrees.[35] Leading figures on the Christian right, such as Tim and Beverly LaHaye, have long insisted that the "natural longing of every woman's heart is to be a homemaker," and yet in Bush's economy, the prospect of a secure salary that can provide for an entire family has become ever more remote.[36]

James Dobson is part of the chorus of Christian right leaders who now see a federal marriage amendment as "the linchpin in efforts to protect marriage in our country."[37] But his massive Christian counseling operation in Colorado Springs likely tells him something quite different. Focus on the Family gets so much mail from its radio listeners that the organization has its own zip code and several hundred employees who spend their days just answering requests for information. They send out magazines, books, tapes, and pamphlets offering advice to families on such topics as how to handle a spouse who is a nonbeliever, cope with job loss in midlife, or avoid piling up debt during the holidays. His operation meets an important need: studies have shown that born-again Christians experience a higher divorce rate than both mainline Protestants and secular couples, and divorce rates are higher throughout the southern Bible belt than in the liberal Northeast. And when born-again Christians do get divorced, they're more likely to experience rejection from their religious community than support.[38]

When I asked Focus on the Family spokesperson Carrie Gordon Earll how the prospect of legalized gay marriage hurt traditional marriages, she had a hard time making the link. "Most of the people who contact us are dealing with abuse, or pornography, or divorce," she said. "Those are their day-to-day concerns, and gay marriage doesn't intersect with that a whole lot." Stephen Crampton, chief counsel for the American Family Association's Center for Law and Policy, had a similar response to the question. "In the instant the first homosexual couples were married, so called, it's not like a married couple in Nevada can feel some ethereal loss," he said. Rather than being a threat to actual marriages, Earll described gay marriage as a threat to a biblical ideal. "For our constituency, marriage is a foundational issue, a biblical issue," she told me, echoing the words of many other Christian right leaders. "We see marriage as a stabilizing influence on the family and society that needs to be protected. The heart of our concern is that civilization as we know it, civilization for hundreds and hundreds of years, could be detrimentally altered. This is not a minor tweak in the social structure. This is a major deconstruction of our social, religious, and legal systems."

Despite such dramatic statements as these, Mel White, the founder of the Christian gay-advocacy group Soul Force, sees the explosion of concern about gay marriage on the Christian right as driven more by politics than by morality. White, a former theology professor, became close to several of the biggest figures on the Christian right in the 1970s when he was tapped by a publisher to ghostwrite biographies of Jerry Falwell, Pat Robertson, and Billy Graham. He became their confidant—until he came out as a gay man. White says that while "they are sincere believers in their own propaganda" that homosexuality is a sin, most of them are far more comfortable with gay people than they let on. After he founded Soul Force, White was invited to Falwell's Lynchburg headquarters to make his case against homophobia to Falwell and his staff; at the end of the meeting, Falwell pulled him aside and said his publisher wanted to do a sequel to the book White had penned. "He asked if I didn't tell anybody, would I write it for him," White recalls. Falwell also mentioned that one of his senior staffers was a gay man who lived with his partner; Falwell said he had told the aide that "if they didn't put Jerry in a corner, he wouldn't put them in a corner." In White's view, the Christian right inter-est in gay marriage isn't, in the end, so different from Bush's: it riles up the base. A February 2004 Pew Research Center survey hints at the politi-cal calculus: among the nearly one-third of Americans who support gay marriage, it's not a deciding issue; only 6 percent would refuse to vote for a candidate who opposed gay marriage. But among the two-thirds of Americans who *oppose* gay marriage, Pew found gay marriage had sur-passed even abortion and gun control as a "make-or-break voting issue": 34 percent would refuse to support a political candidate who did not share their view, a number that jumps to 55 percent among evangelical Christians.[39]

"They are expert on demographic studies," White says of the Chris-tian right. "They know more about finding issues and creating mass mailings than anyone—at knowing what evokes a negative response and thus donations and recruits." He says movement leaders are always looking for "co-belligerency" issues, where people of faith and others can join together in common cause. In the 1970s it was anti-Communism, but when Communism fell, their research pointed to abortion and homosexuality. As they began to push gay marriage, he says, they found out it was extremely effective, "and abortion had to take a back seat. When you spend $1 million to send a mailing out, and you have to bring in $2 million or $3 million a week, as Robertson and Dobson have to do, then you have to have something that really works. And this works. Homosexuality is so unknown to so many people, and so terrifying to them, that this really struck a chord." In February 2004, the right's direct-mail guru, Richard Viguerie, told the *New York Times* he was planning to send out 10 million appeals in the coming months for several social conservative organizations.[40]

"They built their base on an alarmist message, so having their guy in the White House has not been great for fundraising," says Political Re-search Associate's Jean Hardisty, who has researched the far right for more than two decades. And indeed movement patriarch Paul Weyrich said the Christian right had not been gaining members during Bush's tenure, until gay marriage began "turning things around."[41] "The gay marriage issue has been a real gift for them," Hardisty says, "because it's revitalized their base, and revitalized their fundraising. Abortion and gay marriage are really their bread and butter."

For both Bush and his Christian right base, gay marriage also offers the appealing possibility of attracting new constituencies—particularly religious African Americans—to their cause. Indeed, a May 2003 memo by Republican Pollster Richard Wirthlin calls an antigay marriage amendment "an ideal wedge issue."[42] African American Christians have been targeted heavily by the Bush administration through its faith-based initiative, and have been sought out episodically by Christian right leaders as well; in the 1990s, for example, Pat Robertson offered a reward for the capture of anyone responsible for the wave of black church arsons that was spreading through the south. Support for gay marriage is, not surprisingly, lowest among white evangelicals (12 percent), but it is lower among African Americans (28 percent) than among any other racial group taken as a whole.[43] When black ministers such as Boston's Eugene Rivers complained that gay activists had "exploited" the legacy of the civil rights movement to make their claim for marriage rights, leaders on the Christian right—despite their record of opposing African American civil rights initiatives—took their cue.[44] The Family Research Council announced that the group "strongly opposes the hijacking of the civil rights movement by homosexual activists, and believes that homosexual behavior cannot be equated with such innate characteristics as sex or race." Concerned Women for America released a report on the topic, titled *Homosexuals Hijack Civil Rights Bus: Claiming a "Civil Right" to "Marry" the Same Sex Demeans a Genuine Struggle for Liberty and Equality,* while the newly formed Alliance for Marriage courted black endorsements, and succeeded in wooing the African Methodist Episcopal Church and the Church of God in Christ.[45]

While African American legislators almost succeeded in blocking passage of a proposed constitutional amendment in Georgia banning gay marriage, incurring the wrath of the state leader of the Christian Coalition, social conservatives have had more success rallying black clergy. The Georgia Family Council, an affiliate of Focus on the Family, organized thirty black pastors to sign a declaration calling for a state ban on gay marriages; in Boston, while that state's constitutional amendment was being debated, three of the largest associations of black ministers joined to stage press conferences denouncing gay marriage, where they stood shoulder-to-shoulder with the Family Research Council. "This will be a rolling crescendo," warned Richard Land, lead lobbyist for the Southern Baptist Convention, as the gay marriage debate gained momentum. "Politicians who don't know the radioactive nature of this issue now will by November of 2004."[46]

After the 2000 elections, the Family Research Council circulated a paper responding to analyses in the gay press that gay voters had made the difference for Bush in Florida. A *Washington Blade* story, extrapolating from Voter News Service data, estimated that Bush received around 60,000 votes in Florida, enough to provide his margin of victory. "Virtually any special interest group could claim the same," read the Family Research Council paper, which then used the same data to estimate 4.8 million conservative and religious right voters had gone Bush's way in Florida. "If Bush had publicly embraced the homosexual agenda," the paper concluded, "the resulting loss of his socially conservative constituency would have overshadowed any modest gain of homosexual votes."[47] Apparently the Bush team did the very same math.

AIDS, BORN AGAIN

RONALD REAGAN had been president for only a few months when, in June 1981, scientists announced that a cluster of rare cancer cases among gay men signaled a new epidemic. It would be a year before AIDS would have a name, and five years more before the president would utter one word about the disease. Today, in the age of SARS and anthrax, Reagan's silence seems unimaginable, but as the new illness grew from 400 American cases to 70,000 during the 1980s; as it leaped from Los Angeles and New York to Paris, Kampala, and Rio; as it touched nearly one hundred nations and was fast on its way to becoming the most deadly epidemic in human history, the president simply refused to take notice. The Centers for Disease Control, under Reagan's watch, was slow to protect the nation's blood supply from infection. The National Institutes of Health researched only one prospective AIDS drug. Finally, in 1987, facing bipartisan pressure from Congress, civil disobedience in the streets, and increasing criticism in the media, Reagan appointed an AIDS commission to study the issue. Then he ignored the commission's 579 recommendations.[1] By the time Reagan's vice president, George Herbert Walker Bush, succeeded him 1988, the epidemic had killed 38,000 Americans. Yet Bush Sr. consistently fought full funding of the Ryan White CARE Act, a congressional initiative to provide federal assistance to American cities hardest hit by AIDS.

AIDS afflicted society's pariahs—homosexuals and heroin addicts, constituencies with little political power and even less relevance to the Republican Party. Moreover, any serious discussion about AIDS prevention required explicit talk about things most Americans didn't mention in polite company, if at all: vaginal, oral, and anal sex; drug injection; and gay relationships. Popular conservative solutions to AIDS, such as banning infected children from the public schools (forwarded by William Dannemeyer) and tattooing the buttocks of gay men (a William F. Buckley brainstorm), telegraphed conservatives' belief that neither the disease nor the infected had a place in their America. Indeed, several prominent congressional Republicans built their careers on AIDS bashing. Former North Carolina Senator Jesse Helms famously waved safer sex brochures on the Senate floor, branding them obscene; former Oklahoma Representative Tom Coburn, who came to Washington with Newt Gingrich's far-right class of 1994, pushed for such punitive measures as the criminalization of HIV transmission and the mandatory testing of pregnant women and sex offenders (though, a physician himself, he also helped push for Ryan White funds).[2]

Into this decade-long vacuum of political leadership exploded a massive private-sector response, from the street activism of ACT UP to such national advocacy groups as the National Association of People with AIDS, from research institutions like AmFAR to service providers such as Gay Men's Health Crisis. These organizations, it happens, were rooted in the gay and African American communities, constituencies that had held little interest for Republicans. And the more these organizations succeeded in collectively defining the national AIDS agenda to include publicly funded research and care, gay-friendly approaches to prevention, risk reduction for drug users, and efforts to fight stigma, the less interested fiscal and social conservatives became in AIDS.

THE BUSH FACTOR

When George W. Bush entered politics, he seemed destined to ignore AIDS in the Republican style. As governor of Texas from 1994 to 2000, a period when the state's AIDS cases surged to rank fourth in the nation, Bush never mentioned AIDS in a single public address. He appointed a Texas health commissioner who opposed condoms because "it's not what God intended," and Bush was so indifferent to AIDS care in his state he refused to sign letters of support for AIDS grant applications.[3] Little changed as the governor began to entertain presidential ambitions. When Bush held his famous Austin meeting with gay Republicans in April 2000, according to one attendee, Carl Schmid, "Global AIDS wasn't on his agenda and it wasn't on ours." An early draft of the 2000 Republican Party platform, a document the Bush campaign had micromanaged, omitted AIDS entirely.[4] And so it went when Bush first arrived in Washington.

A month into the new administration, Bush's chief of staff, Andrew Card, announced that Bush would shutter the White House office on AIDS policy. The comment made national headlines, forcing Card to retract it. Press Secretary Ari Fleischer claimed Card had simply "made a mistake," but beltway AIDS advocates regarded Card's announcement as a trial balloon, to test how far the administration could go in shunting AIDS to the sidelines.[5] Indeed, months passed before Bush named an AIDS czar, and a full year elapsed before Bush appointed members to his AIDS advisory council. HIV-doctor Scott Hitt, who served as chairman of the AIDS council under President Clinton, told me at the time, "I just don't get the sense that this administration is engaged."

But those AIDS council appointments in early 2002—followed by a series of public AIDS initiatives, secret AIDS strategy sessions, and aggressive audits of publicly funded AIDS service providers—actually signaled something quite extraordinary. George W. Bush was doing what no other Republican president before him had done: he was divining a way to make AIDS his own. Rather than focus on the uncomfortable challenges of the domestic epidemic, where three-fourths of all AIDS cases still occur among gay men, injection drug users, and their partners, Bush turned his sights on the global epidemic, with its millions of infected mothers and children and sympathetic AIDS orphans. At home he might have to grapple with condoms and clean needles, but abroad he could put his energies into mother-to-child transmission, a significant source of new infections in Africa and the Caribbean. Rather than seek advice from the AIDS researchers, doctors, social workers, advocates, and people living with HIV who had set the AIDS agenda in the past, he would listen to pharmaceutical executives intent on preserving drug profits and to social conservatives whose abhorrence of gay and extramarital sex was matched only by their lack of AIDS expertise. Rather than promote public health solutions, he emphasized

"personal responsibility." Rather than condoms, his mantra was abstinence and marriage. In Bush's hands, AIDS was born again—as a conservative issue.

At the heart of this Republican AIDS makeover is an all-out war on
condoms and safer sex, one with deep roots in the teachings of the
Catholic Church and evangelical conservatives. The idea of altering
sexual practices to avoid HIV infection—whether by donning a condom or by engaging only in oral sex and other low-risk activities—
emerged first from within the gay community in 1983 and was only
later adopted by health professionals and the American public as the
key to preventing new infections. By 1995, Americans had so embraced
the idea that 80 percent said they would like to see condom information aired on TV.[6] This was a devastating development for the Christian right. Jerry Falwell spoke for many when he said in the mid-1980s
that homosexuality was a sin and AIDS was God's punishment of gay
men for "violating the laws of nature," a view echoed today in pro-
nouncements by such groups as the Traditional Values Coalition that
homosexuality itself is a "public health hazard" and the only way to
stop HIV is to "stop the behavior." Concerned Women for America extended the argument, insisting that all sex outside of a heterosexual
marriage is "not natural" and that access to condoms would discourage
young people from choosing the only spiritually healthy path: chastity
until marriage. "Why abstain from sex when there can be protection
from disease?" Concerned Women asked in a 1998 article, "Furthering
the Safe Sex Lie." "Once again, 'free love' reigns."[7] Social conservatives
wanted sexual promiscuity and gay sex to carry such a severe cost that
young people would be scared straight. So condoms became the
enemy.

Throughout the late 1990s, Tom Coburn served as a mouthpiece for
this perspective in Congress, insisting that "condom distribution and
similar risk-reduction strategies have been heavily funded and heavily
promoted for the past thirty years with little or no beneficial effect."[8] A
Christian fundamentalist himself who would go on to join the board of
the Family Research Council after his retirement from Congress, Coburn

teamed up with Joe McIlhaney of the Medical Institute for Sexual Health and Shepherd Smith of the Institute for Youth Development to conduct annual slideshows for his congressional colleagues about the scourge of sexually transmitted diseases, where he would rail against "permissive sexuality" and the "safe-sex establishment."[9] He introduced legislation to get warning labels put on condoms and instigated a full-scale investigation into condom effectiveness by the National Institutes of Health (NIH)—in effect, a fishing expedition for damning data. Months before the report came out, Smith, who sat in on some of the NIH meetings, claimed in an editorial that the evidence supporting condoms was so thin that promoting their use amounted to "consumer fraud."[10]

When the NIH report finally came out in July 2001, Bush was in the White House, Coburn was back working as an obstetrician in Oklahoma, and the results didn't quite turn out as planned. After an extensive review of all the scientific data on condoms, the NIH found "strong evidence" for the effectiveness of condoms in preventing HIV, as well as several other sexually transmitted diseases—facts that had already become common sense to most Americans. The scientific literature includes evidence that condoms and safe sex practices cut HIV rates in half among white gay men from 1988 to 1993, hailed by many at the time as a public health coup, and that 98 to 100 percent of uninfected people in a long-term relationship with an HIV-positive partner avoided infection through consistent condom use.[11] But Coburn, McIlhaney, and a group of doctors associated with Focus on the Family calling themselves the Physicians Consortium held a press conference to claim the opposite. They latched onto the inconclusive data about one common sexually transmitted virus, HPV—a lack of data that NIH insisted "should not be interpreted as proof of the adequacy or inadequacy of the condom to reduce the risk of STDs"—to condemn condoms once and for all. McIlhaney declared that the report "reveals that condoms are not a reliable defense against today's epidemic of sexually transmitted diseases."[12] Coburn announced to reporters, "For decades, the federal government has spent hundreds of millions of dollars to promote an unsubstantiated claim that promiscuity can be safe. We all now know for a fact that that is a lie." For good measure, claiming that he was guilty of spreading lies about condom effectiveness, they called for the resignation of Jeffrey Koplan, then the director of the Centers for Disease Control (CDC).[13] Within seven months, Koplan had resigned, and Bush had appointed Coburn, McIlhaney, and Shepherd Smith's wife and colleague Anita to his Presidential Advisory Council on HIV/AIDS.

The CDC estimates that new HIV infections peaked at about 160,000 a year in 1985, and then dropped down to 40,000 by the mid-1990s. Since then, the rate has held steady, a stubborn fact that has been used by McIlhaney, Coburn, Smith, and others to suggest safe sex has run its course. "We've spent hundreds and hundreds and hundreds of millions of dollars [on safe sex]," Coburn said when he was named co-chairman of Bush's AIDS council, "and HIV infection is going up."[14] "Comprehensive sex education programs just weren't performing," McIlhaney told me shortly after he joined the council. "Our feeling was it was time to try another approach, so that's why I supported funding for abstinence." Such arguments alarm long-time AIDS advocates, especially those concerned about rising infections among young gay men. "By going after condoms as a tool, they are destabilizing the whole structure of HIV prevention as we know it," says Daniel Wolfe, a former spokesperson for Gay Men's Health Crisis, the nation's oldest AIDS organization, and author of the gay men's health guide *Men Like Us.* "Their underlying message is that HIV prevention doesn't work and there's no use bothering." David Holtgrave, the CDC's former director of HIV prevention, also became worried about "this mantra that HIV prevention has failed," so he set out to study it.

From his new post as a professor of public health at Emory University, Holtgrave conducted a state-of-the-art analysis of the impact of HIV prevention since the mid-1990s, when that 40,000-infections-a-year rate more or less held steady. He found prevention efforts halted somewhere between 204,000 and 1.5 million new infections during those years, or enough people to fill a city the size of Baton Rouge or Philadelphia. Far from discovering the safe-sex message has failed, Holtgrave found that whenever the CDC's prevention budget rose, infections fell, and when funding leveled off, so did the infection numbers. He says the data prove "you get what you pay for." "What I don't understand," he told me, "is when we're talking about needing to break out of this 40,000 number, and there are people who are either unserved or underserved by our current prevention efforts, why wouldn't you want to provide the resources to do science-based prevention interventions in those populations?" Under previous administrations, members of the president's AIDS council would have called a press conference to make the case for increasing funds for prevention efforts that work. But Bush's council is another sort of animal.

THROUGH THE LOOKING GLASS

In the heyday of AIDS activism, in the late 1980s and early 1990s, AIDS advisory meetings were the targets of protest and scrutiny. Today, very few AIDS advocates and even fewer members of the press monitor the proceedings. When I journeyed to a nondescript Washington, D.C., hotel in June 2002 for an early meeting of Bush's new council, descending into that dimly lit conference room was like falling down a rabbit hole—into a world where AIDS reality had been turned upside down.

The first afternoon, devoted to surveying the status of HIV prevention, lacked a single presentation on injection drug use, which accounts for at least one in four U.S. transmissions, or any mention of the recent spike in infections among black and Latino men who have sex with men. The lineup included one lone presenter on comprehensive sex education, which includes the range of options from condoms to chastity, but she was interrupted repeatedly by council co-chair Coburn, who presided like a family patriarch over Thanksgiving dinner. She was then outflanked by two speakers promoting the benefits of the abstinence-until-marriage message, neither of whom seemed aware that sex between men, who can't marry, causes most U.S. infections, or that many women get HIV from their husbands—marriage offering them little protection from a husband's infidelity or heroin use. Even though he's a member of the council, McIlhaney also snagged a presenter slot, which he used to warn that even 100 percent condom use leaves some "relative risk." He also insisted young people should be told to avoid not just penetrative sex, which carries HIV risk, but "any contact that creates arousal."

After that, Eve Slater, then assistant secretary of Health and Human Services, trumpeted her agency's aggressive audit of HIV-prevention spending. While earlier speakers had accused "so-called AIDS activists" of "actually furthering transmission of HIV," Slater ended her talk with the chilling complaint that "this field [AIDS] has often been plagued by an overenergetic desire to get things done."

The meeting devolved into utter surrealism on day two, when Coburn tossed out the schedule and ceded the floor to the council's staff director, Pat Ware (now a special assistant at HHS), who gave an impromptu twenty-minute monologue on the importance of marriage. "My goal," said the longtime single mom, "is to bring more black men into homes as loving, caring fathers. A two-parent household stabilizes the family, the community, and the nation." When council member Brent Minor, then one of a handful of holdover Clinton appointees, responded, "What about me as a gay man? We have to be included as part of prevention," born-again Christian council member Joseph Jennings erupted: "Is this a gay HIV agenda? Is this a gay thing?" Afterward, Minor told me another council member approached him to say, "Don't take this wrong, but I just don't believe in *that way*." Months later, in a conversation with gay Republican activist Carl Schmid, who frequently lobbies the administration on AIDS policy, Schmid told me, "The community most affected by AIDS in this country is still the gay community. How can you fight AIDS in this world and not mention the word 'gay'?"

The first presidential AIDS council was established in 1987, and began a tradition of articulating prophetic calls to conscience in the face of presidential complacency. Though Ronald Reagan's Presidential Commission on the HIV Epidemic began ignominiously, embroiled in controversy over the appointment of one member who believed HIV was transmitted by mosquitoes and another who called AIDS "the due penalty for [gay men's] perversion," it didn't end that way. When re-tired admiral James Watkins took over as chair, he hired a staff of thirty experienced Capitol Hill operatives and, though a devout Catholic himself, vowed to "keep morals out of this." Within ten months he had held forty-three hearings with hundreds of witnesses and issued a 279-page report that excoriated Reagan for his "sluggish" response to AIDS and called for antidiscrimination legislation, comprehensive K-12 health education, and a big jump in federal funds. Following suit, Bush Sr.'s commission charged that Bush had "seriously underestimate[d] the scale of the AIDS disaster," and when the administration resisted its no-nonsense call for universal health care, drug treatment on demand, and the legalization of hypodermic needles, commissioner Magic Johnson resigned in protest.[15]

Clinton's Presidential Advisory Council was no softer. It expressed "grave concerns" about the government's "overly timid" prevention plan and pushed the administration, in countless memos, reports, and editorials, to endorse needle exchange. It was stacked with people who had devoted their lives to AIDS—from pioneering women-and-AIDS researcher Alexandra Levine, MD, to Ronald Johnson, associate direc-tor of Gay Men's Health Crisis—many of whom were living with HIV themselves.[16] According to Levi Strauss representative Stuart Burden, another Clinton appointee who remained on the council for the early months of the Bush administration, "the Clinton council had big-time wonks who knew the entire history of a bill, who was lined up around it, and the complete political context."

The thirty-four current Bush council members, however, include only one scientist, addiction specialist Beny Primm, and a handful of public health officials from rural states. The dearth of HIV researchers makes Hank McKinnell, CEO of the pharmaceutical giant Pfizer, the most knowledgeable person on HIV drug development in the room, which creates at least the appearance of a conflict of interest. (AIDS ad-vocates have pressured McKinnell's company to reduce the price of its drug Diflucan, used to treat HIV-related fungal infections, and Pfizer contributed $1.4 million in soft money donations to the Republican Party during Bush's presidential campaign.) What's more, the council lacks a single representative from a major national AIDS organization. Instead, it features nine longtime advocates of abstinence-only HIV prevention, a few of whom, such as twenty-six-year-old Dandrick Moton, openly acknowledge that "I'm not an expert on AIDS." Cynthia Gomez, co-director of the Center for AIDS Prevention Studies (CAPS) at the University of California at San Francisco and a Clinton-era council member, says, "For any other advisory group, you'd be hard-pressed to find someone to suggest that a third to a half of the council should be composed of people who don't know the field."

Moton, who directs the Arkansas abstinence-until-marriage group Choosing to Excel, has recruited a group of kids he dubs "The A Team," each of whom has taken a public pledge of abstinence to show other kids that virginity until marriage is "a realistic approach." In effect, Bush had appointed his own A Team to the AIDS council: Moton; Rashida Jolley, a former Miss D.C. and self-proclaimed virgin who once interned at the conservative Heritage Foundation; Mildred Freeman, who directs abstinence education at an association of historically black colleges; Lisa Shoemaker, one of Bush's few HIV-positive appointees, who says she was infected by her dentist and now does the pro-abstinence speaking rounds; Jennings, a former gang member and evangelical "motivational speaker" who uses a scared-straight style to send a message of abstinence from sex and drugs to at-risk youth; Anita Smith, vice-president of the pro-abstinence Children's AIDS Fund, who serves as chair of the council's prevention committee; and McIlhaney, one of the administration's most prolific promoters of questionable condom science. Tom Coburn and Pat Ware—until mid-2003, when Ware took a post at HHS—are the unofficial team captains, united in their goal of unraveling the safer sex consensus.

Coburn has done little to modulate his rhetoric now that he holds this influential AIDS post. While he described himself to me as someone who "understands the sensitivities of the gay community and the Christian right," he also said, "Do I agree with the homosexual lifestyle? No. That's a well-known fact. The attitude in the gay community is unless you have a lifestyle that's promiscuous you're not free. How about abstinence until you have a partner that you want to live with?" Ware, though less of a public figure than Coburn, has also made a career out of hailing abstinence until marriage—with a special emphasis on marriage. She deploys her own story as former single mother from the "inner city" (Raleigh, North Carolina) to argue that chastity and two-parent households are the magic bullets for all that ails the African American community. She and her message were snapped up by the first Bush White House, which awarded her a teen-pregnancy post, and by the Christian right, in the form of a senior position at Americans for a Sound AIDS Policy, best known for its unsuccessful campaign to block people with HIV from protection under the Americans with Disabilities Act. (The group, founded by Shepherd and Anita Smith, was recently renamed the Children's AIDS Fund.) She spoke warmly to me about "male friends" from her days in the theater who got sick from AIDS, saying, "I promised then that I would do something to help stop this suffering." But she insists that her abstinence-until-marriage concept would have applied to them, too. "For young gay men," she said, "it's the same message." According to Greg Smiley, who served as interim director on the council until Ware took over, she exerted a strong hand in stacking the council with like-minded people she met on her extensive travels as an abstinence advocate.

This replacement of experts by ideologues on Bush's AIDS council, mirrored in scientific advisory bodies at the Environmental Protection Agency, the State Department, the Food and Drug Administration, and across the federal government, has opened the door for politics and morality to trump public health throughout the Bush administration. This would prove to be particularly true in the field of AIDS.

LET THE AUDITS BEGIN

The International AIDS Conference, where more than 10,000 researchers and AIDS service providers gather to present new data on treatment and prevention, has been the site of great despair over the years (in 1993, a massive study found the only approved HIV drug at the time, AZT, had done nothing to extend peoples lives) and also great hope (at the 1996 conference, promising combination therapies burst on the scene). It has also, as anyone familiar with the event knows, attracted marches, protests, fiery speeches, and creative acts of disruption, with activists hanging banners over pharmaceutical booths and taking over government press conferences. But Tommy Thompson, Bush's health secretary, is not an AIDS conference habitué.

According to the journal *Science,* when Thompson showed up at the Barcelona conference in July 2002, he immediately tried to politically stage manage his appearance. Thompson insisted conference planners remove a speaker from his session, Mechai Viravaidya, the Thai legislator who has promoted condom use so enthusiastically that he has come to be called "Mr. Condom," a move widely understood to reflect a concern that his message would conflict with the Bush administration's focus on sexual abstinence. The secretary planned to use the packed lunch session to promote the president's contributions to global AIDS (at that time, only a few hundred million dollars to target mother-to-child transmission), but he was shouted down by American AIDS activists, who, calling the U.S. contribution "miserly," whistled, booed, and yelled "Shame!"[17] Headline grabbing, yes, but typical for these contentious conferences.

Not for team Bush. Thompson met with a few of the protesters afterward and, according to several participants, expressed extreme anger at the display. Within days, a dance between far-right members of Congress and the administration began—one that was becoming quite familiar. A dozen members of the Values Action Team—Congress's Christian right caucus—wrote Thompson saying they were outraged at the "rude reception" he got in Barcelona and demanded to know whether any taxpayer dollars had been used to fund the protesters' conference participation. Their like-minded friends in HHS were happy to oblige, and soon the "Barcelona 15"—respected AIDS organizations such as Gay Men's Health Crisis and the National Association of People with AIDS that had participated in the Barcelona protest—got phone calls requesting their financial records. Unconfirmed reports filtered out to AIDS organizations that full-scale efforts to defund the Barcelona 15 were in the works. Anything seemed possible: In September, when a trio of sex education organizations launched a campaign to oppose the president's abstinence-only offensive, another

Values Action Team letter sparked intensive audits of all three groups. And months-long audits of two small but respected gay AIDS organizations—Stop AIDS Project in San Francisco and Us Helping Us, which serves gay men of color, the population most at risk for HIV, in Washington, D.C.—were already in the works.

Us Helping Us, for example, had two auditors from the HHS inspector general's office move in for ten months. One of them, Lisa Blake, a Baptist church leader, carried a Bible with her into meetings, and, says Us Helping Us president Ron Simmons, "her body language said she was very uncomfortable being there." Simmons hoped her time at the organization would make her a little more familiar with the gay community, as she'd pass openly gay staff and clients every day in the halls. Instead, says Simmons, she tried to convert someone on his staff. One morning in May 2002, Blake followed openly gay finance director Jerome Offord to the door and asked him to meet her at the corner store so as not to be seen. She then told Offord homosexuality was a sin that would keep him out of heaven. She mentioned that when she found out her cousin was gay she stopped speaking to him, and explained to Offord that it was her calling to share this information with him. She then wrote on the back of her personal card, which identifies her as an associate minister of Maryland's First Baptist Church of Guilford, a list of Bible verses for him to read, including Leviticus 18, a favorite exhibit in the Christian right case that God condemns homosexuality. At the bottom of the verses she wrote, "I am praying for you." Five days later, Blake called Offord from out of the office. "She said she wanted to check on me personally," he wrote in a memo to his boss, "and to check if I had read the scriptures she suggested."[18] (She was eventually reassigned, in August 2002, after Simmons reported the incident to HHS.)

The Us Helping Us audit was a routine financial review that took an odd turn, but the audit of Stop AIDS was political from its beginnings, back in August 2001. That's when Congressman Mark Souder first wrote to Thompson at HHS, asking about a local HIV-prevention program in San Francisco that his aide Roland Foster had brought to his attention. Stop AIDS is a fairly small, grass roots operation that occupies a challenging niche in the world of HIV prevention: the group targets sexually active gay men living in a city facing a new spike in infections. Stop AIDS receives city, state, and federal monies to conduct anonymous HIV testing and to run workshops tailored for their community, ones that might not exactly play in Peoria. These include sessions on the risks of crystal meth and the relative safety of oral sex; most have colorful names to lure participants. It was one titled "Booty Call" on safe anal sex, and one called "Great Sex," about safe fantasies, that attracted Souder's attention.[19] The director of the San Francisco Department of Public Health, Mitchell Katz, funds them enthusiastically. "We in San Francisco believe that to reach the men who have sex with men who are at highest risk of HIV transmission, we need to speak the same language they do," Katz told the Los Angeles Times after the controversy erupted, "and we need to have workshops that draw them in."[20] That's what Stop AIDS does, and the organization enjoys broad support from the local community. But in May 2001, the Traditional Values Coalition, one of the most explicitly antigay organizations in the family values movement, published a report provocativley entitled Federal AIDS Dollars Fund Homosexual Proms and Fisting Seminars, which singled out Stop AIDS for special condemnation. The report ended with a list of recommendations. At the top of the list: "Defund AIDS groups operated by activist homosexuals." The report was picked up by the conservative Christian news media, and soon Roland Foster was complaining about the explicit Stop SIDS workshops to his influential email list, which goes out to conservatives in Congress and inside the administration. Souder's letter was soon to follow, triggering a relentless series of audits over two years that went to the highest levels of the Bush administration.[21]

Then–HHS Inspector General Janet Rehnquist, the daughter of the Supreme Court justice, headed up the first one, centered on whether Stop AIDS had actively promoted sex or had violated community decency standards. Though the workshops had passed through a rigorous local screening process, Rehnquist concluded in November 2001 that some of Stop AIDS' workshops were "too sexy" and met the "legal definition of obscene," prompting Thompson to promise a full-scale audit of all federally funded AIDS programs across the country, a project he would entrust to his evangelical conservative deputy, Claude Allen.[22]

Soon heavyweights on the Christian right had joined in the attack with Concerned Women for America and the Family Research Council sending out action alerts to their members. Three more auditors from Rehnquist's office arrived the following March for a rigorous follow-up investigation into whether Stop AIDS was correctly reporting its expenditures. This round lasted for six months, as the team poured through records at both Stop AIDS and the city health department. According to one staffer's notes from the period, the auditors told Stop AIDS that it was highly unusual for a second audit to follow so quickly, that most organizations were given a full year to correct any problems, and that they viewed the audit as politically motivated. Before the HHS team had finished its work, Congressman Souder wrote another letter, this time to the Centers for Disease Control, the federal agency that directly funds Stop AIDS. Within weeks the CDC launched round three, sending its own three-man team westward to investigate. This investigation wasn't focused on alleged obscenity or financial impropriety, but on scientific efficacy. "If the program's working, where's the proof?" Foster complained to USA Today. "Shouldn't there be some kind of yardstick we can hold up to see if it's working?"[23]

As a measure of how closely the investigations were being watched by the Christian right, White House AIDS czar Scott Evertz immediately came in for criticism after he spoke out in support of Stop AIDS sometime between audits number one and two. After Christian right groups complained noisily about his comments, the conservative Christian magazine World labeled him "the administration's leader in socially liberal remarks,"[24] an irony, since AIDS advocates had complained that he was insufficiently outspoken. By July 2002 Evertz had been ousted.

The second inspector general's report on Stop AIDS, completed in December 2002, exonerated the organization, finding that even the most explicit of their brochures and workshops had been approved through a local community review process, as mandated by federal law. In February 2003, CDC head Julie Gerberding sent her own all-clear letter to Souder, saying Stop AIDS workshops were "based on current and accepted behavioral science." But apparently some audit results are less acceptable than others. "All [the CDC letter] says is what Stop AIDS is doing is based on currently accepted behavioral theories," complained Foster. "Accepted by who?"[25] If accepted prevention science wasn't good enough for Foster, it also wasn't good enough for his boss, Souder, who demanded Gerberding's resignation.[26] A top CDC official told AIDS advocates that the controversy had percolated all the way up to the White House, with chief of staff Andrew Card pressuring Gerberding to change her tune. In June 2003, Gerberding, a former San Francisco AIDS doctor with years of experience treating gay men, abruptly retracted her conclusions about Stop AIDS and demanded that the group stop conducting explicit HIV workshops or lose hundreds of thousands of dollars in CDC funding. (CDC officials declined to comment on whether the White House was involved in Gerberding's "about-face.") "These audits have politicized sound HIV prevention," Terje Anderson of the National Association of People with AIDS told me. "The chilling impact it has had on community-based prevention across the country is frightening." In May 2004, the other shoe dropped, with a CDC announcement that it would not renew Stop AIDS' annual $225,000 grant, nor would it fund any HIV prevention programs in San Francisco targeting white gay men.

In fall 2003, a new round of intimidation began, when HIV-prevention researchers across the country got warning calls from NIH that their federal funding was in danger. It was little comfort to AIDS advocates when the Traditional Values Coalition eventually claimed credit for drafting a grant hit list that had triggered the calls. When Andrea Lafferty, the group's director, spoke of trying to tear down "this HIV/AIDS scam and sham," it sounded as if she was articulating the goals of the Bush administration.[27]

Behind Closed Doors

While AIDS organizations and AIDS researchers were being threatened with defunding, the Christian right was being invited inside to chart national AIDS policy. The administration's invitation-only HIV Prevention Summit in Atlanta in early December 2002 received no press attention.[28] In fact, no press was allowed, and no tape recorders or laptops for taking notes (even staffers from the Academy for Educational Development

[AED], contracted to produce a meeting summary, were barred from taking notes on their computers). Someone who snapped a few photos was stopped. The AED did write a report of the event, but it was never released publicly, and my Freedom of Information Act request for the event's proceedings was denied on the grounds that it was still "predecisional internal draft material." (CDC spokesperson Kathryn Bina says the restrictions on documentation were put in place to "Foster open and uncensored dialogue" and to "protect participants' privacy.") But the event, as reconstructed through a FOIA'd attendance list and subsequent interviews with participants, signaled a sea change in who shapes the federal response to AIDS policy. Representatives of several major AIDS organizations were invited, from agencies such as Gay Men's Health Crisis, the National Minority AIDS Council, and the National Association for People with AIDS, groups that federal health experts had often turned to for advice over the years because their perspectives on HIV policy are rooted in years of experience serving people with AIDS and preventing infections within high-risk communities. But when these experts arrived, they were confronted by a group of right-wing lobbyists from groups like the Traditional Values Coalition, Focus on the Family, and the Family Research Council with no experience in public health. The event was subtitled "New Perspectives in HIV Prevention," and apparently the new perspectives were intended to come from people entirely unfamiliar with AIDS.

According to Paul Kawata, the openly gay director of the National Minority AIDS Council, Traditional Values Coalition director Andrea Lafferty approached him to say, "I just don't understand—why do you have to have more than one sexual partner in your lifetime?" Peter LaBarbera, then a senior staffer at Concerned Women for America, was more blunt, telling Kawata he was "sick and demented." When participants in a working group on adolescents defended instruction about condoms, Roland Foster, the congressional aide who helped to launch the Stop AIDS audits, dialed Washington on his cell phone to complain that the AIDS experts were being rude. The family values representatives in that working group, according to one participant who asked not to be named, were extremely uncomfortable talking about sex, especially anal sex, and were completely unfamiliar with basic terms of HIV prevention such as "men who have sex with men." At one point, LaBarbera, Lafferty, and others sought to introduce a resolution opposing homosexuality. Several of those in attendance recount that when LaBarbera stood up to make the presentation, he declared homosexuality to be a mental illness, adding that federal dollars should be withdrawn entirely from HIV prevention and spent instead on reparative therapy to turn gay men straight. AIDS advocates were so alarmed, recalls one participant, that the room was "crackling." "What happened was conservatives were invited to one of these things for the first time," LaBarbera, now director of the Illinois Family Institute, a Focus on the Family affiliate, told me. "We proposed language about not promoting homosexual behavior, which some people didn't like."

"In retrospect, that was more of a milestone than we realized at the time," says Terje Anderson, a summit participant from the National Association of People with AIDS. "These were not groups who do any AIDS work or have any background in HIV. They have nothing to offer to the prevention debate except ideological positions. Yet the idea was that somehow these right-wing groups had a credible perspective on HIV prevention—and every idea was given equal weight, whether good or bad." According to a source close to the planning process, the impetus for the event—and the invite list—did not come from the CDC, but rather from the top levels of HHS, or from the White House itself.

Many of these "new perspectives" were soon enshrined at another closed-door meeting—this one at the Department of Health and Human Services in February 2003—convened to institute a paradigm shift in HIV and STD prevention among youth.[29] Speakers included many of the administration's family values luminaries: Deputy Health Secretary Claude Allen, considered the conduit for Christian right priorities within HHS; Alma Golden, the family planning administrator who has coached federally funded clinics to promote abstinence and who has written in disparaging terms about condoms; Margaret Spellings, a domestic policy advisor from the White House; Wade Horn, the architect of the president's various marriage promotion initiatives; and Pat Ware. The meeting was convened, according to a leaked document, to "familiarize decision makers with [the] philosophical and conceptual framework of risk avoidance."

The term "risk avoidance" may appear innocuous to the casual observer, but the room was filled with public health professionals from the CDC and other federal agencies who knew its true import. Traditional HIV prevention, as developed over the past twenty years, has always encouraged young people to avoid drug use and sexual activity if they can. But that's only part of the message. A comprehensive approach accepts that many youth, no matter how they are counseled, will continue to be sexually active and that some use injection drugs—and seeks to prevent those activities from becoming a death sentence. This approach, known as risk *reduction* (not *avoidance*) and proven effective by years of scientific study, involves encouraging those who do use drugs or have sex to take steps to protect themselves, like using condoms or clean needles. Studies have definitively shown that promoting risk reduction does not encourage more sex or more drug use, as opponents once feared. But the message of this February meeting was clear—"just say no" were the administration's new watchwords. The goal, according to the HHS document, was "to establish a common paradigm, across HHS agencies, that embraced avoidance of risks." Lloyd Kolbe, the founder and director of the CDC's division of adolescent and school health, was there to witness the arrival of the new paradigm that would now rule the nation's youth prevention, a program he had shepherded for eighteen years, since the administration of Ronald Reagan. That summer, he resigned.

The modest and soft-spoken Kolbe had been known as an ideological bridge builder. He urged teens to both delay sexual activity *and* learn how to use a condom; he insisted both that the institution of marriage needed support *and* that gay lives not be sidelined. When he arrived at his new post as a researcher at the University of Indiana, I asked him about the events that had preceded his departure—the new approach to HIV prevention laid out at the December and February meetings, the coordinated effort to emphasize condom failure, not condom success. "Over the eighteen years that I worked at CDC, I don't think you could have found a better group of people that were more committed to basing their decisions on science, listening to the American people, and trying to do the right thing, often with enormous pressures from the right and the left," he said. "Part of a pluralistic society is we need to hear from the extremes, but we also need to recognize when they're speaking from the extremes and respond accordingly." When I asked whether the pressure to squeeze science into a political mold had intensified in recent years, he told me, "There's pressure in any administration, but I'm more concerned about the public's health than I have been in the past—about the administration's commitment and focus. I worry," he added carefully, "that we not injure our commitments."

Soon the new paradigms would take the form of official policies and programs, with the weight of billions of dollars behind them.

A MAN, A PLAN, A CABLE

Throughout 2002 and 2003, the campaign to banish condoms in favor of abstinence was making gains in Washington. In early 2002, President Bush proposed to increase federal abstinence funding by a third, to $135 million in 2003. Later that year, top administration officials ordered the CDC to end its Programs that Work project, which identified sex education programs that had been found to be effective in scientific studies—all five of the recommended programs used a comprehensive, risk-reduction approach, and they were deleted from the federal Web site. A CDC Web site that showed how condoms work and emphasized condom effectiveness was also pulled and replaced in October 2002 with one emphasizing condom failure rates and recommending abstinence.[30] According to Terje Anderson, HHS officials even purged any mention of condoms from slide presentations at private meetings with federal AIDS grantees.

And a 2002 Christmas cable from Secretary of State Colin Powell to country-based supervisors of the U.S. Agency for International Development (USAID) issued the first firm policy directive that with AIDS, abstinence should come first. The cable said that U.S.-funded HIV-prevention programs should "support a strong emphasis on campaigns that promote abstinence, faithfulness, and reduction of the number of partners." It asked that USAID do more to engage "faith-based and community organizations." It insisted that all "USAID-funded programs and publications reflect appropriately the policies of the Bush administration," including, specifically, not accepting prostitution as an "employment choice" and not supporting needle exchange. Powell mentioned condoms only in reference to a "fully balanced approach to the ABC's"—short for abstinence, be faithful, use condoms, a moniker lifted from Uganda's successful HIV-prevention program.[31] By then, the ABC approach, cited by everyone from CDC head Julie Gerberding to the president himself, was fast becoming a code for the sidelining of condoms.

Uganda and Thailand are the two best examples of success in developing world HIV prevention—each managed to reduce high rates of infection significantly during the 1990s. Whereas Thailand's program was focused, targeting sex workers with a message of "100 percent Condom Use," Uganda's program cast a wide net, using a combination of messages about abstinence, partner reduction, and condom use to reach the entire population. Uganda's model has been embraced by the far-right rainbow—from family values organizations to *Wall Street Journal* editorial pages to congressional Republicans—but in a conveniently modified form. In their formulation, ABC emphasizes abstinence and monogamy and treats condoms as, in the Eagle Forum's phrase, "only a last resort." Bush's global AIDS bill makes a point of referring to the Uganda model as " 'Abstain, Be faithful, use Condoms' (ABC), *in order of priority*." (Emphasis added.)[32] The only problem with this version of ABC is that it's inaccurate. According to one Ugandan health minister, condom usage rates went from 7 percent in the late 1980s to 42 percent by 1999, contributing heavily to the country's HIV success story. In late 2002, Ugandan health officials announced they would import 80 million condoms the following year to meet "rising demand." They even proposed that Ugandan commercial sex work be legalized to stem the spread of HIV, since the workers "operate underground for fear of being arrested."[33] As for abstinence coming first in ABC and condoms last, "that's just an accident of using the English alphabet," says Milly Katana, an advocate with Uganda's Health Rights Action Group and a former board member of the Global Fund to Fight AIDS, TB, and Malaria. She told me Ugandan public health experts look at ABC "as a stool, which has three legs. You can't have a stool that stands on one or two legs."

President Bush's new global AIDS initiative, announced in his 2003 State of the Union address, was the second major effort to institutionalize a morality-driven federal AIDS policy. Bush described his plan as a $15 billion, five-year effort to treat millions of people living with AIDS and to prevent millions more new infections, and the initial response from the AIDS community was overwhelmingly positive. "It's an incredible step forward," Terje Anderson, director of the National Association of People with AIDS, said at the time, "and I offer Bush unreserved praise."[34] As would soon become clear, in the words of Jeffrey Sachs, chairman of a World Health Organization commission on economics and health, the disappointment was in the fine print.[35] Bush asked Congress to appropriate no more than $2 billion in year one, less than anticipated. Many of the bill's treatment dollars were wasted, because the administration would purchase only name-brand drugs, rather than the cheap generics opposed by the pharmaceutical lobby. His bill starved the United Nation's multilateral Global Fund to Fight AIDS in favor of bilateral aid that could be used for political ends—much of it bound by restrictive "buy American" provisions. Above all, Bush's bold emergency effort was undermined by his allegiance to the Christian right.

In his State of the Union address, Bush called the initiative "a work of mercy," a subtle hint that religious scruples, not science, would shape its priorities. In the end, a third of the initiative's prevention dollars were tagged for abstinence-only-until-marriage messages, which forbid the mention of condoms. (That amendment was introduced by Values Action Team chairman Joe Pitts, but received strong administration support.)[36] A USAID ban on support for syringe exchange was left in place, and a ban on endorsing prostitution was added. Language stipulated that churches and missionary operations should receive special consideration in the awarding of grants, while family planning networks, the main source of community health care in much of the developing world, had already been forced to shutter clinics under the President's 2001 global gag rule. Furthermore, a provision of the bill referred to as a "conscience clause" allows religious groups to reject any HIV-prevention strategy they find morally objectionable and to still receive U.S. funds. With the United States now the largest government donor to international AIDS efforts, these provisions could reverse years of progress, strengthening the hand of the Catholic Church in its global crusade against condoms and leading U.S.-funded programs to abandon serving the hardest hit and most stigmatized populations—sex workers, men who have sex with men, people with multiple sexual partners. The provisions also set the stage for Catholic and evangelical operations to benefit from the new government largesse.

None of this surprised AIDS advocates who were engaged in trying to shape the president's AIDS bill as it moved through Congress. "All the right-wing groups were there lobbying," Terje Anderson says. "And on the abstinence money and the language around sex workers, they completely outgunned us." Throughout 2002, Franklin Graham was positioning his global evangelizing outfit, Samaritan's Purse, to both shape the Bush administration's response to AIDS and become one of its leading grantees. The son of the evangelical icon Billy Graham—the man credited with President Bush's own religious awakening—Franklin Graham organized a major conference in Washington in February 2002 to, according to one announcement, "equip the Church to respond biblically" to AIDS. "At this juncture, only a massive societal change in behavior can stop the spread of AIDS," Graham said to the hundreds of evangelicals in attendance, "and only Jesus Christ can bring about this change." Major administration players attended Graham's event, too, including USAID head Andrew Natsios and Senate Majority Leader Bill Frist, who has traveled to Africa several times with Samaritan's Purse.[37] And in the year that followed, according to the *Times* of London, Graham discussed AIDS regularly with Karl Rove and other White House officials and received a personal briefing from the White House an hour before the president used his State of the Union speech to announce his new AIDS initiative. Chuck Colson, the founder of Prison Fellowship Ministries, asked his followers to urge their representatives in Congress to support provisions to the AIDS bill "that make abstinence first and provide a conscience clause for faith-based organizations," and the Family Research Council and Concerned Women for America did likewise.[38] The National Association of Evangelicals (NAE) also became "deeply involved" in the president's global AIDS initiative; according to the group's press statements, NAE staff strategized with the administration and lobbied Congress to get funds earmarked for sexual abstinence. The NAE convened a forum shortly after the bill was passed, which brought together some 250 evangelical leaders and missionaries to educate them about the "specific prevention, treatment, and care programs in which churches and faith-based communities can participate," that is, receive government grants. A statement of conscience, delivered at the event, included a pledge "to promote abstinence before marriage and faithfulness within marriage as the best way to protect against contracting HIV."[39] Shepherd Smith organized his own global AIDS summit, too, and was invited to join Secretary Thompson on his tour of African nations affected by AIDS.[40]

This was the cast of characters shaping Bush's global AIDS policy. When his bill passed, with the abstinence funds and conscience clause intact, Focus on the Family e-mailed an action alert to its members, saying, "Please give thanks to God that the Congress has passed a bill for fighting AIDS that honors God's principles."[41]

WHAT'S A DEATH, OR TWO?

On the domestic AIDS front, the Bush administration continued to provoke anxiety. Intent on capping his domestic spending package, Bush pushed Republican congressional leaders to flatline funding for the federal AIDS Drug Assistance Program, even though the program was already facing shortfalls in several states. Within months of Bush's State of the Union address, where he declared "we have confronted, and will continue to confront, HIV/AIDS in our own country," two people died of AIDS in West Virginia while on a waiting list for such drug assistance, and five more in Kentucky; nationally, wait lists swelled into the hundreds as doctors described a desperate scramble to access medications. Then, that spring, the Centers for Disease Control announced a radical new prevention initiative.

When the CDC released this controversial plan, "Advancing HIV Prevention," on April 17, 2003, none of the connected AIDS players had heard a whisper it was coming—not Gay Men's Health Crisis, not the National Association of People with AIDS, nobody.[42] "When I was at CDC," says a former AIDS official who served during the Bush Sr. and Clinton years, "key changes in policies were usually accompanied by public consultations, so that concerns could be heard." This time, National Minority AIDS Council director Paul Kawata says, "The plan happened in total secrecy."

Yet Roland Foster, the Republican congressional staffer, sent out an e-mail the very day of the surprise announcement that indicated other beltway players had been very much in the loop. Along with statements dated April 17 from the likes of Concerned Women for America and the Medical Institute for Sexual Health, Foster's e-mail included two press releases dated *before* the prevention plan was announced: one from Anita Smith, in her private capacity as head of the Children's AIDS Fund, congratulating the Bush administration on its "difficult yet bold decisions," dated April 16; and one from Tom Coburn, in his private capacity as an Oklahoma physician, praising the CDC plan as "a major step forward," dated February 21. With an administration obsessive, even vicious, about information control, the timing and coordination of these statements spoke volumes about who is now in the administration's inner circle on AIDS.[43]

The initiative, which has only a threadbare basis in prevention research, focuses almost exclusively on intervening with people who already have HIV, harkening back to a punitive "personal responsibility" approach to AIDS control long advocated by Coburn and the Smiths. It emphasizes testing those who don't yet know they're infected but offers no new treatment dollars for those who learn their status, only to be exiled to an AIDS Drug Assistance Program wait list. It emphasizes preventing mother-to-child transmission, responsible for less than 200 infections a year in the United States, but never mentions gay men or drug users, though these populations experience 20,000 to 30,000 infections each year. As originally drafted, the new measure threatened to upend prevention models, twenty years in the making, that target at-risk individuals and slash funds for some 200 HIV-prevention programs across the country, organizations that have formed the infrastructure for

HIV prevention and AIDS care for decades. CDC prevention dollars are the bread and butter of many HIV-prevention programs, and, coming on the heels of the audits of Stop AIDS, Us Helping Us, and other organizations anathema to the religious right, many AIDS advocates suspected this was the real intent of the CDC initiative: to avoid having to fund, and defend, controversial organizations.

Again, a major new administration AIDS policy had managed to please social conservatives while throwing frontline AIDS experts—and AIDS researchers—into a panic. The initiative strongly echoed the presidential AIDS council's first official communication to the president, in spring 2002. The short letter argued, in an allusion to the abstinence-only agenda, that "we should revisit current strategies to determine if they are, indeed, still the most effective methods of prevention education." And it twice mentioned the "responsibility [of people with HIV] to not infect someone else." Mary Fisher, an AIDS council member known for being the only openly HIV-positive person to have ever addressed a Republican National Convention (she did so in 1992 and 1996), responded angrily when she was sent a draft for review. The letter, she wrote, "strongly infers that evil people are out intentionally infecting innocent folk" and that HIV is "a disease of the guilty."[44] Exactly the message, many AIDS advocates charged, of the CDC's new HIV initiative.

At a major CDC conference in Atlanta that July, Ron Valdiserri, a top HIV official at the agency, insisted that the new plan was sound, and the problem was only that "the CDC has not done an effective job communicating what this is about." But the hallways buzzed with concern. During a speech by HHS's leading social conservative, deputy secretary Claude Allen, hundreds of AIDS professionals raised signs in silent protest that read, "Stop the War on HIV Prevention." That same month, nearly 150 of the country's most respected AIDS organizations sent a letter to President Bush outlining their litany of concerns. They mentioned the flat funding of domestic HIV prevention; the Stop AIDS audits; the administration's emphasis on abstinence-only education; the withdrawal of condom information from the CDC Web site; the intimidating communications with HIV-prevention researchers, who have been "implicitly or explicitly discouraged from doing research that includes any mention of gay or bisexual men"; and of course, the new prevention initiative, which, they said, fails to reach the nation's most at-risk populations: people of color, injection drug users, gay men, and sex workers.[45]

"If you put all these things together," says longtime AIDS advocate Eric Sawyer, a co-founder of both ACT UP and the global AIDS group Health Gap, "the faith-based program, the punitive audits, the abstinence-only funding, you come up with the impression that the administration's policy is to totally dismantle the fight against AIDS."

THE PURITY BRIGADES

IF YOU WANT to get a feel for President Bush's campaign for abstinence-only education, you might want to take a drive out to the peaceful, open farmland of western Tennessee. Here, gently rolling hills are covered by vast soybean and cotton fields and bordered by clusters of trees; at harvest time, tufts of cotton drift along the roadside. For kids growing up in the agricultural counties of Dyer, Crocket, Obion, and Lauderdale, there's little to do besides hang out at the local Sonic Burger or help on the farm. A third or more of these counties' residents never graduated high school, and the counties post some of the highest teen pregnancy rates in the state.

Allicia Ladd is a Dyer County native, and so is her husband. While he spends his days farming soybeans, Ladd, a former social worker, is usually behind the wheel, driving from one school district to another, overseeing a multicounty program that teaches abstinence-only-until-marriage. The program, Right Choices, is funded entirely by the Bush administration; it uses a popular curriculum called "Why kNOw?" that is promoted by the Abstinence Clearinghouse, a national organization advised by such luminaries of the Christian right as Beverly LaHaye, the founder of Concerned Women for America, and televangelist D. James Kennedy, the founder of Coral Ridge Ministries.[1] One day in October 2003, Ladd drove me out to Ridgemont Elementary in Obion County to sit in on an eighth-grade class led by two of Ladd's educators, Holly Powell and Jeremy Shelton, both in their early twenties. They made a lively pair, with their shopping bag full of visual aides, and not a minute passed without them introducing a new prop. But for all the bustle of activity, the two instructors never asked the students about their own lives or encouraged them to pose questions. A good portion of their lesson boiled down to lecturing the kids not to "sell yourself cheap." A typical exercise involved four girls standing before the room wearing made-up name tags prepared by Jeremy. The girl labeled "Nancy," Jeremy told the class, gave love away easily; "Ellen" slept only with boys who used condoms; "Sharon" slept with her boyfriend only after they were engaged; and "Sherry" waited to have sex until she was married. Then he asked each girl to unfold a tiny slip of paper to learn her fate. Guess which one ended up with "a whole heart"—and which three ended up depressed and insecure, plagued by herpes and HPV (human papilloma virus)? Why kNOw's overriding message seemed to be that nothing can protect you from pregnancy and sexually transmitted diseases, not even a condom, so you'd better just avoid sex altogether.

After the class scampered out to a pep rally, Powell and Shelton told me many students have sent them e-mails saying the workshops had inspired them to stay virgins or to become "recycled virgins." But Shelton mentioned one boy who wrote him anonymously asking, "I know one condom don't work, but how about two?" And Powell mentioned a seventh grader who confessed she was having sex with her boyfriend, a high school junior. I asked what advice they planned to offer students like these, the ones who don't choose abstinence. Powell said she hoped to find a moment to encourage the girl to get screened for sexually transmitted diseases (STDs); when I asked whether she would also encourage the girl to use birth control, Ladd interrupted to explain that federal guidelines prohibited her instructors from ever discussing condoms or birth control, even with a sexually active pupil. And Ladd was hardly being a stickler: these strict eight-point guidelines,* written into

---

* The eight-point federal abstinence-only restrictions require a program to: a) have as its exclusive purpose teaching the social, psychological, and health gains to be realized by abstaining from sexual activity; b) teach abstinence from sexual activity outside marriage as the expected standard for all school-age children; c) teach that abstinence from sexual activity is the only certain way to avoid out-of-wedlock pregnancy, sexually transmitted diseases, and other associated health problems; d) teach that a mutually faithful, monogamous relationship in the context of marriage is the expected standard of sexual activity; e) teach that sexual activity outside the context of marriage is likely to have harmful psychological and physical effects; f) teach that bearing children out-of-wedlock is likely to have harmful consequences for the child, the child's parents, and society;

the laws that govern the federal abstinence program, require abstinence instruction to be the "exclusive purpose" of her workshops, and require her instructors to teach abstinence as "the only certain way" to avoid pregnancy and STDs. These restrictions, authored by the conservative Heritage Foundation, promoted by Christian right lobby groups, and quietly slipped into the 1996 welfare reform bill by Republican legislators at the last moment while the bill was in conference, are the least understood aspect of abstinence-only education. They allow instructors to discuss the failure rates of condoms and birth control, because that can further the message that abstinence is best. But any mention that condoms and contraception can prevent pregnancy or STDs is completely out of bounds—even when a student directly asks the question. So Ladd was right: Jeremy Shelton was prohibited by law from correcting his student's notion that condoms "don't work," and Holly Powell was barred from suggesting the pill to her sexually active seventh grader. This is why Representative Henry Waxman has criticized the guidelines as a "gag rule on information."[2]

Experts on sex education have criticized other clauses in the federal guidelines. Adrienne Verrilli is a spokeswoman for SIECUS, the Sexuality Information and Education Council of the United States, a national advocacy group that designed one of the first sex education training manual for teachers in the 1960s. She says the mandate that marriage be taught as the "expected standard of human sexuality" could result in educators "teaching gay kids that they're unacceptable and wrong and teaching sexually abused kids that it's their fault, that they deserve to feel guilty and ashamed." According to a joint report by SIECUS and Advocates for Youth, another organization that promotes sex education, a mandate to teach that having a child out of wedlock "is likely to have harmful consequences for the child, the child's parents, and society" will likely alienate children of single parents and lower

---

g) teach young people how to reject sexual advances and how alcohol and drug use increases vulnerability to sexual advances; h) teach the importance of attaining self-sufficiency before engaging in sexual activity.

their self-esteem. And a requirement to teach that sex outside of marriage is likely to have "harmful psychological . . . effects," according to the report, lacks any public health data to back it up.[3]

As I rode with Ladd back to her office later that day, I asked her again about the seventh-grade girl who was sleeping with her high school boyfriend, and whether Ladd thought the federal restrictions against mentioning birth control made sense. Absolutely, she said, and then, to make her point, she reeled off a series of metaphors that had the burnish of frequent repetition. Just because some people run red lights, she asked, does that mean we should tear down the traffic lights? Just because some people use drugs, should we teach them how to mainline? Then, after a pause, she said, "You know, I have personal friends who have preached abstinence to their kids for a lifetime, and several of them now have teenage kids who are pregnant." I was startled. Did Ladd harbor some doubts after all? She continued: "And every single one of them tells me that if they had to do it again, they would not do it any differently. Because what they were teaching their kids was right. They had taught them the right values."

Ladd's comments said it all. Though abstinence-only education has come under fire from the National Institutes of Health, the Institute of Medicine, the surgeon general, the American Medical Association, the American Academy of Pediatrics, and several other national medical associations for being medically unsound, its advocates are impervious to such criticisms. Ladd's view that teaching values, not preventing pregnancy, is the primary aim of abstinence-only education pervades the Christian right, whose institutions undergird the growing abstinence-only lobby. Materials from the Abstinence Clearinghouse, the nerve center of the abstinence movement, declare that "the goal of abstinence-until-marriage education is to convey the expected standard of waiting until marriage," not to reduce STDs or teen pregnancy, while Clearinghouse president Leslee Unruh is fond of telling young people, "Condoms won't protect your heart."[4] And with Christian right powerhouses such as Focus on the Family and the Christian Coalition playing a leading role in the push for abstinence, it is no surprise that this "values" language has been adopted by the Bush White House as well.

In documents and speeches, Bush has blamed teen pregnancy and sexually transmitted diseases on the 1960s sexual revolution and has promoted abstinence-only education as a "character" issue.[5] Bush was a strong promoter of abstinence-only as governor of Texas, and as president he has pushed to triple abstinence-only funding during his tenure to $270 million. More than once, he has dismissed concerns about its efficacy by joking, "I tell you this, if you're interested in what works, it works 100 percent of the time."[6] No one doubts abstinence works when it's practiced; the problem is scientists and public health experts have found little evidence that abstinence-only education actually results in abstinence—or any other form of risk reduction. The assumption shared by Bush and the abstinence lobby is that if young people embrace the right values, reduced rates of syphilis, teen pregnancy, or HIV will naturally follow. And whenever assumptions aren't good enough, abstinence proponents tap into reports compiled by the Heritage Foundation and Joe McIlhaney's Austin-based Medical Institute for Sexual Health that claim a growing body of evidence shows that abstinence-only works. "This is not about politics or ideology," McIlhaney told Congress in April 2002. "This is about medicine, science, and data."[7]

A Look at the Data

In 1997, Douglas Kirby, one of the nation's leading sex education researchers, conducted a major review of the scientific literature on sex education for the National Campaign to Prevent Teen Pregnancy, a not-for-profit organization that enjoys the respect of advocates on all sides of the issue. Kirby found that "there are no single or simple approaches that will markedly reduce adolescent pregnancy. Because some youths have sex while others do not, programs need to address both postponing sex and using contraception." Kirby cited several peer-reviewed studies showing that a comprehensive approach, which includes messages about avoiding sex and how to prevent infection and pregnancy for those who are sexually active, "delayed the onset of intercourse, reduced the frequency of intercourse, or reduced the number of sexual partners." Moreover, Kirby reported, several of the programs increased condom or contraceptive use. As for abstinence-only programs, he found that "there does not currently exist any published scientific research demonstrating that they may have actually delayed (or hastened) the onset of sexual intercourse or reduced any other measure of sexual activity." In a 2001 follow-up study, after five years of federally funded abstinence-only education, Kirby again found that "evidence is not conclusive"— none of the programs he studied show any reduction in sexual behavior or increase in contraceptive use. In 2000, the Institute of Medicine (IOM), a federal agency, weighed in with its own review of the data. The IOM concluded that comprehensive sex education reduces risky sexual behavior among adolescents and—contrary to the fears of abstinence proponents—does not increase adolescent sexual activity. The IOM concluded that abstinence-only education, however, has "no evidence of effectiveness." The authors found this evidence gap so disturbing they recommended that "Congress, as well as other federal, state, and local policymakers, eliminate requirements that public funds be used for abstinence-only education."[8]

Because of this slim-to-none track record, Congress required the federal government to produce an evaluation of the estimated 700 abstinence-only programs it has funded since 1998. But the Bush administration has made such scientific evaluation optional. According to Mathematica Policy Research, which was contracted to do the research, only programs that state abstinence directors viewed as "promising" were approached about participating in the study, and even then participation was completely voluntary, meaning that nationwide, only eleven programs are being studied.[9] Moreover, administration officials replaced the original evaluation criteria, which would have measured the impact of abstinence programs on sexually transmitted diseases, teen pregnancy, and sexual delay, with vague criteria that scientists do not generally consider to be relevant to public health outcomes, such as attendance, attitudes, and how many youth "commit" to abstaining (not how many actually do).[10] Concern that the evaluation results might not only be inadequate, but biased, surfaced after one of Mathematica's lead researchers, Rebecca Maynard, contradicted scientific consensus in a speech to a CDC conference on HIV prevention in July 2003. "The status of evidence is really not much different for programs focused on abstinence-only or comprehensive sex education," she said. "It all has significant weaknesses."

SIECUS's Adrienne Verrilli reports that when her organization sent out its own evaluation survey to federally funded abstinence programs, Focus on the Family countered with a memo urging abstinence educators, "Do not sign and return." So when Joe McIlhaney, in his new post as presidential AIDS advisor, told me, "Let's increase funding for abstinence programs and see what they can do," he did so in a context where the Bush administration and Christian right lobby groups have joined forces to undermine independent evaluation.

In the face of such poor data, abstinence-only advocates trot out a small handful of non-peer-reviewed studies. One of these is a 1995 evaluation of the Best Friends Program in Washington, D.C.—a politically connected program run by Elayne Bennett, the wife of former Reagan education secretary and *Book of Virtues* author Bill Bennett, which has received visits from Colin and Alma Powell and George and Laura Bush.[11] The evaluation found that only 4 out of 600 participants reported pregnancies, data that has been cited repeatedly in congressional testimony both by McIlhaney (who happens to sit on Best Friends' board of directors) and by Pat Ware, a senior staffer at Health and Human Services.[12] In fact, the Best Friends evaluation wasn't a scientific study at all, but an unpublished graduate student thesis. The closest thing to a legitimately promising finding appears in a 2001 study by Columbia University sociologist Peter Bearman assessing a Southern Baptist program called True Love Waits. Bearman found that some participants who pledged virginity did delay sex for a year and a half (but not until marriage). While the study has become a favorite citation of everyone from McIlhaney to the Heritage Foundation, these abstinence advocates consistently neglect to mention Bearman's caveats: most of the successful pledgers were no more than fourteen years old, indicating that "pledging does not work for adolescents at all ages." And once virginity pledgers did have sex, they were a third *less likely* to use contraceptives than those who'd never pledged in the first place. "Pledgers are less likely to be prepared for an experience that they have promised to forego," Bearman wrote.[13] After a rash of abstinence advocates blared his findings as a vindication of their approach ("Teens Who Say 'No' to Sex Are Less Likely to Have It," read a typical headline in the Christian press), Bearman wrote an angry clarification to the Heritage Foundation with a reminder that virginity pledges offer no long-term benefit unless pledgers later use contraception when they do have sex. "It may be that you are not interested in science, and this letter will fall on deaf ears," he wrote. "[I]t seems obvious to me that all adolescents should learn how to protect themselves."[14]

Abstinence-only advocates make creative use of other scientific data to make their case. For example, a favorite tactic of abstinence-only promoters is to scare young people about the downsides of sex. One curriculum, Facing Reality, asks teachers to "list as many possible harmful consequences of premarital sexual activity as you can."[15] To this end, McIlhaney's Medical Institute for Sexual Health latched onto a 2001 NIH study on condoms that found insufficient data to determine that condoms prevent HPV, a common sexually transmitted virus. Rather than saying, accurately, that the jury is still out, the Medical Institute has spread the word that condoms are useless against HPV, and this pseudo-fact has shown up in abstinence-only materials across the country, including a federally funded brochure distributed by the State of Louisiana. The brochure warns that HPV causes cervical cancer and claims falsely that "there is no cure." It not only asserts that "condoms are useless against HPV," but it also neglects to mention that regular pap smears and early treatment can almost always prevent cervical cancer. It ends by quoting an absurd contention of the Medical Institute that "delaying sex until marriage is the only advice supported by medical research that offers reliable protection from STDs."[16]

When studies fail to produce affirmative data, abstinence proponents claim success by association—pointing out that during the past decade, as abstinence programs exploded, teen pregnancy rates dropped.[17] Indeed by 1997, pregnancy rates had reached their lowest rate in twenty years. Focus on the Family, like other Christian right supporters of abstinence education, claim that "more teens are saying no to sex outside of marriage, and that fact is the primary reason for the drop."[18] But an analysis of data from two large-scale government surveys by the Alan Guttmacher Institute, a Washington, D.C.–based organization that conducts research on sexual and reproductive health, found only a quarter of that drop could be attributed to lower rates of teen sex—while three quarters of the drop in teen pregnancy was due to increased contraceptive use by sexually active teens, especially long-term contraceptives such as Depo Provera—exactly the kinds of tools abstinence-only educators are barred from mentioning in class.[19]

The shoddy abstinence-only data trouble behavioral prevention expert Thomas Coates, a public health researcher with the UCLA Medical Center, who until recently directed the Center for AIDS Prevention Studies at U.C. San Francisco. "Promoting abstinence-only prevention is like a doctor saying, 'I'd rather treat HIV with valerian root,'" he says. "It's that dangerous. Fine, fund studies of abstinence-only—but we should not promote it as a public health policy in the absence of evidence. Especially when we've got so much evidence supporting the comprehensive approach." A former top AIDS official at the CDC, James Buehler, wrote an editorial for the *Atlanta Journal-Constitution* in late 2003 echoing these concerns about the lack of promising abstinence-only data, given the "unequivocal" evidence that condoms are "highly effective." He pointed out that the average American starts having sex at age seventeen, while the average age for marriage is twenty-five to twenty-seven years. "This is a gigantic gap to close," he wrote, and "for homosexual youth, the logic of the abstinence-until-marriage approach would forbid sex entirely."[20] Nevertheless, in the Bush White House, abstinence-only is public health policy.

In late 2002, Human Rights Watch published the first detailed examination of how the federal abstinence-only policy has played out on the ground. The group's report, *Ignorance Only*, comprises interviews with teachers and students in the state of Texas, which, at the pace of $3 million to $5 million a year, is one of the biggest recipients of federal abstinence dollars. Public school teachers there are confined not only by federal abstinence-only restrictions, but by a state law, signed in 1995 by then governor Bush, that requires HIV and sex education to "emphasize that abstinence from sexual activity, if used consistently and correctly, is the only method that is 100% effective in preventing pregnancy, sexually transmitted diseases, infection with [HIV], and the emotional trauma associated with adolescent sexual activity."[21] Since Bush's law made Texas only the third state to institutionalize abstinence education, its record is telling.[22] And since some of Bush's closest Texas abstinence advisers followed the governor to Washington—including Joe McIlhaney, now on his presidential AIDS council, and Alma Golden, now a senior HHS official—the Texas experience will likely prove to be a national bellwether.

The Human Rights Watch account traces the effects of these federal funds, from the questionable science in the curricula they pay for to the impact on teachers and students. The federally funded abstinence materials Human Rights Watch examined include a video, *Sex Is Not a Game*, whose only mention of condoms is the line "Condoms aren't much good against the most common sexual infection anyway," and a scripted pledge ceremony, "A Night to Last a Lifetime," where teens promise "before God . . . to avoid all risk behaviors, knowing that choosing to participate in any of them could lead me to a path of confusion and isolation." Linda Grisham, a science instructor at one Texas high school, said she was told at a teacher training session on abstinence to give students pieces of a condom, a rubber glove, and a plastic bag to "show how condoms were one of the thinnest kinds of plastic [*sic*] and how easy they were to break." Since the training, she says, "I show the percentages of times that condoms don't work and tell the students that most kids that use condoms don't use them correctly . . . I try not to tell them that it's better than nothing." Laura Wilson, a teacher at another Texas high school, says that when students ask about condoms, she limits her answer to what's in her abstinence-only curriculum: "I tell them that they give a false sense of security about protection against STDs, because they're not 100 percent and that condoms may prevent HIV or not."

The results of this combination of self-censorship and extreme misinformation can be seen in the report's many interviews with Texas schoolchildren. Human Rights Watch quotes a sixteen-year-old student identified only as Linda P., who says, "I don't know any other way but abstinence to prevent HIV." Federally funded television ads reinforce Linda's ignorance, including one whose script reads in part:

> Voiceover: In ten seconds, you'll hear this father spread a lie. He's a good dad, who's trying to help his son. But if he doesn't know the truth, he can't tell the truth.
>
> *Screen: HERE COMES THE LIE.*
>
> Father: They'll keep you safe. They'll keep you safe. They'll keep you safe.
>
> Voiceover: Condoms will not protect people from many sexually transmitted diseases and you could be spreading lies to your children.

When the ads aired, during the summer of 2002, a Texas Planned Parenthood staffer told Human Rights Watch several teenage clients came to the clinic saying "condoms aren't as safe as everybody seems to think" and "my boyfriend says they don't work." And there is little opportunity for such abstinence-only misinformation to be countered. The report documents that HIV educators from the Texas Department of Health have been shut out of the public schools by principals concerned their lessons might contradict abstinence-only guidelines, and the state turned down $1.3 million in federal HIV prevention funds because Governor Bush's education commissioner shared the same concern.

The health data describe a total failure: in 2001, six years after Texas mandated abstinence, teen pregnancy rates were one and a half times the national average; while the rate had fallen nationally by 26 percent during the previous decade, the rate dropped by only 13 percent in Texas, one of the smallest declines in the nation. Teen birth rates in Dallas became some of the highest in the nation—the city now ranks number six nationally, up from eighteenth in 1990, according to a 2003 study by the Annie E. Casey Foundation. Sexually transmitted diseases climbed steadily since Bush imposed the abstinence regime, with cases of gonorrhea, syphilis, and chlamydia soaring above the national average, while the state's total AIDS cases grew to fourth in the nation.[23]

With this track record, George W. Bush came to Washington, and nearly doubled federal abstinence spending in three years.

AN ARTICLE OF FAITH

John Marble, the communications director for National Stonewall Democrats, a gay political group, spent much of his youth in Florida as a Southern Baptist churchgoer, a Republican activist, and an abstinence educator. The first political campaign for which he volunteered was Ken Connor's 1994 bid for the Republican gubernatorial nomination in Florida as the far-right alternative to Jeb Bush; Connor went on to become president of the Family Research Council. The son of a Baptist preacher, Marble was fired from his job at a religious afterschool program after some friends in Operation Rescue spotted him at Disney World on the annual Gay Day (they were there to protest the event).

Before then, Marble had often attended youth conferences sponsored by Teen Mania, an evangelizing outfit targeting young people, where he heard motivational speakers such as former gang leader Joseph Jennings (now a member of Bush's AIDS advisory council) promote abstinence until marriage. But the real purpose of these abstinence barnstormers, Marble says, was to save people. "The abstinence-only message is deeply linked with evangelical Christianity," he says. "You're really hoping everyone will come to Christ and wait till marriage for sex. If you're struggling with homosexual thoughts, you need to convert to Christianity and that will cure you. It's a mind-frame that it has to be total in order to be acceptable, so no attempts at compromise will be tolerated." It's a mind-frame that has received significant taxpayer support.

Federal abstinence dollars pour mainly through two channels: the first, SPRANS (special projects of regional and national significance), offers grants directly to community groups; the second, Title V of the federal welfare reform bill, gives block grants to states, who in turn disburse them to community groups. These latter are particularly hard to track and monitor, but a May 2002 suit by the ACLU in the State of Louisiana revealed the degree to which Title V–funded programs there were deeply permeated with Christian evangelical messages. In monthly reports obtained by the ACLU, one grantee, the Rapides Station Community Ministries, wrote, "December was an excellent month for our program. We were able to focus on the virgin birth and make it apparent that God desires sexual purity as a way of life." Another, the Just Say "Whoa" abstinence theater troupe, used a character called "Bible Guy" and told students sex outside of marriage is "offensive to God." A third group, Passion 4 Purity, reported teaching abstinence through "scriptural concepts."[24] In July of that year, a federal judge finally ordered the state to stop giving money to groups such as these that "convey religious messages or otherwise advance religion" with tax dollars.[25] A detailed review by SIECUS of curricula used in federally funded abstinence-only programs found that while many popular guides have recently revised their language to refer to "morality" and "ethics" rather than to explicit biblical mandates, some, such as CLUE 2000, produced by New York City's Pure Love Alliance, continue to claim that "every religious scripture has a clearly worded warning about the dangers of misusing sex" and to ask students to pledge to God that they will remain abstinent until marriage.[26]

In the fall of 2003, I traveled to Slidell, Louisiana, to visit one of the programs highlighted in the Louisiana lawsuit: Passion 4 Purity. While "P4P" no longer receives Title V funding, its director, Cindy Collins, still does, as one of the state's GPA (Governor's Program on Abstinence) coordinators. The P4P Refuge is nestled in the middle of quiet strip mall, with a prom-rental business and a donut shop nearby. The Refuge is housed in a crisis pregnancy center, which Collins also runs, where she counsels young pregnant girls and women against abortion. This tie is hardly unusual, as federal abstinence-only funding has proved to be an enormous boon to these centers, which have received in excess of $6 million in abstinence-only funding since Bush took office.

If you enter the Slidell storefront by one door, you enter the offices of the crisis pregnancy center; if you enter by another, a few feet down, you find yourself in a large open space constituting the P4P Refuge. It's set up like a living room, with couches and rugs; a list of rules posted prominently begins, "Respect 4 God. Respect 4 each other." Collins joined me there with Carly Berbert, an eighteen-year-old senior at Northshore High, who is involved, like Collins, with both P4P and the local GPA club. Collins said her goal at P4P is to introduce each young person to the idea that there is "a destiny, a plan, and a purpose for her life," that choosing abstinence is part of a young person's "walk with Christ." Berbert described her role in more teenage terms, as breaking down "the preconception that Christianity is dull."

When I asked what their message was for kids who are already sexually active when they come to P4P, Berbert told me she has two friends her age who already got pregnant, one of whom had an abortion, and what she tells them is, "God forgives so much." "Unconditional love," adds Collins, "loving people right where they are, that's what Jesus did." Unconditional love, but not unconditional information: whether through P4P or the GPA, Collins does not explain to kids how to use condoms or birth control—whether or not they're sexually active. Collins is clear that unlike P4P, the federally funded GPA clubs provide "a secular public health program" that's "information-based." She sees GPA, with its emphasis on avoiding pregnancy and sexually transmitted diseases, as a good beginning, but limited, because in the end students need to "dig down deep" if they're going to adopt purity as a lifestyle. "If young adults understand that they're of worth and value, intertwined with God's love," she said, "then all of these other issues [such as the risk of pregnancy] become secondary."

But the line between P4P and the GPA clubs often blurs—and not only because they're both run by Collins and Berbert. Berbert mentioned that her favorite event of 2003 was the September P4P Campus-JAM, where a "praise band" came to Northshore to play and spread the message of Jesus Christ. "I had people coming up to me so interested in Christianity," she said, "people who were never involved in religion before who just felt so comforted being there." If this was only a P4P event and received no federal funds, it may have steered clear of the July 2002 court order. But in the September 2003 report Collins filed with the State of Louisiana to account for her federally funded time as a GPA coordinator, she described her top achievement this way: "Assisted in coordinating event on the campus of Northshore High School on September 6th called CampusJAM." The event, she wrote, included speakers, pizza, soft drinks, and "a local college band (AYCE)," the Christian rock band Carly mentioned. At the bottom of the same page, Collins certified that none of her activities had included religious content.[27]

That day, as I was leaving the P4P office, Collins stopped me at the door, and wondered aloud about my name. "Are you Jewish?" she asked. When I answered yes, she took my hands and asked, "May I pray for you?"

The belief held by Cindy Collins and so many abstinence educators across the country that abstinence is part of, as she puts it, "God's plan for this generation" goes far toward explaining their disregard for data on whether such teachings actually reduce teen pregnancy or sexually transmitted diseases. For Christian conservatives, avoiding such public health consequences is secondary; their primary concern is to lead young people away from any sexual activity that God would find unpleasing—meaning any sexual contact outside of marriage. Before Pat Ware joined the HHS staff, she testified before Congress about the dangers of "mutual masturbation"—a sexual activity with no public health consequences at all.[28] Bush AIDS advisor Joe McIlhaney, speaking at a meeting of the president's AIDS advisory council, stated that the goal of abstinence-only education is to prevent not just risky sexual practices but also "any contact that creates arousal."[29] Their comments reveal the gulf between the abstinence-only strategy and approaches guided by public health results: masturbation or a passionate kiss can certainly arouse—maybe, depending upon your perspective, they even displease God—but they just as surely can't spread HIV or cause pregnancy. While providers of comprehensive sex education and promoters of safe sex are in the business of saving lives, abstinence educators are primarily in the business of saving souls. The two camps are not really in a battle over data, but in one over goals: between protecting health here on earth and seeking salvation in the hereafter.

In speaking about abstinence, Bush has been careful to indicate to his base which set of concerns he shares. In a New Hampshire speech during the early days of his 2000 campaign, Bush spoke warmly of the True Love Waits program and then said, "Our teenagers feel the pressures of complex times, but also the upward pull of a better nature"—a reference, of course, to the "upward pull" of God.[30]

Who's in Charge

After years of trying to block taxpayer-supported sex education, the drive for abstinence represented a turnabout in strategy for the Christian right. "They called us Communists in the 1960s for promoting sex education, but they lost that particular battle in the culture wars," says Bill Smith, public policy director for SIECUS. "So they had to shift tactics. They said, instead of fighting programs, let's get funding for our own, and they moved to the content issue." The Heritage Foundation drafted the original legislative language defining the abstinence-only program, and ultraconservative Senator Rick Santorum was the first to introduce it. Soon after it was written into law in 1996, the Christian Coalition entered the fray to lobby for a $150 million increase in funding levels—an amount that's been exceeded under George W. Bush.[31] The Abstinence Clearinghouse, created the following year to coordinate the publicly financed explosion of abstinence programs across the country, is led almost entirely by religious conservatives. Sitting on the advisory board with abstinence educators from such programs as Why kNOw? (Allicia Ladd's curriculum of choice) are representatives of Christian right lobby groups such as Focus on the Family, the Family Research Council, and Concerned Women for America; proselytizing operations such as Summit Ministries and Coral Ridge Ministries; and the Heritage Foundation.[32] While the Heritage Foundation is, to a great extent, the brains behind abstinence-only, publishing papers that seek to link teen sexuality with suicide or that promote model abstinence-only programs, Christian right groups serve as the abstinence lobby's muscle in Washington. Bill Smith, who has lobbied against abstinence-only funding, says that often when he visits the office of a congressional swing voter, lobbyists from the Heritage Foundation, the Family Research Council, the Traditional Values Coalition, the Christian Coalition, Focus on the Family, or Concerned Women for America have beaten him to the door.

The earliest abstinence programs, under Ronald Reagan, were small pilots, averaging only about $4 million a year; during Newt Gingrich's reign in Congress, aided by pressure from a concerted Christian right lobby, that amount rose to around $97 million a year. When Bush got into office, the Heritage Foundation began to argue for significant funding increases for abstinence-only by putting out reports claiming federal and state governments spend $12 on family planning, safe sex, and condom promotion for every $1 spent on abstinence programs, an analysis that was soon being replicated by Bush administration officials.[33] The comparisons are ridiculous—based on lumping together all Medicaid and Title X family planning funding (which covers pricey medical services) and comparing that to dedicated abstinence-only education dollars. A more appropriate comparison would show abstinence dollars loom large: the only federal grants that pay for comprehensive sex education come from the CDC's Division of Adolescent and School Health, whose total prevention budget is around $48 million, an amount dwarfed by current abstinence spending.[34] Nevertheless, George Bush has called for funding parity, seeking early on in his term to double abstinence-only spending and then, in his 2005 budget, to double it again. The funds, in Bill Smith's view, are "*the* deliverable to the party's right-wing base." Smith recalls an informal conversation he had with HHS Secretary Tommy Thompson in early 2003: when Smith brought up his concerns about the abstinence-only funding, Thompson said, "I don't really go for that stuff—but you know it has to be there."

Abstinence-only advocates have made significant inroads across the country. The Southern Baptist Convention claims that in the ten years since it launched its "True Love Waits" program, 2.4 million teens have signed its virginity pledge. According to the Alan Guttmacher Institute, in 1988 only one in fifty sex education teachers taught abstinence-only; by 1995, one in four teachers did. By 1999, 35 percent of all school districts mandated abstinence-only education, and an additional 51 percent required that abstinence be taught as the preferred option.[35] And these programs have multiplied thanks to the Bush administration's generosity.

If Thompson himself isn't an abstinence-only backer, he's a rarity in the federal government these days. Bush has put passionate proponents of the approach in key staff and advisory positions throughout his Department of Health and Human Services, from deputy secretary Claude Allen, an advocate of abstinence-only since his days as health secretary in the state of Virginia, to Alma Golden, supervisor of the department's family planning programs, who used to run an abstinence-only organization called Virginity Rules. Golden has used her Bush administration perch to encourage federally funded clinics to coach abstinence to their clients—even though their mission is to provide medical services, not education. Abstinence-only proponents and practitioners make up nearly half of the president's sprawling AIDS advisory council, and Bush appointed abstinence advocates to an advisory council to CDC director Julie Gerberding and to an FDA advisory council on reproductive drugs. Former White House spokesperson Ari Fleischer once said of the Clinton White House, "If Planned Parenthood wanted it, the previous administration favored it," and Bush has made every effort to turn that around. "We're getting nothing but support from the Bush administration," Leslee Unruh, the Abstinence Clearinghouse president, told the *Washington Post* during Bush's first year in office. "He has personally talked to me about doing anything and everything he can to support abstinence-until-marriage education."[36] He has also sent administration officials to Unruh's conferences to teach her member organizations how to snare federal grants.[37] Beyond his staff picks, President Bush has again and again made it clear that abstinence-only is his own strategy of choice. "In order to help people help themselves, I strongly believe that we must encourage teen abstinence programs," he said at a speech at a South Carolina high school during a July 2002 push for welfare reauthorization. "We've got to help people understand that, one, it's okay to abstain. And, secondly, having a baby out of wedlock early in life is going to make it awfully tough—awfully tough on the child, awfully tough on the mom. We've got to make it clear that we've got a health issue when it comes to sexually transmitted disease, and that we've got to deal with it in an upfront way with our youngsters. You know, I've heard all the talk about the abstinence programs, and this that and the other"—apparently a reference to the lack of supportive research—"but let me just be perfectly plain. If you're worried about teenage pregnancy, or if you're worried about sexually transmitted disease, abstinence works every single time."[38] Indeed, Bush has signaled so clearly abstinence is official White House policy that when anyone in his administration breaks ranks, the Christian right explodes.

In early 2002, Secretary of State Colin Powell appeared on MTV to speak to an international youth audience. When a young woman in Italy asked his thoughts on the Catholic Church's opposition to condoms as a way to prevent AIDS, Powell responded in strong terms. "It is important that the whole international community come together, speak candidly about it, forget about taboos, forget about conservative ideas with respect to what you should tell young people about," he said. "It's the lives of young people that are put at risk by unsafe sex, and therefore, protect yourself. . . . In my own judgment, condoms are a way to prevent infection, and therefore, I not only support their use, I encourage their use among people who are sexually active and need to protect themselves."[39] The response was immediate: Donald Wildmon of the American Family Association excoriated Powell for "tell[ing] the kids of this world to ignore their parents, ignore their pastors and priests and the teachings of Scripture, and instead listen to him and the hedonists of Planned Parenthood" and urged his members to write to Powell and the president. Ken Connor, then president of the Family Research Council, called Powell's remarks "irresponsible" and "reckless" and complained that they "could lead millions of young people to believe that condoms prevent STDs." (They do.) The Traditional Values Coalition, Concerned Women for America, and other family values groups joined Wildmon's group in putting out action alerts. Even though the president has himself voiced support for condoms as an element in HIV prevention, all of them insisted that Powell was, in the words of Focus on the Family's Pete Winn, undermining "the stated policy of the Bush administration." When, in the wake of this outcry, Bush reiterated his support for abstinence as "the only completely effective way to prevent unwanted pregnancies and sexually transmitted diseases," Connor responded, "Bravo!" Concerned Women for America's Michael Schwartz pronounced Bush "the best defender of that program. He was its best defender as governor of Texas, he really believes in it, he understands why it is good, and his words today were fantastic."[40]

Earlier in Bush's tenure, the family values lobby won a similar victory. In July 2001, Surgeon General David Satcher issued a report on teen sexuality that was received by such mainstream medical organizations as the American Academy of Family Physicians as smart and scientifically sound; it was also praised by editorial pages across the country and by religious leaders working in communities at high risk for teen pregnancy and HIV, such as the Washington, D.C.–based Black Church Initiative.[41] Though the report sought to appease the family values lobby by praising the abstinence message and the institution of marriage, it also responded to the data on successful interventions by calling for clear and accurate sex education and easy access to condoms. The report affirmed the conclusions of studies that sex education does not encourage earlier or more sexual activity, abstinence-only education has had no proven successes, and the belief that gay youth can be counseled straight through reparative therapy is a fiction. The very same cast of characters—the Traditional Values Coalition, the Family Research Council, Focus on the Family—responded, with the Family Research Council complaining that Satcher's report sought to "destigmatize so-called sexual orientation" and support "so-called safe sex," and Focus on the Family calling for Satcher's immediate resignation.[42] Foreshadowing Powell's treatment eight months later, the White House distanced itself from the report and began floating names for a possible Satcher replacement, while Ari Fleischer told reporters, "The president continues to believe that abstinence and abstinence education only is the most effective way to prevent AIDS, to prevent unwanted pregnancy." Within four months, in November 2001, Satcher, who had spoken upon release of his report of "a conspiracy of silence when it comes to sexuality," had announced that he would step down at the end of his term.[43]

Follow the Money

Abstinence education has been used as a blunt political tool in other ways. Favored political constituencies have been rewarded with abstinence funds and optional evaluations, while organizations that don't line up behind the abstinence-only approach have been subjected to punitive audits. Abstinence-only state block grants date back to 1996, but the SPRANS funding stream, which allows the federal government to offer grants directly to community groups, was first implemented by the Bush administration in 2001. Congress initially seeded the program with $20 million, a number Bush has sought to nearly quadruple. A quick glance at these grantees during 2001, 2002, and 2003 reveals some disturbing, if familiar, patterns: more than $6 million in grants—some as large as $800,000—to pro-life "crisis pregnancy centers." More than $7 million to overtly Christian organizations, such as Georgia's Metro Atlanta Youth for Christ and Arkansas's Mid-South Christian Ministries. Zero dollars to Muslim, Jewish, Hindu, Buddhist, or other non-Christian religious charities. Several grants to overtly political groups advocating pro-life or family values positions, such as the Tri-County Right to Life Education Foundation in Ohio; the New Jersey Family Policy Council, an affiliate of Focus on the Family; and the Virginia-based Institute for Youth Development, run by Shepherd Smith. Throughout the Bush years, there was one lone SPRANS grant to a Planned Parenthood, for $127,000.[44] These patterns appear far less random when you look at who hands out the money.

While HHS refused to provide a list of grant applications that were denied, the agency did respond to a Freedom of Information Act request for a list of the independent experts the agency tapped for grant review panels from 2001 to 2003. The list is startling. It includes public health officials from nine states, as well as three representatives from legitimate medical bodies such as the American Academy of Pediatrics. But it lacks any nationally respected experts on sexuality education and pregnancy prevention, whether from the Kaiser Foundation, SIECUS, the Alan Guttmacher Institute, Planned Parenthood, or prestigious universities. Instead it includes nine representatives of Christian evangelizing outfits such as Summit Ministries, the Turning Point, and the National Association of Evangelicals—and, as with the grantee list, it doesn't include a single representative of a non-Christian religious organization. There are about fifteen representatives of local abstinence-only providers or clearinghouses, but they are far outnumbered by representatives of overtly political Christian right lobby groups. The list includes two representatives of Focus on the Family; three from the Family Research Council, including Robert Knight, an author of the Defense of Marriage Act; three from Concerned Women for America, including founder Beverly LaHaye and chief lobbyist Michael Schwartz; representatives of the Christian Coalition, the Traditional Values Coalition, the Heritage Foundation, Paul Weyrich's Free Congress Foundation, and such local social conservative lobbies as the New Jersey Family Policy Council (also a grantee). The list also includes five representatives from the Medical Institute for Sexual Health, the Austin-based organization whose director, Joe McIlhaney, claims to debunk condom effectiveness. And it includes congressional operatives for the family values lobby such as House Republican aide Roland Foster, who has used his perch as a Government Reform subcommittee staffer to instigate audits of AIDS groups that promote condom use.[45] The Bush administration has effectively turned over hundreds of millions of dollars to the Christian right to distribute as it sees fit.

While these organizations control the pursestrings, sending money to favored family values groups, organizations with a comprehensive approach to sex education have had their funding threatened. The targeted groups include two AIDS organizations that do explicit HIV prevention among gay men with the aid of the CDC and three organizations that had initiated a lobbying campaign against abstinence-only funding: Planned Parenthood, SIECUS, and Advocates for Youth. (Planned Parenthood receives millions in Title X dollars to provide family planning services at its clinics and the other two organizations receive small CDC grants to produce sex education materials targeting parents and teachers.) Advocates for Youth, which had received grants from the CDC for years without ever undergoing an audit, suddenly underwent three audits by Bush administration officials, two by the CDC and one by the

General Accounting Office. "You don't have to be paranoid," says Advocates for Youth president James Wagoner, "when you have an eighteen-year partnership with the CDC, never having been audited, and then you see three waves of audits in eighteen months." Wagoner says the White House's obsession with his organization seems to date back to an internal memo leaked to the *Washington Post* in July 2001, in which HHS staffer Boyd Work, a Catholic deacon, responded to a guide Advocates for Youth had authored that was designed to help parents discuss sexual health with their kids. "You should know that the secretary [Tommy Thompson] is a devout Roman Catholic. . . . Do you think he'll buy off on the nature and scope of the content?" Work wrote. "Advocates for Youth, on their Web site and in their press releases, are ardent critics of the Bush administration. Mmmm."[46] Wagoner says the group's work to educate members of Congress about the censorship of contraceptive information built into the abstinence-only initiative drew attention as well. "What does it mean when the audit mechanism can be used selectively, politically, whenever agencies use a science-based approach at odds with ideology of people in the administration?" he asks. "In many ways it's our belief that abstinence is becoming the flagship issue driving public health research to the edges. They're so committed to this approach, and it's so outside proven public health methods, that they'll change the science or censor it."

And while Advocates for Youth and other purveyors of comprehensive sex education fight off audits, oversight of abstinence-only programs lags. The federal evaluation of abstinence-only programs was due in 2003, but Mathematica had yet to release its report as of spring 2004, and may not release it until 2005. Meanwhile, the negative independent data continues to accumulate. Peter Bearman, the same Columbia University researcher whose earlier study of True Love Waits had provided a flash of validation for abstinence-only advocates, completed a large-scale NIH-funded study in March 2004 of 12,000 teens. Bearman had first interviewed the teens at ages twelve to eighteen; in this study, he interviewed them again six years later. Bearman found that 88 percent of the teenagers who had pledged virginity-until-marriage years earlier ended up having sex before they married, and that STD rates were identical among those who had pledged virginity and those who had not. He also found that virginity pledgers were less likely to use condoms (40 percent of male pledgers reported condom use, versus 60 percent of male non-pledgers), less likely to seek out medical care for STDs, and less likely to be aware they had an STD at all. "Because pledgers make a public pledge, the sex that they have is more likely to be hidden," Bearman concluded. "It is also more likely to be unsafe."[47]

Evidence has also accumulated that abstinence-only education is unpopular with parents. A nationwide survey by the Kaiser Family Foundation found at least 85 percent of parents would like their teenagers to be given the tools to delay sex and to receive information about how to put on a condom, how to use contraceptives, and where to get them—in other words, comprehensive sex education. Only 15 percent of parents want abstinence-only lessons, a number that's even smaller than the total population of evangelical social conservatives in America. The survey also found that while only one in five Americans support federally funded abstinence education, half of all evangelicals do.[48]

Bush once promised to eliminate all federal programs without proven results, "stopping the cycle of funding decisions based on wishes, rather than performance information."[49] But as the prospect of upbeat abstinence-only data appears ever more remote, Bush has asked Congress to double the amount of federal dollars going to abstinence-only education in 2005 to $270 million, and he has begun to export the abstinence-only approach to Africa. Under pressure from the Christian right, Bush targeted a third of his global AIDS prevention dollars to abstinence-only education, or about 10 percent of its total $15 billion budget, and sold his global AIDS administrator on the idea. "There's no evidence in generalized populations that a broad-based use of condoms as the backbone of prevention efforts has worked," Randall Tobias told *World,* the conservative Christian magazine, in March 2004. "I've come to believe, not just intuitively or by guessing about it, but based on a lot of data that we've been able to collect, that abstinence is the best approach."[50] Bush's global abstinence push came at a time when the abstinence-only movement had already set its sites on Africa. The

Southern Baptist Convention's True Love Waits program has been active in Uganda since 1994, and the religious body has set up some thirty clubs in South Africa, Guyana, and Kenya since then. The Assemblies of God, a Pentecostal denomination, brings the abstinence message into African secondary schools. The Abstinence Clearinghouse launched AbstinenceAfrica.org in 2004 to support abstinence-only campaigns in twenty-three countries across the continent of Africa and to "provide up-to-date information regarding . . . the Global AIDS Initiative."[51] An educator with Why kNOw?, the same curriculum Allicia Ladd uses in western Tennessee, has gone to Uganda to promote the group's lesson plans there. And the interest among evangelical Christian organizations in Bush's global AIDS initiative is high: in the first round of applications, Franklin Graham's group Samaritan's Purse, Chuck Colson's Prison Fellowship Ministries, the Association of Christian Schools, and Campus Crusade for Christ were among the organizations that applied for funds to promulgate the abstinence-only message in Africa.[52] Public health experts doubt these evangelical character-based programs can successfully reduce HIV infections without encouraging condom use as well—but perhaps that was never the point. As Graham said in testimony to the Senate in 2000, "Education is inadequate without the teaching that the only reliable way to avoid contracting AIDS through sexual contact is by maintaining a lifelong monogamous relationship. But just as important, we must recognize that the ability to adopt such dramatic lifestyle changes is almost impossible without the moral conviction that sex outside of a marriage between a man and a woman is contrary to God's law. This crisis will be curbed only when the moral teachings of God's Word permeate African society."[53]

THE GLOBAL CRUSADE

ON JANUARY 22, 2001, the twentieth anniversary of *Roe v. Wade* and his first working day in office, George W. Bush issued an executive order reinstating Ronald Reagan's Mexico City Policy. When Senator Sam Brownback announced Bush's decision that afternoon to 100,000 protesters at the annual March for Life, the crowd burst into cheers.[1] Pro-choice leaders, on the other hand, were caught off guard. Bush had run as a social conservative during a few closely fought primary races, but he had run a disciplined general election campaign in which he convincingly portrayed himself as a moderate. He called himself "pro-life," but relegated the issue to the background; despite pressure from the Christian right, he refused to publicly commit to an anti-abortion litmus test for judicial nominees. He even floated pro-choice Pennsylvania governor Tom Ridge as a possible running mate, prompting some prominent Christian right leaders to issue threats about bolting the ticket.[2] So when Bush arrived in Washington, pro-lifers considered him a cautious ally, at best.[3]

Bush's speedy reinstatement of the Mexico City Policy caused Kate Michelman, president of the pro-choice advocacy group NARAL, to complain that he "has shed the mantle of moderation very quickly." But that was likely Bush's intent. With the simple flick of a pen he had managed to send a very loud message to his base. The conservative *National Review* saw it as "a powerful symbolic gesture," as did the *Washington Times:* "The fact that this was his first order of business as president certainly suggests the importance Mr. Bush attaches to the abortion issue, a fact not lost on pro-abortion groups."[4] The Mexico City Policy itself wasn't a major pro-life priority—Eagle Forum founder Phyllis Schlafly, who served as MC at the March for Life, even grumbled to the crowd that reinstating the policy had never been the march's goal—but

Bush's executive order was received as a timely pledge of allegiance to the anti-abortion cause. Then Family Research Council president Ken Connor called the announcement "a welcome indicator he intends to stick to his pro-life campaign promise."[5]

Bush himself barely seemed to understand what he'd signed. In his memo to the U.S. Agency for International Development (USAID) reinstating the order, he wrote, "It is my conviction that taxpayer funds should not be used to pay for abortions," seeming unaware that direct U.S. funding of overseas abortions had been illegal since 1973, prohibited by a law passed just months after *Roe v. Wade*.[6] Bush press secretary Ari Fleischer, answering questions from reporters, repeated the error, saying the president had reinstated the policy because he "opposes using taxpayer dollars to pay for abortions."[7] In fact, Bush's Mexico City Policy accomplishes something more wide-ranging: it restricts what organizations receiving U.S. aid can do with private funds, or even public funds from their own governments. Now, once an organization accepts a family planning grant from the United States, it can no longer use its own separate funds to provide abortions, refer women for abortions, educate clients that abortion is an option, or even lobby for safe abortion access. The policy is so restrictive that reproductive rights advocates have dubbed it the "global gag rule." Comments he made some days later, during a White House meeting with Catholic charity leaders, only strengthened the perception that Bush hadn't understood the policy he had reinstated. In his remarks, characterized in the *Washington Post* as "halting and notably imprecise," he called it "the money from Mexico, you know, that thing, the executive order I signed about Mexico City."[8] Though a Reagan official had first announced the policy at a Mexico City population conference in 1984, the policy had nothing to do with Mexico in particular, but rather with the fate of tens of millions of family planning dollars destined for the developing world. It seemed that President Bush, in an effort to offer a "symbolic gesture" to his domestic political supporters, had casually imposed an international policy he hadn't bothered to read—one that would have profound effects on women around the globe. In the coming years, he would make several other high-stakes decisions on global health policy, from defunding family planning groups to strong-arming a family values agenda at the United Nations, that were designed only to appease his Christian right basea at home.

In the end, Bush's Mexico City Policy didn't even much excite the Christian right: Judie Brown, president of the American Life League, told reporters, "It's not meaningless, but there is so much more that he could have done."[9] Even more ironically, the ill-conceived policy, whose intent was to reduce the number of abortions in the developing world, may actually increase them. While the impact of the Reagan-era policy was never thoroughly evaluated, this time around, governments and charitable organizations have examined the evidence carefully. According to a September 2003 report on Bush's Mexico City Policy by the European parliament, "As clinics close and access to reproductive services becomes more difficult for lack of funding, less poor women in Europe and worldwide can afford contraception, *leading to an increase in unwanted pregnancies—and consequently abortions. . . .* The impact of the Mexico City Policy thus is the opposite of its intention." (Emphasis added.)[10] Another report issued in late 2003, this one authored by Population Action International and a consortium of other international family planning groups, sketches out exactly how Bush's policy has worked to increase—rather than decrease—abortions in Romania.[11] Deaths from illegal abortions were so common under the rule of Nicolae Ceausescu that the government immediately legalized abortion after his 1989 ouster. Since then, however, a government policy of reimbursing the cost of abortion services, while contraceptives aren't covered at all, has turned abortion into the primary form of family planning—to the point that the average Romanian woman has more abortions than she has children. Against this backdrop, independent reproductive health organizations stepped in to encourage the use of contraception and reduce Romanian women's dependence on abortion. These same organizations— unable to comply with the Mexico City Policy because steering women away from abortion requires talking about it—have now lost access to USAID funds and free contraceptive supplies. "Although everyone working in reproductive health in Romania is committed to reducing rates of abortion," the report concludes, "the Global Gag Rule is compromising efforts to do so."

Disruptions in HIV-prevention work have emerged as another unintended consequence of Bush's policy: In Lesotho, a small southern African nation with one of the planet's highest HIV rates—one in four women there are infected—the country's Planned Parenthood association was the only group serving as a conduit for USAID contraceptive supplies, and the group had distributed nearly half a million of them in the three years before Bush took office. Since Bush's executive order, that supply has been eliminated. Family planning associations in Cameroon and St. Lucia were likewise forced to end HIV-prevention programs serving youth due to the loss of USAID funds.[12]

When Bush first reinstated the Mexico City Policy, Austin Ruse, president of the pro-life Catholic Family and Human Rights Institute (C-FAM), celebrated the maneuver as "a great blow to the other side." And to the extent that Bush's decision was embraced by the Christian right as a policy—not just a symbol—it was in this sense. "Organizations that openly proclaim they believe they have a mission to undermine [anti-abortion] laws have been massively subsidized by the Clinton administration," Douglas Johnson, legislative director for the National Right to Life Committee, told NPR. "It's engendered a lot of resentment."[13]

By this measure, Bush's policy has succeeded quite well. International Planned Parenthood Federation (IPPF), for example, tops the list of groups whose message Right to Life opposes. In the eyes of the Christian right, Planned Parenthood is more than a pro-choice opponent—it is a leading force in the nation's moral degeneration. Life Dynamics, a Texas-based pro-life research and advocacy organization, has claimed that Planned Parenthood is a "pedophile protection racket" and called for the group to be prosecuted.[14] The Family Research Council has described Planned Parenthood as a "leftist organization" engaged in an "assault on religion"; a profit-mad "cartel" that nefariously promotes "rampant sexual promiscuity" among susceptible teenage girls in order to build an abortion and contraception empire.[15] IPPF is indeed formidable: after fifty years in existence, it now comprises the most extensive network of family planning organizations in the world, reaching 180 countries and offering the only reproductive health care of any kind in many impoverished rural areas throughout the developing world. When IPPF refused to comply with Bush's gag rule, the federation and its affiliates lost $12 million a year, more than a quarter of their unrestricted income, as well as a five-year $75 million grant just on the verge of approval—all in all, says director-general Steven Sinding, "a very substantial loss." Sinding says the policy forced a "devastating wedge" into the family planning world, as clinics faced a choice between maintaining their full range of services and rejecting millions of dollars in USAID grants. The Population Action International report cites clinic closures in country after country. In Kenya, for example, five family planning clinics were shuttered after having their USAID funding cut off for refusing to comply with the policy; one facility was the only family planning center serving some 300,000 people in a vast poor neighborhood of Nairobi.[16]

Family planning organizations that decided to comply with Bush's policy and retain American financial support lost their freedom of speech instead. Though deaths from botched abortions are a distant memory in the United States, the developing world's restrictive abortion laws have forced some 20 million illegal procedures every year, causing more than 70,000 deaths annually.[17] In recent years, several nations—even socially conservative Nepal—have responded to this health crisis by liberalizing abortion laws, or at least by opening up the conversation. Ethiopia, which just emerged from decades of military rule in the early 1990s, had just begun to engage in a national debate about reforming its own restrictive abortion laws when the Mexico City Policy came down. Now every family planning organization there that receives U.S. assistance, even the ones who mop up after botched illegal abortions, will be forced to keep mum as the debate unfolds.[18] Barbara Crane, the vice-president of Ipas, which works to expand safe abortion access in the developing world, says that close to twenty countries where USAID supports family planning are engaged in active debates about whether to liberalize their abortion policies. Ipas affiliates in Kenya and Ethiopia—Ipas refused to comply with the Mexico City Policy—are leading campaigns for more abortion access, Crane says, "but it's hard when other organizations, dependent on US-AID funds, hang back, stay on the sidelines, see the problems of unsafe abortions everyday but are prohibited from speaking to the issues."

A former staffer at the State Department's Bureau of Population, Refugees, and Migration told me that as bureau officials prepared to implement the Mexico City Policy, they often had contact with the White House's domestic policy staff, including domestic policy advisor Josh Bolton, an indicator of how much domestic concerns drove the policy. "Under Clinton all of our interactions were with the National Security Council staff," recalls the former State Department staffer, who asked not to be named. "I did wonder what role the Domestic Policy Council had in foreign programs." This curiosity would soon become the norm.

THE PAPER CHASE

When direct-mail expert Richard Viguerie and conservative political activist Howard Phillips launched their campaign to "defund the left" during the early Reagan years, Planned Parenthood was one of their primary targets from the start. In their view, shared throughout the emerging Christian right, Planned Parenthood and other pro-choice organizations were using federal funds to "subsidize liberal antifamily values" and, perhaps more importantly, to oppose the Reagan revolution.[19] The original Mexico City Policy, announced in 1984, came out of this flurry of activity. When their drive to defund the left was revived in the mid-1990s, conservative think tanks such as the Heritage Foundation again singled out Planned Parenthood as a target, while the Gingrich-led Congress consistently passed budgets that reduced contributions to the UN Population Fund, since the UN agency and Planned Parenthood are the two largest family planning funders in the world.[20]

Bush's Mexico City Policy appears in retrospect to have been the first salvo in an attempt by the administration to exercise the power of the purse—the United States being the world's largest government source of family planning funds—over organizations at the top of the pro-life enemies list. When I asked Janice Crouse, a senior staffer at Concerned Women for America, what she saw as the biggest family values victories under George W. Bush, she listed two things: his stepped up activity against sex trafficking, and his effort to "follow the money." "One of the things that has been a problem for us is that the radical nongovernmental organizations are so well funded," she said. "They know how to get grant money, they know the political structures, and they are unified in their purpose to achieve reproductive services worldwide. We have been able to say, 'Where is this money going?' and we have been able to follow the trail. I think tracing the money and insisting that money go to groups that support the administration's values and policy positions is vitally important. And we've made a lot of progress." International Planned Parenthood had been decimated by the Mexico City Policy; the world's other largest provider of international family planning would be next.

In his 2002 budget request, the Bush administration included $25 million for the UN Population Fund, known as UNFPA. When Secretary of State Colin Powell appeared before Congress to make the case for the request, he praised the agency's "invaluable work" in maternal and child health care, family planning, cancer screening, and HIV prevention, and Congress responded in December 2001 by boosting the U.S. contribution to $34 million.[21] But that was before the Christian right lobby decided that blocking the funding would be, in the words of Concerned Women for America policy director Wendy Wright, "one of our big priorities."[22] By January 2002, the Population Research Institute, an organization closely linked with Austin Ruse's C-FAM, issued a report that claimed to document that UNFPA was complicit in China's restrictive population policy—a policy sometimes implemented through coerced abortions and sterilization. Though composed mostly of inconclusive anecdotes, the report made its way to the White House by means of Christian right lobbyists.[23] Meanwhile, Representative Chris Smith, a former executive director of New Jersey

Right to Life who continues to work in close coordination with pro-life activists, authored a letter claiming the UN agency was supporting forced abortions in China, while organizations such as Concerned Women for America launched a grassroots e-mail campaign demanding that Bush block the $34 million. According to the *Washington Post,* Concerned Women for America leaders Sandy Rios and Beverly LaHaye also put pressure on the administration's two leading evangelical liaisons, Tim Goeglein (a former Gary Bauer staffer) and Jay Lefkowitz (a former Dan Quayle aide, known for orchestrating Quayle's condemnation of fictional single-mom Murphy Brown) and on Bush's top political strategist Karl Rove. By the end of January, Bush abruptly announced he would withhold the $34 million pending a State Department investigation.[24]

In May 2002, the U.S. team returned an extremely inconvenient report. After a fourteen-day visit to Chinese officials, local UNFPA staffers, and clinics in five of the thirty-two rural counties where the UN agency is active in China, the investigators found "no evidence that the UNFPA has knowingly supported or participated in the management of a program of coercive abortion or involuntary sterilization." To the contrary, the inspectors found that coercive abortion policies had been altered by UNFPA's presence, replaced in many cases by a fully voluntary approach that offers clients multiple contraceptive choices along with information and counseling. UNFPA had even negotiated to get birth quotas lifted for families living in its pilot counties. The Bush investigators also affirmed that UNFPA consistently voiced "strong opposition" to coercive policies, calling them "contrary to the principles of free choice."[25] A delegation of British parliamentarians, which included an outspoken pro-life leader, came to the same conclusion a few weeks later, finding that "UNFPA's involvement appears to be encouraging reformers within China" and arguing it was "vitally important that UNFPA remains actively involved."[26]

Despite such official exoneration, the Bush administration, in what the *Washington Post* called "an astonishing display of hypocrisy," withheld the $34 million anyway.[27] Lefkowitz was widely credited with drafting an unsigned three-page legal analysis that provided a pretext for the decision, through the creative application of a 1985 law against direct U.S. funding of coerced abortions known as Kemp-Kasten. The analysis claimed that even if UNFPA did not "knowingly" support Chinese population policies, inadvertent support was enough to justify withholding the spending. That the State Department investigation was disregarded; that Lefkowitz, whose bailiwick was domestic politics, was involved in the legal analysis rather than State Department lawyers—these were just the latest measures of how much Bush's international family planning policy was being driven exclusively by domestic political advisors and domestic political concerns. As with the Mexico City Policy, the net effect of this decision would be to increase, not decrease, abortions. The United Nations released estimates that the lost $34 million, constituting 12 percent of its budget, would have prevented some 4,700 maternal deaths, 77,000 infant and child deaths, and 800,000 abortions worldwide.[28] European Union leaders found the decision so "counterproductive" in the fight against poverty and maternal deaths that they launched a campaign to fill the "decency gap" themselves. In July 2002 the EU donated $38 million to UNFPA and IPPF to make up for their lost U.S. funds.[29]

In the closing months of 2002, Chris Smith and his allies turned their sights on two other targets: a $65 million USAID grant for international HIV-prevention work to the Population Council, an international public health organization, and a $3 million congressional appropriation to the World Health Organization (WHO). Each of them, pro-life activists discovered, had ties to the early abortion pill, RU-486, which Smith has called "a baby pesticide."[30] WHO houses a research entity that has conducted studies of the drug, while the Population Council holds the RU-486 patent. Approval of the pill by the FDA in September 2000 was a crushing disappointment to the family values lobby, which had conducted a major campaign against it, led in part by Christian book author and gynecologist David Hager.[31] With Bush on the verge of announcing his global AIDS initiative, Smith didn't gain traction on the Population Council's HIV grant, but before year's end, Bush awarded Hager with a position as an FDA advisor on reproductive drugs, and the administration froze the $3 million slated for WHO. Assistant secretary of state Richard Boucher reached for an even broader interpretation of Kemp-Kasten this time, telling reporters, "We can't support any activity that supports abortion as a method of family planning or that motivates or coerces people into practicing abortion, so we would not use our money to support RU-486 research."[32] Representative Carolyn Maloney and several colleagues wrote to Powell in alarm, charging that the State Department's reading of Kemp-Kasten was so "strained" it could even require the United States to pull its funding from the World Bank.[33]

The following year Bush used the specter of forced abortions in China to defund another highly respected international health program, the Reproductive Health for Refugees Consortium, which had received $1 million from the United States the previous year to provide health services for populations affected by war.[34] In September 2003, even as the president was pushing his global AIDS bill through Congress, the administration cut off funding for a major effort by the consortium to address AIDS and reproductive health among youth in conflict-torn nations such as Angola, the Congo, Liberia, and Sri Lanka. How was it justified? One of the consortium's seven member-organizations, Marie Stopes International, partners in China with the UN Population Fund. Like UNFPA, Marie Stopes has an unequivocal position against coercive abortions and works in China to reduce them, but according to Michael Schwartz of Concerned Women for America, "When you're working hand in glove with people who do what the Chinese do, you can't keep clean."[35] In fact, from the Mexico City Policy to the defunding of UNFPA and Marie Stopes, "this has nothing much to do with efforts to prevent abortion," says IPPF's Steven Sinding. "The actual effect of these policies is to increase abortions." And to hamper Bush's global war on AIDS. "Are contraceptive supplies being held back?" says one USAID official, who asked not to be named. "Yes, they are. Because Marie Stopes and International Planned Parenthood are the two best family planning programs in the world and we can't fund them." But more important to Bush than preventing actual abortions or HIV infections was his success at bankrupting organizations despised by the Christian right. "The goal of defunding us was established more than twenty years ago," says Sinding. "If the global gag rule didn't exist, if Kemp-Kasten didn't exist, the leadership were committed to finding mechanisms to defund us anyway." The same week he defunded the refugee consortium, Bush expanded his Mexico City Policy to cover not only USAID grants, but all State Department funds.[36]

"It Feels Like McCarthyism"

Steven Sinding, the IPPF director-general, headed up USAID's Office of Population back when Reagan devised the original Mexico City Policy—and Sinding was the one responsible for implementing it. Most groups complied to keep their funding, Sinding says, but complying was far easier then. Then USAID administrator Peter McPherson was "absolutely committed" to saving family planning, and so he limited the scope of the policy. "There was a determination to keep our hands off the domestic scene, so they applied the policy only to foreign NGO's [nongovernmental organizations], not NGO's based in the United States, and they didn't apply it to foreign governments, because of the sovereignty principle," Sinding recalls. "And in those days, US-AID was the only place this landed. State wasn't involved, HHS wasn't involved, as they are now. So the extent of the thing is new." Sinding himself freely spoke "anywhere and everywhere" about the impact of the policy and no one tried to muzzle him. Now, he says, "there is an atmosphere of fear and intimidation that exceeds anything I experienced during the Reagan years." The woman who now holds his old job as population director rarely speaks publicly about the policy. And Sinding describes a recent trip to Washington, in the fall of 2003, when US-AID staffers chose not to meet with him in the building and set up a rendezvous in a local coffee shop instead. "It feels like McCarthyism," he says.

The fear factor intensified after Colin Powell sent his Christmas 2002 cable to USAID missions around the world. It read in part, "All operating units should ensure that USAID-funded programs and publications reflect appropriately the policies of the Bush administration.

Careful review of all programs and publications should ensure that USAID is not perceived as using U.S. taxpayer funds to support activities that contradict our laws or policies, including trafficking of women and girls, legalization of drugs, injecting drug use, and abortion. . . . All operating units should review their own websites and any websites fully or partially funded by USAID to ensure the appropriateness of the material. . . . You should also review the appropriateness of the messages on the websites of our cooperating partners."[37] The cable sent administrators and grantees into a panic. One USAID grantee working on HIV prevention among drug users in Eastern Europe was cut off by his program officer during a phone call when the grantee used the term "needle exchange." A family planning grantee phoned her contact at USAID about the term "men who have sex with men," asking, "What do we call this now?" Another began a full audit of its Web site to see how often "abortion" popped up. "We have a strong sense that there's a volunteer staff searching the websites of our partner organizations for references to abortions," the USAID official recalls telling a group of grantees. The official also mentioned that she would be taking "abortion" out of the USAID search engine.

A series of e-mail exchanges in 2003 among USAID staffers and family planning grantees captures the climate that has prevailed at the agency since Powell sent his cable. The term "unwanted pregnancies," one USAID staffer suggested, was unimaginable to pro-lifers and so should be replaced by the more neutral "unintended pregnancies." Use of the term "unsafe abortion," referring to the unhygienic, illegal procedures that kill tens of thousands of women a year, should be avoided, as pro-lifers insist that no abortion is safe—from the embryo's perspective. Another document details a lengthy debate over the term "post-abortion care." The United Nations and international health organizations all share an understanding that the term does not refer to abortion provision, but rather to treating hemorrhages, infections, and other complications of abortions after the fact, as well as counseling women on future contraceptive use. Nevertheless, the word "abortion" carried so much stigma in this administration that public health officials spent months trying to dream up a euphemism.

"Bleeding in pregnancy program," "emergency post-pregnancy care," and half a dozen other alternatives were bandied about in the weeks after Powell's memo before experts finally won the argument to stick with the plain-language term. "If it is so controversial as an intervention that we have to change the name," one government health official wrote during the process, "what are the implications for the programs . . . ?" Sinding says that during his years running USAID's population program under Reagan, he never received a communication like the Powell cable, and "we were never told what language we could or couldn't use."

"In those days, you knew the people in the Reagan White House were just throwing a bone to the religious right," Sinding adds. "In this White House, you have the feeling that the price is much, much higher. The religious point of view is much more entrenched, they're much better organized, much better funded, and their infiltration of key positions at USAID and State means people have to be very careful what they say." According to the source at USAID, these political operatives police every public statement and press release, and in at least one documented case, e-mail communications. The official says this has created "a very fearful climate and a very constrained climate. We're very cautious about what we say on the phone, and we're very cautious about what we say in e-mail. Morale is plummeting."

The operatives include Garrett Grigsby and Les Munson, two former staffers for Senator Jesse Helms—the same senator who sponsored the legislation blocking U.S. foreign aid for abortion services back in 1973 and who proposed a constitutional amendment banning abortions at home. While in the senate, Helms led the attack against so many international treaties the *National Review* called him an "American sovereignty hero."[38] His protégés are now both well positioned as enforcers. Grigsby, who worked for Helms on the Senate Foreign Relations Committee for eleven years, holds the number two position in USAID's humanitarian assistance bureau, while Munson, who served as a Helms spokesperson, is chief of staff in USAID's Bureau for Global Health, which oversees the government's population program. Another important operative was attorney Louise Oliver (she recently moved to the Department of Labor), an abortion opponent who headed up the pro-life Society for Law, Life, and Religion while at Harvard Law. Bush made her a special assistant at the State Department's population bureau, permitting her to monitor U.S. delegations to key international family planning conferences. The pressure these ideologues bring to bear extends far beyond language, according to the USAID source. The official describes "huge pressure" to put money into faith-based organizations at the expense of clinics with health expertise; equally strong pressure not to fund emergency contraceptive pills, even in refugee situations where rape is rampant; and a disproportionate emphasis on "natural family planning," meaning the Vatican-approved rhythm method. In one recent incident, in April 2004, when Focus on the Family, the Traditional Values Coalition, and their far-right allies in Congress blew up after discovering that a federally funded international health conference would feature speakers from IPPF and UNFPA, Les Munson played a role in getting USAID to pull $150,000 it had pledged to the event.[39]

STORMING THE UNITED NATIONS

It's the middle of December 2003 and gusty winds are inverting umbrellas along K Street, Washington's lobbyist corridor, forcing a fierce competition for cabs. Upstairs, in the warm offices of Concerned Women for America (CWA), then–president Sandy Rios sits down for her daily talk radio taping, joking about her unfinished Christmas shopping and updating her studio guests on the prognosis of her severely disabled twenty-eight-year-old daughter, Sasha, hospitalized with sepsis. Rios speaks with real warmth about the hospital staff, who "care so deeply about life" that they talk Sasha through every aspect of her treatment, even though she's unable to respond. Before the taping, Rios asks her guests, Austin Ruse, president of C-FAM, and Jill Stanek, the nurse credited with inspiring the Born Alive Infant Protection Act (a pro-life bill that Bush signed in August 2002), to join her in prayer. She thanks God for bringing "a wonderful partner" into Austin's life (he had recently wed another prominent pro-life activist) and for the "privilege" of being Sasha's mother. "Father," she says, on the verge of tears, "words can't describe the joy it is to bring a child into the world and the lessons that are learned, whether it goes well or goes badly."

Once the taping begins, however, the humility and generosity of the moment evaporate; the language of motherhood and friendship slides into paranoia. Rios describes abortion as "horrific," "painful," and "not natural." Stanek warns that Plan B, the emergency contraceptive pill approved by FDA advisors that morning, will become the tool of teachers who have sex with their students and fathers who have sex with their daughters, of "rapists and male sexual predators" who will "keep a stash in their bedroom drawer or their pocket and give it to their young victim," of "sloppy" people involved in "illicit sex." Ruse tells us proponents of international family planning are "a contentious group of bullies," "sneaky elites" who are "going around democratic institutions," "trying to force their way into governments around the world using UN institutions that nobody has ever heard of . . . to push abortion." Rios mentions only one bright light in this world of aggression, deception, and moral decay: the new, staunchly pro-life delegations Bush has sent to represent the country at UN meetings on women, children, population, and AIDS. These delegations, which have included CWA's own Janice Crouse, have been "very strong" in navigating the United Nations' "treacherous waters," Rios says.

After the show, I sit down with Crouse, the executive director of CWA's Beverly LaHaye Institute, which studies women's issues "from a conservative, faith-based perspective." A former speechwriter for the first president Bush, Crouse has also co-authored a book on femininity with LaHaye, CWA's charismatic founder. As LaHaye's husband, Tim, finished writing his megabestselling series of Left Behind novels, in which he portrays the United Nations as the vehicle for a Satanic attempt to establish "one world government," Beverly LaHaye sought official observer status for her organization at the United Nations, where CWA now teams with organizations such as C-FAM to advocate for Christian fundamentalist values on the world stage. Crouse complains that meetings she attends at the State Department or Health and Human Services still include many liberals, some of whom she describes as bosom buddies of Hillary Clinton. "The one exception is at the United Nations, where the delegates are predominantly conservative and embrace mainstream American values," Crouse says. "This had not been the case previously." Jeanne Head, a leader of the National Right to Life Committee, has said Bush's delegate picks signal "a sea change" in U.S. policy.[40] For years Crouse was only able to attend UN meetings as an observer, "relegated to back rooms"; under Bush she served as an official delegate at a UN Children's Summit in May 2002 and at a meeting of the United Nation's Commission on the Status of Women in March 2003. Head was appointed a U.S. delegate for another event, a May 2001 meeting of the World Health Assembly.[41]

Activism at the United Nations by conservative evangelicals is a relatively new phenomenon, dating back only eight or ten years. The strong stance of many Christian right groups against international organizations made it difficult for them to gain approval as official private sector representatives, a status that allows NGOs to attend and lobby UN meetings. Only about 2,300 NGOs worldwide have won this status, and before Bush got into office, only a few conservative religious groups had done so. President Bush changed that landscape. Not only did he invite several Christian right lobbyists to become official U.S. delegates, but with Bush administration support, Focus on the Family, Priests for Life, Concerned Women for America, and the Family Research Council have all been accredited as NGO observers since 2001.[42]

Bush's newly conservative delegations first burst spectacularly onto the scene at that May 2002 Children's Summit in New York. In the past, delegations to such events typically included experts in the field such as the American Public Health Association, the American Medical Association, and the American Nurses Association; this time Bush chose not only Crouse but Bill Saunders of the Family Research Council and John Klink, a former UN negotiator for the Vatican. Representative Chris Smith served as a congressional observer.[43] The Vatican had long insisted phrases such as "reproductive health service" were code words for abortion, although the term is understood by the United Nations to include safe abortions only in countries where the procedure is legal; now Klink, the most experienced UN negotiator on the U.S. team, had an opportunity to put the weight of the United States behind the Catholic Church's position. Suddenly the U.S. delegation was echoing the Vatican stance, seeking to strike any language touching on reproductive rights in the summit document. "The behavior of the U.S. delegation was a big shock," recalls María Antonieta Alcalde, who attended as an NGO representative from Mexico. "It was ridiculous to see how paranoid the U.S. delegation was about the issue of abortion, looking at every aspect of the document to see where abortion might be hiding. Going to extremes, like saying they won't agree to health services for children living in war conditions, because that could be abortion-related, as many children in war situations face rape."

The U.S. negotiating team's misinterpretation of the language on "reproductive health" did not spring from lack of expertise. According to the former staffer at the State Department Bureau of Population, Refugees, and Migration, part of the staffer's job had been to supply administration officials with background analysis in preparation for the Children's Summit and other international conferences. "We tried to clarify the history of some of the language, such as 'reproductive health services,' what the U.S. position had been, and what the international consensus was on what the language meant," says the former population staffer, a specialist in reproductive health issues. "We literally got those memos bounced back to us with e-mails and phone calls saying, 'These positions are not in line with the administration's positions.' In effect saying, we don't care what you say, or what the facts are. This happened on the Children's Summit, where we as health policy professionals were not only being ignored but told to shut up. Instead they turned to the right-to-life groups, they turned to the Vatican, and they openly discussed with them negotiating strategies and language."

Bill Saunders of the Family Research Council brought along an agenda as well. The group had long condemned a landmark 1989 UN treaty on children's rights—a treaty that would serve as the foundation for discussion at the Children's Summit—as "a threat to the family." Bill Saunders even authored a treatise against it, in which he expressed alarm at its assertion of the right of youth to access health care, contraception, and sex education without parental consent and the right of children to be free of violence, including corporeal punishment. He has also argued that the treaty doesn't sufficiently endorse the husband-wife nuclear family.[44] Starting from an opening statement by Health Secretary Tommy Thompson, who declared that "abstinence is the only sure way of avoiding sexually transmitted disease," and continuing with the push by U.S. delegates for strong language on traditional marriage and parental rights, Family Research Council positions seemed to guide the U.S. stance.[45] Alcalde says U.S. delegates argued incessantly for the "right to life," yet "they were absolutely against people under eighteen being exempt from the death penalty." According to women's health expert Francoise Girard, who also served as an NGO representative at the summit, "It was about protecting a way of life, with strong nuclear families with married parents, and going after family planning, modern conception, sexuality education, and condom distribution."

At a Christian right strategy session in October 2001, Saunders told the crowd that under the leadership of "a pro-family President," the UN Children's Summit offered "a chance to roll back some of the advances of the Clinton Administration and really promote the family"; to do this, he argued, the U.S. delegation would need to "break some of the cohesion among the Latin Americans."[46] This Family Research Council strategy was adopted wholesale by the U.S. team. Leading up to the summit, the State Department cabled U.S. embassies throughout Central and South America, asking them to lobby their host governments to back U.S. efforts to remove language on "reproductive services."[47] During the course of the meeting, according to Loreto Leyton, a Chilean diplomat to the United Nations who represented the "Rio Group" of Latin American countries there, the Chilean foreign ministry in Santiago got calls from Washington "expressing concern about the position of my delegation." Leyton recalls that delegates from Argentina, Costa Rica, Brazil, and Peru received similar pressure. "We had an agreement one day, and the next day they had lobbied something completely different in Chile," Leyton recalls. "I said to one U.S. delegate, 'This is not fair play. This is not the way we negotiate here.' It was not a clean game."

Still, the Rio Group stood firm. "We don't support the thinking that 'reproductive rights' has to do with abortion, because in my country abortion is illegal, so that would be impossible," says Leyton. "We believe that adolescents have the right to have sexual health services, and that includes a wide range of services that a girl from twelve years old needs to have, but that has nothing to do with abortion." The U.S. delegation, finding itself isolated, joined forces with the Vatican and—despite the president's insistence, post-9/11, that "you're either with us or against us in the fight against terror"—with several Islamic countries to forward its agenda. These new alliances included nations suspected of supporting or harboring terrorist operations, such as Sudan, Syria, and Libya, along with "axis of evil" member Iran.[48] When I asked Crouse about the delegation's choice to pursue these alliances, she acknowledged it was "a concern" but added, "It's ironic that the very people who talk about inclusion and diversity are the ones who are critical of cooperating with people on specific issues."

By the close of the Children's Summit, the United States had managed to expunge the term "reproductive health services" from the final document, along with language promoting sex education; block a ban on executing minors; exclude language validating gay families; and downplay the importance of the children's rights treaty that the Christian right so opposes.[49] The delegation also drafted an unusual "Explanation of Position," which it insisted be placed in the official meeting record. It reads as if it had been drafted by representatives of the Holy See or the Family Research Council—which, in effect, it was:

> The United States does not understand any endorsement of these conferences to be interpreted as promoting abortion. . . .
>
> The United States emphasizes . . . the need to stress the practices of abstinence, of delaying sexual initiation, monogamy, fidelity, and partner reduction. . . .

The United States reaffirms that 'The family is the natural and fundamental group unit of society and is entitled to protection by society and the State.' . . .

The United States understands that 'children's rights' are seen at all times in relation to the rights, duties and responsibilities of parents."[50]

"On both family and life issues, it was a big win for us," said Saunders—and to achieve these results, Crouse told me, "it was absolutely pivotal that conservatives were on the U.S. delegation." In a report to its members after the summit, Focus on the Family said, "Pro-family experts are ecstatic at what was accomplished," and called the results "an answer to prayer." The group also urged readers to contact the president and thank him "for holding the line in favor of the culture of life, the traditional family, and sexual abstinence."[51]

Family planning advocates felt beaten. "As far as we could get was just to stop them, to put a line," Alcalde says, "to prevent them from banning sex education or access to health services." Reaction inside the United States was equally grim, as reflected in newspaper editorials such as one from the *Atlanta Journal-Constitution* that argued, "By cleaving to its anti-abortion and pro-abstinence position, the United States has demonstrated a willful ignorance of the desperate plight of young girls in developed countries, most of whom have no real choice about whether to have sex."[52]

The conference had also marked a new era in U.S. diplomacy. Chile's Leyton says U.S. support had been critical in the past in producing documents that put reproductive rights and women's rights at the center of global population policy—and U.S. delegations had been "wonderful, trustworthy partners for negotiation." All that changed at the Children's Summit. "First, they were completely unapproachable," she says. "They showed inflexibility and—how can I put it, to be diplomatic?—arrogance. The people that they send here to negotiate are not people prepared to negotiate. They're people who come to impose things. And then, from the point of view of content, on values issues they've been completely going backwards." The United States' aggressive new style at the United Nations would gain visibility in the months ahead as the United States built its case for war in Iraq. When Chile rotated onto the UN security Council the country would again become a target of intense U.S. pressure. The day I spoke with Leyton in February 2004 in her offices near the United Nations, an inspection ordered by the Chilean ambassador confirmed that their office phones had been tampered with during the prewar period, likely by U.S. intelligence.[53]

The regional population conference in Bangkok seven months later, in December 2002, was even more polarized. By the end, the United States found itself completely alone.

The Bangkok conference was convened to assess Asia's progress on population control—and to forge new goals for HIV prevention. The measuring stick was something called the Cairo Program of Action, adopted in 1994 by 179 nations; the document marked a radical shift from targets and quotas to a population strategy based on the education and economic empowerment of women and on broad access to family planning services. This U.S. delegation, led de facto by Louise Oliver, the pro-life official from the State Department, and by John Klink, the former Vatican negotiator, again charged onto the scene. Before the meeting even began, Oliver announced that the United States would no longer support the Cairo Program, a document the United States had helped to shape—but which the Christian right had avidly opposed. "This hit like a bombshell," a senior UN official told reporters. "People were stunned." Once the meeting began, Oliver insisted on language supporting "the sanctity of life from birth until natural death," a position that synced closely with the Vatican but contradicted not only positions the United States had taken on the international stage but also U.S. laws on abortion and capital punishment.[54] Even as these embarrassments forced the United States to backtrack, the delegation pushed for major changes in the conference report:

delegates insisted language promoting sex education and condom use be removed in favor of language promoting abstinence and "natural" family planning. They demanded references to "reproductive health services" and "reproductive rights" be deleted, claiming—just as they had at the Children's Summit—that these could be construed as references to abortion.[55] "A lot of the language the United States proposed was straight out of the manual of the Holy See," according to one official American observer. "John [Klink] wasn't supposed to negotiate, but he whispered in Louise's ear and she went to negotiate. He was the puppet master." Jeanne Head, who attended as an observer with the National Right to Life Committee, worked closely with the U.S. delegation and apparently served as its muscle.

Lalaine Viado attended as an NGO observer from the Philippines, and consulted closely with her country's delegation. Abortion is constitutionally prohibited in the Philippines, a ban that enjoys the full support of the country's religious conservative president, Gloria Macapagal-Arroyo. So members of the U.S. delegation, and their close allies among pro-life NGOs, expressed particular frustration that the Filipino representatives didn't quickly line up to support the U.S. stance. Viado recalls Head approaching a group of Filipino delegates and shouting, "You are not taking orders!" Viado saw Head insult one Filipino Congressman, Neri Acosta, to his face, and speak rudely and abrasively to the Philippines secretary of health. "We were totally appalled," Viado recalls, "but we were really feeling the pressure." Filipino delegates also got calls from Macapagal-Arroyo's staff, who warned that they had been berated by Washington for not backing the U.S. position. A group of Filipino legislators issued a formal statement decrying "the attempt of the U.S. government to impose its own policies over other nations through a process that violates democracy and the use of threat to exhibit its power in relation to international agreements."[56]

Several others close to the proceedings, including Francoise Girard, who was an advisor with the British delegation, report that these hardball tactics were applied to other Asian governments as well. "During the negotiations, they kept saying, 'We'll report what you said to Washington tonight,' " says Girard. "After the first day, everyone went back to their hotels and got phone calls from their capitols, saying they'd gotten State Department cables saying, 'You're misbehaving.' And when these governments get a letter like that from the United States, it's very high stakes, because these countries depend on the United States for so many things, including military aid." The only comic relief came when U.S. delegate Elaine Jones, a top population staffer from the State Department, stood up to declare, "I've used the Billings method [the rhythm method] for ten years, and it works." Muffled laughter filled the room; an ob-gyn from Iran stood up to point out that the method has a ridiculously high failure rate.[57] "To have a professional diplomat say that something worked for her personally, so why shouldn't it work for every woman in the developing world," says Valerie DeFillipo, an international expert with Planned Parenthood who was present, "it was embarrassing."

In a blatant effort at intimidation, the U.S. delegation forced a vote on its suggested changes—an almost unprecedented strategy at these consensus-driven meetings. But the camaraderie between the Asian governments and their commitment to the principles of Cairo trumped U.S. efforts at coercion. While two nations abstained (including Nepal, which receives significant U.S. military aide for its counterinsurgency efforts), not a single Asian country backed the extreme U.S. stance, even nations with conservative abortion laws such as the Philippines and Iran. The final tally, 32 to 1.[58] "It was one of the most moving experiences of my life to see them stand up, one after another after another, and vote no," recalls DeFillipo. "But for the United States, it was a huge diplomatic failure."

Again the United States filed an unusual clarification, in a three-page General Reservation that restated its insistence on abstinence, fidelity, and monogamy as solutions for AIDS ("any promotion of the use of condoms," the reservation read, "should be interpreted in the context of [the United States'] continued support for, and promotion of, abstinence as the preferred, most responsible, and healthiest choice"). The reservation also asserted the country's commitment to strengthening marriage and its distaste for prostitution, abortion, and terms like "reproductive health." The document overstepped American laws on birth control and abortion, claiming that the "the United States supports innocent life from conception to natural death."[59]

While Christian right lobbies such as Focus on the Family expressed gratitude for the U.S. delegation's "strong pro-life stance,"[60] Terri Bartlett, an NGO observer with Population Action International, came away with "a heavy feeling" about the damage that had been done to the United States' reputation abroad. "Career diplomats were put in such a terrible position with their colleagues," Bartlett says. "For professional career people, that meeting meant years of work down the drain."

Lalaine Viado says the U.S. posture has also strengthened the hand of religious conservatives in the developing world. Immediately after Bangkok, Viado says, the Philippines legislature was debating a reproductive health care bill and many churches strung up banners in response that read, "No to HR 1041. Stop Killing Innocent Lives!" One diocese issued a pastoral letter closely echoing the themes raised by the U.S. delegation in Bangkok, which was read in remote rural churches. "What's new about this is the Church has become more aggressive," she says. Likewise, María Antonieta Alcalde says the stance the United States has taken on reproductive rights at international conferences and the strictures of the Mexico City Policy have combined to dampen political debate in Mexico. "People are very afraid to take the lead on anything related to abortion," she says, even on such issues as emergency contraception or violence against women.

Loreto Leyton, the Chilean diplomat, suggests another concern: the United States' performance at the Children's Summit and at Bangkok has made it acceptable for religious beliefs to be fought out openly on the diplomatic stage. In the past, she says, even the Vatican delegates, who clearly sought to advance a conservative religious agenda, "were professionals and they understood the game." But the delegates from the Christian right representing the United States brought a new religious zeal into the conversation: "You were a sinner," says Leyton, "and they put it on those grounds." Because of this influence, she says, Muslim nations such as Iran, Malaysia, and Sudan have begun to make their case in passionate religious terms as well. "It's opened a door for other delegations to let go more than they used to in the past," she says.

STACKING THE COURTS

AT SIX O'CLOCK in the evening on November 12, 2003, Republican senators began a thirty-hour Justice for Judges marathon debate on the Senate floor to highlight what they characterized as Democratic obstruction of President Bush's judicial nominations. It was, in the words of marathon ringleader Rick Santorum, a social conservative who is third in command in the U.S. Senate, "a reverse filibuster"—a filibuster, he hoped, to end all filibusters. Senate Judiciary Chairman Orrin Hatch charged that Democrats were treating the president's nominees "like dirt" and Republican Judiciary Committee member John Cornyn accused them of "violating the Constitution," charges so colorful they were only a bit overshadowed by the Democrats' giant yellow-and-purple "168-4" sign contrasting the number of Bush nominees approved with the number they'd held up using the age-old Senate tool. The histrionics only got more extravagant as the night wore on. By the end, *Washington Post* reporter Peter Carlson noted, Hatch was beginning to sound like Howlin' Wolf he'd been shouting so loud for so long.[1] But for all their amusing antics, the Republican protestors had very serious supporters behind the scenes.

The talkathon, according to a memo leaked from the office of Senate Majority Leader Bill Frist, was closely coordinated with a right-wing news outlet. "Fox News Channel is really excited about this marathon and Brit Hume at 6 would love to open with all our 51 senators walking onto the floor," read the memo from Manuel Miranda, a Frist staffer who has since resigned. "The producer wants to know will we walk in exactly at 6:02 when the show starts so they get it live to open Brit Hume's show? Or if not, can we give them an exact time for the walk-in start?"[2] The event was also coordinated with the president, who called a simultaneous press conference in the Oval Office. There he appeared with a group of three of his judicial nominees—all of them female—in a pointed attempt to bolster Republican claims from the Senate floor that sexism and bigotry, not his nominees' records, have fueled Democratic dissent. "I have told these three ladies I will stand with them till the bitter end," President Bush said.[3]

Above all, the event was orchestrated in close concert with the Republican Party's conservative Christian base. Former party operative Chuck Muth launched a Web site promoted by Christian right organizations, justiceforjudges.com, where he posted "gavel-to-gavel" coverage of the faux filibuster. Focus on the Family, the Family Research Council, the conservative Southern Baptist Convention, and other family values lobby groups gained, according to a Family Research Council report, "virtually unfettered access to the capitol building," where they conducted prayer circles and press conferences throughout the wee hours. Bill Frist joined in the Family Research Council prayer circle, where the group's president, Tony Perkins, said, "We have volunteered to be here tonight to keep watch while most of America sleeps. . . . We are here because there is a clear and present danger facing America—an out-of-control judiciary that is chipping away at religious liberties in this nation."[4] Conservative Christian radio and television hosts, meanwhile, touted the event over the airwaves.

James Dobson began his radio coverage hours before the talkathon kicked off. Dobson, the conservative Christian psychologist and Focus on the Family chairman, had rounded up his closest political allies for the show: Gary Bauer, former presidential candidate and president of American Values; Don Hodel, a former leader of the Christian Coalition who had just joined Focus on the Family as its new president; and Perkins. He'd gathered them to discuss what Dobson called "the most troubling development in the American government at this time. . . the imperious, arrogant, far leftist character of the federal judicial system who are unelected, unaccountable, and I believe out of control." He called this phenomenon "judicial tyranny," words that have become a catchphrase on the religious right. Bauer laid out the case. "Almost everything that has gone wrong in this country from a pro-life, pro-family standpoint has been caused by our courts," he said. "There's pornography everywhere, but you can't see the Ten Commandments. Our children suffer from abortion on demand, over a million of them a year are losing their lives. We're facing the prospect of men marrying men. The list goes on and on. On all these issues there has never been a vote by the American people or the people of any state to do these things. No state really would push those kinds of radical proposals. In every case it's been these unelected federal judges that have done it, continue to do it, and they're remaking America right in front of our eyes." They all agreed that President Bush had done what he could; "[Bush] said he'd put a different kind of judges on the court, and he's fulfilled that promise," Bauer said. But they saw a conspiracy against Christian values in the efforts by Democratic senators to block even a handful of Bush's nominees. "The candidates who've been stiff-armed," Hodel said, "have nearly all been pro-life, conservative, pro-family people, something every believer ought to be concerned about."[5] George W. Bush is one such believer. And the truth is, few of his nominees have been stiff-armed. Some 98 percent of his "pro-life, conservative, pro-family" nominees who have come up for a Senate vote, many of whom share Dobson, Hodel, and Bauer's vision for America, are now serving on the federal courts. And these judicial appointments, combined with like-minded judges put in place by Bush's father and Ronald Reagan, have the potential to remake the federal courts as a reactionary force for generations to come. Protections for abortion and gays, and protections against state-sponsored religion, all of these could be eroded in the years ahead. That's precisely why getting compatible judicial appointments has become a primary goal of evangelical conservatives—and therefore of Karl Rove and George W. Bush.

The landmark *Brown v. Board of Education* school desegregation decision in 1954 first provoked conservatives to embark on a quest to curb what they saw as the excesses of the Warren Supreme Court. Throughout the 1960s, the court continued to expand the reach of civil rights protections—and to antagonize conservatives—with decisions protecting racial minorities and criminal defendants and strengthening the church/state divide. Christian conservatives joined the cause only after the 1973 *Roe v. Wade* decision legalizing abortion, which so outraged pro-life activists that Nixon appointee Harry Blackmun received death threats. Once efforts to push a constitutional ban on abortion collapsed in 1975, remaking the courts gained currency as the ultimate strategy for reversing *Roe* and protecting conservative Christian values. Ronald Reagan's 1980 presidential campaign embraced this mission. The party's platform that year called for judicial nominees "who respect traditional family values and the sanctity of human life."[6]

Court decisions in the intervening years striking down state restrictions on abortion have made court appointments an increasingly prominent concern on the Christian right. But two sets of events in 2003 brought the issue more attention than it has received since the shock of *Roe v. Wade.* The first concerned Alabama Supreme Court Justice Roy Moore's court battle over a five-ton Ten Commandments monument he had installed in the state courthouse. Few major news organizations noticed when the ACLU sued Moore for its removal back in 2001, but the story struck a chord on the Christian right, who mobilized their constituency to send tens of thousands of e-mails in his support. Once a district court ordered the piece of granite removed in late 2002, the rallies, petitions, and donations for his legal defense multiplied, gaining strength in 2003 as Moore appealed the decision.[7] In an eventful year marked, in the words of Focus on the Family by "miraculous victories and heartbreaking defeats for Christian Americans who advocate for righteousness," Focus members ranked Moore's fight as second in importance only to the signing of the partial-birth abortion ban. "He stayed true to what he knows to be right, just and constitutional—regardless of the consequences," Focus member Sheryl Ridley wrote in from Fresno, California. "His determination to stand for truth is inspiring and motivating to me to be more outspoken about my faith and beliefs. Out of this story emerges a true modern hero of the faith that we can teach our children to emulate."[8] When Focus on the Family head James Dobson spoke at a rally in front of the state courthouse in Montgomery, he said the attacks on Moore signaled that "the liberal elite and the federal court judges and some members of the media are determined to remove every evidence of faith in God from this entire culture."[9]

If Roy Moore's court battle had activated the evangelical base, it was the Supreme Court June 2003 decision in *Lawrence v. Texas,* which struck down sodomy laws as unconstitutional, that got the attention of Christian right leaders. Within weeks of the ruling, Pat Robertson had launched Operation Supreme Court Freedom, an effort to get his millions of followers to pray for a death on the Supreme Court. "The Supreme Court . . . has opened the door to homosexual marriages, bigamy, legalized prostitution, and even incest," Roberston wrote to Christian Broadcasting Network viewers. "But there is a higher tribunal than the United States Supreme Court. There is the Judge of all the earth. We must earnestly come before Him now and cry out for redress of our grievances." Robertson asked that prayers target justices in ill health, noting that "one justice is eighty-three years old, another has cancer, and another has a heart condition," seemingly references to the aging John Paul Stevens and to Ruth Bader Ginsburg, who had surgery for colon cancer in 1999. Robertson kicked off the twenty-one-day "prayer offensive" on his popular *700 Club* cable TV program with the words, "We ask for miracles in regard to the Supreme Court."[10]

The same week Randall Terry, the pro-life radical who led confrontational protests at abortion clinics through Operation Rescue, launched his Impeach the Twisted Six campaign with a series of rallies demanding impeachment of the six justices who voted with the majority in *Lawrence*. His lengthy call-to-arms, which he claims was e-mailed to 3 million Christian activists, employed rhetoric even more ferocious than Robertson's. "God Himself put child-killing, sodomy, and bestiality on the short-list of sins that will cause the destruction of a nation," Terry wrote. "We declare to the 'pagan elite'; to our 'ruling oligarchy' at the Supreme Court; to the politicians and judges who seek compromise and collaboration with baby killers and militant homosexuals: You will be defeated. You have mocked the God of heaven, and thereby sealed your own demise."[11]

This heated oratory found expression in a new crop of right-wing judicial projects—an infrastructure supported in part by the administration's political operatives. Focus on the Family created a new Stop Judicial Tyranny project, complete with action alerts and "religious liberty" rallies around the country, to complement the efforts of the Alliance Defense Fund, an organization Focus on the Family co-founded in 1993 that files legal challenges against abortion access, gay rights, and church/state separation. The Eagle Forum has a Court Watch operation, which once worked to build opposition to Clinton's nominees and now works to gain support for Bush's through "report cards" and lobbying efforts. The Free Congress Foundation and Concerned Women for America have similar projects of their own. Dozens of pro-life organizations, from the American Family Association to Heartbeat International, a network of crisis pregnancy centers, hatched a Shake the Nation campaign, which involved sending tens of thousands of baby rattles to senators as a reminder to support Bush's pro-life judges.[12] Several Christian right groups joined forces with industry lobbies to form the Coalition for a Fair Judiciary. The Coalition, with its seventy-five member-organizations, allows some of Washington's most influential mouthpieces for the Christian right, such as the Family Research Council, Concerned Women for America, the Free Congress Foundation, and the Christian Coalition, to work side-by-side with pro-business lobbies such as Grover Norquist's Americans for Tax Reform, which works to lower corporate taxes; the American Tort Reform Association, which seeks to limit corporate liability for wrongdoing; and the National Association of Manufacturers.[13]

Good for the Goose, Good for the Gander

The most visible of these conservative judiciary watchdog groups is C. Boyden Gray's Committee for Justice, which has run inflammatory television ads accusing Democrats of anti-Catholic bias for opposing the confirmation of such extreme ideologues as Roy Moore–booster William Pryor. (Pryor, like half of the Democrats on the Senate Judiciary Committee, is indeed Catholic; Bush ultimately put him on an appeals court through a recess appointment.) An October 2003 *New Republic* article outlines how Gray, a patrician old-line Republican and prolific Republican fundraiser for whom the phrase "well connected" is an understatement (his father served in the Truman and

Eisenhower administrations, while the junior Gray served in the first Bush White House), found himself so isolated in the ultraright climate the younger Bush ushered into Washington that he had to become an attack dog to maintain political access. When the White House tapped him, through an intermediary, to head a right-wing answer to People for the American Way—the liberal watchdog group famous for blocking Robert Bork's nomination to the Supreme Court—Gray jumped at the opportunity. As the *New Republic*'s Franklin Foer writes, the White House and Senate Republicans effectively subcontracted their dirty work to Gray, allowing them plausible deniability as he defamed the Democratic opposition.[14] So Orrin Hatch, the judiciary committee chairman, could pointedly put Pryor on record about his religion during committee hearings, and then insist that he was "not happy" with Gray's ads accusing the Democrats of anti-Catholic bias. No one in the Bush administration has ever called on Gray to change his tone, either.

In fact, the Bush administration promotes Gray's propaganda. The official Department of Justice (DOJ) Web site includes biographical backgrounders on several of Bush's judicial nominees, most of which come from Gray's committee or one of the various Christian right judicial operations. The DOJ page on Priscilla Owen includes an article by Gray, two articles by the Coalition for a Fair Judiciary, and one article by Concerned Women for America; the only information the DOJ posted on Carolyn Kuhl was produced by Gray's Committee for Justice.[15]

Gray's Committee for Justice has focused its attentions almost exclusively on supporting Bush judicial nominees who are darlings of the Christian right. There's William Pryor, for example, who opposes "the so-called separation of church and state," referred to *Roe v. Wade* as "the day seven members of our highest court ripped the Constitution and ripped out the life of millions of unborn children," and filed a brief opposing gay civil rights protections. There's Janice Rogers Brown, who has likewise disparaged the "wall of separation between church and state" as an "uninformative metaphor." There's Owen, who, as a judge in Texas, refused to grant a judicial bypass for minors seeking abortions. And there's Charles Pickering (who got onto a federal appeals court through another Bush recess appointment), who supports a constitutional amendment to ban abortion.[16] Yet the Committee for Justice isn't led by Christian right leaders, but rather by some of corporate America's most heavy-hitting attorneys. Gray's own law firm, Wilmer, Cutler & Pickering, defended high-tech giant Microsoft in its antitrust case. Committee member Connie Mack, the former Republican senator, is now with Shaw Pittman, a firm that represented R.J. Reynolds against federal charges that it concealed the dangers of smoking, while committee member Fred Fielding, a former Nixon and Reagan official, is a partner in a firm that fights media regulation on behalf of radio powerhouse Clear Channel. Rounding out the roster is former Oklahoma governor Frank Keating, now CEO of the American Council of Life Insurers, and Stan Anderson, vice president of the U.S. Chamber of Commerce, which represents business interests in Washington.[17] None of these men is a card-carrying member of the family values movement. So what's their interest?

Like becoming a top-ranking "ranger" for the Bush/Cheney ticket, attaching their respectable names to the Committee's attack ads is just one more way to curry favor with the administration. But these corporate players will likely receive more direct benefits from lending their support to Bush's judicial candidates. Because in case after case, these conservative Christian nominees are also stalking horses for corporate interests. Claude Allen, an appeals court nominee known for being pro-abstinence, antigay, and anti-abortion down the line, also happens to sit on the board of an organization called Peacemaker Ministries, which takes a hardline position against litigation, favoring "biblically-based mediation" instead. The group encourages individuals and organizations to write language into contracts forswearing the right to sue—a sort of tort reform from below.[18] Appeals court nominee Priscilla Owen, too, is more than just an avid foe of abortion. Before being elected to the Texas Supreme Court, Owen spent her sixteen years in private practice representing oil and gas companies, and once on the court she remained so friendly to these interests she became known as "Judge Enron." According to the watchdog group Texans for Public Justice, "her result-oriented opinions overwhelmingly favor defendants over plaintiffs, businesses over consumers." The Texas AFL-CIO opposed her nomination because she so often ruled against workers injured on the job; the Texas Civil Rights Project opposed her because she always took the side of business in civil rights cases.[19]

Charles Pickering is another anti-abortion true believer who has exhibited a strong pro-business bias. Of the seventeen opinions he turned over to the Senate from his years as a district court judge in Mississippi, Pickering found for the employer in all but three cases, and his decisions often displayed disdain for laws protecting workers from employer discrimination. "The courts are not super personnel managers charged with second guessing every employment decision made regarding minorities," he wrote in one. In another, he accused a sex-discrimination plaintiff of crying wolf: "Some seem to think that every time an adverse employment action is taken against one protected by Title VII that discrimination has occurred. . . . That is unfortunate." William Pryor, an all around favorite of Christian conservatives, has piled up a corporate-friendly record of opposing environmental protections. He filed a Supreme Court amicus brief in support of gutting the Clean Water Act, and he has testified before Congress against federal enforcement of the Clean Air Act, two essential tools for regulating corporate pollution. He is a proponent of tort reform, the effort to limit corporate liability for wrongdoing, and has disparaged trial lawyers as "leftist bounty hunters."[20]

It is this fortuitous convergence of evangelical and corporate interests that has made judicial nominations a Karl Rove special. It was back in Texas that Rove refined his formula for keeping both the party's corporate conservatives and its religious conservatives happy: tax cuts and tort reform for the former; strong opposition to abortion and gays, and support for public funding of religion through vouchers and other schemes, for the latter. While Rove famously applied this formula to George W. Bush's campaign for governor, he also applied it to remaking the Texas judiciary, where he saw early on that tort reform could activate an untapped pool of potential Republican donors. "Karl was talking about how business and medicine had to pull this together on the tort thing" as far back as the late 1980s, Kim Ross, a former lobbyist for the Texas Medical Association, told *Mother Jones*. Rove handpicked Priscilla Owen from her post as an undistinguished corporate lawyer and ran a cash-rich winning campaign, funded in great part by the business community and corporate lawyers, to put her on the Texas Supreme Court. On the court, she repaid her debt to big business several times over, ruling on behalf of insurers, doctors, pharmaceutical companies, energy firms, and land developers, some of whom had contributed to her campaign. She even lent her name to a fundraising appeal by the Texas Civil Justice League, an energy and transportation trade group that advocates tort reform. Conveniently for Rove, she was also flamboyantly anti-abortion, so much so that she was once accused by a fellow Republican on the court of "an unconscionable act of judicial activism" for seeking to thwart a bypass mechanism in state parental consent law. (That jurist, Alberto Gonzales, is now White House counsel to President Bush.) By the time Rove followed George W. Bush to Washington, the entire nine-member Texas Supreme Court comprised Republicans in Owen's image—every single one of them a client of Karl Rove's. Rove accomplished nearly the same feat on Alabama's court. Between 1994 and 2000, campaign spending on state judicial races doubled to nearly $47 million, driven largely by increased corporate donations. The U.S. Chamber of Commerce, for example, secured victories for its candidates in twenty-one of twenty-four judicial elections it worked on in eight states.[21] Karl Rove helped make it all happen.

In Washington, Rove has played a hands-on role in identifying nominees who are attractive to both corporate lobbyists and the Christian right, holding regular strategy sessions with key senators and conservative interest groups—and in orchestrating efforts to use these nominations to energize the GOP base. According to Nan Aron, president of the Alliance for Justice, which investigates judicial nominees, Rove pulled rank on White House council Gonzales to get Owen nominated to the Fifth Circuit Court of Appeals over Gonzales' more moderate pick, Deborah Hankinson.[22] After the Senate Judiciary Committee, then Democratically controlled, rejected Charles Pickering's nomination in March 2002, Rove showed up at a Family Research Council event to denounce the vote as a "judicial lynching" and to defend the appointment of "strong conservatives."[23] That October, the Eagle Forum published a paper entitled "Judicial Activism: The Biggest 2002 Election Issue," which argued that "the entire existence of our constitutional republic hangs in the balance. . . . Activist judges have been advancing a liberal agenda that opposes religious values, conventional morality, the separation of powers, our structure of federalism, and even the right of American citizens to govern ourselves." The paper concluded with words that soon became Rove's marching orders: "November 5th is our big opportunity to restore our constitutional form of government by electing Senators who will confirm good constitutionalist judges."[24] In Rove's gambit to retake the Senate and expand the Republican House majority in the midterm elections that fall, he sent President Bush across the country to support candidates in close races. Bush's standard stump line was that he needed more Republicans so that he could fill the federal bench with judges "who respect the Constitution and understand the limits of judicial power," a not so subtle reference to the Christian right's call to oppose judicial tyranny.[25]

Rove's challenge has been to stoke up Christian right enthusiasm for Bush's most extreme nominees while not generating alarm among swing voters. To this end, Bush deleted the topic of judicial nominees from his stump speech when he appeared beside Republican Senator Susan Collins in Maine, a pro-choice moderate, and held that Oval Office press conference with his three women judicial nominees in an effort to sell his commitment to diversity.[26] When Boyden Gray runs ads reading "No Catholics Need Apply," it is an attempt at diversion aimed at swing voters as well—to convince them that the Democrats are the extremists, not Bush's conservative Christian nominees.[27] All told, judicial nominations are a handy political tool for Rove: even if Bush's nominees get filibustered, he still gets points from the Christian right for defending pro-life ideologues, while the nomination of the occasional woman, Latino, or African American helps to mute any fears among independents of right-wing radicalism.

Litmus Tests, After All

While on the campaign trail during the 2000 presidential race, hoping to avoid triggering swing-voter anxieties, Bush declined to embrace any ideological litmus test for judicial nominees. But along the way he did scatter some clues to the far-right standards he would impose once he took office. He ran on a Republican Party platform that included a plank calling for the appointment of judges who "respect traditional family values and the sanctity of innocent human life,"[28] and during his first debate with Al Gore, Bush signaled his sympathies with the Christian right campaign against judicial tyranny. "I believe that the judges ought not to take the place of the legislative branch of government," Bush said. "They shouldn't misuse their bench. I don't believe in liberal activist judges. I believe in—I believe in strict constructionists. And those are the kind of judges I will appoint."[29] When pressed about who he'd appoint to the highest court, candidate Bush usually mentioned his admiration for Justices Antonin Scalia and Clarence Thomas.[30] People for the American Way released a report during the campaign, "Courting Disaster," in which they imagined what more Supreme Court appointments in the Scalia-Thomas mold would mean for America. Scalia and Thomas's position on the landmark Voting Rights Act of 1965, for example, was criticized by Justices Stevens, Blackmun, Souder, and Ginsberg as so "radical" that it would require overturning at least twenty-eight Supreme Court decisions on everything from jury selection to affirmative action to legislative redistricting. The two men don't trace their views on church/state relations to the Constitution, which bans the establishment of religion, but to what they've characterized as an early American tradition of public prayer. If in the majority, Scalia and Thomas would likely sanction government-sponsored Christian prayer and public funding of pervasively religious institutions and exhibit, according to the report, "complete disrespect for the legitimate rights and interests of people who are not religious or are members of minority faiths." A court guided by Scalia and Thomas would be friendly to corporate America as well, narrowly interpreting antitrust law, limiting consumer protections, and protecting corporations from liability when their products cause harm. It would prioritize property rights over environmental protections, restrict legal defense for the poor, hobble antidiscrimination laws, undercut the rights of the disabled and the elderly, and allow the government to suppress political speech. It would, undoubtedly, overturn *Roe v. Wade*. Altogether, the report concludes, a Supreme Court modeled after Scalia and Thomas— Bush's ideal justices—would be "catastrophic" for equal rights and civil liberties. "On some issues, even one new right-wing candidate will tip the balance," People for the American Way director Ralph Neas writes in the report's introduction. "Three or four justices who share Scalia and Thomas's extreme views would spell disaster."[31]

But it was only after he was elected in the summer of 2002 that Bush articulated an actual judicial litmus test. In comments responding to a federal appeals court ruling that it was unconstitutional to require schoolchildren to recite the Pledge of Allegiance if it included the words "under God," he accused the Ninth Circuit Court of being "out of step with the traditions and history of America" and said the phrase, inserted at the height of Cold War anti-Communism, was merely "a confirmation of the fact that we received our rights from God." The country, he said, needs "commonsense judges who understand that our rights were derived from God. Those are the kind of judges I intend to put on the bench."[32] These remarks, his most explicit to date about his judicial philosophy, implied a fundamental disagreement with the principle of church/state separation. Christian conservatives openly oppose such a separation, and campaign against it in such venues as televangelist D. James Kennedy's annual Reclaiming America for Christ conference, where Kennedy exhorts those in attendance to tear down the "diabolical wall of separation that has led to increasing secularization, godlessness, immorality, and corruption in our country."[33] But it alarms civil libertarians. In effect, says Barry Lynn, executive director of Americans United for the Separation of Church and State, "the president is saying a guy can't be on the bench unless he believes in God. Not only do you have to believe in God, but you have to have a corollary belief that our rights come from God. Well, that sounds like a religious test to me." And it's a test that the president's nominees have met handily.

Of all of Bush's picks for the federal appeals courts, former Alabama Attorney General William Pryor has most aggressively embraced government-endorsed religion, earning opposition to his nomination by the ACLU, People for the American Way, and several Jewish organizations. In Alabama he not only defended Judge Roy Moore's Ten Commandments monument (Pryor became a critic only in late 2003 after being nominated by Bush), he defended Moore's practice of having Christian clergy recite prayers as jurors assembled in the courtroom before trial. When Pryor joined a rally to support "Roy's rock" in the summer of 2003 he told the crowd: "God has chosen, through his son Jesus Christ, this time, this place, for all Christians—Protestants, Catholics, and Orthodox—to save our country and save our courts." Pryor has insisted that "the Constitution of the United States is rooted in a Christian perspective," and he has harshly criticized the Supreme Court's 1962 decision banning school prayer, calling it a sign that "our government has lost God."[34] Pryor speaks the language of state religion, and apparently that's a quality George Bush was looking for in a judge.

And that's only the beginning. For every burning issue on the Christian right agenda, Bush has nominated ferocious advocates to the federal bench. On the decades-old campaign against sex education, the evangelical right has appeals court nominee Claude Allen, one of the nation's most powerful advocates for replacing comprehensive sex ed with abstinence-only-until-marriage programs. On homosexuality, they have confirmed Bush appeals court nominee Michael McConnell, a hero to the religious right for successfully defending the Boy Scouts before the Supreme Court, when the organization sought to exclude gay kids.[35] In Carolyn Kuhl, they have a nominee who defended the right of a cherished religious right institution, Bob Jones University, to practice racial discrimination.

On the question of *Roe v. Wade*, President Bush's nominees virtually closed ranks, their positions varying from Miguel Estrada's begrudging statement that it's "settled law" to open calls for the landmark decision to be overturned. Confirmed appeals-court judge John Roberts represented the Bush administration in two high-profile abortion cases, defending clinic blockades in one case, and arguing in the other that "*Roe* was wrongly decided and should be overruled."[36] Charles Pickering, who got on the federal bench through a recess appointment, voted as a Mississippi state senator for a constitutional convention to overturn *Roe* and helped to draft a Mississippi GOP platform plank calling for abortion to be outlawed entirely. Kuhl has written several legal briefs arguing for restrictions on abortion access, one urging the Supreme Court to "overrule [Roe] and return the law to the condition in which it was before that case was decided." McConnell has signed onto such inflammatory statements as "There is no longer any scientific doubt that an unborn child is a human creature who dies violently in the act of abortion," and has voiced strong opposition to laws protecting clinic patients from violence. Pryor has called *Roe* "the worst abomination in the history of constitutional law," a statement, according to a proud action alert from Concerned Women for America, that he "continues to stand by" today.[37]

Some of Bush's nominees are far more than standard bearers for this or that family values position; they are firm backers of the full Christian right agenda. District-court nominee James Leon Holmes, for example, is the former president of Arkansas Right to Life, an affiliate of the influential National Right to Life Committee, and a member of the far right Federalist Society. He's on record supporting a constitutional amendment banning all abortions, without exception, and he has often employed the inflammatory rhetoric of the pro-life movement, declaring that abortion is as immoral as slavery and comparing abortion advocates to Nazis. He wrote an essay with his wife arguing that the proper role of women in marriage should be a biblical one, in which a "wife is to subordinate herself to her husband" and "place herself under the authority of the man." Conversely, he has disparaged feminism, saying the movement "brought with it artificial contraception and abortion on demand, with recognition of homosexual liaisons soon to follow" and is "contributing to the culture of death."[38]

Deputy Health Secretary Claude Allen, Bush's choice for a seat on the Fourth Circuit appeals court—already one of the most right-wing federal appeals courts in the country—is a Christian homeschooler who gained a reputation as an up-and-coming black conservative back in 1983. That's when he became the first African American staffer for Jesse Helms, the Christian right's champion in the Senate. At the time, Allen said he joined Helms' staff out of admiration for Helms's legislative leadership against abortion, which Allen called a form of "genocide." Later, in the Virginia attorney general's office, Allen worked closely with such conservative religious lobby groups as the Family Foundation and the Virginia Society for Human Life in promoting restrictive abortion laws there concerning mandatory wait periods, restrictions on minors' access, and a ban of "partial-birth" abortion. He aggressively interfered in a right-to-die case involving a local broadcaster reduced to a persistent vegetative state after a car accident, engaging in a legal fight with the man's wife, who has since sharply criticized his "heavy-handed use of government resources to ... further his own personal beliefs." Allen also has a history of hostility to gays; while working as an aide in Helms' intense 1984 reelection campaign, Allen tried to smear Helms' opponent for his links with "the queers."[39]

Several of these nominations have been stalled—Allen's because he's a Virginian nominated for a seat that's traditionally gone to a Maryland judge—and a few have famously been filibustered. But as President Bush began his fourth year in office, 169 of his 175 judicial nominees to reach the Senate floor have been approved, and this list includes such devoted social conservatives as McConnell and Roberts. A January 2004 report from People for the American Way, "Confirmed Judges, Confirmed Fears," begins to document the impact of those 169 judges since they made it onto the bench. Together, People for the American Way found, these judges have used their new posts to undermine civil rights, workers' rights, and environmental protections. Roberts, who had enjoyed religious right support for his nomination to the D.C. circuit appeals court because of his staunch anti-abortion track record, issued a dissenting opinion favoring a real estate developer, which indicated that he found aspects of the Clean Water Act unconstitutional. In a dissenting opinion in another case, he supported Bush administration efforts to suppress records from Vice President Cheney's energy task force. Others have issued opinions giving law enforcement officials immunity for executing unlawful strip searches, refusing workers protection from pressure to refrain from union activities, and refusing disability protections to a woman with multiple sclerosis.[40] "What often winds up happening is that people who are very right wing on one issue often are on others as well," Elliot Mincberg, vice president of People for the American Way, told me. "It's not just abortion or church/state. These appointments constitute an effort by the administration to institutionalize their views on a whole range of issues, because, of course, judicial appointments are for life."

DEMOCRACY AND DISSENT

In their campaign to push these ultraconservative nominees onto the courts, Christian leaders often express a level of urgency verging on deep-seated panic. They seem to believe that the courts as currently configured will not only allow abortion, open the door to gay marriage, and block the promotion of Christianity in public schools and public courts, but will, in the words of James Dobson as he addressed a Roy's Rock rally in Montgomery, "destroy the family and bring down this nation." Tony Perkins, president of the Family Research Council, often calls the judiciary a "black plague."[41] He's referring to judges' black robes, but the metaphor—of a deadly infection with the power to destroy a civilization—captures the fear driving these politics. Though the Christian right represents less than one in five Americans, its ground troops share a conviction that they speak for true American values—values that secular senators and courts are seeking to undermine. The Christian Coalition's Take America Back petition, which supports a constitutional amendment banning gay marriage, a law allowing display of the Ten Commandments in government buildings, and a law allowing tax-exempt religious institutions to endorse candidates, contends that "our federal judges have indeed been overriding the will of the American people and legislating from the bench."[42] It's not surprising, then, that Christian right activism on this issue is steeped in paranoia.

The Traditional Values Coalition, for example, sent an e-mail alert to its members when Republican Senate staffers hacked into the computers of Senate Democratics and leaked what they found to the *Wall Street Journal*. "These memos show a clear pattern of collusion between leftist special interest groups and liberal Senators who are blocking President Bush's judicial nominees," the item read. They linked readers to the Coalition for a Fair Judiciary Web site, which posted reams of the memos in their entirety, and lionized one staffer implicated in the memos' theft as a "whistleblower."[43]

In the six cases when Senate Democrats have resorted to filibuster— in the extreme cases of Pryor and Owen, for example—they have come under particularly venomous attack. Richard Land, a leader in the conservative Southern Baptist Convention and president of its Ethics and Religious Liberty Commission, has condemned the filibusters as "odious tactics," while Concerned Women for America's legal expert Tom Jipping circulated talking points claiming that such filibusters are "hypocritical" and "unconstitutional."[44] In a column timed for the Republicans' all-night Justice for Judges talkathon, Jerry Falwell claimed that Democrats had used the filibuster to send a "frightening" message: "that they will not accept a future U.S. Supreme Court nominee who has deeply held religious beliefs, specifically on abortion." He called the tactic "religious persecution—at its ugliest."[45]

At times this paranoia even verges on the anti-Semitic. In one letter then–Concerned Women for America president Sandy Rios sent to minority leader Tom Daschle, she can barely conceal her distrust of the Jewish junior senator from New York who has led the Democratic opposition. "We recognize that Sen. Schumer has a right to oppose this or any nomination for the reason of his choice," Rios writes in the July 30, 2003, letter. "But we wonder what that reason can be. It certainly cannot be the pro-life views of Mr. Pryor, because Sen. Schumer has said that he applies no 'litmus test.' . . . So it must be something else. And as we review Sen. Schumer's comments, the troubling thought arises that it might be Mr. Pryor's 'deeply held' Roman Catholic faith. Sen. Schumer . . . appeared extremely agitated to confront, in Mr. Pryor, a person who is unapologetic about his beliefs, yet completely responsible in his public role. You know Sen. Schumer. What assurance can you offer that a believing Catholic who comes before him, holding faithfully to the teachings of his church, will be treated fairly and dispassionately?"[46]

When Estrada was filibustered, groups such as Focus on the Family and the conservative umbrella group Coalition for a Fair Judiciary accused the Democrats of a conspiracy against Hispanics. "There's a sign over the Senate that not only says 'Believers need not apply,' " Coalition president Kay Daly told a Christian newsletter. "It also says 'Hispanic immigrants, you need not apply if you don't embrace a liberal philosophy.' " Gray of the Committee for Justice asked, "Are the criteria [that ranking Democrat on the Judiciary Committee Patrick Leahy] is using based on the fact that Estrada is Hispanic?" When religious right favorite Priscilla Owen was filibustered, the Eagle Forum—the same organization built by Phyllis Schlafly to defeat equal rights for women—tried to insinuate a bias against women, complaining that "[Owen's] defeat represents the first time that the Senate has rejected such a [well-qualified] recipient and also a woman nominee."[47] (Such charges, incidentally, have little basis in reality: As of the end of 2002, only 21 percent of Bush's nominees were women, down from 29 percent under Clinton; while a quarter of Clinton's judicial nominees were people of color, only 16 percent of Bush's have been.[48])

The Bush administration has exhibited signs of paranoia as well, circumventing established vetting procedures and trying to shield judicial nominees from public scrutiny and debate. These changes have become a pressing concern for Marcia Kuntz, director of the Judicial Selection Project at the Alliance for Justice, a nonpartisan organization that has served, along with People for the American Way, as one of the country's most avid watchdogs of judicial nominations. The group has published investigative reports both on individual nominees and on the ways this administration has upended the nomination process. The first troubling maneuver was Bush's decision to cut the American Bar

Association (ABA) out of the process. The ABA, the country's leading professional legal association, had been given the names of potential nominees for review ever since the Eisenhower administration. "Previously administrations would refrain from formally nominating somebody until the ABA rating had come out, which meant that the ABA was out there asking questions about people and there was talk in the legal community about who was being considered," says Kuntz, an attorney who served as a Democratic congressional staffer during most of the Clinton years. "Now these things are being conducted much more in secret, and so people are being nominated without having been vetted. Whereas previous administrations would have identified any ethical problems ahead of time and would have simply not nominated that person, now you've got a large number of people who are pretty significantly ethically compromised being nominated and who, in large numbers, are also being confirmed." Now ABA ratings come out only after a name has been forwarded to the Senate—when raising questions about a nominee's ethics or competence threatens to embarrass the president. At that stage, a vast majority of Bush's nominees are confirmed, anyway. Kuntz says even these belated evaluations are compromised, because Senate Republicans and administration officials have shown that they will retaliate against people who speak ill of their nominees. She mentions Arizona State law professor Paul Bender, a former supervisor of nominee Miguel Estrada's who told the press that Estrada "lacks the judgment and is too much of an ideologue to be an appeals court judge." Afterward Judiciary chair Orrin Hatch tried to tar Bender as a supporter of child pornography for positions he'd taken on First Amendment grounds.[49] Kuntz also relates a conversation she had with a former colleague of one nominee. The colleague, who did not want his name used, received a standard prescreening call from the FBI, during which he spoke frankly about the nominee's poor qualifications; shortly thereafter, he got a furious call from the Justice Department asking why he'd "trashed" their nominee. "The intimidation they use to silence people is scary," Kuntz says.

The system of open advice and consent has been undermined in other ways. The "blue slip" policy, which traditionally allowed senators from a nominee's home state a right of refusal, was once a favorite of Hatch's. He helped turn it from a customary courtesy into a formal veto by adding a statement onto the blue slips that "no further proceedings on this nominee will be scheduled until both blue slips have been returned by the nominee's home state senators." But during Bush's tenure, Hatch has changed his view, saying that the slips wouldn't prevent his Judiciary Committee from forwarding a nominee to the floor.[50] And Senate Republicans have sought to change the filibuster rule to streamline confirmations of even Bush's most controversial nominees—a tactic that has received enthusiastic support from the Christian right. "It's time for the Republican Party to see the game is hardball and put down their Wiffle bat," Jan LaRue, chief counsel for Concerned Women for America, told a Christian newsletter in the fall of 2003. "The Senate has authority over its own rules, which includes determining how many votes are needed to invoke cloture to end a filibuster of a nominee."[51]

Bush and the GOP have done more than remove obstacles to the approval of nominees sympathetic to the Christian right; they have invited far right ideologues into the nomination process on the front end. While the Bush administration has exiled the 400,000-member American Bar Association, it has rolled out the red carpet for the once marginal, 25,000-member Federalist Society. The Federalist Society was founded in 1982, just as Christian right dreams of remaking the federal judiciary were taking shape in the early Reagan years; a prominent leader was ultraconservative law professor Robert Bork, who would later be denied a place on the Supreme Court for his extreme views of the law. The Society advocates strict federalism, which includes a belief that neither the federal government nor the federal courts should have a say in laws protecting the environment, civil rights, or workplace safety, and its leaders have consistently taken positions amenable to the Christian right, backing government funding of religion through voucher programs and strongly opposing *Roe v. Wade*. Its members now occupy every key position surrounding judicial nominations: Attorney General John Ashcroft, Solicitor General Ted Olsen, Hatch, and a significant number of high-powered staffers in the Justice Department and the office of the White House Counsel.[52] Their influence has been pervasive: some 40 percent of the president's nominees to the federal appeals courts are Society members, including some who have sparked broad-based opposition: Carolyn Kuhl, Priscilla Owen, and Michael McConnell.[53]

One of the Christian right's most effective opponents of "judicial tyranny," Tom Jipping, is now on the inside, too. For years he led attacks on Clinton judicial nominees from his perch at the Free Congress Foundation, excoriating Republican senators for "selling our freedom down the river" for approving too many. He ranted that "the time has come to throw them out" and distributed Christian Coalition voter guides to turn up the heat.[54] He then led the charge in favor of Bush's pro-life nominees for Concerned Women for America, warning Republicans that the evangelical grass roots would remember if they didn't fight hard enough for their approval. "This had better be a march-to-victory strategy, rather than going down waving the white flag," he told *Congressional Quarterly*. In September 2003, Senate Judiciary Chair Orrin Hatch, a frequent Jipping target in the past, hired the enforcer onto his personal staff.[55]

THE PERMANENT REVOLUTION

Throughout the night on November 12, 2003, as Republican senators held their antifilibuster filibuster, the talk on the floor, in the president's Oval Office press conference, in the prayer circles, and in the speechifying of the social-conservative lobbyists and clergy who filled the corridors, was of Democratic obstructionism. At the prayer circle, Family Research Council president Tony Perkins called Bush's judicial confirmation rate "the worst of any modern president"; at his press conference, Bush complained of the "ugly politics in the United States Senate," insisting that his nominees deserved an "up or down vote" and that use of the filibuster is "wrong, and it's shameful, and it's hurting the system." Hatch, meanwhile, on the Senate floor, howled that "a militant minority is thwarting the will of the majority."[56] But for all this bluster, and despite the nomination of several underqualified and ethically challenged candidates, almost every single one of Bush's nominees have sailed through the Senate. Six of Bush's nominees have been filibustered (two of which he appointed anyway while the Senate was in recess), while as of spring 2004, 169 had been approved in open votes on the Senate floor. Compare this with the 63 Clinton nominees who were prevented from "up or down" votes—refused either hearings or referrals to the Senate floor—by Republicans. In a major Rose Garden address in May 2003, Bush claimed that there is a "crisis in our judiciary," due to the extreme number of vacancies; yet the high rate of approval of the president's nominees brought vacancies down from more than 9 percent at the end of the Clinton administration to a little above 5 percent by the end of 2003. While Bush and his right-wing base complain often of a "liberal, activist" judiciary, by the end of 2003, Republican appointees accounted for 57 percent of all federal judges—a ratio that will continue to rise throughout 2004, and perhaps beyond. When Bush first took office that number was 46 percent; when Ronald Reagan took office, the number was 40 percent.[57]

As legal scholar Herman Schwartz documents in his 1988 book, *Packing the Courts,* presidents typically seek to nominate judges who reflect their worldview, but Ronald Reagan was the first to insist on ideological purity. His 1980 Republican Party platform laid out detailed criteria for judges, insisting that nominees embrace a judicial philosophy of states' rights, "traditional family values," and "the sanctity of innocent human life," standards that Reagan often emphasized during his campaign. Reagan, along with Senate Republican leaders, made a special effort to push through young judges, who would, in the words of Senator Phil Gramm, be "making rulings after I'm dead." While 2 to 3 percent of Eisenhower, Kennedy, Johnson, and Carter's appointees were under age forty, 10 percent of Reagan's were. More than a third of Reagan's second-term nominees were rated as barely qualified by the ABA (compared with 6 percent for Carter), but they were all true blue conservatives: During the Reagan years, Senator Orrin Hatch devised an elaborate thirty-question test for nominees to make sure their positions on such issues as abortion, labor law, and church/state separation fit the mold.[58] The senior President Bush continued these efforts, assigning Boyden Gray to screen potential nominees for their conservative bona fides, and the younger Bush has approached his nominations with Reaganesque fervor.

Compare this, says Marcia Kuntz, with Clinton's approach to nominations. Ever the triangulator, Clinton generally avoided liberals in favor of well-qualified, centrist, establishment judges.[59] According to Kuntz, his screeners at the Justice Department knocked out anyone who would raise a red flag for Republican senators: "If someone was an active member of the ACLU, that was disqualifying, from their perspective," she recalls. "They were so careful about not offending Republicans that they nominated only middle-of-the road moderates." As of early 2004, out of 812 sitting federal judges, only 41 remained who were appointed before Reagan became president.[60] So virtually our entire federal judiciary is composed of two kinds of judges—Reagan/Bush/Bush hard-line conservatives in one camp and Clinton moderates in the other. "So even though Clinton served for two terms, and got more than 350 judges confirmed, they don't begin to balance out in terms of ideology," Kuntz says, "and now in terms of sheer numbers they don't balance out either." In early 2004, Republicans formed a majority on ten out of thirteen federal appeals courts; of the three others, one is evenly split and another has seven Democratic appointees and five Republican appointees, with nominees pending. By the end of 2004, it's likely that Republicans will dominate every federal appeals court but one.[61]

"In terms of our basic rights, to be free from discrimination on the basis of religion or race, or to have freedom of speech, or to have environmental protection, the federal courts of appeal are at least as important as the United States Supreme Court," says legal scholar Cass Sunstein, a professor at the University of Chicago Law School. "The reason is there are so many of them, and cases are so frequent, that they're effectively final. The Supreme Court can get involved only rarely." Federal appeals courts decide some 28,000 cases a year; maybe 80 make it up to the Supreme Court. Sunstein recently published data he has collected about the role of party affiliation in predicting judicial decisions in his book, *Why Societies Need Dissent*.[62] He says the path taken by Supreme Court Justice David Souter, a Reagan nominee who has proved to be fairly liberal on the bench, is quite unusual. In most cases, Sunstein found the correlation between the party of the president who nominated a judge and the performance of that judge on the court to be remarkably dependable. "If a Democratic president wants to get liberals on the court, as some Democratic presidents have wanted to do, say Roosevelt, then the judges are generally going to follow him," he says. "And Republican presidents in recent years have been spectacularly successful—I'm thinking here especially of Reagan and Bush—at getting on the bench judges who are conservative. On issue after issue there's an unmistakable link between the political party of the president who appoints the judge and the judge's point of view on the great legal issues of the day." J. Michael Luttig, a Bush Sr. appointee to the Fourth Circuit Court of Appeals, the most conservative appeals court in the country, acknowledged this tendency in an interview with the *New York Times*. "Judges are told, 'You're appointed by us to do these things,'" he said. "So then judges start thinking, well, how do I interpret the law to get the result that the people who pushed for me to be here want me to get?"[63]

In addition to political partisanship, Sunstein also discovered a powerful pattern of conformity. Most appeals court cases are decided by three-judge panels, drawn randomly from the pool of judges in a given district. He found that when a Republican sits with two Democrats, the Republican votes fairly liberal, and when a Democrat sits with two Republicans, the Democratic appointee's voting pattern tends to be quite conservative. "The more striking, and to me alarming finding," Sunstein says, "is if you get a Republican sitting with three Republicans, that judge's voting patterns become extremely conservative, far more conservative than Republican voting patterns when Republicans are sitting with one Republican and one Democrat." This is exactly the kind of panel—three Republicans—that will become more and more common as every appeals court in the nation gains a Republican majority.

"There's a human tendency, when you're talking to like-minded people, to get more extreme," Sunstein says. "This helps explain terrorism, violence, radicalism, and some of the worst forms of current American democracy. The courts of appeals need a dissenter and they often end up blundering if they don't have one. On all Republican panels, and that is the current danger, you won't have someone who will draw those judges' attention to the strong legal arguments on the other side, so their ideology will carry them away." Ever since *Roe v. Wade* in 1973, but especially since *Lawrence v. Texas* in summer 2003, leaders of the Chritian right have been stoking fears among their followers that "judicial tyranny" will erode the moral character of the nation. But Bush's stacking of the federal courts with extreme social conservatives, who have joined a growing right-wing Republican majority on the bench, could produce judicial tyranny of a quite different kind.

CODA

FIVE YEARS AFTER Paul Weyrich's despairing letter, in which he mourned the death of his dream of an American "moral majority" and called on conservative evangelicals to retreat from political life, the Christian right is profoundly reenergized.[1] When George W. Bush became president, he provided the movement with a new leader, a moral center, unprecedented access in Washington, millions of dollars in federal grants, and, most importantly, a string of important wins. "The Bush administration came along just in time to save many of these pro-family organizations," Weyrich told the conservative Christian magazine *World* in February 2001. "Four more years of a Gore administration—of being on the outside—and I think a lot of them wouldn't have made it." The president has strengthened the Christian right, and evangelical conservatives have remained his most loyal supporters, through thick and thin. "We are so thankful that our Father did not give us the president we deserve," Andrea Lafferty, director of the Traditional Values Coalition, told the crowd at an inaugural party in January 2001. "He gave us a better one. Amen."[2]

In an interview with the *New Yorker,* Karl Rove spoke of the sixteen-year period of Republican rule that was ushered in by William McKinley's election in 1896. "Somebody will come along and figure out a new governing scheme through which people could view things," he said, "and could, conceivably, enjoy a similar period of dominance."[3] Thanks to the intimate alliance between Bush, his party, and the Christian right, that period of dominance may already have arrived.

The White House, Senate, and Congress are all now in Republican hands, and most states have Republicans in the governor's office. In 2002, Republicans won enough local races to outnumber Democratic state legislators for the first time in fifty years.[4] Control over these state bodies will likely tilt the U.S. Congress in an increasingly Republican direction as well, since state legislators, in most states, draw the lines for congressional districts. And with the Republican Party decisively under the sway of evangelical conservatives, who now run everything from state parties to the national party platform committee, Republican Party rule means ongoing political influence by the Christian right.

Even if George Bush loses the presidency, the muscle he has put behind the Christian right agenda will have a lasting impact. In agency after agency, relentless pressure from Christian conservatives has drained the federal government of talent and expertise. "The strain has become increasingly difficult at USAID and the State Department," says Terri Bartlett of Population Action International, who has worked with these agencies for years on international family planning. "We have quite a number of key people where this should be the last four or six years of a stellar career and all they do all day is fight back and answer questions, and at some point you can't blame them when they leave. They're career, they've given their lives to this, they've worked in countries all over the world, and they're leaving without even taking advantage of retirement." Morale is likewise plummeting in the sciences. Margaret Scarlett, a former Centers for Disease Control (CDC) AIDS scientist, says, "The brain drain has been just incredible. It's a tremendous loss of years of investment." The researcher who founded the federal government's adolescent health program and ran it through four administrations has departed, and so many AIDS scientists have left most of the CDC's top AIDS posts empty. Scientists in fields that have experienced the most pressure under the Bush administration, such as HIV and stem cell research, are not only leaving the government—they're leaving the field, or leaving the country to conduct their work in a more hospitable climate. "You are going to start picking up *Nature* and *Science* and all the great [research] journals, and you are going to read about how South Koreans and Chinese and Singaporeans are making advances that the rest of us can't even study," Stanford University professor Irving Weissman, a leading stem cell researcher, told the *Boston Globe*. In February 2004, South Korean researchers became the first to extract stem cells from a cloned embryo, a scientific quest that was barred from receiving tax-payer support here.[5]

Meanwhile, Bush's politically driven science appointments have lent credibility to Christian right advocates with no fealty to the scientific process. "Putting people like Joe McIlhaney and Tom Coburn, who re-fuse to acknowledge the scientific consensus on condoms, in advisory positions not only gives them direct power," says Michael Cover, a spokesperson for Washington, D.C.'s Whitman Walker AIDS clinic, "but it gives them entree into public health policy and opens the door for the Traditional Values Coalition, for Concerned Women for America, for Focus on the Family—groups that have no background in public health—to be recognized as experts by local school boards and small newspapers across the country." Abroad, the administration's strong campaign against abortion and condoms has strengthened the hand of social conservatives throughout the Catholic and Muslim worlds. While the Vatican has always opposed condoms, it did so for doctrinal reasons. But in October 2003, Cardinal Alfonso Lopez Trujillo, presi-dent of the Pope's Council for the Family, took up the fake science tools of Bush's Christian right advisors. He told the BBC that HIV "can easily pass through the 'net' that is formed by the condom," the kind of patently false claim that has become wearifully familiar in this country.[6]

While a new administration could reverse executive orders allowing churches to discriminate in hiring, or denying family planning funds to clinics that offer abortions, killing unsound programs is harder. Now that faith-based social service providers, marriage promoters, and absti-nence educators are accustomed to federal funds, they will likely defend that income stream in the future, and pressure their congressional rep-resentatives to do the same. Joe Cook, executive director of the Louisiana ACLU, says there were few abstinence-only programs in the state before the federal money stream started; now there are several dozen, whose leaders won't be happy if their funds are threatened with termination. "It's like an epidemic, you can never go back," says Donna Crane of the pro-choice lobby group NARAL. "The abstinence money will never disappear, because of legislative inertia. The provisions that the president allowed the religious right and the social conservatives to put into effect for a first-ever global AIDS policy will be really hard to reverse. You create a constituency for this funding and it never goes away."

Then, Crane adds, "there are effects on the ground that can never be reversed." There are the civilian dead in Iraq, caught up in a religiously inspired war, and those lost to AIDS or botched abortions due to the administration's moralistic public health policies at home and abroad. A former State Department staffer points out that Bush's defunding of Marie Stopes, a health care provider to refugees, over unfounded accusations that the group supported coerced abortions has had "a ripple effect impacting war refugees and people in need," scaring other organizations away from providing controversial services. Adrienne Verrilli of the sex education group SIECUS points out that after spending half a billion dollars telling young people condoms don't work, HIV and other STD rates are on the rise.

Democracy and Theocracy

A few weeks after the American invasion of Iraq, deputy defense secretary Paul Wolfowitz spoke about the potential for democracy there on *Meet the Press*. He said the administration's "democratic goal" would require building on a variety of existing Iraqi institutions, "institutions that are a significant rudimentary step toward a representative democratic government," and that it also "requires the Iraqis being free to speak." Here at home, just as in Iraq, the spirit of democracy requires far more than just the right to vote. It requires a true valuing of pluralism, opposing views, and different belief systems. And it requires a true balance of powers, a complex system of checks and balances that encourages open debate, protects dissent, and sustains independent power bases that can challenge each other. The back-and-forth between Congress and the president, and between legislators and the courts are certainly part of this, but so is the back-and-forth between labor and business interests; between science, policy, and politics; between government, the media, and private sector advocates.

This White House is deeply uncomfortable with opposing views.

The president has not only stifled serious debate inside his own administration—whether from former terrorism chief Richard Clarke, or former faith czar John DiIulio, or former treasury secretary Paul O'Neill—he's sought to stifle public debate as well, especially on issues of importance to his most favored constituency. When the National Head Start Association sent a mailing to parents outlining the perils of Head Start funds going to religious groups, the Bush administration issued a threatening letter in response, warning of possible sanctions against those who engaged in such "political activities." When activists disrupted a speech by Health Secretary Tommy Thompson at an international AIDS conference in Barcelona, HHS conducted an audit of every single AIDS service organization associated with the protest. When three nonprofit organizations joined forces to oppose funding for abstinence-only programs, they received government audits, too. "We agree that we have a right to be audited, since we receive government funds," says James Wagoner, president of Advocates for Youth, one of the targeted groups. "But what does it mean when the audit mechanism can be used selectively and politically?"

Independent voices have been silenced in other ways. Since public employee unions are identified with the Democratic Party, Bush targeted federal workers for privatization, under the rubric of a Department of Homeland Security restructuring. Since plaintiffs' lawyers are identified as important Democratic Party donors, the president has nominated federal judges who would limit the power of attorneys to file suits. The American Bar Association, which has long provided independent assessment of potential nominees to the federal courts, was pushed out of the process by President Bush. On scientific advisory panels, Bush replaced mainstream medical associations, who would offer independent scientific perspectives, with associations that are explicitly Christian or pro-life. The private sector advisors who accompany government officials to UN negotiations once included recognized policy experts such as the American Medical Association; now they feature leaders of the Christian right. All of these actions hew to Karl

Rove's vision for defanging institutions that lean Democratic and building long-term Republican rule. The goal is not to engage your opponents in the public square, but to kneecap them, or send them into exile.

The Bush White House also has little respect for the balance of powers. When the courts contradict an important stance of the administration, Bush accuses them of overstepping. Bush signed a partial-birth abortion ban that plainly did not pass Supreme Court muster—lacking an exemption to protect a woman's health—and then vowed his administration would "vigorously defend this law against any who would try to overturn it in the courts."[7] On same-sex marriage, Bush backed an effort to circumvent the courts through a constitutional amendment, railing against "activist judges" and insisting that "the voice of the people must be heard."[8] On the other hand, when the people's representatives in the Senate blocked a handful of his judicial nominees as too extreme, he did an end-run around the Senate and made two recess appointments, claiming the dissenting senators were abdicating their "constitutional responsibility and are hurting our judicial system" by refusing to rubber stamp his nominees.[9] When Congress wouldn't okay his faith-based bill because, among other things, it would have allowed for discrimination in hiring, he went around the Congress, signing the whole package into effect through a series of executive orders.

The administration launched a preemptive war on Iraq without support from the United Nations, and it has refused to accept the recognized meaning of language in international conventions that the United States itself helped draft. His Mexico City Policy has prevented family planning advocates in the developing world from entering into their own national debates about abortion law reform. At home, he has refused to honestly make the case for his policies to the American people, selling a tax cut as a jobs program, deregulation as an environmental initiative, and a war for regime change as a war about weapons of mass destruction.

The Christian right movement, as a whole, is not enamored of democracy, if democracy leads away from their biblical values, and they have found in George W. Bush a sympathizer. This is a president who once told reporters in Texas that only Christians have a place in heaven, and who has claimed that he was called by God to run for office. He launched a faith-based initiative with much multicultural talk about it not mattering "if there is a rabbi on the board, or a cross on the wall or a crescent on the wall," but evidence suggests that every penny of those religious funds has gone to Christian organizations. In the name of Christian morals he has blocked potentially lifesaving research and endorsed religious discrimination. In case after case, his attorney general has intervened to tear down the separation of church and state.

To Bush's primary constituency, Christian fundamentalism is the only true faith. In the eyes of Franklin Graham, Pat Robertson, and other leaders of the Christian right, Islam is evil, Judaism is an incomplete form of Christianity, and minor religions are cults. And such intolerance is not confined to the movement's leadership. A 1994 study of the membership of two of the Christian right groups that have emerged in the Bush years as the beltway's most influential, found that only 6 percent of Focus on the Family members and only 2 percent of Concerned Women for America members agree with the statement "A diversity of moral views is healthy."[10] Even Christians who pursue a social gospel, rather than a social conservative hard line, are beyond the pale in the eyes of the Christian right. The National Right to Life Committee, which has enjoyed many special audiences with the president, has published ads attacking pro-choice Catholics in the Senate, warning that Ted Kennedy and his ilk will go to hell for their votes.

Bush has offered up countless signs that he may think the same way. In comparing the rhetoric of George Bush and Osama bin Laden with regard to September 11, theologian Bruce Lincoln found far more in common than one might expect. "Both men constructed a Manichaean struggle," he writes in his book *Holy Terrors*, "where Sons of Light confront Sons of Darkness, and all must enlist on one side or another, without possibility of neutrality, hesitation, or middle ground."[11] Whether in the Islamic world or here in the United States, this worldview is profoundly incompatible with the give-and-take and compromises of democracy.

New York Times columnist Paul Krugman, in his book *The Great Unraveling*, writes, "It seems clear to me that one should regard America's right-wing movement—which now in effect controls the administration, both houses of Congress, much of the judiciary, and a good slice of the media—as a revolutionary power. . . . That is, it is a movement that does not accept the legitimacy of our current political system."[12] Krugman was speaking mostly of the administration's relentless efforts to upend the nation's tax system to serve an economic elite and dismantle what remains of the welfare state. But these "revolutionary" changes to benefit the few at the expense of the many have only been made possible by efforts to keep the administration's Christian right base not only appeased, or even satisfied, but inflamed.

Just as Israel's ruling Likud Party is in thrall to ultra-Orthodoz settlers who are convinced the occupied territories were given to them by God, as India's former prime minister Atal Bihari Vajpayee found it politically necessary to support the violent Hindu nationalism of his party's religious followers, as Egypt and other moderate governments in the Arab world must tread carefully in the face of a growing Muslim fundamentalism, so our governing Republican Party is unmistakably in the grips of its own Christian theocratic base. We are all, in broad strokes, aware of this relationship, but there has so far been too little public debate about its corrosive effects on our democracy.

NOTES

<small>INTRODUCTION</small>

1. "President-Elect George W. Bush Holds Media Availability with Congressional Leaders," December 18, 2000, available from the Federal Document Clearing House.

2. Frederick Clarkson, "Robertson Redux," *Salon*, February 24, 1999; Liz Szabo, "Christian Coalition Losing Clout; Fractured Organization Showing Little Effect on Campaign So Far," *Virginian-Pilot*, February 19, 2000.

3. The letter is posted on the Free Congress Foundation Web site at www.freecongress. org/misc/990216ltr.asp.

4. Kevin Phillips, *American Dynasty: Aristocracy, Fortune, and the Politics of Deceit in the House of Bush* (New York: Viking, 2004), 128.

5. Fred Barnes, "The Emerging 9/11 Majority," *Weekly Standard*, November 18, 2002.

6. "Third National Survey of Religion and Politics," University of Akron Survey Research Center, Fall 2000, data presented in John C. Green and John DiIulio, "How the Faithful Voted," *Center Conversations*, Ethics and Public Policy Center, March 2001; Lyman A. Kellstedt, Corwin E. Smidt, Jame L. Guth, and John C. Green, "Cracks in the Monolith: Evangelical Protestants and the 2000 Elections," *Books & Culture*, May/June 2001, a publication of *Christianity Today*.

7. Quoted in Gwen Ifill, "Faith Initiative," *Newshour with Jim Lehrer*, December 25, 2002.

8. "Reform Jewish Movement Expresses Dismay over Introduction of Anti-Gay Marriage Amendment," Religious Action Center of Reform Judaism press release, July 12, 2001; Thomas J. Allio et al., "Unity Statement on Overcoming Poverty," May 24, 2004, available at www.calltorenewal.org.

9. David Frum, *The Right Man: The Surprise Presidency of George W. Bush* (New York: Random House, 2003), 3–4.

10. Hamil R. Harris, "Putting Worship into Their Workday: More Federal Employees Participating in Prayer Services at the Office," *Washington Post*, November 19, 2001.

11. Fred Barnes, "Conservatives Love George W. Bush: But Will the Romance Last?" *Weekly Standard*, March 5, 2001.

12. George W. Bush, "Radio Address by the President to the Nation," Bush ranch, Crawford, Texas, August 11, 2001, available at www.whitehouse.gov.

13. Randall A. Terry, letter to "Christian activists nationwide," July 12, 2003.

14. Jim Whittle, "All in the Family: Top Bush Administration Leaders, Religious Right Lieutenants Plot Strategy in Culture 'War,'" *Church & State*, May 2002.

15. Dana Milbank, "Religious Right Finds Its Center in Oval Office; Bush Emerges as

Movement's Leader After Robertson Leaves Christian Coalition," *Washington Post,* December 24, 2001.

16. Joel C. Rosenberg, "Political Buzz from Washington," *World,* October 6, 2001.

17. Frum, *The Right Man,* 30.

CHAPTER 1: YES, VIRGINIA, IT IS A HOLY WAR

1. These details are drawn largely from John Kifner, "The Back Page: Unsettling; The Bush Plan: Put the Toughest Hurdles First," *New York Times,* June 8, 2003.

2. Arnon Regular, " 'Road Map Is a Life Saver for Us,' PM Abbas Tells Ha'aretz," *Ha'aretz,* June 26, 2003.

3. Ari Fleischer, Press Briefing, James S. Brady Briefing Room, Washington, DC, July 1, 2003.

4. Mitch Potter, "Bush: My Vision for the Mideast," *Toronto Star,* June 4, 2003.

5. Francine Kiefer, "The Private Faith of a Public Man," *Christian Science Monitor,* September 6, 2002.

6. Stephen Mansfield, *The Faith of George W. Bush* (New York: Penguin, 2003), 162, confirmed in a follow-up interview in Paul Harris, "Bush Says God Chose Him to Lead His Nation," London *Observer,* November 2, 2003.

7. Deborah Sontag, "The Erdogan Experiment," *New York Times Magazine,* May 11, 2003.

8. Bill Keller, "God and George W. Bush," *New York Times,* May 17, 2003.

9. Tony Carnes, "A Presidential Hopeful's Progress," *Christianity Today,* October 2, 2000.

10. Mansfield, *The Faith of George W. Bush,* 109.

11. Jim Wallis, "George W. Bush's Theology of Empire," *Sojourners,* September-October 2003.

12. Mansfield, *The Faith of George W. Bush,* 110–111.

13. Reed quoted in Dana Milbank, "Religious Right Finds Its Center in Oval Office; Bush Emerges as Movement's Leader After Robertson Leaves Christian Coalition," *Washinton Post,* December 24, 2001; Goeglein quoted in Joel C. Rosenberg, "Political Buzz from Washington," *World,* October 6, 2001.

14. David Frum, *The Right Man: The Surprise Presidency of George W. Bush* (New York: Random House, 2003), 4, 284.

15. Michael Duffy, "Marching Alone," *Time,* September 9, 2002.

16. Bob Woodward, *Plan of Attack* (New York: Simon & Schuster, 2004), 421.

17. Howard Fineman, "Bush and God," *Newsweek,* March 10, 2003.

18. Ron Suskind, *The Price of Loyalty: George W. Bush, the White House, and the Education of Paul O'Neill* (New York: Simon & Schuster, 2004), 292.

19. Transcript of Pat Robertson's interview with Jerry Falwell on the *700 Club,* September 13, 2001, reprinted in Bruce Lincoln, *Holy Terrors: Thinking About Religion After September 11* (Chicago: University of Chicago Press, 2003), 106.

20. Graham in "Graham Stands by Characterization of Islam as 'Wicked,' " Associated Press, November 19, 2001; Vines in Deborah Caldwell, "Should Christian Missionaries Heed the Call in Iraq?" *New York Times,* April 6, 2003; Robertson in Matthew Lee, "US Evangelist Says Muslims 'Worse than Nazis,' Urges Jews to Know Enemy," Agence France Presse, November 12, 2002; Falwell in "Nine Dead, 100 Injured in Western Indian City After Riots," Agence France Presse, October 13, 2002.

21. "Evangelical Views of Islam," Beliefnet and Ethics and Public Policy Center, April

7, 2003, available at www.beliefnet.com/story/124/story_12447_1.html; "Americans Struggle with Religion's Role at Home and Abroad," Pew Research Center for the People and the Press, March 20, 2002, available at people-press.org.

22. Laurie Goodstein, "Seeing Islam as 'Evil' Faith, Evangelicals Seek Converts," *New York Times*, May 27, 2003.

23. On the 10–40 window, see Window International Network at win1040.com; on Nazarene, see "What Is the 10/40 Window?" Nazarene Missions International, at www.nazarenemissions.org/prayer/10_40_window.htm; on the Baptist seminary and the number of missionaries see Caldwell, "Should Christian Missionaries Heed the Call in Iraq?"; for the survey data see "Evangelical Views of Islam," Beliefnet.

24. Johanna Neuman, "Bundling of Aid, Christianity Stirs Concerns; Evangelical Groups' Plans to Spread the Gospel Along with Food and Medicine in Iraq Could Complicate Rebuilding Efforts," *Los Angeles Times*, April 9, 2003.

25. Caldwell, "Should Christian Missionaries Heed the Call in Iraq?"

26. John Blake, "Aid vs Evangelism: Some Say Christian Missionaries to Iraq Should Provide Food, But Not Force-Feed Their Message," *Atlanta Journal-Constitution*, May 10, 2003.

27. Blake, "Aid vs Evangelism."

28. Laurie Goodstein, "Groups Critical of Islam Are Now Waiting to Take Aid to Iraq," *New York Times*, April 4, 2003, and Jean Marbella, "Graham's Appearance at Pentagon Draws Fire: It Sends 'Wrong Message' to Muslims, Critics Say," *Baltimore Sun*, April 19, 2003.

29. On Christian Missionary Alliance see Neuman, "Bundling of Aid"; on In Touch see Nicholas Wapshott, "Alarm at American Crusade to Convert Muslims," *Times* of London, April 19, 2003; on Arab World Ministries see Goodstein, "Seeing Islam as 'Evil' Faith, Evangelicals Seek Converts."

30. Michelle Cottle, "Bible Brigade," *New Republic*, April 21, 2003 and Neuman, "Bundling of Aid."

31. Neuman, "Bundling of Aid."

32. George W. Bush, "President Welcomes Aid Workers Rescued from Afghanistan," Rose Garden, White House, Washington, DC, November 26, 2001, available at www.whitehouse.gov.

33. On the pamphlets, see Dana Milbank, "In Brief," *Washington Post*, April 1, 2003 and Max Blumenthal, "Onward Christian Soldiers," *Salon.com*, April 15, 2003. On the baptisms, see Meg Laughlin, "Water Shortage Works to Chaplain's Advantage," *Miami Herald*, April 7, 2003, and Gill Donavan, "Army Probe Clears Chaplain of Coercive Baptisms," *National Catholic Reporter*, April 25, 2003. On Abu Ghraib, see Steven Lee Myers, "Testimony from Abu Ghraib Prisoners Describe a Center of Violence and Fear, *New York Times*, May 22, 2004.

34. "Defaming Islam," *Washington Post*, October 6, 2002.

35. Ari Fleischer, Press Briefing, October 9, 2002, available at www.whitehouse.gov/news/releases/2002/10/20021009-3.html.

36. George W. Bush, "Remarks by the President Upon Arrival," South Lawn, White House, Washington, DC, September 16, 2001, available at www.whitehouse.gov; Ari Fleischer, Press Briefing, September 18, 2001, available at www.whitehouse.gov/news/releases/2001/09/20010918-5.html.

37. On the Pentagon speech see Maureen Dowd, "A Tale of Two Fridays," *New York Times*, April 20, 2003; Eltantawi's quotation from Tosin Sulaiman and Sumana Chatterjee,

"Muslims Demand Pentagon Rescind Graham Invitation," Knight Ridder/Tribune News Service, April 16, 2003.

38. Jim Wallis, "Dangerous Religion: George W. Bush's Theology of Empire," *Sojourners*, September-October 2003.

39. George W. Bush, "President Bush Announces Major Combat Operations in Iraq Have Ended," aboard USS *Abraham Lincoln* off the coast of San Diego, California, May 1, 2003, available at www.whitehouse.gov.

40. See, e.g., Messianic Prophecy at www.messianic-prophecy.net/.

41. John Ashcroft, "Prepared Remarks of Attorney General John Ashcroft," National Religious Broadcasters Convention, Nashville, Tennessee, February 19, 2002, available at www.usdoj.gov/ag/speeches/2002/021902religiousbroadcasters.htm.

42. "Arab Americans Call on President to Insist Ashcroft Clarify Offensive Remarks," Arab American Institute press release, February 8, 2002, available through PR Newswire.

43. *The Status of Muslim Civil Rights in the United States 2002*, Council on American-Islamic Relations, 2002.

44. Richard T. Cooper, "General Casts War in Religious Terms: The Top Soldier Assigned to Track Down Bin Laden and Hussein Is an Evangelical Christian Who Speaks Publicly of 'the Army of God,'" *Los Angeles Times*, October 16, 2003, and Lisa Myers, "Controversial Views Could Complicate Mission of Newly Promoted Deputy Undersecretary of Defense, Lieutenant General William Jerry Boykin," on *NBC Nightly News*, hosted by Tom Brokaw, October 15, 2003.

45. Gary L. Bauer, president, American Values, letter addressed to the author, November 25, 2003.

46. Ibish on *CNN Crossfire*, hosts Tucker Carlson and Paul Begala, October 22, 2003; Rumsfeld and Myers at Defense Department Operational Update Briefing, Pentagon Briefing Room, Arlington, Virginia, October 16, 2003; Warner and Rumsfeld's investigation in Bradley Graham, "Pentagon to Probe Remarks by General: Boykin Angered Muslims, Lawmakers," *Washington Post*, October 22, 2003.

47. Remarks on Malaysian prime minister Mahathir, Interview of the President by the Press Pool, Air Force One, en route to Canberra, Australia, October 22, 2003; remarks on Boykin at Press Conference by the President, Rose Garden, White House, Washington, DC, October 28, 2003.

48. Bauer in Gary L. Bauer, "Boykin's Fate," *End of Day*, e-mail to members of American Values, October 23, 2003; petition, addressed to Secretary of State Donald Rumsfeld and entitled "Support Lieutenant General William G. Boykin," was posted on the Christian Coalition Web site at www.cc.org; Dobson on Focus on the Family syndicated radio program, November 12, 2003; Awad in "Top U.S. General Says Muslims Worship 'Idol'; Islamic Group Calls for Reassignment Over 'Extremist' Views," Council on American-Islamic Relations press release, October 16, 2003, available from U.S. Newswire.

49. Garance Franke-Ruta, "Jews in Play?" *American Prospect*, May 1, 2003.

50. George W. Bush, "President Bush Calls for New Palestinian Leadership," Rose Garden, White House, Washington, DC, June 24, 2002, available at www.whitehouse.gov.

51. E.J. Kessler, "Bush Bid for Jews' Votes Zeroes in on Gen X," *Forward*, July 11, 2003.

52. Richard W. Stevenson, "Bush Campaign Plays up Pro-Israel Stance," *New York Times*, May 15, 2004.

53. Upton from Rick Perlstein, "The Jesus Landing Pad," *Village Voice*, May 18, 2004; "Proclamation of the Fourth International Christian Congress on Biblical Zionism," February 22, 2001, available at christianactionforisrael.org/4thcongress3.html.

54. "American Christians and Support for Israel," executive summary, the Tarrance Group, October 9, 2002; "Religion and Politics: Contention and Consensus," Pew Forum on Religion and Public Life, July 24, 2003.

55. "Israeli Government Officials to Speak Across U.S. on Oct. 26 Day of Prayer and Solidarity with Israel," Stand for Israel press release, October 22, 2003.

56. "What We Believe," Mount Paran Church of God, at www.mtparan.org/whatwebelieve.asp.

57. David C. Cooper, *Apocalypse! A New Look at the Book of Revelation* (Cleveland, TN: Pathway Press, 1999).

58. Jerry Falwell, *Listen America!* (Garden City, NY: Doubleday and Company, 1980), 113, quoted in Michael Lienesch, *Redeeming America: Piety & Politics in the New Christian Right* (Chapel Hill: University of North Carolina Press, 1993), 231.

59. "What Is CIPAC?" Christians' Israel Public Action Campaign, at www.cipaconline. org/.

60. The rally numbers were reported in Tatsha Robertson, "Evangelicals Flock to Israel's Banner; Christian Zionists See Jewish State Bringing Messiah," *Boston Globe,* October 21, 2002, and the rally text is from the Christian Coalition rally flier entitled, "Christian Support for Israel Rally"; Americans for a Safe Israel advertisement, December 20, 2002, available at www.afsi.org/ADS/ad-2002dec19.htm; the letter quoted is Gary L. Bauer et al., letter to President of the United States George W. Bush, May 19, 2003; postcards from Perlstein, "The Jesus Landing Pad."

61. Robertson, "Evangelicals Flock."

62. Joseph Farah, "My Meeting with President Bush," WorldNetDaily.com, August 7, 2001; Scott Thompson and Jeffrey Steinberg, "The 'Mega-Maniacs' Steering Sharon's Mideast War Drive," *Executive Intelligence Review,* November 16, 2001; Perlstein, "The Jesus Landing Pad."

63. These details are drawn from Joan Didion, "Mr. Bush & the Divine," *New York Review of Books,* November 6, 2003 and from LaHaye's official Web site, www.leftbehind.com.

64. The 1995 essay is Phyllis Schlafly, "The United Nations—An Enemy in Our Midst," *Phyllis Schlafly Report,* November 1995, available at eagleforum.org/psr/1995/psrnov95.html; on the defunding drive, see "United Nations Attempts to Steal U.S. Sovereignty," Concerned Women for America press release, March 5, 1997; the video is for sale through the Eagle Forum at www.eagleforum.org/order/video/gg.html.

65. On the women's rights treaty, see Wendy Wright, "CEDAW: A Global Tool that Would Harm Women," Concerned Women for America, August 27, 2002; on the children's rights treaty, see "The New World Order Wants Your Children," Eagle Forum, March 1993 and Austin Ruse, "Toward a Permanent United Nations Pro-Family Bloc," address to the World Congress of Families, Geneva, November 14–17, 1999.

66. Tim LaHaye, *The Coming Peace in the Middle East* (Grand Rapids, MI: Zondervan Publishing, 1984), quoted in Lienesch, *Redeeming America,* 315. For a discussion of the meaning of the "new world order" on the Christian right, see Lienesch, *Redeeming America,* 237.

67. Brent Scowcroft, "Don't Attack Saddam," *Wall Street Journal,* August 15, 2002.

68. George W. Bush, "State of the Union Address," U.S. Capitol, Washington, DC, January 20, 2004, available at www.whitehouse.gov.

69. "World Summit for Children: February 1, 2001," Concerned Women for America, January 1, 2002.

CHAPTER 2: CHRISTIAN NATION

1. Judy Bachrach, "John Ashcroft's Patriot Games," *Vanity Fair,* February 2004.

2. David Johnston and Neil A. Lewis, "Religious Right Made Big Push to Put Ashcroft in Justice Department," *New York Times,* January 7, 2001.

3. Vicki Haddock, "Son of a Preacher Man," *San Francisco Chronicle,* August 4, 2002.

4. Jeffrey Toobin, "Ashcroft's Ascent," *New Yorker,* April 15, 2002.

5. Bachrach, "John Ashcroft's Patriot Games."

6. Steve Benen, "One Nation, Easily Divisible?" *Church & State,* July-August 2002.

7. People for the American Way, *Two Years After 9/11: Ashcroft's Assault on the Constitution,* September 9, 2003.

8. Amicus brief, *Locke v. Davey,* at www.usdoj.gov:80/osg/briefs/2003/3mer/1ami/2002-1315.mer.ami.html.

9. "Transcript: Interview with the Secretary of Education," *Baptist Press,* April 11, 2003, www.bpnews.net/bpnews.asp?ID=15707.

10. "Guidance on Constitutionally Protected Prayer in Public Elementary and Secondary Schools," U.S. Department of Education, February 28, 2003.

11. Michael Foust, "Federal Prayer Guidelines Resulting in Fewer Complaints, Sekulow Says," *Baptist Press,* May 15, 2003, www.lifeway.com/lwc/article_main_page/0,1703,A%253D153365%2526M%253D50011,00.html.

12. National Gay and Lesbian Task Force, "Gale Norton, Secretary of the Interior," www.thetaskforce.org/federal/wwnorton.htm.

13. From Frank Rich, "Apres Janet, a Deluge," *New York Times,* March 21, 2004, and Paul Farhi, "FCC Commissioner's Mission: Cleaning Up Radio, Television," *Washington Post,* March 22, 2004.

14. The e-mails cited refer to: Gary L. Bauer, "End of Day,"e-mail to the membership of American Values, February 2, 2004; Gary Schneeberger, editor, "CitizenLink,"e-mail to the membership of Focus on the Family, February 4, 2004; and Tony Perkins, "Washington Update," e-mail to the members of the Family Research Council, February 2, 2004.

15. "Ashcroft Urges States, Charities, and Churches to Embrace Landmark Reforms in New Welfare Law," Sen. John Ashcroft press release, October 10, 1996, available through the Federal Document Clearing House.

16. George W. Bush, "President's Remarks at Faith-Based and Community Initiatives Conference," Los Angeles Convention Center, Los Angeles, California, March 3, 2004, available at www.whitehouse.gov.

17. National Religious Broadcasters, "Statement of Faith," available at www.nrb.org.

18. George W. Bush, "President Bush Discusses Faith-Based Initiative in Tennessee," Opryland Hotel, Nashville, Tennessee, February 10, 2003, available at www.whitehouse.gov.

19. "A Resolution to Honor President George W. Bush," Resolution 2003-3, National Religious Broadcasters, February 8, 2003, available at www.nrb.org.

20. Rebecca Carr, "Leading the (Faith-Based) Way," *Austin American-Statesman,* April 9, 2001.

21. See the Values Action Team roster for this and other identifications of Values Action Team members, available at www.house.gov/pitts/vat.htm.

22. Biographical information is mostly pulled from White House Faith-Based and Community Initiatives, *White House Office of Faith-Based and Community Initiatives and the Agency Centers.*

23. Texas Freedom Network Education Fund, "The Texas Faith-Based Initiative at Five Years," October 10, 2002.

24. Jim Towey, "Ask the White House," November 26, 2003, available at www.whitehouse.gov.

25. Paul Krugman, "The Tax-Cut Con," *New York Times,* September 14, 2003.

26. John DiIulio Jr., "Text of a Speech Delivered Before the National Association of Evangelicals," March 7, 2001, available through U.S. Newswire.

27. Myron Magnet, *The Dream and the Nightmare: The Sixties Legacy to the Underclass* (San Francisco: Encounter Books, 1993), 51.

28. Magnet, *The Dream and the Nightmare,* 74.

29. Marvin Olasky, *Compassionate Conservatism: What It Is, What It Does, and How It Can Transform America* (New York: Free Press, 2000), xi.

30. Olasky, *Compassionate Conservatism,* xxi.

31. Ibid, 102.

32. For example, Bush, "President Bush Discusses Faith-Based Initiative," February 10, 2003.

33. Joseph Loconte, *God, Government, and the Good Samaritan: The Promise and Peril of the President's Faith-Based Agenda* (Washington, D.C.: Heritage Foundation, 2001).

34. Mary Leonard, "Bush Targets Support of Blacks: Faith-Based Efforts Focus on Churches," *Boston Globe,* March 11, 2001.

35. Mary Leonard, "Faith-Based Office Chief Under Fire; White House Responds to Conservatives," *Boston Globe,* March 17, 2001.

36. Jackson and Scott quotations from Leonard, "Faith-Based Office Chief."

37. Thomas B. Edsall and Alan Cooperman, "GOP Using Faith Initiative to Woo Voters: Office's Officials Have Appeared with Republican Candidates in Tight Races," *Washington Post,* September 15, 2002.

38. Leonard, "Faith-Based Office Chief."

39. Fallwell comments in Deborah Caldwell, "Falwell: Deep Concerns," Beliefnet, March 6, 2001, www.beliefnet.com/story/70/story_7040_1.html; Robertson comments in Steven Waldman, "Doubts Among the Faithful," *New York Times,* March 7, 2001.

40. DiIulio, "Text of a Speech."

41. Leonard, "Faith-Based Office Chief."

42. This is a reference to the Coalition Against Religious Discrimination, which began criticizing the faith-based initiative in January 2001; see, e.g., their January 30, 2001, letter to the president, available at www.house.gov/scott/c_choice/coalition_against_ religious_discrimination_letter_01_30_01.htm.

43. Steve Benen, "On a Wing and a Prayer," *Church & State,* May 2001.

44. Connie Marshner, "Statement for Distribution at Coalition for Compassion Press Conference," April 11, 2001, available at www.freecongress.org/media/2001/010411.asp.

45. Steve Benen, "Pat Gets Paid," *Church & State,* November 2002.

46. "President Bush Is Joined by Labor Secretary Elaine L. Chao and Attorney General John Ashcroft for Discussion on Job Training Programs for Ex-Offenders," U.S. Department of Labor press release, June 18, 2003, www.dol.gov/opa/media/press/opa/OPA2003321.htm.

47. Grant information from U.S. Department of Health and Human Services press releases, "HHS Awards $17.1 Million in Abstinence-Only Education Grants," July 6, 2001; "HHS Awards Grants Nationwide to Support Abstinence Education, Services to Teens," July 2, 2002; "HHS Awards New Grants to Support Abstinence Education Among

Nation's Teens," July 2, 2003; quotation from Metro Atlanta Youth for Christ newsletter, September 2003, available at www.atlantayfc.org/newsletter/default.asp?content=active.

48. DiIulio, "Text of a Speech."

49. Rivers quotation from Dana Milbank, "DiIulio Resigns from Top 'Faith-Based' Post," *Washington Post,* August 18, 2001; Falwell quotation from Joseph Conn, "DiIulio Departs," *Church & State,* October 2001.

50. Ron Suskind, "Why Are These Men Laughing?" *Esquire,* January 2003.

51. Operation Blessing, "Statement of Faith," available at www.ob.org/about/statement_of_faith.asp.

52. Daniel Zwerdling, "Colorado Program Tests Church-State Divide," National Public Radio, November 1, 2003.

53. White House Faith-Based and Community Initiatives, *Guidance to Faith-Based and Community Organizations on Partnering with the Federal Government.*

54. George W. Bush, "State of the Union Address," U.S. Capitol, Washington, DC, January 28, 2003, available at www.whitehouse.gov.

55. David Frum, *The Right Man: The Surprise Presidency of George W. Bush* (New York: Random House, 2003), 283.

56. Joseph Conn, "Presidential Altar Call: Bush Urges Addicts to Find Miracles at 'Faith-Based'Addiction Programs, Proposes HUD Funds for Church Construction," *Church & State,* March 2003.

57. Castellani's attendance in "Attendees at Faith-Based Event," White House press release, January 26, 2001; Castellani comment in Conn. "Presidential Altar Call."

58. U.S. General Accounting Office, *Drug Abuse: Research Shows Treatment Is Effective but Benefits May Be Overstated,* March 1998, and Eyal Press, "Lead Us Not into Temptation," *American Prospect,* April 9, 2001.

59. See "Teen Challenge's Proven Answer to the Drug Problem: A Review of a Study by Dr. Aaron T. Bicknese,"available at www.teenchallenge.com/tcreview.html.

60. See Press, "Lead Us Not into Temptation," and Emily Pyle, "Faith-Based Homes on Trial," *Austin Chronicle,* December 15, 2000.

61. Maia Szalavitz, "Why Jesus Is Not a Regulator," *American Prospect,* April 9, 2001.

62. *The Texas Faith-Based Initiative at Five Years,* Texas Freedom Network Education Fund, October 10, 2002, available at www.tfn.org.

63. Matt Porio, "Keeping the Faith Has Its Cost," *Newsday,* March 23, 2003.

64. "President Bush Puts Forward Final Installment of Faith-Based Plan: ACLU Opposes Tax-Payer Funded Religious Discrimination," American Civil Liberties Union press release, September 22, 2003.

65. Steve Benen, "Faith-Based Barricade," *Church & State,* February 2002.

66. *American Civil Liberties Union of Louisiana v. Governor M.J. Foster,* Memorandum of Law in Support of Motion for Preliminary Injunction.

67. "ACLU Applauds Decision by State Health Officials to Recall Religious AIDS Education Brochures," American Civil Liberties Union of Florida press release, April 8, 2003.

68. " 'Faith-Based' Initiative Threatens Church-State Separation: AU's Lynn Tells Congressional Panel," Americans United for Separation of Church and State press release, March 23, 2004.

69. Coalition Against Religious Discrimination, letter to the president, January 30, 2001, available at www.house.gov/scott/c_choice/coalition_against_religious_discrimination_letter_01_30_01.htm.

70. Olasky, *Compassionate Conservatism,* 127.

71. D. James Kennedy, *The Gates of Hell Shall Not Prevail* (Nashville, Nelson Reference, 1997), quoted in Rob Boston, "D. James Kennedy: Who Is He and What Does He Want?" *Church & State,* April 1999.

72. This belief on the part of Robertson, Dobson, and LaHaye is widely documented, including in Randall Balmer, "Bush and God," *Nation,* April 14, 2003; the Falwell quotation is from a March 1993 sermon, reported in "The Falwell Follies," *Church & State,* May 2000.

73. Sara Diamond, *Roads to Dominion: Right-Wing Movements and Political Power in the United States* (New York: Guildford Press, 1995), 246–48.

74. Rep. Bobby Scott, "Statement at Press Conference on Opposition to Charitable Choice," Washington, DC, April 24, 2001, available at www.house.gov/scott/c_choice/statement.at.nadler.press.conf.htm.

75. Dana Milbank, "Charity Cites Bush Help in Fight Against Hiring Gays: Salvation Army Wants Exemption from Laws," *Washington Post,* July 10, 2001, and Mike Allen and Dana Milbank, "Rove Heard Charity Plea on Gay Bias: White House Denied Senior Aides Had Role," *Washington Post,* July 12, 2001.

76. "Comments of People for the American Way Foundation Regarding Proposed Rule on Participation in HUD Programs by Faith Based Organizations: Providing for Equal Treatment of All HUD Program Participants," submitted March 7, 2003 and "Comments of People for the American Way Foundation Regarding Proposed Regulation on Charitable Choice Provisions Applicable to Programs Authorized Under the Community Services Block Grant Act," submitted February 20, 2003, available at www.pfaw.org. Salvation Army rule documented in "NYCLU Says No to Salvation Army Discrimination," *NYCLU News,* Spring/Summer 2004.

77. Gary D. Bass, Kay Guinane, and Ryan Turner, *An Attack on Nonprofit Speech: Death by a Thousand Cuts,* OMB Watch, July 2003, 2.

78. Bill Peterson, "Coalition Pushes Block Grants to 'Defund' the Left," *Washington Post,* July 2, 1981.

79. George J. Church, "Seeking Strategy on Social Issues: Rightists Agree on Policy, But They Differ on Ways and Means," *Time,* September 14, 1981.

80. "Washington Update," *National Journal,* January 16, 1982.

81. Susan Cohen, "Debate Over Abortion, Family Planning Expected During Next 100 Days," *Washington Memo,* Alan Guttmacher Institute, April 25, 1995.

82. See "Greenpeace Under Ashcroft Attack," *Watcher,* OMB Watch, November 17, 2003; "Complicated and Expensive Reporting for Labor Unions Is Put on Hold," *Watcher,* OMB Watch, January 12, 2004; and "Administration Threatens Head Start Programs," *Watcher,* OMB Watch, June 4, 2003. Additional information from interviews with Kay Guinane, manager, Community Education Center, OMB Watch, and Paul Kawata, executive director, National Minority AIDS Council.

83. Chris Brennan, "Government Funds Philadelphia Program to Educate Parents on School Options," *Philadelphia Daily News,* October 16, 2002.

84. *The USA Patriot Act and Its Impact on Nonprofit Organizations,* OMB Watch, September 10, 2003.

85. "Faith-Based Initiative Gets a Push with Set Aside Funds," *Watcher,* OMB Watch, January 26, 2004.

86. Ralph G. Neas, *Five Years and Counting: A Closer Look at the Cleveland Voucher Program,* People for the American Way, September 25, 2001.

87. George W. Bush, "Remarks by the President in a Conversation on Parental

Options and School Choice," Archbishop Carroll High School, Washington, DC, February 13, 2004, available at www.whitehouse.gov.

88. For this figure and the $14 million figure above, see for example, "Bush Repeats Support for School Vouchers," Associated Press, February 13, 2004.

CHAPTER 3: MOST FAVORED CONSTITUENCY

1. Stephen Mansfield, *The Faith of George W. Bush* (New York: Penguin, 2003), 68.

2. Bill Minutaglio, *First Son: George W. Bush and the Bush Family Dynasty* (New York: Crown, 1999), quoted in Mansfield, *The Faith of George W. Bush*, 76, 83, and Kevin Phillips, *American Dynasty: Aristocracy, Fortune, and the Politics of Deceit in the House of Bush* (New York: Viking, 2004), 213.

3. Mansfield, *The Faith of George W. Bush*, 69.

4. The quotation is from Marvin Olasky, "In from the Cold," *World*, February 10, 2001.

5. James Moore and Wayne Slater, *Bush's Brain: How Karl Rove Made George W. Bush Presidential* (Hoboken: John Wiley, 2003), 146.

6. Lou Dubose, Jan Reid, and Carl M. Cannon, *Boy Genius: Karl Rove, the Brains Behind the Remarkable Political Triumph of George W. Bush* (New York: Public Affairs, 2003), 167.

7. Nicholas Lemann, "The Controller: Karl Rove Is Working to Get George Bush Reelected, But He Has Bigger Plans," *New Yorker*, May 12, 2003.

8. Ibid.

9. Moore and Slater, *Bush's Brain*, 161–62.

10. Fred Barnes, "Conservatives Love George W. Bush: But Will the Romance Last?" *Weekly Standard*, March 5, 2001.

11. Dubose et al., *Boy Genius*, 133; Mansfield, *The Faith of George W. Bush*, 107.

12. Mansfield, *The Faith of George W. Bush*, 109–12.

13. Dubose et al., *Boy Genius*, 167; Barnes, "The Impresario: Karl Rove, Orchestrator of the Bush White House," *Weekly Standard*, August 27, 2001.

14. Lemann, "The Controller."

15. Moore and Slater, *Bush's Brain*, 255–56.

16. Karen Armstrong, *The Battle for God: A History of Fundamentalism* (New York: Ballantine, 2001), 275.

17. Excellent sources on this history are Sara Diamond, *Roads to Dominion: Right-Wing Movements and Political Power in the United States* (New York: Guildford Press, 1995) and Jean Hardisty, *Mobilizing Resentment: Conservative Resurgence from the John Birch Society to the Promise Keepers* (Boston: Beacon Press, 1999).

18. Jim Whittle, "All in the Family: Top Bush Administration Leaders, Religious Right Lieutenants Plot Strategy in Culture 'War,' " *Church & State*, May 2002.

19. Kimberly H. Conger, John C. Green, "Spreading Out and Digging In: Christian Conservatives and State Republican Parties," *Campaigns & Elections*, February 2002.

20. Jim Jones, "Moderates Unite? The Future of Southern Baptist Dissidents," *Christian Century*, August 14, 2002.

21. Hardisty, *Mobilizing Resentment*, 19.

22. Jones from Walter H. Capps, *The New Religious Right: Piety, Patriotism, and Politics* (Columbia: University of South Carolina Press, 1990), 98; Southern Baptists from "Baptists Seek to Convert Mormons, Other 'Cult' Members," Associated Press, January 22, 2000.

23. Chip Berlet, "Religion and Politics in the United States," *Public Eye*, Summer 2003, based on research by the Glenmary Research Center.

24. Robin Toner, "Biding Time, Conservatives Hold Breath and Brimstone," *New York Times*, August 3, 2000.

25. Voter News Service data, November 11, 2000.

26. "Third National Survey of Religion and Politics," University of Akron Survey Research Center, Fall 2000, quoted in John C. Green and John DiIulio, "How the Faithful Voted," *Center Conversations*, Ethics and Public Policy Center, November 11, 2000; Reagan comparison from 1984 and 1988 exit polls quoted in Herman Schwartz, *Packing the Courts: The Conservative Campaign to Rewrite the Constitution* (New York: Scribner's, 1988), 24.

27. Lyman A. Kellstedt, Corwin E. Smidt, James L. Guth, and John C. Green, "Cracks in the Monolith? Evangelical Protestants and the 2000 Election," *Books & Culture*, May/June 2001, a publication of *Christianity Today*.

28. C. Hart, "Mobilizing Against the 'Road Map,'" CBN.com, July 15, 2003.

29. Elisabeth Bumiller and Richard W. Stevenson, "A Trusted Bush Aide to Return, But Not to Washington," *New York Times*, March 28, 2004.

30. Moore and Slater, *Bush's Brain*, 146.

31. Ibid, 258.

32. Ibid, 267.

33. Phillips, *American Dynasty*, 147.

34. Barnes, "The Impresario."

35. DuBose et al., *Boy Genius*, 193; Barnes, "The Impresario."

36. Dana Milbank, "Religious Right Finds Its Center in Oval Office: Bush Emerges as Movement's Leader After Robertson Leaves Christian Coalition," *Washington Post*, December 24, 2001.

37. Don Parker, "National Right to Life Leaders Meet with President Bush," *National Right to Life News*, February 2002, reprinted from the *National Catholic Register*.

38. Bruce Lincoln, *Holy Terrors: Thinking About Religion After September 11* (Chicago: University of Chicago Press, 2003), 99.

39. Ibid, 30.

40. Steve Burger, executive director, Association of Gospel Rescue Missions, in *Rescue Happenings*, February 2002.

41. Ceci Connolly, "AIDS Panel Director Leaves Amid Controversy Over Activist," *Washington Post*, February 5, 2003.

42. See, e.g., "White House Disavows Christian View on Homosexuality," American Family Association press release, January 24, 2003.

43. David D. Kirkpatrick, "In Fight Over Gay Marriage, Evangelicals Are Conflicted," *New York Times*, February 28, 2004.

44. "Top Bush Aide Assures Religious Right About White House Agenda," *Church & State*, March 2001.

45. Barnes, "Conservatives Love George W. Bush."

46. Olasky, "In from the Cold."

47. Barnes, "Conservatives Love George W. Bush."

48. Whittle, "All in the Family"; Robin Toner, "Conservatives Savor Their Role as Insiders at the White House," *New York Times*, March 19, 2001.

49. Joel C. Rosenberg, "Political Buzz from Washington," *World*, May 19, 2001.

50. Barnes, "Conservatives Love George W. Bush."

51. Jim Vandehei and Elizabeth Crowley, "Bush Keeps the Faith with Religious Right: Attracts a Spirited Following Father Lacked," *Wall Street Journal*, June 13, 2001.

52. Whittle, "All in the Family."

53. Rosenberg, "Flash Traffic," *World*, March 24, 2001.

54. Rosenberg, "Political Buzz from Washington," *World*, October 6, 2001; "Graham Stands by Characterization of Islam as 'Wicked,'" Associated Press, November 19, 2001.

55. Whittle, "All in the Family."

56. Ron Suskind, "Why Are These Men Laughing?" *Esquire*, January 2003; John DiIulio Jr. "Text of a Speech Delivered Before the National Association of Evangelicals," March 7, 2001, available through U.S. Newswire.

57. Ryan Lizza, "Salvation," *New Republic*, April 23, 2001; Vandehei and Crowley, "Bush Keeps the Faith."

58. Toner, "Conservatives Savor Their Role as Insiders at the White House."

59. Liz Marlantes, "Bush's Alter Ego with a Sense of History," *Christian Science Monitor*, January 24, 2003.

60. Mansfield, *The Faith*, 117; David Frum, *The Right Man: The Surprise Presidency of George W. Bush* (New York: Random House, 2003), 24.

61. Jonathan E. Kaplan, "Think Tanks Survey Policy Landscape in Post-Iraq, Pre-Election Environment: From AEI to PPI, Policy Wonks Jockey for Influence in the Bush Administration," *Hill*, June 11, 2003; Ron Suskind, *The Price of Loyalty: George W. Bush, the White House, and the Education of Paul O'Neill* (New York: Simon & Schuster, 2004), 34.

62. Whittle, "All in the Family."

63. See the National Fatherhood Initiative Web site at fatherhood.org.

64. DuBose et al., *Boy Genius*, 194; Barnes, "Conservatives Love George W. Bush."

65. Grover Norquist, "Conservatives Grow Up; Bush's Tactics Don't Incite Fears of Betrayal," *American Spectator*, April 2001.

66. Phillips, *American Dynasty*, 226.

67. *State of the Administration 2003*, National Stonewall Democrats, January 28, 2003.

68. Phillips, *American Dynasty*, 227.

69. Carla Marinucci, "Gays Protest Choice for GOP Faith Summit," *San Francisco Chronicle*, April 25, 2001.

70. Milbank, "Religious Right."

71. Toner, "Conservatives Savor Their Role as Insiders at the White House."

72. Vandehei and Crowley, "Bush Keeps the Faith."

73. Lemann, "The Controller."

74. Christine Whitman, "The Vital Republican Center," *New York Times*, January 12, 2004.

75. Suskind, "Why Are These Men Laughing?"; DiIulio e-mail to Suskind, subject "Your Next Essay on the Bush Administration," October 24, 2002.

76. Suskind, *The Price of Loyalty*, 107–109.

77. Ibid, 117.

78. Ibid, 121.

79. Ibid, 124.

80. Ibid, 130.

81. Ibid, 149.

82. Moore and Slater, *Bush's Brain*, 317.

CHAPTER 4: WEIRD SCIENCE

1. The details surrounding the Grand Canyon incident primarily come from interviews with Jeff Ruch, director, Public Employees for Environmental Responsibility, who blew the whistle on the story.

2. Murphy role in Kimberly Edds, "At Grand Canyon Park, a Rift Over Creationist Book," *Washington Post,* January 20, 2004.

3. Steve A. Austin, editor, *Grand Canyon: Monument to Catastrophe* (Santee, CA, Institute for Creation Research, 1995) as quoted in "Grand Canyon: Monument to the World-Wide Flood," *Creation Magazine,* March 1996.

4. Ron Strom, "E-mails on Creation Flap 'Swamp' Park Service," WorldNetDaily.com, January 14, 2004.

5. Alliance Defense Fund, "Our Mission," alliancedefensefund.org/about/.

6. Edds, "At Grand Canyon Park, a Rift over Creationist Book."

7. Letter from Dale M. Schowengerdt, staff attorney, Alliance Defense Fund, to Gale A. Norton, secretary of the interior, January 9, 2004.

8. Letter from David B. Shaver, chief, Geologic Resources Division, U.S. Department of the Interior, to Chick Fagan, Office of Policy, January 25, 2004.

9. "Creationist Book Re-Ordered and Offered as 'Natural History': Geologists Rebuffed," Public Employees for Environmental Responsibility press release, February 26, 2004.

10. Nicholas D. Kristof, "For Bush, His Toughest Call Was the Choice to Run at All," *New York Times,* October 29, 2000.

11. "Survey: Nat'l Park Service Workers See Parks Jeopardized by Political Interference, Special Interest Deals," Campaign to Protect America's Lands press release, November 13, 2003. The survey was conducted by Edge Research.

12. Philip W. Anderson et al., letter to President George W. Bush, February 18, 2004, initiated by the Union for Concerned Scientists and available at www.ucsusa.org/global_environment/rsi/page.cfm?pageID=1320.

13. John H. Marburger III, "Statement of the Honorable John H. Marburger III on Scientific Integrity in the Bush Administration," April 2, 2004, available at www.ostp.gov/html/ucs.html.

14. James Glanz, "At the Center of the Storm Over Bush and Science," *New York Times,* March 30, 2004.

15. Early coverage included Sabin Russell, " 'Scientific McCarthyism': AIDS, Sex Scientists on Federal List Fear Their Research Is in Jeopardy," *San Francisco Chronicle,* October 28, 2003, and Mark Sherman, "NIH Questions Researchers on AIDS Grants," Associated Press, October 28, 2003.

16. Rich McManus, "Hill Hearing Airs NIH Needs, Congress' Concerns," *NIH Record,* October 28, 2003.

17. "NIH Funds,"made available by the Republican Study Committee to conservative columnist Chuck Colson and posted at www.townhall.com/columnists/chuckcolson/cc20030924.shtml.

18. Jeff Miller, "Toomey Tries to Block Study of Prostitutes' HIV Risk," Allentown *Morning Call,* July 11, 2003.

19. Shirley Haley, "House Passes FY 2004 Health and Human Services Funding Measure After Floor Attempt to Defund NIH Research Grants," *Washington Fax,* July 11, 2003.

20. "HHS Grant Projects," a document for which the Traditional Values Coalition claim authorship.

21. Letter from Rep. Henry A. Waxman, ranking minority member, House Committee on Government Reform, to Tommy Thompson, secretary of health and human services, October 27, 2003.

22. Sherman, "NIH Questions Researchers on AIDS Grants", and Rick Weiss, "NIH Faces Criticism on Grants," *Washington Post,* October 30, 2003.

23. Letter from Tommy Thompson, secretary of health and human services, to Rep. Henry A. Waxman, October 28, 2003.

24. Ramesh Ponnuru, "Values for Sale," *National Review* online, July 17, 2003.

25. On Moloney's background, see, e.g., Piper Fogg, "People," *National Journal,* April 1, 2000. On Pitts, see "Rep. Pitts Wins 'True Blue'Award for Consistent Support of Family," Rep. Joe Pitts press release, October 23, 2003.

26. Grover Norquist, "Dobson and the GOP," *American Spectator,* July 1998.

27. Values Action Team roster, available at www.house.gov/pitts/vat.htm.

28. Ceci Connolly, "U.S. Warns AIDS Groups on Funding: CDC Cites S.F. Programs that 'Appear to Encourage' Sex," *Washington Post,* June 14, 2003.

29. Sally T. Hillsman, "Statement by Sally T. Hillsman, Executive Officer of the American Sociological Association, on NIH-Funded Research and the Peer-Review Process," American Sociological Association press release, November 3, 2003.

30. See, for example, *Politics and Science in the Bush Administration,* House Committee on Government Reform, Special Investigations Division, August 2003; George Monbiot, "The Covert Biotech War," London *Guardian,* November 19, 2002; and Monbiot, "The Fake Persuaders," London *Guardian,* May 14, 2002.

31. "Precautionary Principle Campaign Proposal," proposal from public relations firm Nichols-Dezenhall to the American Chemical Council, March 16, 2004.

32. Eric Pianin, "Moving Target on Policy Battlefield: Increasingly, 'Science' Used by Proponents and Critics to Score a Shot," *Washington Post,* May 2, 2002.

33. *State of Misinformation About Climate Science,* Union of Concerned Scientists, February 2000.

34. On the arsenic episode, see, e.g., Eric Pianin and Cindy Skrzycki, "EPA to Kill New Arsenic Standards: Whitman Cites Debate on Drinking Water Risk," *Washington Post,* March 21, 2001, and Edward Walsh, "Arsenic Drinking Water Standard Issued: After Seven-Month Review, EPA Backs Clinton-Established Scientific Review Levels," *Washington Post,* November 1, 2001.

35. Andrew C. Revkin and Katharine Q. Seelye, "Report by EPA Leaves Out Data on Climate Change," *New York Times,* June 19, 2003.

36. "Greenpeace Obtains Smoking-Gun Memo: White House/Exxon Link," Greenpeace press release, September 9, 2003.

37. Karen Armstrong, *The Battle for God: A History of Fundamentalism* (New York: Ballantine, 2001), 140.

38. "Belief that Jews Were Responsible for Christ's Death Increases," Pew Research Center for the People and the Press, April 2, 2004.

39. Steve Benen, "From Genesis to Dominion, Fat-Cat Theocrat Funds Creationism Crusade," *Church & State,* July-August 2000.

40. Christian Medical and Dental Associations, "Our Mission," "Our Statement of Faith," "Our Core Values," available at www.cmds.org.

41. See the Web site of the National Association for the Research and Therapy of Homosexuality, at www.narth.com.

42. National Gay and Lesbian Task Force, "Gale Norton, Secretary of the Interior," www.thetaskforce.org/federal/wwnorton.htm.

43. See the Web site of the Medical Institute for Sexual Health, at www.medinstitute. org.

44. See the Web site of the Institute for Youth Development at www.youthdevelopment. org.

45. "CDC: Physicians, Politicians Seek Chief's Resignation," *American Health Line*, July 25, 2001.

46. Robert E. Rector, Kirk A. Johnson, and Lauren R. Noyes, *Sexually Active Teenagers Are More Likely to Be Depressed and to Attempt Suicide*, Heritage Center for Data Analysis, June 2, 2003.

47. David Michaels et al., "Advice Without Dissent," *Science*, October 25, 2002.

48. Donald Kennedy, "An Epidemic of Politics," *Science*, January 31, 2003; "NIH Litmus Test?" *Science*, December 13, 2002; and *Scientific Integrity in Policymaking: An Investigation into the Bush Administration's Misuse of Science*, Union of Concerned Scientists, February 2004.

49. Dan Ferber, "Critics See a Tilt in a CDC Science Panel," *Science*, August 30, 2002.

50. Laurie Garrett, "Science vs. Ideology," *Seed*, March-April 2003.

51. Rick Weiss, "HHS Seeks Science Advice to Match Bush Views," *Washington Post*, September 17, 2002.

52. Ferber, "Critics See a Tilt."

53. *Scientific Integrity in Policymaking*, Union of Concerned Scientists; Sheryl Gay Stolberg, "Bush's Science Advisors Drawing Criticism," *New York Times*, October 10, 2002.

54. Garrett, "Science vs. Ideology"; Christian Medical and Dental Associations, www.cmds.org; Center for Bioethics and Human Dignity, "About the Center," www.cbhd.org.

55. Nancy L. Jones, letter to the President's Council on Bioethics, February 20, 2002.

56. Charter, Secretary's Advisory Committee for Human Research Protections, October 1, 2002, available at http://ohrp.osophs.dhhs.gov/sachrp/charter.pdf; for the Johnson quotation see Rick Weiss, "New Status for Embryos in Research," *Washington Post*, October 30,2002.

57. Stolberg, "Bush's Science Advisors Drawing Criticism."

58. "Public Contact Information for Presidential Advisory Council on HIV/AIDS (PACHA) Members," February 11, 2003, available at www.pacha.gov/staff/ members/members.html, and "Secretary Thompson Appoints Nine to CDC Advisory Committee," U.S. Department of Health and Human Services press release, February 20, 2003.

59. Joe S. McIlhaney Jr., testimony before the Subcommittee on Health of the Committee on Energy and Commerce, U.S. House of Representatives, April 23, 2002; "Federal Panel on Condoms Offers Crucial Warnings to Sexually Active Americans, Says the Medical Institute for Sexual Health," Medical Institute for Sexual Health press release, July 19, 2001.

60. "Secretary Thompson Appoints Nine to CDC Advisory Committee," HHS; "Public Contact Information for Presidential Advisory Council on HIV/AIDS (PACHA)

Members," PACHA; On Marilyn Billingsly's association with Focus on the Family, see, for example, "Doctor Care 101," *Physician* magazine, Focus on the Family, available at www.family.org/physmag/issues/a0010543.html; additional information from an interview with Pat Ware and e-mails sent by Roland Foster.

61. "FDA Names 11 Physicians to Advisory Committee for Reproductive Health Drugs," U.S. Food and Drug Administration press release, December 24, 2002; "HHS Announces Six New Appointments to CDC Advisory Committee on HIV and STD Prevention," U.S. Centers for Disease Control and Prevention press release, September 6, 2002; see Freda McKissic Bush biographical notes at the Medical Institute for Sexual Health Web site, at www.medinstitute.org.

62. On Coburn's affiliation with the Family Research Council, see "Ken Connor Named as Family Research Council President: Additional Leadership Changes Include New Board Member, Rep. Tom Coburn, and the Creation of National Advisory Committee," Family Research Council press release, September 26, 2000, available through PR Newswire; for Marilyn Billingsly's affiliation with *Adolescent & Family Health*, see the Web site of the Institute for Youth Development at www.youthdevelopment.org.

63. Garrett, "Science vs. Ideology."

64. "Potential Reviewers, SPRANS Abstinence Education Grants, 2003," U.S. Department of Health and Human Services.

65. Amy Goodman, host, "Scientific McCarthyism: Is the Bush Administration Compiling a Hit List of AIDS Scientists?" *Democracy Now,* syndicated radio program, November 5, 2003.

66. Michaels, et al., "Advice Without Dissent."

67. "Keeping Scientific Advice Non-Partisan," *Lancet,* November 16, 2002.

68. Karen Tumulty, "Jesus and the FDA," *Time,* October 5, 2002; W. David Hager et al., "Roundtable on Abstinence," *Physician* magazine, Focus on the Family, available at www.family.org/physmag/issues/a0011783.html; on Hager's refusal to prescribe RU-486, see Maureen Dowd, "Tribulation Worketh Patience," *New York Times,* October 9, 2002.

69. W. David Hager, *As Jesus Cared for Women* (Grand Rapids, MI: Fleming H. Revell, 1998), 57–58. Previous citation, 41–43.

70. W. David and Linda Carruth Hager, *Stress and the Woman's Body* (Grand Rapids, MI: Fleming H. Revell, 1996).

71. Tumulty, "Jesus and the FDA"; Tim Graham, "Political Science," *World,* August 31, 2002.

72. Minutes, Advisory Committee for Reproductive Health Drugs, September 29, 2003, at Center for Drug Evaluation and Research, Food and Drug Administration, U.S. Department of Health and Human Services, available at www.fda.gov/cder.

73. "Faith-Based Reasoning," *Scientific American,* June 2001.

74. Joseph B. Stanford, "Sex, Naturally," *First Things,* November 1999.

75. See the Web sites of the American Association of Pro-Life Obstetricians and Gynecologists at www.aaplog.org and the American College of Obstetricians and Gynecologists at www.acog.org.

76. "Rep. Slaughter Expresses Disappointment with the FDA Announcement to Delay Its Decision on Emergency Contraception," Rep. Louise Slaughter press release, February 13, 2004.

77. Bill Clinton, "Remarks by the President During the National Medal of Science and

Technology Awards Ceremony," Presidential Hall, Old Executive Office Building, Washington, DC, April 27, 1999, available at clinton4.nara.gov/WH/New/html/19990427-4646.html.

78. Madeline Drexler, "A Pox on America," *Nation,* April 28, 2003.

79. Chris Clarke, "Bush's Bizarre Science," *Earth Island Journal,* June 22, 2003.

80. This message is available on the Web site of the U.S. Centers for Disease Control and Prevention at www.cdc.gov/nccdphp/dash/rtc/.

81. Rep. Henry Waxman et al., letter to Tommy Thompson, secretary, U.S. Department of Health and Human Services, December 18, 2002.

82. Based on a September 1999 version of the U.S. Centers for Disease Control and Prevention Web page, entitled "Condoms and Their Use in Preventing HIV Infection and Other STDs," and the current version of the Web page, "Male Latex Condoms and Sexually Transmitted Diseases," available at www.cdc.gov/nchstp/od/latex.htm.

83. *Scientific Integrity in Policymaking,* Union of Concerned Scientists; email from CDC spokeswoman Kathryn Bina to the author.

84. "Physician's Group Calls on U.S. Government to Stop Promoting Pornography to Children," Physicians Consortium press release, April 10, 2002; statement of Joe S. McIlhaney, Hearing Before the Subcommittee on Health of the Committee on Energy and Commerce of the U.S. House of Representatives, April 23, 2002.

85. Based on a March 6, 2002 version of the U.S. National Cancer Institute Web page, entitled "Abortion and Breast Cancer," and the current version of the Web page, "Abortion, Miscarriage, and Breast Cancer Risk," available at http://cis.nci.nih.gov/fact/3_75.htm.

86. Both incidents are documented in *Politics and Science in the Bush Administration,* House Committee on Government Reform.

87. Department of Health and Human Services, program announcement 04004, *Federal Register,* August 28, 2003.

88. The description of this incident is based on sources close to the process inside and outside of the administration.

89. Kenneth J. Arrow et al., letter to George W. Bush, president of the United States, February 21, 2001.

90. "Majority of Americans Say Embryonic Stem Cell Research Morally OK," Religion News Service, August 8, 2003.

91. For the meetings with Karl Rove et al. see "Stem Cell Line in the Sand," *World,* August 18, 2001; for George Bush's campaign statements see, e.g., Ceci Connolly, "Bush 'Agonizing' Over Funding of Embryo Research," *Washington Post,* July 15, 2001.

92. David Frum, *The Right Man: The Surprise Presidency of George W. Bush* (New York: Random House, 2003), 106. The extended quotation below is from page 110.

93. "Stem Cell Line in the Sand," *World.*

94. James C. Dobson, "Dear friends" letter, dated September 2001, available at www.family.org/docstudy/newsletters/a0017576.html.

95. Karen Tumulty and James Carney, "Bush's Fuzzy Science?" *Time,* September 10, 2001.

96. Constance Holden and Gretchen Vogel, " 'Show Us the Cells,' U.S. Researchers Say," *Science,* August 9, 2002.

97. See also Wayne Arnold, "Singapore Goes for Biotech," *New York Times,* August 26, 2003.

98. *Scientific Integrity in Policymaking,* Union of Concerned Scientists.

CHAPTER 5: GOOD-BYE *ROE*

1. For descriptions of the scene, see Dave Andrusko, "A Day to Remember," *Today's News & Views,* National Right to Life Committee, November 6, 2003; Robin Toner, "For G.O.P., It's a Moment," *New York Times,* November 6, 2003; Roberta Combs, "Partial Birth Abortion Ban Signed into Law by President Bush," *Washington Weekly Review,* Christian Coalition, November 7, 2003.

2. These quotations are from "Partial-Birth Abortion Ban Becomes Law," Family Research Council press release, November 5, 2003; "Thank President Bush for Signing the Partial-Birth Abortion Ban!" Concerned Women for America action alert, November 5, 2003; Andrusko, "A Day to Remember"; Tony Perkins, "A Historic Day for Life," *Washington Update,* e-mail to members of the Family Research Council, November 5, 2003; "Issues Update," Focus on the Family syndicated radio program, November 7, 2003.

3. George W. Bush, "President Bush Signs Partial Birth Abortion Ban Act of 2003," Ronald Reagan Building, Washington, DC, November 5, 2003, available at www.whitehouse.gov.

4. Andrusko, "A Day to Remember."

5. Perkins, "A Historic Day"; Andrusko, "A Day to Remember"; "North Korea Pt. 2," Concerned Women Today, syndicated radio program, November 6, 2003, available at www.cwfa.org/radio.asp?broadcastID=2060; "Issues Update," Focus on the Family.

6. "Issues Update," Focus on the Family.

7. The image appeared in a pop-up window on the National Organization for Women Web site at www.now.org; the quotations are from Kim Gandy, "Bush Takes Away Women's Reproductive Rights—Feminists Promise to Vote Him out of Office," NOW press release, November 5, 2003.

8. Sara Diamond, *Roads to Dominion: Right-Wing Movements and Political Power in the United States* (New York: Guilford Press, 1995), 136; Derek Arend Wilson, editor, *The Right Guide: A Guide to Conservative, Free-Market, and Right-of-Center Organizations* (Ann Arbor, MI: Economics America, 2000), 114, 132.

9. Focus on the Family Web site at www.family.org; American Life League Web site at www.all.org; National Right to Life Committee Web site at www.nrlc.org.

10. "FRC to Join Pro-Life Coalition to Rally Support for Pro-Life Plank in GOP Platform," Family Research Council press release, June 27, 2000, available from PR Newswire.

11. Senate scores from National Right to Life Committee Scorecand, 108th Congress, U.S. Senate, available at www.capwiz.com/nrlc/home/; Rep. Joe Pitts, letter to Wanda Franz, president, National Right to Life Committee, November 20, 2003.

12. "U.S. Catholic Bishops' Guide to Washington, D.C.," advertisement sponsored by the American Life League, available at www.all.org/crusade.htm.

13. Much of this history is summarized in the National Right to Life Committee's "Abortion Timeline," available at www.nrlc.org/abortion/timeline1.html.

14. *Who Decides? A Reproductive Rights Issues Manual,* the NARAL Foundation, October 2002.

15. The data on violence is from "NAF Violence and Disruption Statistics," National Abortion Federation, June 30, 2003; the reduction in providers is drawn from Stanley K. Henshaw, et al., "Abortions Services in the United States, 1991 and 1992," *Family Planning Perspectives,* May-June 1994, and Henshaw, "Abortion Incidence and Services in the United States, 1995–1996," *Family Planning Perspectives,* November-December 1998.

16. See, e.g., *George W. Bush's War on Women: A Chronology,* Planned Parenthood Federation of America, January 27, 2003.

17. David Johnston and Neil A. Lewis, "Religious Right Made Big Push to Put Aschroft in Justice Dept.," *New York Times,* January 7, 2001.

18. Burke J. Balch, "Federal Judge Overturns Ashcroft Assisted Suicide Ruling: Appeal Expected," *National Right to Life News,* May 2002.

19. Richard B. Schmitt, "U.S. Anti-Porn Effort Is Found Wanting: Obscenity Foes Say Their Support for Atty. Gen. John Ashcroft Hasn't Translated into the Aggressive Crackdown They Expected," *Los Angeles Times,* November 23, 2003; *George W. Bush's War on Women,* Planned Parenthood.

20. Rep. John Conyers et al., letter to John D. Ashcroft, attorney general of the United States, November 6, 2003.

21. Eric Lichtblau, "Ashcroft Defends Subpoenas," *New York Times,* February 13, 2004.

22. "U.S. House Upholds Bush Policy Against Aid to Pro-Abort Groups," *National Right to Life News,* June 2001.

23. Bob Jones, "Out of the Wilderness?" *World,* February 3, 2001.

24. National Advisory Board Members, Medical Institute for Sexual Health, www.medinstitute.org; "HHS Names New Deputy Assistant Secretary for Population Affairs," Department of Health and Human Services press release, October 7, 2002.

25. Mark Crutcher, "Child Predators," Life Dynamics, July 2002, available at www.ChildPredators.com/ReadReport.cfm.

26. Judith M. DeSarno et al., *Orange Alert for Reproductive Health: Congressional and Federal Regulatory Action in 2003,* National Family Planning and Reproductive Health Association, January 15, 2004.

27. Letter from the supervisor of a California Title X training program, January 20, 2004.

28. DeSarno et al., *Orange Alert for Reproductive Health.*

29. *George W. Bush's War on Women,* Planned Parenthood.

30. "Attend University Faculty for Life's 10th Annual Meeting," *National Right to Life News,* April 2000.

31. "Maggie Wynne, Congressional Aide," Thomas Aquinas College, available at www.thomasaquinas.edu/alumni/profiles/wynne.htm.

32. Tim Graham, "The Trouble with Tommy," *World,* May 4, 2002.

33. See, for example, "A Barren Plan for Women," *Boston Globe,* February 6, 2002.

34. Rick Weiss, "New Status for Embryos in Research," *Washington Post,* October 30, 2002.

35. Arthur Caplan, "The Problem with 'Embryo Adoption,' " MSNBC, June 24, 2003, available at www.msnbc.msn.com/id/3076556/.

36. Information on the nominees is drawn from Ellen Marshall, *Bush's Other War: The Assault on Women's Sexual and Reproductive Health and Rights,* International Women's Health Coalition, August 1, 2003, and Planned Parenthood's *George W. Bush's War on Women.*

37. Dana Milbank, "Lott's Promise to Bring Up Abortion Worries Bush Aides," *Washington Post,* November 12, 2002.

38. Judy Keen and Kathy Kiely, "Bush: USA Isn't Ready for Total Abortion Ban," *USA Today,* October 29, 2003.

39. George W. Bush, "President's Phone Call to March for Life Participants," January 22, 2002, available at www.whitehouse.gov.

40. Don Parker, "The President's Vision for the Future: National Right to Life Leaders Meet with President Bush," *National Right to Life News,* February 2002, reprinted from *Catholic Register.*

41. Mary Cunningham Agee et al., "The America We Seek: A Statement of Pro-Life Principle and Concern," *First Things,* May 1996.

42. "Stem Cell Line in the Sand," *World,* August 18, 2001.

43. Richard Lacayo, "How Bush Got There," *Time,* August 20, 2001; James C. Dobson, "Dear friends" letter, dated September 2001, available at www.family.org/docstudy/newsletters/a0017576. html.

44. This information on crisis pregnancy centers is drawn from *Deceptive Anti-Abortion Crisis Pregnancy Centers,* NARAL Foundation, April 13, 1999.

45. Marvin Olasky, *Compassionate Conservatism: What It Is, What It Does, and How It Can Transform America* (New York: Free Press, 2000), xiii.

46. Karla Dial, "Focus Launches Ultrasound Program," *CitizenLink,* Focus on the Family, January 19, 2004.

47. "HHS Awards $17.1 Million in Abstinence-Only Education Grants," July 6, 2001; "HHS Awards Grants Nationwide to Support Abstinence Education, Services to Teens," July 2, 2002; "HHS Awards New Grants to Support Abstinence Education Among Nation's Teens," all U.S. Department of Health and Human Services press releases.

48. "Tennessee Abstinence Only Education Program: Funded Projects,"Abstinence Only Education Program, State of Tennessee, August 19, 2003.

49. David Crary, "Religious, Anti-Abortion Groups Among the Winners as Abstinence-Only Funding Increases," Associated Press, March 13, 2004.

50. Agee et al., "The America We Seek."

51. *Abortion, Breast Cancer, and the Misuse of Science,* NARAL Pro-Choice America, January 1, 2004.

52. *Who Decides?,* NARAL Foundation.

53. "Goals," Concerned Women for America, available at cwfa.org/goals-concerns.asp.

54. Rep. Henry Waxman et al., letter to Tommy Thompson, secretary, U.S. Department of Health and Human Services, December 18, 2002.

55. "Abortion, Miscarriage, and Breast Cancer Risk," National Cancer Institute, available at http://cis.nci.nih.gov/fact/3_75.htm.

56. Texas and Minnesota episodes drawn from Kris Axtman, "Texas Tilts Right on Abortion and Other Issues," *Christian Science Monitor,* June 9, 2003; Jennifer Kabbany, "Abortion's Risks Stir New Debate; Possible Link to Breast Cancer Prompts Texas Law," *Washington Times,* June 5, 2003; Sarah Fleener, "Pawlenty Signs Women's Right to Know Act," University Wire, June 6, 2003.

57. George W. Bush, "President Bush Signs Unborn Victims of Violence Act of 2004," East Room, the White House, Washington, DC, April 1, 2004.

58. These details are drawn from "President Bush Signs Unborn Victims of Violence Act ('Laci and Conner's Law') with Members of Victims Families," National Right to Life press release, April 1, 2004; Pete Winn, "Good News, Bad News Day for Pro-Lifers," *CitizenLink,* Focus on the Family e-mail to members, April 1, 2004; "FRC Praises Signing of 'Unborn Victims of Violence Act,' " Family Research Council press release, April 1, 2004; and Tony Perkins, "Two Good News Stories for Pro-Lifers and Unborn Children," *Washington Update,* Family Research Council e-mail to members, April 2, 2004.

59. See, e.g., Pamela Manson, "Rowland Waives Preliminary Hearing; Anger and

Suspicion: South Weber Mother Confronts Prosecutor, Demanding 'To Know Where It Stops,' " *Salt Lake Tribune,* April 6, 2004.

60. "NOW Condemns Utah Murder Prosecution for Delayed Cesarean Delivery," National Organization for Women press release, March 12, 2004.

61. Quotations drawn from Lee Romney and John J. Goldman, "3 Trials Tackle Curb on Abortion: Cases Challenging a New Federal Ban on Late-Term Procedures Are Expected to Turn Almost Solely on the Dueling Testimony of Medical Experts," *Los Angeles Times,* March 30, 2004, and Terry Phillips, "Do Preborn Feel Pain During Partial-Birth Abortion?" *CitizenLink,* Focus on the Family e-mail to members, April 2, 2004.

Chapter 6: Whose Gay Agenda?

1. Robert Dreyfuss, "The Double-Edge Wedge; Republicans Used to Win Points With Antigay Politics, But This Year the Traditional Wedge Issue May Cut the Other Way," *American Prospect,* August 28, 2000.

2. "Bush Says: 'I Welcome Gay Americans': Sexual Orientation 'Not a Factor' in Hiring," Carl Schmid press release, April 13, 2000.

3. Jill Lawrence, "Bush Leaves GOP Door Ajar for Gays, Lesbians," *USA Today,* April 17, 2001.

4. Chris Bull, "The Margin of Victory," *Advocate,* December 19, 2000.

5. On AIDS appointments "Public Contact Information for Presidential Advisory Council on HIV/AIDS (PACHA) Members," February 11, 2003, available at www.pacha. gov/staff/members/members.html; on Greer, see Lou Chibbaro Jr., "Bush Appointee Resigns Over Marriage Issue," *Washington Blade,* March 5, 2004; on Ashcroft, see Eric Lichtblau, "Justice Dept. Draws Heavy Criticism Over Cancellation of Gay Rights Event," *New York Times,* June 7, 2003.

6. See, e.g, Susan Baer, "Daughters Liz and Mary Drop Everything to Help Their Father Campaign Not Just Out of Family Loyalty but Because They Believe in the Message," *Baltimore Sun,* April 1, 2004.

7. "The Lieberman-Cheney Vice Presidential Debate," October 5, 2000, transcript available from the Commission on Presidential Debates, www.debates.org/pages/trans2000d.html.

8. Robert Dreyfuss, "The Double-Edge Wedge," *American Prospect,* August 28, 2000.

9. "Is the White House Drifting Away from Pro-Family Values?" American Family Association action alert, April 20, 2001; "Do We Fight AIDS By Spreading It?" Traditional Values Coalition, January 25, 2001; *The Bush Administration's Republican Homosexual Agenda: The First 100 Days,* Culture & Family Institute, Concerned Women for America, May 29, 2001.

10. On Kay Cole James, *State of the Administration 2003,* National Stonewall Democrats, January 28, 2003; on audits, "Report Documents Misuse of Federal AIDS Funds," Family Research Council, February 22, 2002.

11. On McConnell, *State of the Administration 2003*; on Tymkovich, *State of the Administration 2002,* National Stonewall Democrats, January 29, 2002; on Pryor, "Alliance for Justice Report in Opposition to the Nomination of William H. Pryor to the United States Court of Appeals for the Eleventh Circuit," Alliance for Justice; on Allen, "Claude A. Allen," National Organization for Women, May 19, 2003.

12. George W. Bush, "President Bush Discusses Faith-Based Initiative in Tennessee,"

Opryland Hotel, Nashville, Tennessee, February 10, 2003, available at www.white-house.gov.

13. Dana Milbank, "Charity Cites Bush Help in Fight Against Hiring Gays: Salvation Army Wants Exemption from Laws," *Washington Post,* July 10, 2001, and Mike Allen and Dana Milbank, "Rove Heard Charity Plea on Gay Bias: White House Denied Senior Aides Had Role," *Washington Post,* July 12, 2001.

14. See, e.g., "Homosexual Agenda: Resources," American Family Association, available at afa.net/homosexual_agenda/resources.asp.

15. Lou Chibbaro Jr., "Bush Appoints Anti-Gay Member to AIDS Panel: New PACHA Member Runs Christian Ministry to 'Rescue' Gays," *Washington Blade,* January 17, 2003; Ceci Connolly, "AIDS Panel Choice Wrote of a 'Gay Plague': Views of White House Commission Nominee Draw Criticism," *Washington Post,* January 23, 2003; Press briefing by Ari Fleischer, Washington, DC, January 23, 2003, available at www.whitehouse.gov/news/releases/2003/01/20030123-3.html.

16. "CWA's Rios Calls on Fleischer to Apologize for Bashing Christian," Concerned Women for America press release, January 24, 2003.

17. "CWA Condemns 'Gay Thought Police' for Attacks on Sen. Santorum," Concerned Women for America press release, April 23, 2003.

18. Sheryl Gay Stolberg, "White House Aides Confer with 200 Gay Republicans," *New York Times,* May 10, 2003.

19. Kenneth L. Connor, "Staying Home in '04," *National Review* online, May 22, 2003; Robert Knight, "GOP Chairman Racicot Defends Meeting with 'Gay' Pressure Group," Culture & Family Institute, Concerned Women for America, May 7, 2003, available at http://www.cwfa.org/articles/3903/CFI/cfreport/index.htm.

20. "Supreme Court Declares Perversion a Right: Activist Court Strikes Down Reasonable Texas Law; Others at Risk," Concerned Women for American, June 26, 2003; Joel Belz, "Pro-Family Voters Cannot Compromise on Homosexual Marriage," *World,* July 19, 2003; Dobson quotations from James C. Dobson letter to members of Focus on the Family, dated September 2003 and available at www.family.org/docstudy/newsletters/a0027590.html.

21. "The Threat to Marriage from the Courts," U.S. Senate Republican Policy Committee, July 29, 2003.

22. On the mailings, Evelyn Nieves, "Family Values Groups Gear Up for Battle Over Gay Marriage," *Washington Post,* August 17, 2003; on Dobson, see Greg Pierce, "Dobson's Decision," *Washington Times,* October 6, 2003.

23. Terry quotations from Randall A. Terry letter to "Christian activists nationwide," July 12, 2003, posted at www.twistedsix.com.

24. Tony Carnes, "Ken Connor Resigns from Family Research Council," *Christianity Today,* July 30, 2003.

25. On Arlington Group, see Mary Leonard, "Gay Marriage Stirs Conservatives Again; Right Wing Braces for Mass. Ruling," *Boston Globe,* September 28, 2003; Perkins quotation from "Love and Marriage . . . and Mobilization," *CongressDaily,* March 17, 2004.

26. See www.marriageprotectionweek.com.

27. George W. Bush, "Marriage Protection Week 2003, by the President of the United States of America, a Proclamation," dated October 3, 2003, but not released until Monday, October 6, available at www.whitehouse.gov/news/releases/2003/10/20031003-12.html; on coordination with Concerned Women for America, "NSD Denounces Presidential Attack on American Families: Radical Anti-Gay Group Today Confirms

Bush to Proclaim 'Marriage Protection Week,' " National Stonewall Democrats press release, October 3, 2003.

28. Joel Belz, "Something to Scream About," *World*, October 11, 2003; on Traditional Values Coalition, see John Gittelsohn, "Evangelicals' Moral Dilemma: Schwarzenegger Forces Christians to Weigh Values vs. Economics," *Orange County Register*, September 1, 2003, and Carla Marinucci, "Religious Right Opposes Schwarzenegger: Conservative Groups Say Actor Is No Different than Gov. Davis," *San Francisco Chronicle*, October 1, 2003.

29. Robert Pear and David D. Kirkpatrick, "Bush Plans $1.5 Billion Drive for Promotion of Marriage," *New York Times*, January 14, 2004; Zogby from Mary Leonard, "Bush Seeks $1.5B to Back Marriages," *Boston Globe*, January 15, 2004.

30. Perkins quotation from Leonard, "Bush Seeks $1.5B to Back Marriages"; Stanton and mobilization from Pear and Kirkpatrick, "Bush Plans $1.5 Billion Drive."

31. George W. Bush, "President Calls for Constitutional Amendment Protecting Marriage," Roosevelt Room, White House, Washington, DC, February 24, 2004, available at www.whitehouse.gov.

32. Debra Rosenberg and Mark Miller, "A Falling Out Among Friends," *Newsweek*, March 8, 2004.

33. Dobson response from Pete Winn, "President Bush Backs Marriage-Protection Amendment," *CitizenLink*, e-mail to Focus on the Family members, February 2, 2004; Gary L. Bauer, *End of Day*, e-mail to American Values members, February 24, 2002; White House aide from Rosenberg and Miller, "A Falling Out."

34. Bauer from David Von Drehle and Alan Cooperman, "Same-Sex Marriage Vaulted into Spotlight," *Washington Post*, March 8, 2004; "The Institution of Marriage Amendment," Concerned Women for America action alert, February 6, 2004; Stanton from John Cloud, "The Battle Over Gay Marriage," *Time*, February 16, 2004.

35. On minimum wage and overtime, see the AFL-CIO at aflcio.org; on unemployment rates see the Economic Policy Institute at www.epinet.org.

36. The LaHayes' quotation from Michael Lienesch, *Redeeming America: Piety and Politics in the New Christian Right* (Chapel Hill: University of North Carolina Press, 1993), 66.

37. Bob Kemper, "Bush: Protect Marriage: Calls for Constitutional Amendment to Bar Gay Couples from Marrying," *Chicago Tribune*, February 25, 2004.

38. Data from Barna Research Group, 1999, as referenced in Rob Boston, "My Big Fat GOP Wedding," *Church & State*, February 2003.

39. "Gay Marriage a Voting Issue, but Mostly for Opponents," Pew Research Center for the People & the Press, February 27, 2004.

40. David D. Kirkpatrick, "Conservatives Using Issue of Gay Unions as a Rallying Tool," *New York Times*, February 8, 2004.

41. Ibid.

42. Mark O'Keefe, "Gay Marriage Debate Yields Alliance Between Blacks, White Evangelicals," Newhouse News Service, October 6, 2003.

43. "Religious Beliefs Underpin Opposition to Homosexuality," Pew Research Center for the People & the Press, November 18, 2003.

44. Ron DePasquale, "Gay Debate Splits Black Community," *Chicago Tribune*, March 14, 2004.

45. "Gay Activist Groups 'Hi-Jacking' Rev. King's 'I Have a Dream' Anniversary," Family Research Council press release, August 22, 2003; "Homosexuals Hijack Civil

Rights Bus," Concerned Women for America press release, March 25, 2004; on Alliance for Marriage see O'Keefe, "Gay Marriage Debate."

46. On Christian Coalition, see Andrew Jacobs, "Black Legislators Stall Marriage Amendment in Georgia," *New York Times*, March 3, 2004; on Georgia Family Council, see Mark Niesse, "Black Clergy Rally to Dispel Comparisons Between Civil Rights, Gay Marriage," Associated Press, March 22, 2004; on Family Research Council, see De-Pasquale, "Gay Debate Splits," and "FRC Joins National Alliance of Black Pastors at Boston State House," Family Research Council media advisory, March 9, 2004; on Land, see Cheryl Wetzstein, "Groups Pledge to Protect Marriage," *Washington Times*, October 3, 2003.

47. Timothy J. Daily, "Talking Points: Did the Gay Vote Elect President Bush?" Family Research Council, available at www.frc.org/get/if01f1.cfm.

CHAPTER 7: AIDS, BORN AGAIN

1. On Reagan's commission, see, e.g., *MacNeil/Lehrer NewsHour*, June 2, 1988, when Watkins was a guest and Sally Squires, "Setting the Course on AIDS: How an Admiral Turned Around the President's AIDS Commission," *Washington Post*, June 7, 1988.

2. On Buckley, see, e.g., "Stigmatizing the Victim: Homosexuals, AIDS," *Nation*, April 12, 1986; on Dannemeyer, see, e.g., Joan Mower, "Dannemeyer Urges Steps to Curb Spread of AIDS," Associated Press, October 30, 1985; on Helms, see, e.g, "AIDS Booklet Stirs Senate to Halt Funds," *Los Angeles Times*, October 14, 1987; on Coburn see "Rep. Tom Coburn, M.D. to Announce the Introduction of a Comprehensive HIV Prevention Proposal," Rep. Tom Coburn press release, August 1, 1996, available from PR Newswire.

3. Doug Ireland, "What Dubya Stands For," *POZ*, September 1999, and Ireland, "Grin and Cast It," *POZ*, November 2000.

4. Interview with Carl Schmid, a delegate to the 2000 Republican National Convention.

5. Mimi Hall and Judy Keen, "Bush to Close Offices on AIDS, Race; Advocates Say Move Sends Wrong Message," *USA Today*, February 7, 2001; press briefing by Ari Fleischer, James S. Brady Briefing Room, February 7, 2001.

6. A 1995 public opinion poll by Chilton Research, as cited by the U.S. Centers for Disease Control and Prevention, www.cdc.gov/hiv/pubs/facts/compyout.htm.

7. Falwell in Fred Bayles, "AIDS: Virus of Fear; Clergy Mixed in Response to AIDS Crisis," Associated Press, September 15, 1985; *Federal AIDS Dollars Fund Homosexual Proms and Fisting Seminars*, Traditional Values Coalition, November 2002; " 'Safe' Sex Is False Concept," Concerned Women for America press release, February 8, 1999; "Furthering the Safe Sex Lie," Concerned Women for America, May 11, 1998.

8. Jim Myers, "Coburn Outraged Over Condom Promotion," *Tulsa World*, December 15, 1999.

9. "Tom Coburn: Lawmaker Hosts Slide Show on Dangers of STDs," American Health Line, July 27, 2000.

10. Alma Golden and Shepherd Smith, "Warning Labels for Condoms?" *Washington Times*, February 11, 2001.

11. National Institute of Allergy and Infectious Diseases, Workshop Summary: Scientific Evidence on Condom Effectiveness for Sexually Transmitted Disease (STD) Prevention, July 20, 2001; additional data from the Centers for Disease Control and Prevention.

12. "Scientific Review Panel Confirms Condoms Are Effective Against HIV/AIDS,

but Epidemiological Studies Are Insufficient for Other STDs," U.S. Department of Health and Human Services press release, July 20, 2001; "Federal Panel on Condoms Offers Crucial Warnings to Sexually Active Americans, Says the Medical Institute for Sexual Health," Medical Institute for Sexual Health press release, July 19, 2001.

13. Coburn from "Report Raises Questions About Condoms—Post," Reuters, July 20, 2001; Koplan from "10,000 Physicians to Ask for Resignation of CDC Director, End of Cover-Up," Physicians Consortium press release, July 23, 2001, available from PR Newswire.

14. Laura Meckler, "Conservative Ex-Congressman to Head AIDS Advisory Panel," Associated Press, January 23, 2002.

15. On Reagan's commission, see, e.g., Judy Foreman, "AIDS Panel Chief Paints Dire Future," *Boston Globe,* November 19, 1998; on Bush Sr.'s commission, see, e.g., Robert Pear, "As Bush Defends AIDS Policy, Its Critics See Flaws," *New York Times,* October 18, 1992.

16. "Council Raps Clinton for Not Moving on Needle Exchanges," *AIDS Policy and Law,* August 9, 1996; see AIDS council roster at www.pacha.gov.

17. Jon Cohen, "HIV/AIDS Meeting: Tough Challenges Ahead on Political and Scientific Fronts," *Science,* July 19, 2002; "Protesters Call Administration's AIDS Spending Unacceptable, Drown Out Thompson's Speech in Barcelona," *Daily HIV/AIDS Report,* July 10, 2002, available at www.kaisernetwork.org.

18. Based on conversations with and documents from Ron Simmons, executive director, Us Helping Us.

19. Sabin Russell, "AIDS Czar Backs Embattled Program: S.F. Safe-Sex Program Called 'Good Work' at Researcher Meeting," *San Francisco Chronicle,* January 25, 2002.

20. Charles Ornstein, "AIDS Group Told to End Classes," *Los Angeles Times,* June 14, 2003.

21. *Federal AIDS Dollars Fund Homosexual Proms and Fisting Seminars,* Traditional Values Coalition, May 2001; for an example of Christian news coverage, see John Rossomando, "AIDS Activist Charges CDC with Negligence," CNSNews.com, and "AIDS Funding Investigation Is Long Overdue," *Worthy Opinions,* www.worthyopinions.com/commentary/aids-2.html.

22. "CDC Asks Stop AIDS Project to Discontinue 'Controversial' HIV Prevention Programs," *Daily HIV/AIDS Report,* June 16, 2003, available at www.kaisernetwork.org.

23. This account draws on Robert Stacy McCain, "AIDS Official Dubs Scrutiny of Program a CDC 'Witch Hunt': Compliance with Federal Rules Eyed," *Washington Times,* August 16, 2002; Steve Sternberg, "AIDS Program Could Lose Funding Over Explicit Material," *USA Today,* June 16, 2003; and interviews with a Stop AIDS Project staffer.

24. "TeamBush AIDS Policy Point Man Defends Federal Funding for Obscene Workshops," *World,* March 9, 2002.

25. Gerberding in Ornstein, "AIDS Group"; Foster in McCain, "AIDS official."

26. Jennifer Block, "Science Gets Sacked," *Nation,* August 14, 2003.

27. On defunding, Sabin Russell, "Priorities for AIDS Funds Shift," *San Francisco Chronicle,* May 22, 2004; Lafferty quote from Russell, " 'Scientific McCarthyism': AIDS, Sex Scientists on Federal List Fear Their Research Is in Jeopardy," *San Francisco Chronicle,* October 28, 2003.

28. "HIV Prevention Summit: New Perspectives in HIV Prevention," Sheraton Colony Square Hotel, Atlanta, Georgia, December 4–5, 2002.

29. "DHHS Risk Avoidance Meeting," Humphrey Building, Washington, DC, February 5, 2003.

30. *Scientific Integrity in Policymaking: An Investigation into the Bush Administration's Misuse of Science,* Union of Concerned Scientists, February 2004.

31. "Implementation of USAID Policies and Programs on HIV/AIDS and Trafficking," action cable from Secretary of State Colin Powell to U.S. Agency for International Development mission directors and population, health and nutrition officers, December 24, 2002.

32. Eagle Forum from "What Happened in the 108th Congress, 1st Session?" *Eagle Forum News,* January 2004, available at www.eagleforum.org/alert/2004/108thCongress-session1.html; and H.R. 1298: An Act to Provide Assistance to Foreign Countries to Combat HIV/AIDS, Tuberculosis, and Malaria, and for Other Purposes, 108th Congress, 1st Session.

33. "Ugandan Health Officials to Import 80 Million Condoms to Stem HIV Spread," *Daily HIV/AIDS Report,* October 29, 2002, available at www.kaisernetwork.org.

34. Sarah Baxter, "AIDS Cash Inspired by Christian Right," *Times* of London, February 9, 2003.

35. Jeffrey Sachs, "Lone Rangers No Use in AIDS War," Business Day (South Africa), February 5, 2003.

36. "House Readies AIDS Bill for President's Signature," Rep. Joe Pitts press release, May 21, 2003.

37. Baxter, "AIDS Cash."

38. Chuck Colson, "Africa's AIDS Crisis," Townhall.com, May 2, 2003.

39. "Evangelicals Respond to the Global AIDS Crisis," National Association of Evangelicals press release, June 11, 2003; the statement of conscience is available at worldvision.org/worldvision/wvususfo.nsf/stable/globalissues_aids_conscience.

40. "Programs: IYD, USAID HIV Meeting," notice posted on the Institute for Youth Development Web site, at www.youthdevelopment.org/articles/pr100103.htm.

41. Pete Winn, "Victory Declared on Global AIDS Bill," *CitizenLink,* Focus on the Family e-mail to members, May 16, 2003.

42. "Advancing HIV Prevention: New Strategies for a Changing Epidemic—United States, 2003," *MMWR Weekly,* April 18, 2003.

43. E-mails forwarded by Roland Foster to his e-mail contact list, April 17, 2003.

44. Mary Fisher letter to Pat Ware, undated.

45. David C. Harvey et al. letter to George W. Bush, president of the United States, June 20, 2003.

CHAPTER 8: THE PURITY BRIGADES

1. Abstinence Clearinghouse, National Advisory Council, available at abstinence.net/member/advisorycouncils.php.

2. Statement of Rep. Henry Waxman, Hearing Before the Subcommittee on Health of the Committee on Energy and Commerce of the U.S. House of Representatives, April 23, 2002.

3. *Toward a Sexually Healthy America: Roadblocks Imposed by the Federal Government's Abstinence-Only-Until-Marriage Education Program,* Advocates for Youth and Sexuality Information Council of the United States, 2001.

4. Abstinence Clearinghouse, "Opinions and Facts About Abstinence-Until-Marriage

Education," www.abstinenceAFRICA.com/about/101.php; Unruh quotation from Steve Sternberg, "Sex Education Stirs Controversy," *USA Today*, July 10, 2002.

5. On the sexual revolution, see *Working Toward Independence*, White House, February 2002, available at www.whitehouse.gov/news/releases/2002/02/welfare-reform-announcement-book.html, and on character see George W. Bush, "State of the Union Address," U.S. Capitol, Washington, DC, January 20, 2004.

6. George W. Bush, "Remarks by the President at a Conversation on Welfare Reform," Church at Rock Creek, Little Rock, Arkansas, June 3, 2002, available at www.whitehouse.gov.

7. Statement of Joe S. McIlhaney, Hearing Before the Subcommittee on Health of the Committee on Energy and Commerce of the U.S. House of Representatives, April 23, 2002.

8. Douglas Kirby, *No Easy Answers*, National Campaign to Prevent Teen Pregnancy, 1997; Kirby, *Emerging Answers*, National Campaign to Prevent Teen Pregnancy, 2001; *No Time to Lose: Getting More from HIV Prevention*, Institute of Medicine (Washington: National Academies Press, 2001), 8, 116–18.

9. Barbara Devaney et al., "Evaluation of Abstinence Education Programs Funded Under Title V, Section 510: Interim Report," Mathematica Policy Research, available at http://aspe.hhs.gov/hsp/abstinence02.

10. *Politics and Science in the Bush Administration*, House Committee on Government Reform, Special Investigations Division, August 2003.

11. Best Friends, "Media Coverage," at www.bestfriendsfoundation.org/new.html.

12. See, e.g., McIlhaney, Hearing Before the Subcommittee on Health.

13. Peter S. Bearman, "Promising the Future: Virginity Pledges as They Affect Transition to First Intercourse," Columbia University, July 15, 1999.

14. Terri Lackey, "Teens Who Say 'No' to Sex Are Less Likely to Have It," *Baptist Press News*, January 4, 2001; Peter Bearman, letter to Robert Rector, the Heritage Foundation, undated. Bearman was responding to Robert E. Rector, "The Effectiveness of Abstinence Education Programs in Reducing Sexual Activity Among Youth," Heritage Foundation, April 8, 2002.

15. Martha E. Kempner, *Toward a Sexually Healthy America: Abstinence-Only-Until-Marriage Programs that Try to Keep Our Youth "Scared Chaste,"* Sexuality Information Council of the United States, 2001.

16. "Do You Have a Girlfriend, Sister or Daughter Who Has Died from HPV?" Governor's Program on Abstinence, Baton Rouge, Louisiana.

17. See e.g., Candi Cushman, "Freedom from Fear," *World*, January 22, 2000.

18. "Study Credits Abstinence with Lowering Birth and Pregnancy Rates," Focus on the Family press release, April 14, 2003.

19. "Teen Pregnancy: Trends and Lessons Learned," Alan Guttmacher Institute, *Issues in Brief*, 2002 series, no. 1.

20. James W. Buehler, "Condom Use: Naysayers Aside, Research Has Confirmed Effectiveness," *Atlanta Journal-Constitution*, August 22, 2003.

21. Rebecca Schleifer, *Ignorance Only: HIV/AIDS, Human Rights, and Federally Funded Abstinence-Only Programs in the United States*, Human Rights Watch, September 2002.

22. Ceci Connolly, "Texas Teaches Abstinence, with Mixed Grades," *Washington Post*, January 21, 2003.

23. Data drawn from Connolly, "Texas Teaches"; the Kaiser Family Foundation's

"State Facts Online, at www.statehealthfacts.org; and *Teen Births in America's Largest Cities: 1990 and 2000,* Annie E. Casey Foundation, 2003.

24. *American Civil Liberties Union of Louisiana v. Governor M.J. Foster,* Memorandum of Law in Support of Motion for Preliminary Injunction.

25. Connolly, "Judge Orders Changes in Abstinence Program; La. Groups Found to Be Promoting Religion," July 26, 2002.

26. Kempner, *Toward a Sexually Healthy America.*

27. Regional Directors Monthly Report 2003–2004, Governors Program on Abstinence, Baton Rouge, Louisiana, signed by Cindy Collins, October 6, 2003.

28. "Prepared Testimony of Ms. Patricia Funderburk Ware, President and CEO, PFW Consultants, Inc.," delivered to a hearing of the House Small Business Committee, July 16, 1998, and available at www.house.gov/smbiz/hearings/105th/1998/980716/ware.htm.

29. Presidential Advisory Council on HIV/AIDS meeting, Wyndham City Center Hotel, Washington, DC, June 21, 2002.

30. Stephen Mansfield, *The Faith of George W. Bush* (New York: Penguin, 2003), 162.

31. "Exclusive Purpose: Abstinence-Only Proponents Create Federal Entitlement in Welfare Reform," *SEICUS,* vol. 24, no. 4.

32. Abstinence Clearinghouse, National Advisory Council.

33. On the Heritage Foundation, see Issues 2004: The Candidate's Briefing Room, "Abstinence," the Heritage Foundation, available at www.heritage.org/Research/Features/Issues2004/Abstinence.cfm; the numbers were echoed in a presentation by Maggie Wynne, a legislative analyst with the Department of Health and Human Services, at the Presidential Advisory Council on HIV/AIDS meeting, June 21, 2002.

34. Cynthia Dailard, "Abstinence Promotion and Teen Family Planning: The Misguided Drive for Equal Funding," *The Guttmacher Report on Public Policy,* February 2002.

35. The True Love Waits number is from Erin Curry, "Leaders: True Love Waits 'Different' from Other Programs," *Baptist Press News,* March 10, 2004; the Guttmacher data is from "Sex Education: Politicians, Parents, Teachers, and Teens," Alan Guttmacher Institute, *Issues in Brief,* 2001 Series, no. 2.

36. Fleischer and Unruh quotations from Ceci Connolly, "Administration Promoting Abstinence: Family Planning Efforts Are Being Scaled Back," *Washington Post,* July 30, 2001.

37. Christina Larson, "Pork for Prudes," *Washington Monthly,* September 2002.

38. George W. Bush, "President Urges Senate to Pass Compassionate Welfare Reform Bill," West Ashley High School, Charleston, South Carolina, July 29, 2002, available at www.whitehouse.gov.

39. "Be Heard: An MTV Global Discussion with Colin Powell," transcript available at www.state.gov/secretary/rm/2002/8038.htm.

40. Wildmon from "Secretary of State Disparages Abstinence, Promotes Condom Use to World's Young People," American Family Association action alert, February 15, 2002; Ken Connor, "Powell's Reckless Remarks Put Young Lives at Risk," Family Research Council, February 15, 2002; Pete Winn, "Powell Pushes Condoms to Youth," *CitizenLink,* Focus on the Family, February 15, 2002; Connor and Schwartz quoted in Winn, "Using the 'Bully Pulpit,'" *CitizenLink,* Focus on the Family, February 26, 2002.

41. On physician endorsements see Tom Teepen, "Satcher's Sane Sex Stand Surely Will Doom Him," Cox News Service, July 2, 2001; on religious support see Caryle Murphy,

"Satcher Hailed by Black Clergy: Forum Endorses Report on Sex-Ed," *Washington Post,* July 14, 2001.

42. Ceci Connolly, "Surgeon General Urges Thorough Sex Education," *Washington Post,* June 29, 2001, and Karen S. Peterson, "Satcher Urges Sex Dialogue: Critics Urge Ouster," *USA Today,* June 29, 2001.

43. Fleischer in Bill Press, "The Surgeon General Teaches Bush About Sex," Tribune Media Services, July 6, 2001; Satcher in Connolly, "Surgeon General Urges Thorough Sex Education."

44. Grant information from U.S. Department of Health and Human Services press releases, "HHS Awards $17.1 Million in Abstinence-Only Education Grants," July 6, 2001; "HHS Awards Grants Nationwide to Support Abstinence Education, Services to Teens," July 2, 2002; "HHS Awards New Grants to Support Abstinence Education Among Nation's Teens," July 2, 2003.

45. "Potential Reviewers, SPRANS Abstinence Education Grants, 2003," U.S. Department of Health and Human Services.

46. Connolly, "Administration Promoting Abstinence."

47. "Just Saying No: Study Shows Virginity Pledgers Have Same STD Rates as Non-Pledgers," *Policy Update,* Sexuality Information and Education Council of the United States, March 2004, available at siecus.org/policy/PUpdates/pdate0094.html.

48. *Sex Education in America,* National Public Radio/Henry J. Kaiser Family Foundation/Harvard University John F. Kennedy School of Government, January 29, 2004.

49. Office of Management and Budget, *Budget of the United States Government, Fiscal Year 2003,* as quoted in Krista Kafer, "Making Good on Promises to Increase Funding for Special Education," Heritage Foundation Reports, September 10, 2002.

50. Priya Abraham, "Putting Money Where His Mouth Isn't," *World,* March 27, 2004.

51. True Love Waits from Chris Turner, "True Love Waits Fosters Success in Abstinence Pledges, Leaders Say," *Baptist Press,* March 15, 2004; Assemblies of God from Life-Way.com, "Cooperating Ministries," www.lifeway.com/tlw/ldr_coop_home.asp; Abstinence Clearinghouse from Abstinence Africa at abstinenceafrica.com.

52. Abraham, "Putting Money."

53. Franklin Graham, "Prepared Statement of Rev. Franklin Graham President of Samaritan's Purse Before the Senate Committee on Foreign Relations Subcommittee on African Affairs," February 24, 2000, available from the Federal News Service.

CHAPTER 9: THE GLOBAL CRUSADE

1. Bob Jones, "Out of the Wilderness?" *World,* February 3, 2001.

2. "Conservatives Threaten GOP Revolt: A Ridge Over Troubled Waters," *World,* June 3, 2000.

3. See, e.g., Jones, "Out of the Wilderness?"

4. Michelman in Eric Brazil, "Abortion 'Gag Rule' Returning: Bush Says He'll Limit International Aid," *San Francisco Chronicle,* January 22, 2001; "The Week," *National Review,* February 19, 2001; Helle Bering, "Rebirth of Foreign Policy: Clinton's Sins Are Being Aborted," *Washington Times,* January 31, 2001.

5. Jones, "Out of the Wilderness?"

6. George W. Bush, "Memorandum for the Administrator of the United States Agency for International Development," January 22, 2001, available at www.whitehouse.gov/news/releases/20010123-5.html; for the full text of the Mexico City Policy, see

"Memorandum for All Contracting Officers and Negotiators," U.S. Agency for International Development, March 29, 2001, available at www.usaid.gov/procurement_bus_opp/procurement/cib/pdf/cib0108r.pdf.

7. Jim Lobe, "Bush Reinstates Abortion Curbs on Overseas Aid," Inter Press Service, January 22, 2001.

8. Mike Allen, "Bush on Stage: Deft or Just Lacking Depth?" *Washington Post,* February 19, 2001.

9. Kathy Gambrell, "Bush Not 'Pro-Life,' Group Says," United Press International, January 24, 2001.

10. "Impact of the 'Mexico City Policy' on the Free Choice of Contraception in Europe," Parliamentary Assembly, Committee on Equal Opportunities for Women and Men, September 11, 2003.

11. "The Impact of the Global Gag Rule in Romania," *Access Denied: U.S. Restrictions on International Family Planning,* the Global Gag Rule Impact Project, led by Population Action International in partnership with Ipas and Planned Parenthood Federation of America, 2003.

12. On Lesotho, "The Global Gag Rule & Contraceptive Supplies," *Access Denied* and Susan A. Cohen, "Global Gag Rule Revisited: HIV/AIDS Initiative Out, Family Planning Still In," *Guttmacher Report on Public Policy,* October 2003; on Cameroon and St. Lucia, "The Global Gag Rule & HIV/AIDS," *Access Denied.*

13. Ruse in Andrew Cain and Julia Duin, "Order Cuts Funding for Abortion Overseas," *Washington Times,* January 23, 2001; Johnson on *Talk of the Nation,* National Public Radio, January 24, 2001.

14. "Why New Restrictions on Abortion? LDI Says States Should Enforce Laws Already on the Books," Life Dynamics Incorporated press release, April 17, 2003.

15. See, e.g., Suzanne Chamberlin, "With Planned Parenthood's Latest Programs, You Choose, You Lose," Family Research Council, undated, available at www.frc.org/get.cfm?i=PV02L1.

16. "The Impact of the Global Gag Rule in Kenya," *Access Denied.*

17. World Health Organization data.

18. "The Impact of the Global Gag Rule in Ethiopia," *Access Denied.*

19. Bill Peterson, "Coalition Pushes Block Grants to 'Defund' the Left," *Washington Post,* July 2, 1981 and George J. Church, "Seeking Strategy on Social Issues; Rightists Agree on Policy, But They Differ on Ways and Means," *Time,* September 14, 1981.

20. Susan Cohen, "Debate Over Abortion, Family Planning Expected During Next 100 Days," *Alan Guttmacher Institute Washington Memo,* April 25, 1995.

21. Powell in David S. Broder, "Deadly Politics," *Washington Post,* July 28, 2002.

22. Terry M. Neal, "Downplaying Politics at the White House," Washingtonpost.com, July 24, 2002.

23. Douglas A. Sylva, *The United Nations Population Fund: Assault on the World's Peoples,* Catholic Family and Human Rights Institute, 2002.

24. Neal, "Downplaying Politics."

25. "Report of the China UN Population Fund (UNFPA) Independent Assessment Team," Bureau of Population, Refugees, and Migration, U.S. Department of State, May 29, 2002, available at www.state.gov/g/prm/rls/rpt/2002/12122.htm.

26. "China Mission Report by UK MP's," July 2, 2002.

27. Broder, "Deadly Politics."

28. "UNFPA Welcomes US Congress Support, Urges Administration to Release Funds," United Nations press release, January 23, 2004.

29. "EU Humanitarian Aid for Reproductive Health in Developing Countries," European Union press release, July 24, 2002.

30. Jackie Koszczuck, "White House Gives Nod to Abortion-Inducing Pill," Knight Ridder, September 29, 2000.

31. *George W. Bush's War on Women: A Chronology,* Planned Parenthood Federation of America, January 27, 2003.

32. Richard Boucher, State Department Regular Briefing, November 7, 2002, available through the Federal News Service.

33. Rep. Carolyn B. Maloney et al., letter to Secretary of State Colin Powell, October 31, 2002.

34. Arlene Superville, "Bush Broadens Global Gag Rule on Abortion," Associated Press, August 29, 2003.

35. Steve Jordahl, "U.S. Pulls Funding from AIDS Organization," *Family News in Focus,* Focus on the Family, August 29, 2003.

36. Superville, "Bush Broadens Global Gag Rule."

37. "Implementation of USAID Policies and Programs on HIV/AIDS and Trafficking," action cable from Secretary of State Colin Powell to U.S. Agency for International Development mission directors and population, health, and nutrition officers, December 24, 2002.

38. Doug Domenech, "Hands Off Our Children," *National Review* online, June 11, 2001.

39. Ceci Connolly, "HHS Withholds Funds for Global Health Meeting," *Washington Post,* April 27, 2004, and leaked emails from USAID.

40. Dave Andrusko, "Huge Pro-Life Win at Children's Summit," *National Right to Life News,* June 2002.

41. Karen DeYoung, "Organizations Find Big Changes in Bush's A-List: Professional Groups Lose Delegate Spots," *Washington Post,* May 17, 2001.

42. "List of Accredited NGOs," Global Policy Forum, August 2003, www.globalpolicy.org/ngos/ngo-un/index.htm; see also Candi Cushman, "A World of Difference," *Citizen,* Focus on the Family, undated, available at www.family.org/cforum/citizenmag/features/a0020431.cfm.

43. For previous participants see DeYoung, "Organizations Find Big Changes"; current participants from "United States Delegation to the Special Session of the United Nations General Assembly on HIV/AIDS, New York, June 25–27, 2001," U.S. State Department.

44. William Saunders, "The UN Threat to the Family," remarks prepared for the World Congress of Families, Washington, DC, October 26, 2001, available at www.frc.org/get.cfm?i=PD02G1.

45. Thompson quotation from Somini Sengupta, "U.N. Forum Stalls on Sex Education and Abortion Rights," *New York Times,* May 10, 2002.

46. William J. Saunders, "The Family at the United Nations—What Went Wrong and What Can We Do About It," transcript of address to the World Congress of Families, Washington, DC, October 26, 2001, available at www.efamilyaction.org/wcf/William_Saunders.htm.

47. Dafna Linzer, "Bush to Alter Child Summit Policy," Associated Press, August 29, 2001.

48. Linzer, "Bush"; Jennifer Block, "Christian Soldiers on the March," *Nation,* February 3, 2002; interview with Loreto Leyton, First Secretary of the Chilean Mission to the United Nations.

49. Sengupta, "Goals Set by U.N. Conference on Children Skirt Abortion," *New York Times,* May 11, 2002.

50. Ambassador Sichan Siv, "Statement in Explanation of Position by Ambassador Sichan Siv, United States Representative on the United Nations Economic and Social Council, at the Special Session of the United Nations General Assembly on Children, following Adoption of the Outcome Document, May 10, 2002," U.S. Mission to the United Nations, May 15, 2002, available at www.un.int/usa/02_070.htm.

51. Saunders and Focus on the Family quotations from Pete Winn, "An Answer to Prayer," *CitizenLink,* Focus on the Family, May 14, 2002.

52. "Blinders Won't Solve Global Ills," *Atlanta Journal-Constitution,* May 14, 2002.

53. "Chile's UN Phones 'Were Tapped,' " BBC News, February 10, 2004.

54. Bombshell from Jodi Enda, "U.S. Ending Support of World Health Plan: White House, in Move Against Abortion Rights, Rejects Global Accord on Population Control," *San Jose Mercury News,* November 2, 2002; Oliver from James Dao, "Over U.S. Protest, Asian Group Approves Family Planning Goals," *New York Times,* December 18, 2002.

55. See, e.g., Dao, "U.S. Raises Abortion Issue at Conference on Families," *New York Times,* December 15, 2002.

56. Philippines statement quoted in "U.S. 'Non-Negotiable' Demands Roundly Rejected," Population Action International press release, December 14, 2002.

57. Block, "Christian Soldiers."

58. Dao, "Over U.S. Protest, Asian Group Approves Family Planning Goals," *New York Times,* December 18, 2002.

59. "The United States of America General Reservation Submitted for Inclusion in the Report of the Conference," Fifth Asia and Pacific Population Conference, December 16–17, 2002.

60. Ben Taylor and Pete Winn, "2002 in Review," *CitizenLink,* Focus on the Family, December 31, 2002.

CHAPTER 10: STACKING THE COURTS

1. Peter Carlson, "The Big Filibluster," *Washington Post,* November 14, 2003; additional details from Chuck Muth, "Gavel-to-Gavel JFJ Marathon Blog," November 12–14, 2003, posted at justiceforjudges.com.

2. Klaus Marre, "Senate Debate on Judicial Nominees Has Fractious Start," *The Hill,* November 13, 2003.

3. George W. Bush, "President Reiterates Call for Fairness in Judicial Confirmation Process," appearance with judicial nominees Carolyn Kuhl, Janice Brown, and Priscilla Owen, Oval Office, White House, Washington, DC, November 13, 2003, available at www.whitehouse.gov.

4. On Justice for Judges see Muth, "Gavel-to-Gavel"; find a Focus on the Family link to Justice for Judges at www.family.org/cforum/feature/a0024283.cfm; the Perkins details are from Tony Perkins, "Senate Dems Offer Myth After Myth at Judges Debate," *Washington Update,* e-mail to Family Research Council members, November 13, 2003.

5. Focus on the Family syndicated radio program, November 12, 2003.

6. Much of this history is drawn from Herman Schwartz, *Packing the Courts: The*

Conservative Campaign to Rewrite the Constitution (New York: Scribners, 1988), Blackmun death threats, 16; party platform, 5.

7. Televangelist D. James Kennedy's Reclaiming America posts a detailed timeline of the Moore events at www.reclaimamerica.org/PAGES/10Commandments/MooreTime. asp.

8. "Readers' Top Ten Stories of 2003," *CitizenLink*, e-mail to Focus on the Family members, December 31, 2003.

9. James Dobson, "Restoring the Foundations: Repealing Judicial Tyranny," address to the Restore the Foundation rally on the steps of the Montgomery, Alabama State Courthouse, August 28, 2003, available at family.org/fmedia/misc/a0027564.cfm.

10. Pat Robertson, letter to fellow Americans, text reprinted in "Robertson's Rage—There He Goes Again," People for the American Way press release, July 8, 2003, available at www.pfaw.org/pfaw/general/default.aspx?oid=11421; *700 Club* account from "Broadcaster Pat Robertson Calls for Retirement of Justices," Associated Press, July 15, 2003.

11. Randall A. Terry, letter to "Christian activists nationwide," July 12, 2003, posted at www.twistedsix.com.

12. See, e.g., Stop Judicial Tyranny at family.org/cforum/judicial_tyranny/; Alliance Defense Fund at alliancedefensefund.org; Eagle Forum's Court Watch at eagleforum.org/court_watch/; Shake the Nation at shakethenation.org.

13. Members are listed on "Priscilla Owen Press Conference," Coalition for a Fair Judiciary press release, July 15, 2002, and Kay Daly, president, Coalition for a Fair Judiciary, et al., letter to Noel Hillman, U.S. Department of Justice, February 10, 2004.

14. Franklin Foer, "What It Takes," *New Republic,* October 20, 2003.

15. See these Department of Justice Web pages: for Owen, usdoj.gov/olp/owen.htm; for Kuhl, usdoj.gov/olp/kuhl.htm.

16. "Alliance for Justice Report in Opposition to the Nomination of William H. Pryor to the United States Court of Appeals for the Eleventh Circuit," Alliance for Justice, available at independentjudiciary.com; "Senate Panel Should Reject Janice Rogers Brown for U.S. Appeals Court Seat, Says Americans United," Americans United for Separation of Church and State press release, October 22, 2003; "Texas Supreme Court Justice Priscilla Owen Nominee to the U.S. Court of Appeals for the Fifth Circuit," Alliance for Justice, available at independentjudiciary.com.

17. For a list of Committee for Justice members, see committeeforjustice.org/contents/about/members.shtml.

18. For an account of Claude Allen endorsing these views, see "Highlights of the Day," an article about Peacemaker's annual conference, Conforming to Christ, November 2–5, 2000, at www.hispeace.org/html/AC2000/AC_Updt_Nov4.htm.

19. "Texas Supreme Court Justice Priscilla Owen: A Summary of Judicial Career & Opinions," Texans for Public Justice, July 2002, available at www.tpj.org.

20. "The Case Against the Confirmation of Charles W. Pickering, Sr., to the U.S. Court of Appeals for the 5th Circuit," Alliance for Justice, available at independentjudiciary.com; "Alliance for Justice Report in Opposition to the Nomination of William H. Pryor to the United States Court of Appeals for the Eleventh Circuit."

21. On Rove's influence on the Texas courts, see Michael Scherer, "The Making of the Corporate Judiciary: How Big Business Is Quietly Funding a Legal Revolution," *Mother Jones,* November 1, 2003, and Lou DuBose et al., *Boy Genius: Karl Rove, the Brains Behind the Remarkable Political Triumph of George W. Bush* (New York: PublicAffairs, 2003), 108; with regard to Alabama, see Nicholas Lemann, "The Controller: Karl Rove Is

Working to Get George Bush Reelected, but He Has Bigger Plans," *New Yorker*, May 12, 2003.

22. Nan Aron, "You Too Can Be a Judge," *Los Angeles Times*, May 19, 2003.

23. John Nichols, "Karl Rove's Legal Tricks," *Nation*, July 22, 2002, and Ken Connor, "Senator Leahy Mangles the Truth—Again," Family Research Council, www.frc.org.

24. "Judicial Activism: The Biggest 2002 Election Issue," Eagle Forum, October 2002.

25. DuBose, *Boy Genius*, 220.

26. On Collins, see DuBose, *Boy Genius*, 225.

27. The Committee for Justice ads are available at committeeforjustice.org/contents/commercial/.

28. The Republican Party platform is posted at www.gop.com/About/PartyPlatform/Default.aspx.

29. "Transcript of Debate Between Vice President Gore and Governor Bush," *New York Times*, October 4, 2000.

30. "Governor George W. Bush, Republican from Texas and a GOP Presidential Candidate, Talks About His Bid for the Presidency, Other Presidential Candidates and His Political Career," *Meet the Press*, Tim Russert, host, November 21, 1999, available from NBC News Transcripts.

31. This information is drawn from an updated version of the report, Ralph G. Neas, *Courting Disaster II: How a Scalia-Thomas Court Would Endanger Our Rights and Freedoms*, People for the American Way, June 2003.

32. Larry Downing, "Bush Calls Pledge Ruling 'Out of Step,'" Reuters, June 27, 2002.

33. Wyatt Olson, "Onward, Christian Soldiers: TV Preacher D. James Kennedy and His Religious Right Cohorts Want to 'Reclaim America for Christ'—and the GOP," *Church & State*, January 2004.

34. Background on Pryor drawn from "Alliance for Justice Report in Opposition to the Nomination of William H. Pryor to the United States Court of Appeals for the Eleventh Circuit"; Jeremy Leaming, "Pryor Offenses," *Church & State*, June 2003; "William Pryor: Unfit to Judge," People for the American Way, 2003, available at www.pfaw.org/pfaw/general/default.aspx?oid=10900.

35. *State of the Administration 2003*, National Stonewall Democrats, January 28, 2003.

36. "John G. Roberts," National Organization for Women, report available at www.now.org/issues/legislat/nominees/roberts.html.

37. On Roberts, Kate Michelman, "NARAL Pro-Choice America Letter Opposing the Confirmation of John Roberts to the United States Court of Appeals for the District of Columbia," NARAL Pro-Choice America, February 12, 2003; on Pickering, *Judicial Selection in the First Two Years of the George W. Bush Administration*, Alliance for Justice Judicial Selection Project 2001–2002 Biennial Report, Spring 2003, available at www.allianceforjustice.org; on Kuhl, "Alliance for Justice Report in Opposition to the Nomination of Judge Carolyn Kuhl to the U.S. Court of Appeals for the Ninth Circuit," Alliance for Justice, available at independentjudiciary.com; on McConnell, *Judicial Selection in the First Two Years of the George W. Bush Administration*; on Pryor, "We Must Protect the President's Judicial Nominees!" Concerned Women for America action alert, July 2003.

38. "James Leon Holmes," National Organization for Women report, available at www.now.org/issues/legislat/nominees/holmes.html and "James Leon Holmes," NARAL Pro-Choice America report, available at www.naral.org/facts/holmes_facts.cfm.

39. "Report of the Alliance for Justice in Opposition to the Nomination of Deputy Secretary of Health and Human Services Claude Allen to the U.S. Court of Appeals for the Fourth Circuit," Alliance for Justice, available at independentjudiciary.com.

40. Ralph G. Neas, *Confirmed Judges, Confirmed Fears*, People for the American Way Foundation, January 23, 2004.

41. Dobson, "Restoring the Foundations"; remarks of Tony Perkins, president of the Family Research Council, at a press conference announcing Marriage Protection Week, October 2, 2003, available at www.frc.org/get.cfm?i=PR03J02&f=PR04C08.

42. "Take America Back—Stop Judicial Tyranny in America," Christian Coalition petition, posted at www.cc.org/printpetition.htm.

43. "Coalition for a Fair Judiciary Exposes Democrat Memos on Judges," Traditional Values Coalition, available at www.traditionalvalues.org/modules.php?name=News&file=article&sid=1303.

44. Land from "Judiciary Committee Sends Justice Owen to the Full Senate," Ethics & Religious Liberty Commission of the Southern Baptist Convention press release, March 28, 2003; Jipping from Thomas L. Jipping, "Fight the Filibuster Campaign Talking Points," Concerned Women for America, April 23, 2003.

45. Jerry Falwell, "The Dark Motive Behind the Democrat Filibuster," NewsMax.com, November 14, 2003.

46. Sandy Rios, president, Concerned Women for America, letter to Sen. Thomas Daschle, July 30, 2003.

47. Daley in Pete Winn, "Estrada Withdrawal a 'Tragedy,' " *CitizenLink*, Focus on the Family e-mail to members, September 5, 2003; Gray in Jonathan Groner, "Privilege Fight Looms Over Estrada; Leahy's Request for Memos: May Spark a Showdown," *Legal Times*, June 3, 2002; Eagle Forum from "Senate Democrats Continue Scorched Earth Policy Toward Courts," Eagle Forum's Court Watch action alert, October 4, 2002.

48. *Judicial Selection in the First Two Years of the George W. Bush Administration*, Alliance for Justice Judicial Selection Project.

49. Bender quotation from David Montgomery, "A Man on Hold: While the Senate Debates, Judicial Nominee Miguel Estrada Waits. And Waits," *Washington Post*, March 14, 2003; Hatch accusation in Audrey Hudson, "Democrats Raise Issue of Estrada's Politics: Nominee Targeted Over 'Ideology,' " *Washington Times*, September 27, 2002.

50. "The Senate, the Courts, and the Blue Slip," People for the American Way, available at www.pfaw.org/pfaw/general/default.aspx?oid=7611.

51. Winn, "Estrada Withdrawal a 'Tragedy.' "

52. Amy Bach, "Movin' on Up with the Federalist Society," *The Nation*, October 1, 2001.

53. Martin Garbus, "A Hostile Takeover," *American Prospect*, March 1, 2003.

54. Thomas L. Jipping, "Judiciary-Selling GOP Senators Deserve to Be Thrown Out," EnterStageRight.com, June 5, 2000; on voter guides, Robert Marquand, "Will War Over Judges Become Permanent?" *Christian Science Monitor*, December 19, 1997.

55. Emily Pierce, "Hatch Hires a Longtime Critic," *Roll Call*, September 18, 2003.

56. Perkins, "Senate Dems Offer Myth After Myth at Judges Debate"; Bush, "President Reiterates Call for Fairness in Judicial Confirmation Process"; Hatch from Carlson, "The Big Filibuster."

57. Bush number from *Judicial Selection in the First Two Years of the George W. Bush Administration*, Alliance for Justice Judicial Selection Project; Reagan number from Schwartz, *Packing the Courts*, 58.

58. On party platform, Schwartz, *Packing the Courts,* 5, 18; on Gramm, ibid, 59; on age ratios, ibid, 60; on Hatch's test, ibid, 83–84.

59. *Judicial Selection in the First Two Years of the George W. Bush Administration,* Alliance for Justice Judicial Selection Project.

60. "Federal Judiciary by Court and Appointing President," Alliance for Justice, www.allianceforjustice.org/judicial/judicial_selection_resources/selection_database/by CourtAndAppPres.asp.

61. *Judicial Selection in the First Two Years of the George W. Bush Administration,* Alliance for Justice Judicial Selection Project.

62. Cass R. Sunstein, *Why Societies Need Dissent* (Cambridge: Harvard University Press, 2003).

63. Deborah Sontag, "The Power of the Fourth," *New York Times Magazine,* March 9, 2003.

Coda

1. The letter is posted on the Free Congress Foundation Web site at www. freecongress.org/misc/990216ltr.asp.

2. Bob Jones, "Out of the Wilderness?" *World,* February 3, 2001.

3. Nicholas Lemann, "The Controller: Karl Rove Is Working to Get George Bush Re-elected, but He Has Bigger Plans," *New Yorker,* May 12, 2003.

4. Tim Storey and Gene Rose, "GOP #1: First Time in 50 Years," *State Legislatures Magazine,* December 2002.

5. Gareth Cook and Scott Allen, "US Researchers Losing Edge in Stem Cell Work," *Boston Globe,* February 13, 2004.

6. "Condoms Don't Prevent AIDS, Vatican Official Says," Reuters, October 10, 2003.

7. George W. Bush, "President Signs Partial Birth Abortion Ban Act of 2003," Ronald Reagan Building, Washington, DC, November 5, 2003, available from www.whitehouse.gov.

8. George W. Bush, "President Calls for Constitutional Amendment Protecting Marriage," Roosevelt Room, White House, Washington, DC, February 24, 2004, available at www.whitehouse.gov.

9. George W. Bush, "Statement by the President," January 16, 2004, available at www.whitehouse.gov/news/releases/2004/01/20040116-19.html.

10. Jean Hardisty, *Mobilizing Resentment: Conservative Resurgence from the John Birch Society to the Promise Keepers* (Boston: Beacon Press, 1999), 20.

11. Bruce Lincoln, *Holy Terrors: Thinking About Religion After September 11* (Chicago: University of Chicago Press, 2003), 20.

12. Paul Krugman, *The Great Unraveling: Losing Our Way in the New Century* (New York: Norton, 2003), quoted in Russell Baker, "The Awful Truth," *New York Review of Books,* November 6, 2003.

INDEX